Mental Health *Still* Matters

Edited by

Jill Reynolds
Rosemary Muston
Tom Heller
Jonathan Leach
Mick McCormick
Jan Wallcraft
Mark Walsh

Compilation, original and editorial material © The Open University 2009
The Open University, Walton Hall, Milton Keynes MK7 6AA, United Kingdom

First published 2009 by
PALGRAVE MACMILLAN

Palgrave Macmillan in the UK is an imprint of Macmillan Publishers Limited,
registered in England, company number 785998, of Houndmills, Basingstoke,
Hampshire RG21 6XS

Palgrave Macmillan in the US is a division of St Martin's Press LLC,
175 Fifth Avenue, New York, NY 10010.

Palgrave Macmillan is the global academic imprint of the above companies
and has companies and representatives throughout the world.

Palgrave® and Macmillan® are registered trademarks in the United States,
the United Kindgom, Europe and other countries.

ISBN–13: 978–0–230–57730–5   hardback
ISBN–10: 0–230–57730–X   hardback
ISBN–13: 978–0–230–57729–9   paperback
ISBN–10: 0–230–57729–6   paperback

This book is printed on paper suitable for recycling and made from fully
managed and sustained forest sources. Logging, pulping and manufacturing
processes are expected to conform to the environmental regulations of the
country of origin.

A catalogue record for this book is available from the British Library.

A catalog record for this book is available from the Library of Congress.

10   9   8   7   6   5   4   3   2   1
18   17   16   15   14   13   12   11   10   09

Printed and bound in Great Britain by
CPI Antony Rowe, Chippenham and Eastbourne

Mental Health *Still* Matters

Books are to be returned on or before
the last date below.

This Reader forms part of the Open University courses *Challenging ideas in mental health* (K272) and *Diverse perspectives on mental health* (K225). Both are 30-point second-level undergraduate courses and are options in the BA/BSc (Hons) Health and Social Care, the Diploma in Health and Social Care, and the Foundation Degree in Health and Social Care. They are also compulsory courses in The Open University's pre-registration nursing programme (mental health branch) and options in the BA (Hons) Social Work.

Details of these and other Open University courses can be obtained from the Student Registration & Enquiry Service, The Open University, PO Box 197, Milton Keynes MK7 6BJ, United Kingdom: tel. +44(0)845 300 6090, e-mail general-enquiries@open.ac.uk

Alternatively, you may visit The Open University website at http://www.open.ac.uk where you can learn more about the wide range of courses and packs offered at all levels by The Open University.

Contents

Acknowledgements

The editors, contributors and publishers wish to thank the following for permission to use copyright material: Richard Bentall for material from R. Bentall 'Roll over Kraepalin', first published in *Mental Health Today*, Pavilion Publishing (Brighton) Ltd (2004); Blackwell Publishing Limited, for material from K. Wright, K. Haigh and M. McKeown, 'Reclaiming the humanity in disorder', *International Journal of Mental Health Nursing*, 11 (2007), from M. Flanagan, 'The challenge of shared care' in G.H. Rassool (ed.), *Dual Diagnosis*, Blackwell (2002), and from N. Bowles et al., 'Formal observations and engagement: a discussion paper', *Journal of Psychiatric and Mental Health Nursing*, 9 (2002), and from T. Freeman and E. Peck, 'Evaluating partnerships: a case study of integrated specialist mental health services', *Health and Social Care in the Community*, 14(5) (2006); The Royal College of Psychiatrists, for material from R.E. Kendell, 'The distinction between mental and physical illness', *British Journal of Psychiatry*, 178 (2001), from D. De Leo, 'Why are we not getting any closer to preventing suicide?', *British Journal of Psychiatry*, 181 (2002), from P. Trivedi and T. Wykes, 'From passive subjects to equal partners', *British Journal of Psychiatry*, 181 (2002), from A. Faulkner and P. Thomas, 'User-led research and evidence-based medicine', *British Journal of Psychiatry*, 189 (2002); Taylor & Francis Ltd (wwwtandf.co.uk/journals), for material from P. Beresford, 'Thinking about "mental health": towards a social model', *Journal of Mental Health*, 11(6) (2002), from P. Thomas, 'Big boys don't cry? Mental health and the politics of gender', *Journal of Mental Health*, 5(2) (1996), and from A. Borthwick et al., 'The relevance of moral treatment to contemporary mental health care', *Journal of Mental Health*, 10(4) (2001); Psychosocial Rehabilitation Journal, the Trustees of Boston University and IAPSRS for the material from P.E. Deegan, 'Recovery: the lived experience of rehabilitation', in *Readings in Psychiatric Rehabilitation*, Centre for Psychiatric Rehabilitation (1994); Taylor & Francis Books UK, for material from S. Fernando, 'Spirituality and mental health', in *Mental Health and Psychiatry: The Struggle against Racism*, Brunner-Routledge (2003), from J. Laurance, 'Life stories', in *Pure Madness: How Fear Drives the Mental Health System*, Routledge (2003), and from I. Leudar and P. Thomas, 'Hearing voices and psychopathology', in *Voices of Reason, Voices of Insanity*, Routledge (2000); Professor Jane Ussher for material from J.M. Ussher, 'Madness and misogyny: my mother and myself' in *Women's Madness: Misogyny or Mental Illness?* Harvester Wheatsheaf,

(1991); World Health Organization, for the material from E. Lahtinen et al., 'Strategies for promoting the mental health of populations', *Promoting Mental Health: Concepts, Emerging Evidence, Practice*, WHO (2005); Baillière-Tindall (Elsevier), for material from J. Repper and R. Perkins, 'Challenging discrimination: promoting rights and citizenship' in *Social Inclusion and Recovery: A Model for Mental Health Practice*, Baillière Tindall (Elsevier) (2003); the editorial board of Medical Sociology Online for material from H. Spandler, 'From social exclusion to inclusion? A critique of the inclusion imperative in mental health', *Medical Sociology Online*, 2(2) (2007); Open University Press, for material from H. Kemshall, 'Mental health, mental disorder, risk and public protection', in *Risk, Social Policy and Welfare*, Open University Press (2002), and from M. Duker and R. Slade, 'Getting through', in *Anorexia Nervosa and Bulimia: How to Help*, Open University Press (2003) (all rights reserved); Nacro, for material from D. Brown, 'Black communities, mental health and the criminal justice system', *Nacro Mental Health and Crime Briefing* (2007); John Gunn for material from J. Gunn, 'Reflections on British forensic psychiatry in 2003', first published in *Mental Health Review*, Pavilion Publishing (Brighton) Ltd (2003); Jessica Kingsley Publishers, for material from M. Webber, 'Social capital and mental health' in G. Tew (ed.), *Social Perspectives on Mental Health*, Jessica Kingsley (2005), and from D. Brooker, 'What is person-centred care in dementia?', in *Person-Centred Dementia Care: Making Services Better*, Jessica Kingsley (2007); Jeanette Henderson for material from J. Henderson, 'Experiences of "care" in mental health', first published in *Journal of Adult Protection*, Pavilion Publishing (Brighton) Ltd (2002); Palgrave Macmillan, for material from M. O'Hagan, 'Two accounts of mental distress', in J. Read and J. Reynolds (eds), *Speaking Our Minds: An Anthology of Personal Experiences of Mental Distress and its Consequences*, Palgrave Macmillan (1996); Yale University Press, for material from P. Barham, 'Wresting his own future', in *Forgotten Lunatics of the Great War*, Yale University Press (2007); Mind (National Association for Mental Health – *www.mind.org.uk*), for material from J. Thomas and J. Holloway (with E. Craig), 'Time sharing' and 'Learning from voices', *Openmind*, 103, May/June (2000) and from A. Wells, 'My right to choose', *Openmind*, 123, Sept/Oct (2003); the editor of the Kent Journal of Mental Health, for material from A. Williams, 'The recovery of hope', *Kent Journal of Mental Health*, 2 (2007); Asylum Associates, for material from V. Dewan, 'Two hours fifty five minutes', *Asylum*, 14(4) (2004) (the author would also like to thank Angela Linton-Abulu of the Black Women's Mental Health Project), from P. Trivedi, 'Are we who we say we are – or who you think we are?', *Asylum*, 14(4) (2004), and from P. Chambers, 'What black women want from the mental health services', *Asylum*, 14(4) (2004); the editors and PCCS Books Ltd for material from L. Pembroke, 'Harm minimisation: limiting the damage of self-injury' in H. Spandler and S. Warner (eds), *Beyond*

Fear and Control (2007); Peter Lehmann, for material from R. May, 'Reclaiming mad experience' in P. Stastny and P. Lehmann (eds) *Alternatives Beyond Psychiatry*, Peter Lehmann Publishing (2007); the editor of Community Care, for material from K. Parton, 'Users caught in the "service trap"', *Community Care*, Feb (2003); John Wiley & Sons, for material from J. Wallcraft, 'Holistic therapies: service users' perspectives and research' in T. Stickley (ed.), *Learning about Mental Health Practice*, John Wiley & Sons Limited (2008); BMJ Publishing Group Ltd, for material from P. Bracken and P. Thomas, 'Postpsychiatry – a new direction for mental health', *British Medical Journal*, 322 (2001), and from J. Holmes, 'All you need is cognitive behaviour therapy?', *British Medical Journal*, 324 (2002); Sage for material from S. Ramon, B. Healy and N. Renouf, 'Recovery from mental illness as an emergent concept', *International Journal of Social Psychiatry*, 53, Sage Publications (2007). Every effort has been made to trace the copyright-holders, but if any have been inadvertently overlooked the publishers will be pleased to make the necessary arrangements at the first opportunity.

General Introduction

It is a great pleasure to introduce this collection of writings on a wide range of mental health topics. Our task throughout this collection has been to present a variety of stimulating readings that will spark debate and offer opportunities for serious discussion among people who are involved in the field of mental health. You may not be in agreement with the opinions expressed in all of the articles; indeed it would be surprising if you were. We have chosen authors and articles that represent a wide range of views, often challenging rather than accepting official views or statutory orthodoxy. Our earlier Open University Reader, *Mental Health Matters* (Heller et al., 1996), has continued to be popular. Feedback from readers has indicated that they have found it valuable to have access to a diverse compendium of stimulating interdisciplinary writing. We are convinced that this new volume will offer the same opportunities.

Since that earlier publication, debates on various ways that mental health problems can be conceptualised, as well as discussions on policy and practice, have both developed and intensified. At the same time a normative, centralised view has become even more dominant; mental health services are expected to work in partnership, towards a national service framework (see, for instance, Department of Health, 1999), with shared essential capabilities demonstrated by mental health workers. It has therefore become more important than ever that people studying and working in mental health understand the provenance and terms of the wider debates relating to mental health and ill-health. In particular, we're pleased to note that even within central health and social care policy directives there are expectations of partnership with users of mental health services that now extend across a range of disciplines: service users are considered as partners and leaders in research and teaching. Sharing their experiences and perspectives so that others can learn from them is seen as an essential part of this volume.

The book is in four parts:

Debates and theories introduces some key theories on mental ill-health. The part presents a range of critiques relating to mental health theories and opens up many of the contemporary debates in the field of mental health. The debates presented are not purely theoretical, but encompass the impact of the service user movement, spiritual and cultural dimensions as well as gendered experiences of mental distress.

Inequality and policy considers the consensus on social inclusion as a goal for mental health services and reviews different aspects of the services in which inequality continues to predominate. Does mental health policy tend to be focused solely on dealing with 'mental illness' rather than concerning itself with providing individuals and communities with the resources they need to lead satisfactory lives?

Service users' experiences and perspectives offers compelling stories and accounts of mental distress together with examples where service users have been able to use their experience in order to become teachers, researchers and innovators in mental health work.

Challenges for practice considers how a wide range of practitioners respond to some of the seismic changes in the landscape of mental health.

Collecting together more than 50 readings has defied a neat and rigorous classification into these four parts, so you will find both areas of overlap and contrast within and between them. The opinions expressed in the articles represent the views of the original authors and should not necessarily be taken to be the views of the editors of this collection, or of The Open University. We suggest that you look at the contents pages for areas that interest you, and take the opportunity to dip into the book according to your needs rather than reading it from cover to cover in the order laid down.

This collection of readings is part of the study materials for two Open University courses: K225 *Diverse perspectives on mental health*, and K272 *Challenging ideas in mental health*, so finding material relevant for students of mental health has been part of the motivation behind our editorial selections. K225 considers the person in relation to prevailing social, environmental, economic and political factors within a context of ethics and values. The K272 holistic model looks at the person in relation to their physical, social, psychological, emotional and spiritual dimensions. So both courses focus on models that emphasise the social, while not dismissing the importance of understanding more biomedical explanations for mental health and ill-health. We hope that the same approach followed in this Reader will prove useful to mental health students and practitioners more generally.

It has been an exciting period for the seven editors, deciding what to reprint from the vast accumulation of previously published material and who to commission to write new material for this volume. Two of the editors who worked on the original *Mental Health Matters*, and whose insights we benefited from, are no longer with The Open University. Three of the newcomers to our editorial team either chair, or manage and deliver our mental health courses, and we are also delighted to welcome Dr Jan Wallcraft, who has extensive experience as a service user consultant and has written widely on mental health. It was of great help to us that much of the developmental work for the collection was funded by a grant from The Open University's Practice-Based Professional Learning Centre for Excellence in Teaching and Learning.

As editors, we concluded that while we would look for articles that covered similar kinds of territory to the selection chosen for the earlier volume (and indeed include work from many of the original authors) this new work is best thought of as a companion collection, rather than a second edition, in the sense of simply updating original items. The title *Mental Health Still Matters* forges the link with the earlier volume while indicating that there are new things to say in this fresh look at mental health. The aim has been to cover a wide range of current concerns in the world of mental health and explore contrasting explanations, experiences, strategies and practices. Many of the earlier readings have become 'classics' of their genre, and it seemed sensible to continue to make that volume available to readers. Nine articles in this new volume are either new commissions or specially-commissioned versions of work featured elsewhere. Some articles that we have edited and reprinted might be considered as classics that were overlooked in our earlier edition: we hope that others will go on to become classics in their turn.

In order to be able to include the wealth and diversity of perspectives represented here, most readings are either extracts from the original work, or abridged from a longer piece. The original sources of reprinted work are noted for each reading. We have not used abridgement symbols to show the precise location of text that has been omitted. If you want to follow an author's detailed argument, we recommend that you read the work from which it originated. We hope that this Reader will introduce you to many authors whose ideas intrigue or excite you, and that the extracts will give you an appetite to become better acquainted with their work.

References

Department of Health (1999) *National Service Framework for Mental Health: Modern Standards and Service Models*, London, DH.

Heller, T., Reynolds, J., Gomm, R., Muston, R. and Pattison, S. (eds) (1996) *Mental Health Matters: A Reader*, Basingstoke, Macmillan/Palgrave.

Part **I**

Debates and theories

1

Introduction

Jonathan Leach

The first part of this book reviews and provides examples of some of the key debates in mental health theory. However, these debates are not purely theoretical; many of the authors' ideas about mental health and distress have been influenced by their experiences of providing and using mental health services. In turn these ideas and theories can influence the nature of mental health services and more generally the understanding of mental health issues in the wider society. The themes and debates introduced here recur elsewhere in the rest of the book.

Reading 2 outlines some aspects of social, psychological and biomedical theories and their relationship to each other. Over the last 50 years or so the mental health field could be likened to an intellectual battleground, with challenges to psychiatry originating from within the profession itself in the form of anti-psychiatry, post-psychiatry and critical psychiatry movements, as well as from external challenges posed by psychological, sociological and service user/survivor approaches. Despite Engel's (1980) attempted synthesis of some of these different approaches in the biopsychosocial model, it does not seem to have been widely adopted as a holistic approach to practice (Pilgrim, 2002). Is this because the biomedical, psychological and social approaches are theoretically incompatible with each other, or does the issue lie with the conflicting interests of different players in the mental health field? A number of these different approaches are discussed in more detail in the readings that follow and you may like to consider whether the approaches may be seen as competing with or complementing each other.

Although experiences such as anxiety and depression are widespread throughout the population, much of the debate about mental health has centred around the subject of schizophrenia, possibly because it is seen as typifying 'madness'. The standard psychiatric view of schizophrenia has been that it is an illness with its own distinctive features and category of symptoms, the causes of which are likely to be found within the physical structures or operations of the brain. Richard Bentall (Reading 3) challenges this view suggesting that psychotic symptoms are distributed among members of the non-psychiatric population with a continuum of experiences rather than there being discrete categories of 'well' and 'ill'. He argues that apparent 'symptoms' can be explained as understandable psychological mechanisms rather than as indicators of an underlying disease process. As a consequence of this approach Bentall believes that it is important to take people's life histories into account, including the environmental factors that may have affected them. This would not be seen as so necessary from a biomedical point of view, but if past traumas are accepted as a causal factor then a different approach is indicated.

One of the most challenging diagnoses in mental health has been that of personality disorder. Karen Wright and her colleagues (Reading 4) found that the views of clinical staff tend to overlap with those lay perspectives involving moral judgements concerning this group and their behaviour, seeing them as less deserving of care than people with other diagnoses. The authors argue for raising awareness of the common human characteristics and positive attributes of members of this group. However, the policy background is one which associates personality disorder with public risk and pushes for compulsory detention of those with dangerous severe personality disorder. There is an ambivalence, among both practitioners and policy makers, about whether people with this diagnosis need containment or care. Personality disorder has been seen as untreatable and therefore not the business of mental health services. It is also viewed as deviating from the normal or ideal self, and thus casts those diagnosed as 'other'.

The tensions between psychiatric explanations for certain types of experiences and social and psychological explanations are explored by Lucy Johnstone (Reading 5). As a clinical psychologist who has seen the effects of trauma such as childhood abuse on mental health, Johnstone has been frustrated at the dominance of medical views in determining treatment. Having gone back to work part-time in the hospital system after nine years in an academic setting, she found that the biomedical model was still strong despite other changes that had occurred. Improvements in community services seem to have been at the expense of the most vulnerable patients who find themselves in overstretched hospital wards. Service users' voices are more prominent but the author fears that initiatives which have come from this quarter, such as 'Hearing Voices' groups, become incorporated into mainstream provision and lose their radical impact in the process. While psychiatrists may have lost some of their former power, the gap has been filled by managers rather than by a significant empowerment of service users.

Writing from a biomedical perspective Robert Kendell (Reading 6) argues that distinctions between illness of the mind and the body are fruitless and confusing. People are both minds and bodies, and it is people who have ill-nesses. The author makes the point that it is who gets to treat certain conditions which determines whether they are classed as mental or physical. Kendell believes that there is a biological basis to what are referred to as mental and physical illnesses. This seems an attractive argument for a number of reasons: stigma and blame are less likely if illness is seen as having a biological origin, and scientific procedures are more easily applied to biological and physiologi-cal processes than they are to psychological ones. However, there are also drawbacks to this approach, some of which have already been mentioned in relation to Bentall's and Johnstone's readings. Evidence can be interpreted dif-ferently depending on the perspective taken, and in extreme circumstances genetics can lead to eugenics. The biomedical approach tends to look at symp-toms rather than the person and the context of their life, which is often a source of frustration to service users and survivors.

An important voice in challenging the psychiatric approach, which tends to look for symptoms and place people into diagnostic categories, has been the service user and survivor movement. The development of an active service user movement in the mental health field has challenged previous ideas of mad-ness, sanity and the ability of those experiencing mental distress to contribute to rational debates. In Reading 7 Peter Campbell charts the growth of a move-ment of service users finding their own voice and their presentation of different ways of viewing mental health and distress. As in any group there is a diversity of views, particularly concerning whether it is possible or desirable to bring about fundamental changes in mental health services. What seems to unite dif-ferent kinds of service user activists is a belief in the abilities of people who have been on the receiving end of diagnoses and services to define their own lives and to engage in self-organisation. Campbell points to a significant growth in the numbers of people involved in service user movements, and to a shift from involvement in relatively minor decision-making to engagement in debates about the meaning of mental health and madness itself. Despite these advances, it remains to be seen how much this expression of ideas trans-lates into real power to influence mental health policy and practice at a funda-mental level.

Disability activists have transformed thinking about disability, moving the debate away from notions of personal tragedy and loss to considerations of dif-ference, discrimination and civil rights. Peter Beresford (Reading 8) argues that the mental health service user movement could embrace the social model as it offers an alternative to the individualised biomedical approach. A social model of madness and distress is not as well developed as either social models of disability relating to physical and sensory impairments or in comparison to biomedical and psychological models of mental health and distress. However, the social model fits well with much current thinking on tackling social exclu-sion in areas such as education, employment, housing and access to services.

It also fits with the provision of non-medical support that enables service users and survivors to lead lives of their choosing.

In common with these service user perspectives on mental health, which challenge the dichotomy between the expert professional and the passive patient, the concept of recovery asserts the importance of the individual's own actions and desires. To a certain extent there are parallels with the social model of disability, as the recovery approach places less emphasis on finding a cure than on leading a valued life, even if distress is experienced at times. The recovery approach had its foundation in service users' writings and experiences, as illustrated in the reading by Patricia Deegan (9), but has been subsequently adopted as a model for professional practice featuring in a number of publications aimed at mental health practitioners. The challenge to services now is to recast professionals in a facilitative role, a role that encourages the users of services to have hope in the power of their own efforts and actions.

The social aspects of mental health become particularly apparent when diverse cultural factors are considered in relation to mental health and distress. One aspect of this is the spiritual dimension which Suman Fernando explores in Reading 10 as part of understanding the cultural context of mental distress. This is a key area in the debate because of the contrast between the biomedical model's conception of mental ill-health as a physical fact and other approaches which see mental health and illness as being culturally defined and determined. A western approach based on objective science does not easily find a place for spirituality in understanding mental health and distress. Fernando shows, with particular reference to Buddhism, how in other cultures it would be difficult to ignore the spiritual aspects of life in any discussion of suffering. In contrast to western approaches that tend to dissect and atomise phenomena, eastern approaches are more likely to emphasise holism and connectedness. This has implications not only for how people understand mental health in general, but also for creating mental health services that are responsive to the needs of people from different cultural and ethnic backgrounds.

The social and cultural expectations associated with gender are explored in two readings that reflect on men's and women's experiences of mental distress. Philip Thomas (Reading 11) suggests that men suffer as a result of stereotypical expectations that inhibit their ability to talk about their feelings. Jane Ussher (Reading 12) reflects on her mother's experiences of madness to consider the effects on women of living in a world that is largely shaped by expectations and understandings arising from the power of men. The viewing of mental distress as influenced by gender again raises questions of biological, psychological and social differences. Both authors see the social experiences of each gender as being particularly significant in their effects upon mental health.

The term 'mental health' has commonly come to mean its opposite particularly in relation to services. However the field of mental health promotion proposes models of mental health that go beyond avoiding illness and which are not targeted solely at those who have been given a diagnosis of mental ill-health or disorder. In Reading 13 Eero Lahtinen and his colleagues advocate a positive view of mental health and a targeting of actions at the population level with a strong emphasis on the influence of environmental factors on mental health. This approach overlaps with social models of mental health and the authors express their belief in the capacity of all people to flourish within supportive environments.

These readings, rather than providing the certainty of textbook explanations for mental distress, raise many questions that are difficult to answer definitively. However, the ideas presented here stimulate useful debates about what we mean by mental health, what causes mental distress or 'madness', and what are the most appropriate ways of responding to people who are in crisis. There are still exciting opportunities to take understanding forward, particularly by bringing together academic and professional insights with those of service users and survivors. This part of this book and those that follow are central to that process.

References

Engel, G. (1980) 'The clinical application of the biopsychosocial model', *American Journal of Psychiatry*, vol. 137, pp. 535–44.

Pilgrim, D. (2002) 'The biopsychosocial model in Anglo-American psychiatry: past, present and future?', *Journal of Mental Health*, vol. 11(6), pp. 585–94.

2

Diverse approaches to mental health and distress

Jonathan Leach

There are many theories concerning the definitions and causes of mental ill-health. In fact it can be difficult even to find agreement on the use of terms to describe the experiences which are the subject of this reading. Words such as disorder, disease, pathology and illness when preceded by the word 'mental' tend to imply acceptance of an explanatory framework transferred from physical medicine. For this reason other terms such as 'mental distress' and 'mental health problems' or 'difficulties', although less precise, tend to be used in non-medical publications, while the term 'madness' has been embraced by some service user groups. Compared with other areas of health practice, the mental health field is particularly subject to heated debates, not only about what to call its core subject, but also what it is, what influences it and how, if at all, it should be treated. The various different answers to these questions come not only from the evaluation of evidence and the persuasiveness of competing theories, but also from the perspectives of particular groups in society who seek the power to influence how people whose behaviour causes concern should be treated.

Biomedical approaches

Medical explanations for experiences of madness or mental distress may well have provided a more sympathetic response than those based on earlier theories of demonic possession or moral weakness. However, despite the well-intentioned desire to relieve suffering through the application of medical science, there has been much disagreement about the role of biophysical and biochemical factors in mental health.

Researchers using functional imaging scans have drawn attention to differences in the activities of the brains of people with various psychiatric diagnoses (Jackson, 2006). Similarly, the results of magnetic resonance imaging scans have been used to suggest that some people diagnosed with schizophrenia have noticeable differences in certain aspects of their brain structures compared to others without that diagnosis (Frith and Johnstone, 2003); but as yet these results have not provided conclusive proof for physical origins of mental distress (for example, they may rather demonstrate the impact of mental distress upon the structures of the brain). Both depression and schizophrenia have been linked to differences in brain chemistry, and researchers have suggested genetic patterns of inheritance for these conditions. However, each of these claims has been met with scepticism by some writers in the field and, so far, no reliable physical tests have been developed for use in diagnosing mental ill-health. Kingdon, a consultant psychiatrist, goes so far as to suggest that biological research has made no significant contribution to the practice of psychiatry and is unlikely to do so (Kingdon and Young, 2007). Others believe that we are on the edge of significant discoveries that will identify the genetic, chemical and physiological mechanisms involved in mental illness, to the point where psychiatry, neurology and neuroscience will come together as one discipline (Yodofksy and Hales, 2002).

A fairly purist biomedical approach (Baker and Menken, 2001) proposes that there is no such thing as mental illness, stating that what we call mental illnesses are only the mental symptoms of physical damage or malfunctioning within the brain tissues, and are thus really physical illnesses. Kendell (Reading 6) similarly argues against divorcing the mind from the body. A commonly accepted view in the medical field (Goldberg and Huxley, 1992) is that some people are biologically vulnerable to mental ill-health, but that life events or living conditions may trigger the first appearance of, and subsequent relapses into, these conditions. This is the model that underpins much of the treatment offered by medical services: medication to control or reduce unpleasant symptoms, combined with advice on avoiding, or coping with, stress to avoid triggering further relapses.

In common with physical medicine, medical approaches to mental health follow a process of diagnosis and categorisation of symptoms before treatment is prescribed. In the absence of reliable physical tests, it is through questioning and observing the patient's behaviour and appearance that the medical practitioner will arrive at a diagnosis of mental illness or disorder. The clusters of symptoms found by this process are compared to those given in diagnostic manuals in order to identify conditions such as depression, anxiety, schizophrenia or bipolar disorder. However, there have been suggestions that most mental conditions do not present the discrete clusters of symptoms found in physical medicine (Bentall, 2004; Read et al., 2004).

Criticisms of the medical approach tend to focus on the negative side-effects arising from psychiatric medication (Moncrieff, Reading 47), and the distraction of attention away from the impact of important life events (Carr, 2001). Despite this, medical approaches form the main basis for intervention for many people who have been diagnosed as having mental health problems.

Psychological approaches

Psychological practitioners have not tended to play a defining role in making mental health diagnoses, this has remained largely the preserve of general practitioners and psychiatrists. However, many psychological and psychotherapeutic approaches have been developed, some of which have found a place within mental health services, particularly in recent years with the strengthening of the role of clinical psychologist. This section will look briefly at psychoanalytic and cognitive-behavioural approaches to mental health. This is not to say that other approaches such as client-centred counselling, cognitive therapy, cognitive analytical therapy and family and systems therapy are unimportant.

The terms 'psychoanalytic' and 'psychodynamic' tend to be used interchangeably in relation to therapy. In practice 'psychodynamic' is often applied to a model of brief counselling interventions whereas 'psychoanalytic' generally refers to longer-term psychotherapy. These approaches have their origins in the work of Freud, Jung and Adler (Tyrer and Steinberg, 1999). Psychoanalytic approaches tend to focus on the client's thoughts and feelings, while recognising that the client may not be conscious of what influences these; they may, of course, be unaware of their true feelings. The relationship between the therapist and the client is considered an important part of the process as it provides valuable clues about the subconscious processes going on in the client's mind, many of which will relate to early developmental processes and experiences.

Despite psychoanalysis playing a prominent part in British and American psychiatry in the first half of the 20th century, there has been a certain amount of scepticism within medical circles about the effectiveness of these approaches in dealing with severe mental illness. They have also been criticised for requiring lengthy and intensive periods of therapy and for creating dependence on the therapist. However, brief intervention models (Coren, 1996) have been developed and are used in student counselling services and other settings where long-term therapy is not appropriate or possible.

Cognitive-Behavioural Therapy (CBT) has developed from the cognitive and behavioural traditions and is widely used within NHS services. The basic premise of this approach is that an individual's appraisal of personal life events largely determines how she or he feels and behaves (Szymanska and Palmer, 2000). The treatment explores the person's present situation and, although it might be useful to examine where distressing thoughts, feelings and behaviours come from, the main concern is what reinforces them now and how they could be changed (Hawton et al., 1989). One of the key purposes of the therapy is to help the client look at their self-defeating beliefs or 'automatic thoughts' (also termed 'thinking errors') that they may have come to accept as a given. According to Carr (2001) some cognitive-behaviourists reject the notion of schizophrenia as a disease, instead viewing psychotic experiences as being on a continuum with normal experiences. A person's 'delusions' are not seen as meaningless, but as strongly held irrational beliefs, formed under the influence of cognitive biases and misperceptions and thus susceptible to treatment, a view similar to that of Bentall (Reading 3).

The National Institute for Health and Clinical Excellence's (NICE) guidelines for the treatment of depression and schizophrenia recommend CBT over other forms of counselling and psychotherapy (NICE, 2002; NICE, 2004). Despite the popularity of CBT in health services, some critics feel that this approach has not been proved to address the underlying causes of unpleasant symptoms, potentially leaving those treated vulnerable to future distress (Holmes, Reading 48). Stickley (2004) has a different concern that CBT is potentially a coercive method of promoting the 'right kind' of thinking.

The collection of reliable evidence on the effectiveness of any one psychological treatment is complicated by the tendency among practitioners to combine different approaches, as well as other variables including the skills, the level of training and the personality of the practitioner. It is also likely that the quality of the therapeutic relationship and the client's belief in the efficacy of the treatment are significant factors in reaching a positive outcome.

Social approaches

The biomedical and psychological approaches described above are closely linked to professions such as psychiatry, psychotherapy and clinical psychology. By contrast, social approaches to mental health have tended to come from service user activists (some of whom use the term 'survivors' to describe themselves) and academic theorists (a number of whom are also service users and survivors), with contributions from the social work field. These social approaches, or perspectives, may not yet come together in the form of a commonly agreed social model of mental health (Tew, 2005), but they do offer other ways of viewing the subject.

Service users' and survivors' approaches have advocated alternatives to medication, including crisis support centres and mutual support groups for people who share experiences such as hearing voices or feeling depressed (Stastny and Lehmann, 2007). One key theme in the service user literature has been that behaviour and speech, viewed by psychiatrists as seemingly meaningless other than as symptoms of an underlying disorder, can in fact possess meaning. These 'symptoms' can alternatively be viewed as a way of expressing distress caused by past or current events. This view is close to that of many psychologists, but some service users and survivors advocate peer support and the development of self-management strategies as an alternative to individual psychological therapy (Wallcraft and Michaelson, 2001).

Another social strand in the mental health field has been that of service users and survivors campaigning for civil rights, challenging stigma, seeking recognition of the value of personal experience and working for involvement in service planning and delivery (Campbell, Reading 7). This has links with a social model of disability (Oliver, 1990) which does not deny the existence of physical and mental conditions affecting people's lives, but distinguishes between individual impairments and disabling societal barriers. The model draws attention to how people are discriminated against because they are different and how this intolerance of diversity can cause greater limitations in daily life than factors directly linked to the person's diagnosed medical condition.

Academic writers have highlighted the role social factors play in the way that mental ill-health is experienced in populations. There is strong evidence that the incidence of mental illness varies between social classes (Rogers and Pilgrim, 2005; Gomm, Reading 15), that unemployment is associated with poorer mental health (Singleton et al., 2001) and that the incidence of depression is affected by life events and the presence or lack of social support (Brown, 1996). These and other factors have been used to suggest that there is a social dimension to mental health and this has been reflected to some extent in recent policies in the UK including the National Service Frameworks for Mental Health (Department of Health, 1999) and the social inclusion agenda (Social Exclusion Unit, 2004).

It is questionable whether there is a social model equivalent to psychological or biomedical models, i.e. that could account for all forms of mental ill-health or distress without recourse to either or both of those other explanatory frameworks. A social model probably sits most comfortably alongside psychological approaches, but the social model of disability can accommodate medical approaches, while refusing to give them a privileged position.

Different approaches to mental health in practice

While the biomedical, psychological and social approaches outlined here reflect philosophical and theoretical debates in the mental health field, there are also very practical issues of resource allocation and power relations between different groups allied to these approaches (Colombo et al., 2003). Much of the debate on the nature of mental health problems has centred around schizophrenia, although far fewer people are diagnosed with this condition than with the more common conditions of anxiety and depression. Psychiatrists Goodwin and Geddes (2007) suggest that psychiatry has done itself no favours in making schizophrenia its 'heartland', partly because the controversy surrounding its definition and diagnosis has led to uncertainty about the role of medicine in its treatment, especially as demands for psychological and social care have increased. In contrast they believe that bipolar disorder, which affects more people, provides a better example of what psychiatric medicine can contribute and how this can be balanced with psychological and social care.

The anti-psychiatry debates of the 1960s and 1970s seem to have largely been replaced with 'post-psychiatry' (Bracken and Thomas, Reading 44), critical psychiatry (Double, 2006) and by biopsychosocial (Engel, 1980) biosocial (Goldberg and Huxley, 1992) and psychosocial models (Bebbington, 1991), all of which acknowledge that the distressed individual cannot be viewed in isolation of external factors. Pilgrim (2002) suggests that the biopsychosocial model was an attempt to save psychiatry from its critics, and indeed the model has been criticised by Read et al. (2004) for allowing biological perspectives too great a role in defining and treating schizophrenia, which they see as explainable by social and psychological factors.

Despite these differences, diverse approaches are found combined in the work of community mental health teams, and other services that bring together medical, psychological and social support for mental distress. However, tensions between these approaches seem ever present, leading to changes over time in the relative influence of different professions and service user and survivor groups on how mental distress is understood and responded to.

References

Baker, M. and Menken, M. (2001) 'Time to abandon the term mental illness', *British Medical Journal*, vol. 322, p. 937.

Bebbington, P. (1991) *Social Psychiatry: Theory, Methodology and Practice*, New Brunswick, Transaction Publishers.

Bentall, R. (2004) *Madness Explained: Psychosis and Human Nature*. London, Allen Lane.

Brown, G. (1996) 'Life events, loss and depressive disorders', in Heller, T., Reynolds, J., Gomm, R., Muston, R., and Pattison, S. (eds) *Mental Health Matters: A Reader*, Basingstoke, Macmillan.

Carr, A. (2001) *Abnormal Psychology*, Hove, Psychology Press.

Colombo, A., Bendelow, G., Fulford, B. and Williams S. (2003) 'Evaluating the influence of implicit models of mental disorder on processes of shared decision making within community-based multi-disciplinary teams', *Social Science and Medicine*, vol. 56, pp. 1557–70.

Coren, A. (1996) 'Brief therapy – base metal or pure gold?', *Psychodynamic Counselling* vol. 2(1), 22–38.

Department of Health (1999) *National Service Framework for Mental Health: Modern Standards and Service Models*, London, Department of Health Publications.

Double, D. (2006) *Critical Psychiatry: The Limits of Madness*, Basingstoke, Palgrave Macmillan.

Engel, G. (1980) 'The clinical application of the biopsychosocial model', *American Journal of Psychiatry*, vol. 137, pp. 535–44.

Frith, C. and Johnstone, E. (2003) *Schizophrenia: A Very Short Introduction*, Oxford, Oxford University Press.

Goldberg, D. and Huxley, P. (1992) *Common Mental Disorders: A Bio-social Model*, London, Routledge.

Goodwin, G. and Geddes, J. (2007) 'What is the heartland of psychiatry?', *British Journal of Psychiatry*, vol. 191, pp. 189–91.

Hawton, K., Salkovskis, P., Kirk, J. and Clark, D. (1989) *Cognitive Behaviour Therapy for Psychiatric Problems: A Practical Guide*, Oxford, Oxford University Press.

Jackson, G. (2006) 'A curious consensus: "Brain scans provide disease"?', *Ethical Human Psychology and Psychiatry*, vol. 8(1), pp. 55–60.

Kingdon, D. and Young, A. (2007) 'Research into putative biological mechanisms of mental disorders has been of no value to clinical psychiatry', *British Journal of Psychiatry*, vol. 191, pp. 285–90.

NICE (2002) *Schizophrenia: Core Interventions in the Treatment and Management of Schizophrenia in Primary and Secondary Care, Clinical Guideline 1*, London, NICE.

NICE (2004) *Depression: Management of Depression in Primary and Secondary Care, Clinical Guideline 23*, London, NICE.

Oliver, M. (1990) *The Politics of Disablement*, Basingstoke, Macmillan.

Pilgrim, D. (2002) 'The bio-psychosocial model in Anglo-American psychiatry: Past present and future?', *Journal of Mental Health*, vol. 11(6), pp. 585–94.

Read J., Mosher, L. and Bentall, R. (2004) *Models of Madness: Psychological, Social and Biological Approaches to Schizophrenia*, Hove, Brunner-Routledge.

Rogers, A. and Pilgrim, D. (2005) *A Sociology of Mental Health and Illness*, Maidenhead, Open University Press.

Singleton, N., Bumpstead, R., O'Brien, M., Lee, A. and Meltzer, H. (2001) *Psychiatric Morbidity among Adults living in Private Households 2000*, London, Office for National Statistics.

Social Exclusion Unit (2004) *Mental Health and Social Exclusion*, London, HMSO/Office of the Deputy Prime Minister.

Stastny, P. and Lehmann, P. (2007) *Alternatives Beyond Psychiatry*, Berlin: Peter Lehmann Publishing.

Stickley, T. (2004) 'Why is cognitive behavioural therapy so popular?', *Openmind*, vol. 130, 11.

Szymanska, K. and Palmer, S. (2000) 'Cognitive counselling and psychotherapy' in Palmer, S. (ed.) *Introduction to Counselling and Psychotherapy: The Essential Guide*, London, Sage.

Tew, J. (ed.) (2005) *Social Perspectives in Mental Health*, London, Jessica Kingsley.

Tyrer, P. and Steinberg, D. (1999) *Models for Mental Disorder: Conceptual Models in Psychiatry*, Chichester, Wiley.

Wallcraft, J. and Michaelson, J. (2001) 'Developing a survivor discourse to replace the "psychopathology" of breakdown and crisis', in Newnes, C, Holmes, G. and Dunn C. (eds) *This is Madness Too: Critical Perspectives on Mental Health Services*, Ross-on Wye, PCCS Books.

Yodofsky, S. and Hales, R. (2002) 'Neuropsychiatry and the future of psychiatry and neurology', *American Journal of Psychiatry*, vol. 159(8), pp. 1261–5.

3

Roll over Kraepelin

Richard Bentall

The history of physical medicine is littered with clinical and scientific break-throughs. Psychiatric medicine, in contrast, has few achievements to boast about. Indeed at times psychiatrists have advocated treatments that can fairly be described as cruel and barbaric: the incarceration of millions in crowded asylums, the introduction of brain damaging 'therapies' such as insulin coma and the pre-frontal leucotomy, to list but a few. The greatest horror of all was the introduction of killing as a form of treatment for 'lives not worth living' by German psychiatrists in the Nazi period, who despatched 70,000 adult psychiatric patients and a much greater number of children with behavioural and intellectual difficulties

Today, in the case of the most severe mental illnesses at least, the outcomes obtained are little better than those obtained at the end of the 19th century. Even with the help of antipsychotic drugs, many people suffer from persisting symptoms and are socially isolated, economically non-productive and therefore poor. About ten per cent take their own lives. Astonishingly, cross-cultural comparisons show that people with mental health problems in the developing world have a greater chance of recovering from their difficulties than do those in the industrialised nations (Jablensky et al., 1992).

In the face of these disappointing results, modern psychiatrists still sometimes resort to extreme remedies. For example, antipsychotic drugs have very severe side effects such as Parkinsonian symptoms, diabetes, sexual dysfunction, obesity and a risk of sudden death through a variety of rare adverse reactions. Yet about 30 per cent of people who are given them fail to obtain any benefit at all, for reasons that are not known, and so are being exposed to these risks for no good cause. Of those who do benefit, about 50 per cent are currently prescribed more than one antipsychotic, against accepted good

Edited from R. Bentall, *Mental Health Today*, March 2004.

practice, and a similar proportion are probably given the drugs at a higher than optimum dosage (Cohen, 1997), thereby increasing the risk of side effects with no greater impact on symptoms (Bollini et al., 1994).

It could be argued that these poor practices reflect limited resources; it might also be argued that they are a consequence of poor professional training. However a greater impediment to progress is a poverty of ideas. The failures of psychiatry today reflect false assumptions about the nature of severe mental illness that were formulated more than a century ago and have gone unquestioned ever since.

The Kraepelinian paradigm

During the 20th century most attempts to explain and treat madness were guided by a set of assumptions made by early German psychiatrists, and Emil Kraepelin in particular. These can be summarised (briefly) as:

- madness is qualitatively different from normal functioning
- there is a finite and countable number of varieties of madness
- these are best understood as biological illnesses.

Over the course of his career Kraepelin famously came to believe that he had identified three major types of severe psychiatric disorder: dementia praecox (later renamed schizophrenia by Bleuler), manic depression (covering all the serious mood disorders), and paranoia (recently renamed delusional disorder), in which the patient experiences only delusions.

It is hard to overstate the historical significance of this organising framework. According to Shorter (1997), it is Kraepelin, not Freud, who stands at the centre of the history of psychiatry. Thus any evidence that undermines Kraepelin's framework shakes the whole edifice of psychiatric theory at its foundations.

In fact, evidence of this kind exists in abundance (Bentall, 2003). For example, studies demonstrated as long as 20 years ago (Chapman et al., 1980; Claridge, 1987) that may otherwise healthy individuals, when questioned, report attenuated psychotic experiences such as transient hallucinations or beliefs in magical forces. There is, it seems, a continuum running from the extreme experiences of people with psychosis, through eccentricity and New Age beliefs, to the mundane beliefs and attitudes of ordinary people. More recent studies by epidemologists have similarly revealed that a surprising proportion of the population, when given psychiatric interviews, report experiences that appear to be fullblown symptoms of psychiatric disorder (van Os et al., 2000). One per cent of the population is admitted to psychiatric hospital with a diagnosis of schizophrenia; nearer ten percent experience auditory hallucinations at some point in their lives but, as they are not actually distressed by their voices, do not end up in psychiatric care.

The idea that psychiatric disorders fall into discrete types is challenged by a variety of lines of evidence. It has been known for a long time that psychiatric diagnoses are highly unreliable, in the sense that two psychiatrists assessing the same patients will often disagree about their diagnoses. It was to resolve these differences that DSM-111 was devised in the 1970s. Yet agreement between psychiatrists has hardly improved. In one recent study researchers applied several competing sets of diagnostic criteria to the same group of 700 patients (van Os et al., 1999). Depending on the definition used, the numbers diagnosed as suffering from mania varied between 18 and 87, while the numbers suffering from schizophrenia varied between 268 and 387.

Matters become even more confusing when other tests of the validity of psychiatric diagnoses are used. The application of most definitions of schizophrenia and bipolar disorder seems to produce more people with a mixture of both sets of symptoms than 'pure' cases. Indeed, many researchers now accept that there is a spectrum of conditions running from schizophrenia, through the so-called 'schizoaffective' conditions, to pure bipolar disorder. Even this is probably an oversimplification. Examined in detail, the symptoms of people diagnosed with schizophrenia fall into at least three independent groups: the positive symptoms, symptoms of cognitive disorganisation, and the so-called negative symptoms such as social withdrawal, apathy and the inability to experience pleasure. So, just to account for 'schizophrenia', we require not one theory but at least three.

But there is even worse news for the Kraepelinian system. Diagnoses are supposed to predict how the patient will fare in the future and which treatments are likely to be effective. Psychiatric diagnoses singularly fail in this regard. For example, although antipsychotic drugs are widely regarded as the treatment of choice for schizophrenia, many people with a diagnosis of schizophrenia fail to respond to them, whereas the drugs can work for people with a bipolar diagnosis. Conversely, lithium carbonate, a treatment for bipolar disorder, can benefit people with schizophrenia who experience mood swings. Nor do diagnoses predict outcome: in the cases of both schizophrenia and bipolar disorder, some people recover completely, some remain ill for all their adult lives, and many have intermediate outcomes – periods of partial or full recovery interspersed with episodes of illness. In this respect psychiatric diagnosis is not dissimilar to astrology: both systems attempt to tell us something about people and to predict what will happen to them in the future, and both fail miserably.

It is sometimes said that diagnoses are nothing more than a crude shorthand by which clinicians communicate with each other about their patients. Does it matter if they are less than scientific? It does matter, for three reasons. First, a crude diagnosis of schizophrenia, say, conveys much less information about the person than a simple list of their difficulties. Second, psychiatric research uses diagnoses to group together people with widely differing problems and compare the groups for the purposes of research. No wonder there has been little progress in understanding the causes of severe mental illness. Finally, theories of psychiatric disorder guide psychiatric practice and the attitudes of its practitioners towards their patients. Without the belief that there is a hard and fast line between sanity and madness, without the assumption that psychiatric disorders are brain diseases that are unconnected with problems of living in the world, it would not have been possible for generations of psychiatrists to advocate crude brain operations, or even killing, as treatment. Moreover, by dismissing patients' comments about their lives and treatment as expressions of diseased brains, psychiatrists have been able to deny them a voice that otherwise might have been raised in protest against the horrors perpetrated on them over the past 150 years.

A new understanding

Until recently no obvious alternative way of thinking about psychiatric disorders has been available to challenge the dominance of the Kraepelinian school. However in the last ten years or so a new understanding of madness has begun to emerge, from psychological research. This understanding starts from the premise that we should study, attempt to explain and ultimately offer treatment for the actual problems that people bring into the clinic. It seems that what psychiatrists refer to as 'symptoms' can be readily explained in terms of well-understood psychological mechanisms. And when they have been explained in this way, there remains no 'schizophrenia' or 'bipolar disorder' that also requires an explanation.

For example, auditory hallucinations of voices commenting on or telling a person what to do are usually regarded as symptoms of schizophrenia, but are also often reported by patients diagnosed with bipolar disorder or major depression. Recent research has converged on the idea that these voices are in fact inner speech – the internal dialogue we all conduct – misattributed to an alien or external source (Bentall, 1990). Using electromyography, it has long been possible to record small electrical currents in the speech muscles, known as subvocalisations, that are present when someone who is hallucinating hears their voices. Recent neuro-imaging studies have similarly shown that the parts of the brain responsible for language production 'light up' when people with hallucinations hear their voices. Overall, these findings suggest that hallucinations result from a breakdown in source monitoring: that is, the process by which we distinguish between self-generated sensations and events in the external world.

Some delusions, it seems, are the consequence of using normal reasoning processes to explain anomalous experiences. For example, people suffering form Capgras syndrome (where the person believes a loved one has been replaced by an imposter or doppelganger) have, it is now known, a subtle impairment of the cognitive mechanisms involved in recognising faces: they know whose face it is but do not get the feeling of familiarity that is normally experienced when encountering someone well known. Their delusion seems to arise from the patient's attempt to explain this unsettling phenomenon.

However, most delusions seem to reflect reasoning biases. Garety and colleagues (1991) have shown that deluded patients in general appear to jump to conclusions about the meaning of evidence they encounter: i.e. when puzzled they do not seek more information to resolve their puzzlement. Other research has found that people with persecutory delusions have a particular style of reasoning about the causes of events (Bentall et al., 2001). Depressed patients tend to attribute negative experiences to causes that are excessively global (affecting all areas of life), stable (unchangeable) and internal (to do with the self). This pessimistic style of reasoning is, of course, partially responsible for their depression. Patients with persecutory delusions tend to attribute negative events to causes that are global, stable and external to the self, and are also more likely than ordinary people to attribute blame to the actions of other people. So, for example, an ordinary person arriving late for a meeting will apologise and explain that the traffic was dreadful. A depressed person might apologise for their poor timekeeping. A paranoid person might say that the police had turned all the traffic lights red.

Why paranoid patients reason in this way is not yet fully understood. A combination of motivational and cognitive factors may well be involved. That ordinary people are more likely to attribute negative events externally is known to be a mechanism for regulating self-esteem: if we do this we don't have to feel bad about ourselves and we don't have to feel bad about other people either. Arguably paranoid delusions arise when this self-regulatory mechanical malfunctions.

Other psychotic complaints – notably language disorders, delusions of being controlled and mania – have begun to yield to psychological analysis in the same way. Negative symptoms have been less often studied but there is no reason why there should not also be a psychological story to tell about them. The point is that there can be no one-size-fits-all model of schizophrenia or bipolar disorder; we need a separate theory for each type of complaint. Nor is there anything 'anti-biological' about this account of madness. Indeed, it can lead to interesting biological research: for example, when modern neuro-imaging technology is used to study which parts of the brain become active when people generate causal explanations for different kinds of events.

From complaints to aetiology

It has sometimes been objected that complaint-orientated research does not lead to aetiological discoveries, which are the main goal of the Kraepelinian research programme. Again, this can be challenged. The standard way of thinking about the aetiology of severe mental illness is in terms of genetics. Indeed, it has been said that the effects of inheritance on psychosis are so strong that major environmental influences are precluded. This belief is incorrect, for two reasons: first, because the genetic evidence is nowhere near as strong as is sometimes supposed (it now accepted that many genes make minor contributions towards psychosis); second, because the standard genetic research strategies have failed to take into account gene–environment correlations (the tendency of people with particular genes to be exposed to particular environments). In fact, the best genetic evidence supports the idea of strong gene–environment interactions, and that specific complaints may be related to particular combinations of environmental and genetic influences. For example, a study in Finland (Wahlberg et al., 2000) found that adopted-away children of people with schizophrenia were more likely to become language disordered in adulthood than adopted-away children of healthy parents, but only if they were raised by adopting parents who communicated with them in a dysfunctional way. This finding concords with other studies showing that the language disorders of people with psychosis are heavily influenced by genes, whereas other symptoms, particularly paranoia, appear to be much less so (Cohen, 1997).

Specific pathways to different complaints begin to become evident when we look at environmental influences on psychosis. It seems that people with paranoia in particular often have difficulties with emotional attachments, which suggests a failure of the normal process of bonding between parent and child. Consistent with this hypothesis, a longitudinal study of a large group of children born in Finland found that, if their mothers described their pregnancy as unwanted when interviewed before childbirth, there was a four-fold increased risk of psychosis by the time the children had reached 26 years of age (Dozier et al., 1991).

Environmental influences also seem to be important in the case of paranoia. In the last ten years or so it has been discovered that immigrant groups – for example, Afro-Caribbeans living in the UK – are highly vulnerable to psychosis, and especially to paranoid and manic symptoms (Boydell et al., 2001). Growing up in a city environment, or in circumstances associated with powerlessness and victimisation, also seems to have the same effect (Mirowsky and Ross, 1983). Perhaps these kinds of environments foster the paranoid person's assumption that negative experiences must be caused by malevolent others. In other words, perhaps there is often a kernel of truth in their paranoid ideas.

Other types of experiences seem to confer a vulnerability to auditory hallucinations. Recent studies have consistently found that a very large proportion of severely ill psychiatric patients report having been sexually abused or to have suffered other traumas (Goodman et al., 1997): a phenomenon that was largely over-looked by Kraepelinians because they did not think it important to quiz patients about their life histories. Most of the relevant studies have concerned people with a diagnosis of schizophrenia but one investigation has also found an association between hallucinations and reports of childhood sexual abuse in people with a diagnosis of bipolar disorder (Hammersley et al., 2003). Presumably traumatic experiences affect the source monitoring processes by which we distinguish between our own thoughts and external stimuli.

Post Kraepelin psychiatry

An account of madness can be developed on the basis of an analysis of individual complaints that is at once more scientific, more philosophically satisfactory and more humane than that of Kraepelin and his adherents. It is more scientific because it is not based on the dubious assumptions about the nature of psychiatric disorder embraced by Kraepalin, and also because it is supported by a large volume of research. It is more philosophically satisfactory because it does not assume a Cartesian division between biological and psychological processes. It is more humane because it places the individual's experiences at the centre of psychiatric inquiry and therefore restores to patients the voice that was denied to them by the Kraepelinian system. This is obvious, for example, in the way that the new approach treats people's life histories. Dreadful experiences that were ignored by the Kraepelinians come sharply into focus.

One final objection that is sometimes raised against this new approach is that it offers few guidelines for the practising psychiatrist. In fact the approach's full implications have yet to be properly explored, but a few obvious ones can be stated at this juncture.

First, by abandoning the Kraepelinian myths, we make less probable the kinds of barbaric practices cited above. We begin to talk to our patients, to enquire into their life histories, and to take their attitudes towards treatment more seriously. We do not smother them with irrational doses of medication; indeed, we withdraw medication that is ineffective. In short, we treat them as human beings, investigate their individual needs and tailor our interventions accordingly.

Second, this new approach is also leading to specific treatment strategies. Cognitive behaviour therapy has shown great promise when targeted at specific problems such as hallucinations and delusions, although it requires further development. The findings from research into the psychological processes involved in these complaints are being used to refine this kind of treatment. What we will be able to achieve in even ten years' times will comfortably exceed what we can achieve today. Third, the discovery that many people live relatively happy lives despite their psychotic experiences raises the possibility that some may do best without treatment of any kind. Marius Romme, the Dutch social psychiatrist who has formed a national organisation in Holland for people who hear voices, once told me he thought that 'voice-hearers' (to use his preferred term) were like homosexuals in the 1950s: more in need of liberation than cure. Now that really is a radical thought.

References

Bentall, R.P. (1990) 'The illusion of reality: a review and integration of psychological research on hallucinations'. *Psychological Bulletin*, 107: 82–95.

Bentall, R.P. (2003). *Madness explained: psychosis and human nature*. London: Penguin.

Bentall, R.P, Corcoran R, Howard R. et al. (2001) 'Persecutory delusions: a review and theoretical integration', *Clinical Psychology Review*, 21: 1143–92.

Bollini, P, Pampallona S, Orza M.J et al. (1994) 'Antipsychotic drugs: is more worse? A meta analysis of the published randomised controlled trials'. *Psychological Medicine*, 24: 307–16.

Boydell, J., van Os, J. McKenzie, J. et al. (2001) 'Incidence of schizophrenia in ethnic minorities in London: ecological study into interactions with environment'. *British Medical Journal*, 323: 1–4.

Chapman, L.J., Edell, E.W., Chapman, J.P. (1980) 'Physical anhedonia, perceptual aberration and psychosis proneness'. *Schizophrenia Bulletin*, 6: 639–53.

Claridge, G.S. (1987). 'The schizophrenias as nervous types revisited'. *British Journal of Psychiatry*, 151: 735–43.

Cohen, D. (1997) 'A critique of the use of neuroleptic drugs in psychiatry'. In: Fisher S., Greenberg R.P. (eds). *From placebo to panacea: putting psychiatric drugs to the test*. New York: John Wiley & Sons.

Dozier, M, Stevenson, A.L, Lee, S.E. et al. (1991) 'Attachment organisation and familiar over-involvement for adults with serious psychopathological disorders. *Development and Psychopathology*, 3: 475–89.

Garety, P.A., Hemsley, D.R., Wessely, S. (1991) 'Reasoning in deluded schizophrenic and paranoid patients. *Journal of Nervous and Mental Disease*, 179, 4: 194–201.

Goodman, L.A., Rosenberg, S.D., Mueser, K. et al. (1997) 'Physical and sexual assault history in women with serious mental illness: prevalence, correlates, treatment, and future research directions. *Schizophrenia Bulletin*, 23: 685–96.

Hammersley, P., Dias, A., Todd, G. et al. (2003) 'Childhood trauma and hallucinations in bipolar affective disorder: a preliminary investigation. *British Journal of Psychiatry*, 182: 543–7.

Jablensky, A., Sartorius, N., Ernberg, G. et al. (1992) 'Schizophrenia: manifestations, incidence and course in different cultures'. *Psychological Medicine*, supp. 20: 1–97.

Mirowsky, J., Ross, C.E. (1983) 'Paranoia and the structure of powerlessness'. *American Sociological Review*, 48: 228–39.

Shorter, E. (1997) *A history of psychiatry*, New York: John Wiley & Sons.

van Os, J., Gilvarry, C., Bale, R. et al. (1999) 'A comparison of the utility of dimensional and categorical representations of psychosis'. *Psychological Medicine*, 29: 595–606.

van Os, J., Hanssen, M., Bijl, R.V. et al. (2000) 'Strauss (1969) revisited: a psychosis continuum in the normal population? *Schizophrenia Research*, 45: 11–20.

4

Reclaiming the humanity in personality disorder

Karen Wright, Kevin Haigh and Mick McKeown

The notion of personality disorder is prominent in both of the diagnostic systems, DSM (APA, 2000) and ICD, (WHO 1992), currently favoured across Western psychiatric services. Distinct challenges in how to organize services to best meet relevant care and treatment needs, including the vexed question of treatability for some individuals, have been fairly common across different national jurisdictions.

In 1999, when the UK government announced plans to introduce legislation in England and Wales for compulsory detention of people with dangerous severe personality disorders (DSPD), speculation soared within the media and public services. The term 'dangerous severe personality disorder', which is used as both a noun and an adjective, has no universally accepted definition. The Royal College of Psychiatrists (1999) suggest that DSPD should be characterised by 'gross societal disturbance', as well as 'gross severity of personality disorder within the flamboyant group and a personality disorder in at least one other cluster also' (p. 11). Diagnosis is highly controversial, and issues of reliability and validity exist, because diagnosis is frequently made by interview and disagreement may be common. A postal survey revealed that such diagnoses were rarely based upon structured diagnostic instruments (Milton, 2000). The high prevalence of substance misuse and comorbidity further complicates presentations, and decisions tend to be made in respect of the individual's perceived risk to public safety rather than any specificity of mental disorder (Chiswick, 2001; Morrall, 2000).

Edited from K. Wright, K. Haigh and M. McKeown, *International Journal of Mental Health Nursing* (2007), vol. 11, pp. 236–46.

In policy terms, 'personality disorder', already cloaked in pejorative and disparaging connotations, was now inextricably linked with terminology which implied the public at large were vulnerable to a group of individuals for whom there seemed to be no solution other than containment.

Representations of personality disorder

The policy ambivalence, simultaneously promoting containment and care, is mirrored in mass media representations of personality disorder. All mental health service users are subject to stigmatizing and stereotypical representation and constructions of otherness, whether in the discourse of the lay public, in the pages of the print media, or on TV and cinema screens. Quite often, these accounts fail to differentiate between the various medical categories of mental disorder, with terms such as psychotic and psychopathic used interchangeably in a context of public fear of violent madness. Various commentators have noted the range of media depictions of people with a mental illness, with individuals described as monsters, homicidal maniacs, or narcissistic parasites, raving mad, bad, or absolutely evil. Different stories suggest a public reaction ranging from horror to sympathy, with various stops along the way through ridicule and titillation. Inevitably, the media prescription for policy is for containment: either these people are dangerous and in need of secure detention, or they present a risk to themselves and are in need of the emotional security of asylum (see Gleeson, 1991; Hyler et al., 1991; McKeown and Clancy, 1995). This fits with a perception that many of those individuals who are considered violent and criminal should rationally be incarcerated as a moral and justifiable action to protect a vulnerable and blameless society.

A recent UK national newspaper featured experiences at a high-security prison. Various individuals spoke of the identity issues at stake in receiving the status of dangerous and severe personality disorder:

> At the end of the day, all of us sitting here are monsters, whether we're armed robbers, child molesters, or killers – we're monsters.

> You know when things are getting bad when you're released from a stretch and you go back to your own estate and the hard men you used to know there seem scared, when they treat you like a psycho. (Anonymous interviewees, quoted in Rose, 2005; p. 21)

In the past, prisoners with a personality disorder who were incarcerated for their crimes but were not provided with treatment have been released only to reoffend, further contributing to public and governmental demands for indefinite detention for some. Unfortunately, the term 'personality disorder' often becomes inextricably linked with concepts of dangerousness and evil in lay consciousness.

The construction of difference

The available media representations of madness and personality disorder are sustained within a broader set of social constructs which expose a dynamic relationship between idealised selfhood and denigrated otherness. The anthropologist Geertz (1977) articulated a succinct definition of the self in modern society as:

> bounded, unique, more or less integrated motivational and cognitive universe, a dynamic centre of awareness, emotion, judgement and action, organised into a distinctive whole and set contrastively against other such wholes and against a social and natural background. (p. 483)

This particularly western conceptualisation of the self has proved to be very much compatible with the prevailing hegemony of science and capitalism, and has become increasingly dominant and prominent in psychologised and lay discourse (Ingleby, 1985; Rose, 1990). This notion of the self is the archetypal subject of much counselling and psychotherapy (Venn, 1984), which can, indeed, be described as self-celebratory (Sampson, 1993). In human interaction, this version of the self can be seen, at least in part, to take shape via its relationship to its antithesis – that which encapsulates a sense of 'otherness'. Young (1999) has argued that this construction of difference is almost inevitably accompanied by a demonisation of the 'other'. Otherness in the context of stigmatised or demonised groups suggests some essential denial of common attributes or shared characteristics, it is all or nothing: it casts the other as essentially different: as less than human.

The diagnosis and institutional containment of different versions of personality disorder further establishes the behaviour of the individuals concerned as 'other'. These diagnostic acts operate to restore order to the prevailing symbolic framework, at least in part by reinforcing what is deemed to be normal, or morally appropriate. This is enacted in a process of making clear the boundary between this normality and what is not: that which is different, and 'other'. Hence, categories of personality disorder, especially the extreme variants, are presented as completely distinct from a prevailing view of what constitutes normal and common humanity. These disordered 'selves' are not like 'ourselves', and explicit knowledge that this is so, is comforting and allays anxiety about extremes of behaviour and the nature of ourselves. Indeed, one clear function of the construction of difference is that it allows for the projection of unwanted parts of the ideal self into the denigrated other (Dalal, 2001; Timmi, 1996). Awareness of such processes ought to enable us to deconstruct our notions of self and personality disorder (as an exemplar of otherness) and move towards reclaiming the common humanity in individuals so labelled.

Of course, the notion of otherness in mental health, other health contexts, or wider society for that matter, is not restricted to discursive practices surrounding personality disorder, and numerous scholars have utilised social constructionist theories to illuminate this (Canales, 2000; Hamilton and Manias, 2006; Holmes, 2003; Johnson et al., 2004; Maccallum, 2002; Peternelj-Taylor, 2004; Warner and Gabe, 2004). Constructions of otherness arguably pervade the mental health system, with many other kinds of patients, members of population groups, or diagnostic groups cast as 'other' by virtue of the formal and informal categories used to define them, or even to simply refer to them (Crowe, 2000; Maccallum, 2002). Prime examples of such discourse construct difference relating to categories of ethnicity, gender, and age: utilising constructionist theory and associated methodologies, studies of our own have addressed social constructions of mental health and race (Stowell-Smith and McKeown, 1999a), psychopathy and race (Stowell-Smith and McKeown, 1999b), gender and challenging behaviour (McKeown et al., 2003), and risk in mental health services (McKeown et al., 1999).

The consequences of such constructions of difference are keenly felt by service users with diagnoses of personality disorder:

> We get stigma from medical professionals – many older psychiatrists still live with the PD as a dustbin diagnosis – we can't get them better therefore let's give them a label that means they are awkward then we can kick them out. Many psych nurses have the same impressions as they are not trained in PDs so they have no idea how to handle us. They accuse us of 'acting out' when we are doing anything that they do not understand . . . as this is some psychobabble word that they have heard but do not understand truly. (Anderson, 2004)

Service users' narratives can also suggest openings for care and treatment strategies and can focus upon the relevance of social and developmental factors in case histories, A personal account by Hopkinson (2002) suggests that her diagnosis of personality disorder was in her view, a consequence of childhood experiences specifically witnessing her father beat her mother, who was herself a heavy drinker. Such reflections have the potential to initiate engagement with psychologically or psychodynamically informed therapeutic understandings and interventions. Conversely, however, practitioner reliance upon powerful constructions of difference and otherness can lead to distinct therapeutic pessimism and inertia, and may, at least in part, account for the substance of the critique that historically, UK psychiatric institutions relied upon personality disorder as a diagnosis of exclusion (NIMHE/ DH, 2003).

A plea to escape the imposition of difference and otherness is found in this statement from Lucy, the eponymous author of the myboderline life website (http://www.myborderlinelife.co.uk):

I would love for non-borderlines to somehow be able to taste this foreign territory from the inside.

Implicit here is the sense that Lucy is not typically responded to empathically and has perhaps herself internalised the imposition of difference that accompanies her diagnostic label. Other recipients of personality disorder diagnoses question the process of diagnosis and remark upon the implications of being defined in terms of negative traits (Main, 2002, p. 38):

Rightly or wrongly I interpreted the label as a sign that I was fundamentally flawed, that the bad parts of me far outweighed any good attributes that might also be part of my personality.

Staff discourse

Interestingly, lay and professional accounts can intermingle, leaving open the real possibility that care staff are equally conversant in the pejorative colloquial as well as the psychiatric and psychological. For example, Barrett (1996) observed commonplace utterances in Australian inpatient units to include 'mad as cut snake' (p. 149) and 'away with the birds' (p. 147). Concepts of deservingness and entitlement are also redolent in many studies of staff attitudes. Feather and Johnstone (2001), for instance, concluded that the client with a personality disorder would be blamed more for aggressive behaviour and excused less when compared with the person diagnosed with schizophrenia.

This is exaggerated in studies of staff attitudes to people admitted to high-secure hospitals under the category of psychopathic disorder, where care staff deployed the terminology of 'evil' in reference to the offence behaviour of such individuals (Bower, 2002; Mason and Mercer, 1998). Staff were likely to be more understanding of the behaviour and more likely to explain it in clinical terms when the protagonists were identified as being mentally ill, and, conversely, were more likely to make sense of things in moral terms when considering the same behaviour by those deemed to be personality disordered (Feather and Johnstone, 2001).

Arguably, the categorical approach to definition and diagnosis embodied within psychiatric classification systems is itself an example of the social processes of constructing difference and otherness (Castillo et al., 2000; Crowe, 2000; Harper, 2002). Hence, it is not surprising if there is correspondence between lay and professionalised discourse in this regard. Beresford (2002; p. 29) has argued that standard psychiatric diagnostic systems operate to reinforce the 'strange difference' of otherness by emphasizing abnormality and biologically defined pathology; consequently, the diagnosed become 'divorced from the rest of humanity'. The categories of personality disorder can function to suggest that various negative characteristics are the sole province of those diagnosed, which is palpably not the case. Given this, one service user has wondered if:

> it wouldn't be worse to be diagnosed as having an 'ordered personality' . . . because it seems to me that the traits that make up a personality disorder are the traits of life. (Main, 2002; p. 38)

In a user-led study utilizing emancipatory research methods, service users carrying a diagnosis of personality disorder constucted their own definitional framework, distinct from the accepted clinical taxonomies (Castillo et al., 2000). This new construct moved beyond symptoms and traits to include reference to contextual factors, triggers, coping strategies, and insights into effectiveness of treatments. The authors conclude that there is an 'overwhelming need for a reframing and renaming of personality disorder, to offer a better understanding of this human condition' (Castillo et al., 2000; p. 20).

While the very real challenges which arise in the care of this client group ought not to be minimised, there would seem to be an unhelpful polarisation of viewpoint evidently at play. It would seem that there has been very little shift in the attitudes held by workers since the 1980s, when Lewis and Appleby (1988) concluded that suicide attempts and other behaviours displayed by the personality disorder client were viewed as manipulative and under voluntary control.

References

American Psychiatric Association (2000). *Diagnostic and Statistical Manual of Mental Disorders (DSM-IV-TR)*. Washington, DC: APA.

Anderson, P. (2004). *Personality Disorder and Service User Involvement*. [Cited 17 Feb. 2005]. Available from: URL http://www.nimhenorthwest.org.uk

Barrett, R. (1996). *The Psychiatric Team and the Social Definition of Schizophrenia: An Anthropological Study of Person and Illness*. Cambridge: Cambridge University Press.

Beresford, P. (2002) 'Encouraging caring communities'. *Mental Health Today*, February, 28–30.

Bowers, L. (2002). *Dangerous and Severe Personality Disorder: Response and Role of the Psychiatric Team*. London: Routledge.

Canales, M. (2000). 'Othering: Toward an understanding of difference. [Vulnerability and empowerment: part 1]'. *Advances in Nursing Science*, 22, 16–31.

Castillo, H., Allen, L. and Warner, K. (2000). 'Crossing the borderline'. *Openmind*, 106 (Nov/Dec), 20–21.

Chiswick, D. (2001). 'Dangerous severe personality disorder: from notion to law'. *Psychiatric Bulletin*, 25, 282–3.

Crowe M. (2000). 'Constructing normality: a discourse analysis of the DSM-IV'. *Journal of Psychiatric and Mental Health Nursing*, 7, 69–77.

Dalal, F. (2001). 'Insides and outsides: a review of psychoanalytic renderings of difference, racism and prejudice'. *Psychoanalytic Studies*, 3(1), 43–66.

Department of Health (DH) (2000). *Reforming the Mental Health Act*. London: HMSO.

Feather, N. and Johnstone, C. (2001). 'Social norms, entitlement, and deservingness: differential reactions to aggressive behavior of schizophrenic and personality disorder patients'. *Personality and Social Psychology Bulletin*, 27(6), 755–67.

Geertz, C. (1977). 'From the native's point of view: on the nature of anthropological understanding'. In: J. Dolgin, D. Kemnitzer and D. Schneider (eds). *Symbolic Anthropology: A Reader in the Study of Symbols and Meanings* (pp. 480–92). New York: Columbia University.

Gleeson, K. (1991). Out of our minds: the deconstruction and reconstruction of madness (Unpublished PhD Thesis). University of Reading.

Hamilton, B. and Manias, E. (2006). ' "She's manipulative and he's right off ": a critical analysis of psychiatric nurses' oral and written language in the acute patient setting'. *International Journal of Mental Health Nursing*, 15, 84–92.

Harper, D. (2002). 'The tyranny of expert language'. *Openmind*, 113 (Jan/Feb), 8–9.

Holmes, D. (2003). 'Constructing monsters: correctional discourse and nursing practice'. *International Journal of Psychiatric Nursing Research*, 8, 942–62.

Hopkinson, C. (2002). *My Theory of the Cause of Personality Disorder*, Dialogue, 11, Summer, 4. [Cited 11 Apr 2005]. Available from: URL: http://www.dh.gov.uk/hspch/visped.htm

Hyler, S., Gabbard, G. and Schneider, I. (1991). 'Homicidal maniacs and narcissistic parasites. stigmatisation of mentally ill persons in the movies'. *Hospital and Community Psychiatry*, 42(10), 1044–8.

Ingleby, D. (1985). 'Professionals as socializers: the "psy complex" '. *Research in Law, Deviance and Social Control*, 7, 79–109.

Johnson, J., Bottorff, J., Browne, A., Grewal, S., Hilton, B. and Clarke, H. (2004). 'Othering and being othered in the context of health care services'. *Health Communication*, 16, 253–71.

Lewis, C. and Appleby, L. (1988). 'Personality disorder: the patients psychiatrists dislike'. *British Journal of Psychiatry*, 153, 44–9.

Maccallum, E. (2002) 'Othering and psychiatric nursing'. *Journal of Psychiatric and Mental Health Nursing*, 9, 87–94.

McKeown, M. and Clancy, B. (1995). 'Images of madness: media influence on societal perceptions of mental illness'. *Mental Health Nursing*, 15(2), 10–12.

McKeown, M., Hinks, M., Stowell-Smith, M., Mercer, D. and Forster, J. (1999). 'Q methodology, risk training and quality management'. *International Journal of Health Care Quality Assurance*, 12(6), 254–66.

McKeown, M., Anderson, J., Bennett, A. and Clayton, P. (2003). 'Gender politics and secure services for women: reflections on a study of staff understandings of challenging behaviour'. *Journal of Psychiatric and Mental Health Nursing*, Special Forensic Edition, 10, 585–91.

Main, L. (2002). 'This life'. *Mental Health Today*, August, 38.

Main, T. (1957). 'The ailment'. *British Journal of Medical Psychology*, 30, 129–45.

Mason, T. and Mercer, D. (1998). *Critical Perspectives in Forensic Care: Inside Care*. London: Macmillan.

Milton, J. (2000). 'A postal survey of assessment procedure in forensic settings'. *Psychiatric Bulletin*, 24, 254–7.

Morrall, P. (2000). *Madness and Murder*. London: Whurr.

National Institute for Mental Health in England (NIMHE) (2002), *Services for People with Personality Disorder: The Thoughts of Service Users*. [Cited 21 Oct. 2004] Available from: URL: http://www.nimhe.org/downloads/Rex_Haigh.doc

National Institute for Mental Health in England /Department of Health (2003). *Personality Disorder: No Longer a Diagnosis of Exclusion*. Leeds: NIMHE/DH.

Peternelj-Taylor, C. (2004) 'An exploration of othering in forensic psychatric and correctional nursing'. *Canadian Journal of Nursing Research*, 36, 130–46.

Rose, D. (2005). 'It's a prison within a prison. A unit designed to treat the country's most dangerous men'. An exclusive report from the Westgate by David Rose, *The Observer*, 20 November 2005, pp. 21–9.

Rose, N. (1990). *Governing the Soul: The Shaping of the Private Self*. London: Routledge.

Royal College of Psychiatrists (1999). *Council Report 71: Offenders with Personality Disorder*. London: Gaskell.

Sampson, E. (1993) *Celebrating the Other: A Dialogic Account of Human Nature*. New York: Harvester Wheatsheaf.

Stowell-Smith, M. and McKeown, M. (1999a). 'Locating mental health in black and white men: A Q methodological study'. *Journal of Health Psychology*, 4(2), 209–23.

Stowell-Smith, M. and McKeown, M. (1999b). 'Race, psychopathy and self: a discourse analytic study'. *British Journal of Medical Psychology*, 72, 459–70.

Timmi, S. (1996). 'Race and colour in internal and external reality'. *British Journal of Psychotherapy*, 13, 183–92.

Venn, C. (1984). 'The subject of psychology'. In: J. Henriques, W. Hollway, C. Urwin, C. Venn and V. Walkerdine (eds). *Changing the Subject* (pp. 19–152). New York: Methuen.

Warner, J. and Gabe, J. (2004). 'Risk and liminality in mental health social work'. *Health, Risk and Society*, 6, 387–99.

World Health Organization (1992). *International Classification of Mental and Behavioural Disorders*. Geneva: World Health Organization.

Young, J. (1999). *The Exclusive Society*. London: Sage.

5

Twenty-five years of disagreeing with psychiatry

Lucy Johnstone

I qualified as a clinical psychologist in 1983, and subsequently authored a book and various papers taking a critical view of biomedically based psychiatry (for example, Johnstone, 2000). Here, I present snapshots of my experiences in psychiatry based on articles published in 1993 and 2001, with up to date reflections from 2008.

In 1993, disillusioned with 10 years' full-time work in adult mental health, I left to take up an academic post instead. My parting shot (Johnstone, 1993) generated a large postbag of sympathetic responses. The condensed extract below makes the general tone and viewpoint clear:

> One of the questions that all mental health professionals come to expect at parties is, 'Doesn't it get depressing working with all those unhappy people?' Sometimes it does, of course, but for me the main source of frustration, anger and despair comes from other professionals, or to be more accurate, those of them who support a medical understanding of mental distress ... In order to survive and maintain some kind of foothold in psychiatry, I tended to save speaking out for the more important situations. My NHS career thus consisted of long periods of suppressed frustration and relatively muted comment, interspersed with brief periods of open conflict. The following genuine examples illustrate the typical tactics that I and like-minded colleagues had to face:
>
> *Ignoring or discounting non-medical input.* The contributions of non-medical staff are rarely acknowledged, and their work is often regarded as a kind of fringe recreational activity ('doing painting' with the art therapist or 'keeping occupied' with the OTs.) This assumption was betrayed by one consultant who, after hearing an OT's detailed description of one woman's progress in group therapy, commented, 'That's all very well, but we really need to start treating her depression'.

Attributing all improvement to medical intervention. Since medication is constantly being adjusted, any change for the better is bound to coincide with a new dosage and can be attributed to it. Conversely, progress in counselling is attributed to other factors. When I reported a very successful outcome to a long period of therapy with one in-patient, the consultant commented: 'These conditions do go into remission sometimes'.

Belief in medical interventions is also maintained by *disqualifying the counter-evidence.* If ECT appears to 'work', it will be used again. If it doesn't 'work', then it will still be used again in case it 'works' next time. There are no circumstances that would count as indications against its use. This is in marked contrast to non-medical interventions, where a single failure (for example, a family who did not respond to family therapy) will be quoted for years to come.

Quoting important-sounding research: for example, 'It's been proven that schizophrenics have lesions in their brains'. This frequently bamboozles non-medical staff, who may not realise that there is no proven correlation, that even if there were it would not necessarily indicate a causal link, and that any research based on a dubious concept like "schizophrenia" is seriously compromised from the start. And psychiatrists will not hesitate to undermine your ideas with the dismissive remark 'That's only a hypothesis'. You will not be thanked for pointing out that the theory that mental distress has a physiological cause is 'only a hypothesis'.

The category error. This is the technical term for an error of thinking identified by the philosopher Gilbert Ryle, who described an American tourist being shown around all the various parts of Oxford University – the library, the colleges, the lecture halls – and asking, 'But where's the university?'. This kind of error underlies a great deal of psychiatric thinking. I recall a long discussion in which I attempted to show that all of a certain young woman's behaviour – her anger, her changeable moods, her distrust of staff – could be understood in the light of her statement that she had been sexually abused. The consistent response was, 'Yes, but she may also have a manic-depressive illness that needs to be treated'.

The category error is part of a more general *complete inability to comprehend alternative viewpoints*, which runs deeper than simple disagreement. For example, my occasional confession of disbelief in the concept of schizophrenia was invariably met by responses such as, 'But in the case of Mrs Jones the diagnosis was clear-cut', or 'But people have a right to know what's wrong with them'. The idea that one might not subscribe to this kind of thought-system at all is incomprehensible to many.

Finally, there is the blatant attempt to discredit your views by implying that they are bizarre individual aberrations, by calling you an extremist or by attributing them to personal pathology, for example, 'You're just an angry young woman who likes provoking hostility'.

However, what concerns me is that beyond all these reactions there is a point at which dissenters from the orthodoxy are told not only that they are wrong, but that such views should not be held or expressed at all. The credibility of psychiatry has to be maintained by an appearance of consensus, and cracks in the façade can arouse a deeply defensive and threatened response.

I subsequently spent nine years working in a university, introducing some of these dangerous ideas to undergraduates, social workers, counselling students and psychiatric nurses. Academic posts come with guaranteed freedom of thought and expression under Section 41 of the 1986 Education Act, and these years were fairly free of conflict; indeed, the inclusion of a critical perspective on mental health added to the popularity of the teaching sessions.

In 2001 I returned part-time to psychiatry and found a mixed picture. Some things had changed dramatically, and yet the biomedical assumptions were still alive and well underneath (Johnstone, 2001):

> In the intervening years, much has altered. There has been a plethora of reorganisations and new policies: Health of the Nation targets, clinical governance, National Service Frameworks, clinical audit, and so on. There are new treatments: SSRIs, atypical neuroleptics, relapse prevention, early intervention and Dialectical Behaviour Therapy. There are even some new 'illnesses' such as body dysmorphic disorder. But how much has really changed?
>
> The hospital is now housing a far more disturbed and damaged population than before, and this is having knock-on effects on everything else. It is, I believe, good policy to keep people out of hospital where possible, and only admit those in acute need; but if you have entire wards consisting only of such people, with too few staff, beds and resources and too little support, training and supervision, then you have a recipe for disaster. Entire shifts consist of crisis management, with no time for staff support or debriefing or doing anything remotely therapeutic with the patients. Nursing staff are stretched to their absolute limits; my former students, now out on the wards, seem to be struggling to hold on to some shreds of idealism and compassion.
>
> Squalid and untherapeutic inpatient settings abound all over Britain (Mind, 2000), while surveys confirm that the number of compulsory admissions almost doubled between 1984 and 1996. Reduced numbers of beds may partly explain the higher concentration of craziness, as may increased use of drugs and alcohol and a more defensive attitude towards risk, but surely not all of it. What has happened?
>
> There are other mysteries too. None of the patients I knew 15 years ago seems to be around any more; they have been replaced by a completely new generation of desperate people. Later, I did come across some familiar files, and discovered that the former 'schizophrenics' are rapidly being re-classified as 'borderline personality disorders'. This diagnosis is definitely on the up and up, for reasons that are unclear to me. I suspect that at least three factors are at work. One is the desire to justify keeping out of hospital people whom the staff find difficult, on the grounds that they are 'personality disordered' rather than 'mentally ill' (Castillo, 2000). The second factor is the need to find a way of tacitly acknowledging that many of the most disturbed people have a history of such extreme trauma that an 'illness' diagnosis is totally implausible as an explanation. Who wouldn't be driven crazy by the torments that they have suffered? The third is

the convenience of the term of a government agenda of responding to public anxieties about dangerousness (Pilgrim, 2001).

This brings me on to another point. Sexual abuse was widely acknowledged as a feature in many patients' early lives last time I was around, but surely it wasn't, or at least wasn't known to be, quite as common as now? Just about all the women, and a good proportion of the men, have appalling abuse histories, frequently involving multiple physical and sexual assaults spanning many years.

It isn't all bad. I spend one day a week in a community mental health team. We no longer see any of those slightly anxious people who can't use buses or dislike spiders or aren't very happy with their husbands (where do they all go now?), so a lot of the work is quite demanding, but the team is extremely friendly and cohesive and offers a range of excellent psychological and practical forms of help – along with diagnosis and medication, of course, which seem to be necessary preconditions to being seen by any team.

Cognitive-behaviour therapy, always a winner in terms of claimed evidence-base and effectiveness, has gone from strength to strength. Service users are far more prominent. There is a very active patients' council at the hospital, which sends representatives to meetings and runs a drop-in for inpatients. Hearing Voices groups (staff-led) are widely agreed to be a good thing. Mental health staff are now officially allowed, indeed encouraged, to talk to mad people about their madness, under the general heading of Family Intervention or Cognitive Therapy in Psychosis. Some of the things we are meant to say to them when we meet them are, in my opinion, pretty dubious; still, this does provide another useful permit to gain entry to a world previously closed to us.

Consultant psychiatrists are definitely less powerful than they used to be. I take referrals directly from nursing staff on the ward, and work alongside and report back to them; the once obligatory attendance at ward rounds feels like an irrelevance. On the other hand, the power that has now been transferred to the managers is often used just as damagingly.

Moreover, the adherence to an unfounded biomedical model of mental distress is as rampant as ever. Although in the community it is diluted with (but not replaced by) new therapeutic approaches and a more democratic hierarchy, the dire hospital situation means that 'treatment', whether by choice or default, consists almost entirely of medication. Medical jargon still abounds. One consultant introduced himself to a patient at the start of a CPA with the words, 'You do accept that you are a paranoid schizophrenic?' Refusing your medication or questioning your diagnosis is still sternly opposed, and at the last case conference I attended the audience was still playing the old game of 'What's her label?'. Bewildered SHOs still try to cling to some semblance of usefulness by taking detailed lists of 'symptoms'. Ward rounds still consist largely of juggling medication in a doomed attempt to create sense and order out of the overwhelming human despair and chaos ... Progress in community treatment has been gained at the cost of a worse deal than ever for the most vulnerable group of all.

The Borderline Personality Disorder literature, if you disregard the insulting and nonsensical term itself, actually implies that it makes more sense to regard such people as suffering from traumas with psychological consequences than illnesses with biological causes, and to develop interventions accordingly. Taken to its logical conclusion, this would imply that a trauma model should replace medical diagnosis and treatment for most, perhaps nearly all, psychiatric inpatients. Health of the Nation targets and National Service Frameworks notwithstanding, I have little confidence that a visitor in ten years' time will find much to celebrate.

As I write this chapter, it is seven rather than ten years on, but some definite trends can be detected.

There has been a proliferation of reorganisation; most areas now boast not only a Community Mental Health Team (probably renamed as a Primary Care Liaison Team) but also a crisis team, a home treatment team, an early intervention team, and an assertive outreach team. While each of these in theory meets a genuine need, very little thought has gone into the philosophy underpinning them, or the way they relate to each other and to the hospital. As a result, they still deliver essentially the same diagnosis-and-medication based interventions, with the additional stress of having to negotiate with all the other new services. This is a recipe for constant bickering about boundaries and responsibilities, coupled with desperate attempts to find non-existent beds for those in most need.

CBT's status has been endorsed by the Layard report (Layard, 2006) which recommends setting up a new range of therapy centres across the nation. I can clearly recall psychologists' enthusiastic attempts, in the 1980s, to recruit clients from GP services for the brand new community-based services. This quickly produced an overwhelming number of the so-called 'worried well' who, as I noted in 2001, then had to be rigidly excluded from CMHTs by revising the admissions criteria. Now we have come full circle and they will once again get a community service. It would be nice to think that this is motivated entirely by client need, but Layard makes it disturbingly clear that it is driven by the economic imperative to get people back to work – an outcome that he is confident will inevitably follow the standard 16 sessions of CBT. I, along with other sceptics, will be watching with interest.

The service user movement continues to gain in strength. The international Hearing Voices Network is flourishing, and affiliated groups are deconstructing and demedicalising the areas of paranoia and unusual beliefs as well. The Critical Psychiatry Network has launched an attack on biomedical thinking from within the profession.

On the other hand, the epidemic of Borderline Personality Disorder shows no sign of abating. It seems incredible that in 1993 I had never met anyone with this diagnosis; even the 2000 edition of my book contains only a passing reference to the condition. BPD has been joined by an even more recent outbreak of manic-depression, now re-branded as bipolar disorder, and accompanied by a stream of new publications and, more unusually, a queue of celebrities claiming to suffer from it.

How can we account for this? It may be significant that these conditions are proliferating in parallel with the gradual disappearance of the focus of all those critiques from the 1960s onwards, the diagnosis of schizophrenia. The UK branch of the International Society for the Psychological Treatments of Schizophrenia and the other Psychoses (ISPS) voted last year to drop the word 'schizophrenia' from its title. The Campaign to Abolish the Schizophrenia Label (CASL) has groups across the country. Instead, we are invited to use the woollier and more user-friendly term 'psychosis'. While this may be less stigmatising, a moment's thought will show that it is equally, if not more, problematic in terms of reliability, validity, etc. In sum, I see this as a classic case of shifting the goalposts. It constitutes a new way of defusing and disguising the critiques without actually doing away with the concept of psychiatric diagnosis itself.

This newly-fashionable term also makes an appearance in the growing literature on trauma and psychosis. In brief, John Read and his colleagues have shown remarkable energy and determination in investigating the role of trauma (broadly defined) in those diagnosed as psychotic, and have established beyond any reasonable doubt that it is a causal factor in the majority of cases of psychosis (Read et al., 2006). The implications for the practice of psychiatry are of course profound, as I suggested in 2001. But here again, there are dangers. One is that 'trauma' will simply be added to the list of 'trigger factors' for the underlying biologically based 'illness', which is then treated in much the same way as before. We will not have to face up to the possibility that the pseudo-medical condition 'psychosis' is, in many cases, simply the long-term reaction to abuse.

So, what is the overall verdict? It seems to me that the last 25 years of psychiatry are a classic case of 'the more things change, the more they remain the same'. The major positive development is the service user/survivor movement, which was virtually non-existent in the early 1980s. There are certainly more alternative discourses available, to use a jargon term, for both professionals and service users. On the other hand, this quarter century is also an illustration of what Pilgrim (1990) has called 'the British cultural tradition of incorporating new ideas and practices in order to obstruct more radical shifts of thought or practice'. We are more aware of the role of trauma, but only as the precipitant of a disease process. Hearing Voices groups are turned into cognitive therapy ('your voices are the symptom of an illness that is triggered by stress'). Familiar medications are found to be ineffective and/or damaging, but are simply replaced by other medications, which in their turn are found to be equally ineffective and/or damaging. Dubious diagnoses are dropped, but other equally dubious ones are revived to take their place. The psychiatrists take a step back, but the managers take a step forward. We have many more psychologists, hundreds of new teams, lots of new interventions, but the will to re-examine and change the fundamental assumptions on which all this is based, is still lacking.

There is, I believe, more possibility of disagreeing, but just as much to disagree about. For myself, I plan to carry on disagreeing.

References

Castillo, H. (2000) 'You don't know what it's like', *Mental Health Care*, vol 4(2), 42–3.

Johnstone, L. (1993) 'Psychiatry: are we allowed to disagree?', *Clinical Psychology Forum*, vol 56, 30–2.

Johnstone, L. (2000) (2nd edn) *Users and Abusers of Psychiatry: A Critical Look at Psychiatric Practice*, London, Routledge.

Johnstone, L. (2001) 'Psychiatry: still disagreeing', *Clinical Psychology*, vol 7, 28–31.

Layard, R. (2006) The case for psychological treatment centres, http://cep.lse.ac.uk/layard/psych_treatment_centres.pdf [accessed 23/07/2008].

Mind (2000) *Environmentally Friendly?*, London, Mind publications.

Pilgrim, D. (1990) 'Competing histories of madness: some implications for psychiatry', in Bentall, R. (ed.) *Reconstructing Schizophrenia*, London, Routledge.

Pilgrim, D. (2001) 'Disordered personalities and disordered concepts', *Journal of Mental Health*, vol 10(3), 253–65.

Read, J., Rudegeair, T. and Farrelly, S. (2006) 'Relationship between child abuse and psychosis', in Larkin, W. and Morrison, A. (eds) *Trauma and Psychosis: New Directions for Theory and Therapy*, London, Routledge.

The distinction between mental and physical illness

Robert E. Kendell

Conditions that now would be regarded as 'mental illnesses', such as mania, melancholia and hysteria, have figured in classifications of disease since the time of Hippocrates, and for over 2000 years were treated by physicians with much the same range of potions, medicaments and attempts to correct humoral imbalance as they employed for other more obviously medical disorders. Although Plato attributed some forms of madness to the Gods, and medieval theologians like Thomas Aquinas attributed hallucinations and insanity to demons and other supernatural influences, from the Renaissance to the second half of the 18th century melancholia and other forms of insanity were generally regarded as bodily illnesses, not differing in any fundamental way from other diseases. When the mid-18th century *belle lettriste* Lady Mary Wortley Montagu commented that 'madness is as much a corporeal distemper as the gout or asthma', she was simply expressing the 'commonplace of high and low, lay and medical opinion alike' (Porter, 1987).

Origins of the distinction

The idea that insanity was fundamentally different from other illnesses, that it was a disease of the mind rather than the body, only developed towards the end of the 18th century. The scene was set by Cartesian dualism, the dominant philosophical influence of the time, but medical opinion and medical impotence also played crucial roles. The development first of private mad-houses

Edited from R. E. Kendell, *British Journal of Psychiatry* (2001), vol. 178, pp. 490–3.

and later of large, purpose-built lunatic asylums took the management of the insane out of the hands of the general run of physicians; and because the managers of these new institutions were concerned only with insanity it was relatively easy for them to regard it as different from other illnesses that did not concern them. At the same time it was becoming clear that insanity was not accompanied by the obvious pathological changes that post-mortem examination was revealing in other diseases. It was increasingly apparent also that although the armamentarium of 18th century medicine – special diets, bleeding, purging, emetics and blistering – was as effective in the management of hypochondriasis and hysteria as it was in other disorders, it had little effect on madness itself. In England the success of the clergyman Francis Willis in curing the King (George III) of his madness after the conspicuous failure of his physicians to do so, and the remarkable success of the York Retreat (opened by the Quaker William Tuke in 1796) in calming and curing its inmates despite using few medicaments or restraints, both had a considerable influence on public opinion. It was in this climate that the terms 'disease of the mind', 'disorder of the mind' and 'mental illness' first began to be widely used. Indeed, the York Retreat was explicitly for 'persons afflicted with disorders of the mind' (Hunter and Macalpine, 1963).

Mental and physical illness in contemporary medicine

A distinction between mental and physical illness is still made, both by the lay public and by many doctors, and the terms 'mental disorder' and 'mental and behavioural disorder' are still used in the two most widely used official nomenclatures, the World Health Organization's *International Classification of Diseases* (ICD) and the American Psychiatric Association's *Diagnostic and Statistical Manual* (DSM). This has the unfortunate effect of helping to perpetuate two assumptions that have long since been abandoned by all thinking physicians, namely that mental disorders are disorders of the mind rather than the body, and that they are fundamentally different from other illnesses.

In reality, neither minds nor bodies develop illnesses. Only people (or, in a wider context, organisms) do so, and when they do both mind and body, psyche and soma, are usually involved. Pain, the most characteristic feature of so-called bodily illness, is a purely psychological phenomenon, and the first manifestation of most infections, from influenza to plague, is also a subjective change – a vague general malaise (Canter, 1972). Fear and other emotions play an important role in the genesis of myocardial infarction, hypertension, asthma and other bodily illnesses, and bodily changes such as fatigue, anorexia and weight loss are commonplace in psychiatric disorders. That most characteristic of all psychiatric disorders, depressive illness, illustrates the impossibility of distinguishing between physical and mental illnesses.

There is good evidence from both family and twin studies (Andreasen et al., 1986; Kendler et al., 1992) that genetic factors make an important contribution to the aetiology of the whole range of depressive disorders, from the mildest to the most severe. This necessarily implies that there must be innate biological differences between those who are and are not prone to depression, and this is confirmed by the fact that drugs that have no effect on mood in normal people relieve depression in those who are ill, and the observation that a depressed mood can be precipitated in people who are prone to depressive illnesses simply by manipulating the tryptophan content of their diet (Delgado et al., 1990). There is unassailable evidence, therefore, of somatic abnormalities in this most typical and common of mental illnesses. Analogous evidence could be presented for schizophrenia, obsessional disorder and panic disorder. Indeed, in the case of schizophrenia there is extensive evidence of widespread, albeit subtle, brain pathology as well as strong evidence of genetic transmission.

The fact is, it is not possible to identify any characteristic features of either the symptomatology or the aetiology of so-called mental illnesses that consistently distinguish them from physical illnesses. Nor do so-called physical illnesses have any characteristics that distinguish them reliably from mental illnesses. If pathological changes and dysfunctions are restricted to organs other than the brain, as is often the case, effects on mentation and behaviour are relatively restricted, but this is an inconstant and purely quantitative difference, and in any case does not apply to diseases of the brain or situations in which there is a secondary disturbance of cerebral function. There are many differences between 'mental' and 'physical' disorders, of course. Hallucinations, delusions and grossly irrational behaviour, for example, are a conspicuous feature of the former. But they occur only in a small proportion of mental disorders, and also feature in the confusional states that may complicate many physical disorders. The mechanisms underlying hysterical amnesia or paraplegia are very different from those underlying the amnesia of dementia or the paraplegia of spinal injury and are commonly described as 'psychogenic'. But a myocardial infarction precipitated by fear or anger is equally 'psychogenic', and in both cases there are good grounds for assuming that the emotional predicament generates neuronal or endocrine changes that play a critical role in producing the loss of access to memories, loss of voluntary movement or inadequate oxygenation of the myocardium. In reality, the differences between mental and physical illnesses, striking though some of them are, are quantitative rather than qualitative, differences of emphasis rather than fundamental differences, and no more profound than the differences between diseases of the circulatory system and those of the digestive system, or between kidney diseases and skin diseases.

Why then do we still talk of 'mental' illnesses, or indeed of 'physical' illnesses? The answer is provided in the introduction to the current (1994) edition of the *Diagnostic and Statistical Manual of Mental Disorders* (DSM-IV):

> The term *mental disorder* unfortunately implies a distinction between 'mental' disorders and 'physical' disorders that is a reductionistic anachronism of mind/body dualism. A compelling literature documents that there is much 'physical' in 'mental' disorders and much 'mental' in 'physical' disorders. The problem raised by the term 'mental disorders' has been much clearer than its solution, and, unfortunately, the term persists in the title of DSM-IV because we have not found an appropriate substitute.

Mental and physical disorders in contemporary classifications

Against this background it is instructive to examine the status of mental and physical disorders, and the allocation of individual syndromes to broad groupings of disease, in contemporary classifications of disease.

The *International Classification of Diseases* is by far the most widely used comprehensive classification. It is important to appreciate, though, that it is not a textbook of medicine, sanctified by international approval. Its status and role are more modest; it is essentially 'a statistical classification of diseases and other health problems, to serve a wide variety of needs for mortality and health-care data' (World Health Organization, 1992). Like its predecessors, the current revision, ICD–10, does not draw a fundamental distinction between mental and physical diseases. 'Mental and behavioural disorders' (F00–99) are simply the fifth of seventeen categories of disease (World Health Organization, 1992). Several of these seventeen broad groupings (for example, infectious and parasitic diseases; neoplasms; and congenital malformations, deformations and chromosomal abnormalities) are based on aetiology. Others (such as diseases of the circulatory system; diseases of the respiratory system) are based on the organ system primarily affected. Some (such as conditions originating in pregnancy, childbirth and the puerperium; and possibly mental and behavioural disorders as well) are heterogeneous and determined mainly by the medical speciality primarily responsible for treatment. None of the three underlying principles consistently takes precedence over the other two. Carcinoma of the bronchus (C34), for example, is classified by its aetiology – as a neoplasm – rather than as a disease of the respiratory system. Vascular dementia (F01), on the other hand, is classified as a mental disorder, despite the fact that in aetiological terms it is explicitly a vascular disorder. The distinction between diseases of the nervous system (G00–99) and mental and behavioural disorders (F00–99) is particularly illuminating. Most diseases of the brain, such as encephalitis and epilepsy, are classified as diseases of the nervous system. Others, like the postencephalitic and postconcussional syndromes, are classified as mental disorders. Some, like Alzheimer's and Parkinson's diseases, are listed as diseases of the nervous system and also, if they lead to dementia (as Alzheimer's disease, of course, invariably does), as mental diseases.

The American Psychiatric Association's *Diagnostic and Statistical Manual*, like other classifications produced by professional bodies, is essentially a classification of the disorders seen and treated by contemporary American psychiatrists and clinical psychologists. If, for example, child psychiatrists are asked to treat defiant, disobedient adolescents, as they are, the *Manual* has to contain a category – oppositional defiant disorder – for such patients. The same reasoning applies to substance-related disorders, somatoform disorders and sleep disorders, and would do so even without the statement quoted above, making it clear that the Association regards the distinction between mental and physical disorders as a meaningless anachronism.

Overall, it seems clear that in both ICD–10 and DSM–IV, the two most widely used classifications of so-called mental disorders, the allocation of individual disorders to broad categories of disease or disorder is determined to a considerable extent by practical considerations – mainly which kind of medical specialist usually treats patients presenting with the syndrome in question – rather than by fundamental aetiological considerations. This is particularly true of the distinction between mental diseases and diseases of the (central) nervous system in ICD–10, which reflects little more than a pragmatic distinction between conditions generally treated by psychiatrists and cerebral disorders usually treated by neurologists.

Public attitudes

Unfortunately, the linguistic distinction between mental and physical illnesses, and the mind/body distinction from which this was originally derived, still encourages many lay people, and some doctors and other health professionals, to assume that the two are fundamentally different. Both are apt to assume that developing a 'mental illness' is evidence of a certain lack of moral fibre and that, if they really tried, people with illnesses of this kind ought to be able to control their anxieties, their despondency and their strange preoccupations and 'snap out of it'. It is true, of course, that most of us believe in 'free will'; we believe that we ourselves and other people can exercise a certain amount of control over our feelings and behaviour. But there is no reason, justified either by logic or by medical understanding, why people suffering from, say, phobic anxiety or depression should be able to exert more control over their symptoms than those suffering from myxoedema or migraine. There is a further and equally damaging assumption that the symptoms of mental disorders are in some sense less 'real' than those of physical disorders with a tangible local pathology. As a result, people experiencing intense fatigue, or pain that is not accompanied by any obvious local lesion, are often dismayed or affronted by being told that they are suffering from neurasthenia, the chronic fatigue syndrome or 'psychogenic' pain, and interpret such diagnoses as implying that their doctor does not believe that they are really in pain or exhausted by the slightest effort, and is dismissing their complaints as 'all in the mind'.

Conclusions

Misunderstandings of this kind are important and frequent. They undermine the relationship between doctor and patient and often result in a refusal to consult a psychiatrist or clinical psychologist, or to countenance a potentially effective treatment. The answer to such problems lies in painstaking explanation and gentle persuasion, and in the longer run in better education of both the general public and doctors themselves, not in conniving with patients' convictions that their symptoms are caused by 'real' or 'physical' illnesses. It may be sensible sometimes to do this as a holding tactic in an individual patient. It is never appropriate in other contexts. Not only is the distinction between mental and physical illness ill-founded and incompatible with contemporary understanding of disease, it is also damaging to the long-term interests of patients themselves. It invites both them and their doctors to ignore what may be important causal factors and potentially effective therapies; and by implying that illnesses so described are fundamentally different from all other types of ill-health, it helps to perpetuate the stigma associated with 'mental' illness. We should talk of psychiatric illnesses or disorders rather than of mental illnesses; and if we do continue to refer to 'mental' and 'physical' illnesses we should preface both with 'so-called', to remind ourselves and our audience that these are archaic and deeply misleading terms.

References

American Psychiatric Association (1994) *Diagnostic and Statistical Manual of Mental Disorders* (4th edn) (DSMIV), Washington, DC: APA.

Andreasen, N.C., Scheftner, W., Reich, T. et al. (1986) 'The validation of the concept of endogenous depression – a family study approach', *Archives of General Psychiatry*, 43, pp. 216–51.

Canter, A. (1972) 'Changes in mood during incubation of acute febrile disease and the effects of pre-exposure psychologic status', *Psychosomatic Medicine*, 34, pp. 424–30.

Delgado, P.L, Charney, D.S., Price, L.H., et al. (1990) 'Serotonin function and the mechanism of antidepressant action: reversal of antidepressant-induced remission by rapid depletion of plasma tryptophan', *Archives of General Psychiatry*, 47, pp. 411–18.

Hunter, R. and Macalpine, I. (1963) *Three Hundred Years of Psychiatry 1535–1860*. London: Oxford University Press.

Kendler, K.S., Neale, M.C., Kessler, R.C., et al. (1992) 'A population-based twin study of major depression in women: the impact of varying definitions of illness', *Archives of General Psychiatry*, 49, pp. 257–66.

Porter, R. (1987) *Mind-forg'd Manacles*, London, Athlone Press, 39.

World Health Organization (1992) *International Statistical Classification of Diseases and Related Health Problems*, Geneva, WHO.

7

The service user/survivor movement

Peter Campbell

One of the most significant developments in the mental health field over the last 25 years has been positive change in the role and status of mental health service users. While it would be hard to deny long-term service users remain a powerless and disadvantaged group in society, or claim anti-discrimination legislation and public education have yet led to substantial improvements in public attitudes and behaviour towards 'the mentally-ill', there have been important shifts within mental health services. Services now set out to 'put the user at the centre'. Information and opportunities for individuals to influence their care and treatment have increased. Collectively, service users are extensively involved, indeed are required to be involved, in the monitoring of existing services and the planning of new ones. It is now hardly possible to embark on major mental health debates without at some point seeking out the views of those with direct, personal experience of madness and mental health services. Whether their contributions in all these areas receive sufficient attention or are deflected and devalued in comparison to other participants is a key and controversial issue. But their presence in important places where, until quite recently, they were conspicuously absent, is irrefutable. That such a transformation has taken place is partly due to action by service users within the service user/survivor movement.

The origins of the service user/survivor movement in the United Kingdom are often traced to the mid-1980s, linking it particularly to the introduction of the market into health service provision with its new attention to patients as consumers. Nevertheless, while the extent and character of action by mental health service users did change significantly during the latter half of the 1980s, its roots should probably be placed in the previous decade if not earlier.

The mad have always been protesting at the way society responds to them (and protest remains a powerful element in service user activism even in our current age of involvement and partnership). Literature is filled with the personal and often self-justificatory accounts of mad individuals (Porter, 1987). There are isolated examples of collective action in this country going back to the seventeenth century. The Alleged Lunatics' Friend Society (1845–1863), whose leadership included former asylum inmates, was influential and has been seen as the first mental health advocacy group (Hervey, 1986). While links between such contributions and the activities of the 1980s are probably spiritual rather than practical, this is much less true of the Mental Patients Union established in 1971 and, until recently, frequently overlooked. Although it did not survive into the 1980s, it can claim more direct links and could rightfully be seen as the foundation group of the current movement (Crossley, 2006). When looking for the roots of the service user/survivor movement we should certainly be researching the 1970s as well as the 1980s.

Many factors shaped the initial growth of action and it is impossible to examine them in detail here. New approaches to health service provision initiated by the Conservative government after 1979 were certainly important, as was the imminent closure of the old asylums and the move towards community care. The institutional base of psychiatry was on shifting sands and rival professions with different perspectives, psychology for example, were becoming more assertive. At the same time the potential of self-help was increasingly recognised and deference to medical authority eroding. Collective political action by disadvantaged groups had become extensive and now included disabled people. The 1983 Mental Health Act had placed a greater focus on individual rights and, indeed, would later be seen by influential commentators as having swung the pendulum too far in that direction. In these circumstances, it was always likely that significant numbers of service users would find the possibilities for successful action more attractive than doing nothing.

One interesting question around service user action in the 1980s and since is the extent to which it was influenced by 'anti-psychiatry'. A number of writers, often not themselves service user activists, have seen 'anti-psychiatry' as a key factor in the development of the service user/survivor movement in the United Kingdom. It is certainly true that professionals influenced by R.D. Laing, David Cooper and other 'anti-psychiatrists' played a significant role in the British Network for Alternatives to Psychiatry which was a home for some service user activists in the early 1980s. It is also a fact that 'anti-psychiatry' provided much of the key vocabulary for radical protest over mental health services in the 1980s. On the other hand, 'anti-psychiatry' was a movement dominated by professionals. It did not emphasise service users becoming involved in running services or providing their own services. It did not say much about advocacy or self-organisation. All these have become important to the service user/survivor movement. While the links are there, service users who were activists in the 1980s will often emphasise the differences between the two movements and say they learnt more from each other or from service user activists in other countries like USA and the Netherlands.

Any examination of the diversity of service user action must consider how meaningful the term 'movement' is. The On Our Own Terms research into the movement in England, using a very broad definition that said the term implies 'individuals, groups and organisations share some common goals and are moving in a similar direction', found most respondents felt there was a movement and they were part of it (Wallcraft et al., 2003). On the other hand, a minority of activists felt there was no such movement, or they were not included, or did not want to be. The impression that organisation has often been stronger at a local than national level has been frequently reported and has some bearing on how coherent the movement has been. Recent initiatives like Voices of Experience (VOX), a Scotland-wide group, and the National Survivor User Network (NSUN) in England show that such issues are a continuing concern. The situation of service users in particular parts of the United Kingdom has often been somewhat different and this has been accentuated in Scotland and Wales since devolution. It is not clear how possible or relevant a UK-wide 'voice' would be.

But the question of coherence and direction remains. Service user activists' priorities are often not the same. While this does not usually lead to them working in open and declared opposition to each other, they may in truth be moving in different directions and this can justifiably lead observers to wonder whether important goals are shared. One aspect of these differences relates to how radical a change is thought desirable or possible in mental health services. The movement contains a spectrum of positions, including those who want more choice and better services essentially from the same providers, those who see constructing service user-led alternatives as the key way forward and those who see traditional biomedical psychiatry as the main barrier to progress. None of these positions are necessarily mutually exclusive and have in fact co-existed with varying degrees of support from activists over the last 30 years. For most of that time they have not prevented people from working together. Whether this has made the movement more or less effective and whether it will remain possible to continue working like this is open to debate.

There are certainly a number of broad perspectives, positions and beliefs that are widely shared and help to give coherence to diverse actions. Shared personal experience, both of mental distress and being on the receiving end of services and social attitudes, is fundamental. Although it has become more obvious over the years that different groups of service users actually have substantially different experiences, the bond remains. A belief in, and commitment to, the essential competence of people with a mental illness diagnosis is also important and feeds into the pursuit of self-help and self-advocacy approaches and a continuing interest in self-organisation. Most activists are opposed to any extension of the use of compulsion in mental health services, sceptical about 'the medical model' and the reliance on psychiatric medications it encourages and see discrimination as a key negative factor in their lives. Underlying action are propositions that people with a mental illness diagnosis are misunderstood, have a right to have their own descriptions of their lives respected and are a force for positive change (Campbell, 1999).

One simple indication of the development of the service user/survivor movement is the growth in the number of independent service user-led groups that have always played a significant role within it. In 1985, when service user activists existed, but only on the margins, there were less than a dozen. By 1990 the number had risen to 50. The On Our Terms research project on the movement in England produced in 2003 had a cleaned database of 896 groups. Although it is increasingly difficult to be accurate about the numbers or true character of groups, estimates approaching 2000 groups throughout the United Kingdom are now being made. The resources available to groups have also expanded greatly. In 1990, most groups were small and had little money. Often they had no premises of their own. They rarely had paid workers. By the time of the On Our Own Terms research, although most groups remained fairly small, 77 per cent of the 318 groups surveyed received annual funding (mostly less than £40,000), 70 per cent had premises and 55 per cent had a paid worker. It is quite likely that these percentages are being maintained. There is now a good deal of money tied up in service user involvement. Although by no means all of it ends up in the hands of service user-led organisations and unpaid work remains vital, the days when influential action groups could be run from someone's front room, as they were in the 1980s, are probably over.

The history of service user action in the United Kingdom can partly be seen as a move from the margins to the mainstream, a journey that may be welcome overall but has attendant difficulties. By the late 1990s the service user/survivor movement had achieved a degree of permanence. Although a number of minority groups, in particular people from black and ethnic minorities, were not well-involved, a situation which has not been resolved in the subsequent decade, the pioneering days of spreading the word, fighting for the space for service user-only groups and forums, challenging for places in the same auditoriums and on the same platforms as professionals had largely ended. The argument was no longer about the desirability of service user involvement but its extent and quality. At the time New Labour assumed power, legislation, policy pronouncements, Department of Health guidance and initiatives by the major mental health professions had already made it clear it was no longer acceptable not to involve service users.

During the 1990s, many service user groups became closely tied to the mental health service system, often in response to official enthusiasm for consultation. The On Our Own Terms report found 72 per cent of groups involved in consulting with decision-makers, second only to self-help and social support at 79 per cent. The money groups received often depended on supplying input into consultative processes or providing advocacy services. Groups might worry whether they were seen to be delivering the goods or if some of their other activities might be jeopardising 'their contract'. Being on the agenda and being able to set your own agendas were not necessarily the same thing. It was not only the most radical who started questioning whether the movement had become too closely identified with the system and too 'consumerist'.

At the same time, the movement had become much larger, more widespread and more complicated – a trend that has continued in the current decade. By 1997 there were not only many local groups and a number of regional and national ones but also important specialist groups like the National Self-Harm Network and the Hearing Voices Network. The Manic Depression Fellowship, a large national organisation, had become service user-led. A number of leading mental health charities already had well-established service user networks like Mindlink within Mind and the Voices Forum within the National Schizophrenia Fellowship. Mindlink's membership alone was over 1000 at that point.

As the number and variety of groups and activities has grown, it has become more difficult for activists to keep an overall sense of what is going on in the movement. It is less likely that people will personally know key people in other parts of the country. The expectations and tensions attached to taking action, to being part of delivering service user involvement, have also grown, partly because some service users can now forge a decent paid career doing it. In order to have a real impact, it is now increasingly necessary for activists to have or to learn relevant skills and there are signs that specialising in particular issues is more common. The movement has undoubtedly had to become more 'professional' in its approach not just to be effective but to survive.

Unsurprisingly, the welcome service user action has received has varied. In the 1980s government began by wanting more information from 'consumers' about what it is like to receive services, and, like other powerful groups in mental health services, it probably remains keener on this aspect than on service user-led organisations or service user-led services or independent advocacy. Some activists say that what those with power most want are answers to their questions from atomised service users rather than collective analysis and proposals from organised groups. The feeling that service users are somehow cheating by getting organised still lingers on after 30 years and may help explain why the spectre of the 'professional user' is still regularly invoked in connection with service user involvement.

What is clear is that a significant number of service user activists have not confined themselves to issues to do with the quality (or existence) of services or access to information and independent advocacy but have inserted themselves into discussions about the nature of madness/mental illness itself. The

National Self Harm Network and the Hearing Voices Network are notable examples of this trend, while the rediscovery of spirituality as an important issue in the mental health field is undoubtedly connected to the increasing number of activists prepared to communicate openly about their interior worlds. Resistance to the idea that people with a mental illness diagnosis may have useful understandings in such challenging areas is understandably strong and the debate is by no means yet an equal one. Nonetheless, the service user movement can claim some credit for the fact that it is occurring at all.

Assessing the overall impact of action is difficult. The yardsticks by which to judge it are varied and by no means universally accepted. If the movement has simply been about improving the degree of individual involvement in care and treatment then recent indicators suggest involvement is only 50 per cent – about the same as in the NHS as a whole. If action is measured by the change it produces then at a local level there are positive signs although these have often not been well documented. At a national level, many of the significant changes have been driven by other factors. The provision of independent advocacy, an important development that would not have occurred so rapidly or at all without service user action, is one clear achievement even if clouded by the reality that now a right to advocacy has been partly recognised in new mental health legislation, service user influence over its provision is diminishing.

In many respects, it is a choice between viewing the glass as half empty or half full.

Service users are certainly part of the decision-making process, the research and training initiatives, but they usually have influence rather than power. It takes a long time to change mental health services so, although there have been responses to service user concerns, delay is sometimes more notable than progress. Why did it take 30 years for service users' desire for more talking and listening to lead to significant new provision of talking treatments? Why were service user activists' protests about acute care in the 1980s ignored until more 'legitimate' agencies woke up to the issue ten years later? It remains relatively rare for service users' views to be decisive on major issues.

This account has focused on the service user/survivor movement in relation to mental health services and this reflects the overall bias of activity. Nevertheless, action has taken place elsewhere. Discrimination has become a more important concern since the late 1990s. Although the movement was not significantly involved in campaigns leading to the Disability Discrimination Act 1995, it has recently become more common to hear activists speak of discrimination as being the real problem in their lives. In the 1980s they were more likely to describe mental health services themselves in this way. As equal citizenship, the move towards individual budgets and the impending crisis in social care attract greater attention, the movement may be starting to address wider issues and becoming drawn into new alliances and greater contact with the wider society which remains substantially unaware of what service users have been doing and achieving in the last thirty years. Entering effectively in these new fields while not deserting older and unresolved concerns, developing new agendas and the ability to really influence more powerful partners in the change process, will be an enormous challenge over the coming years.

References

Campbell, P. (1999) 'The service user/survivor movement', in Newnes, C., Holmes, G. and Dunn, C. (eds) *This is Madness*, Ross-on-Wye, PCCS Books.

Crossley, N. (2006) *Contesting Psychiatry: Social Movements in Mental Health*, London, Routledge.

Hervey, N. (1986) 'Advocacy or folly: the Alleged Lunatics' Friend Society, 1845–63', *Medical History*, vol 30, pp. 254–75.

Porter, R. (1987) *A Social History of Madness*, London, Weidenfeld & Nicolson.

Wallcraft, J. Read, J. and Sweeney, A. (2003) *On Our Own Terms: Users and Survivors of Mental Health Services Working Together for Support and Change*, London, Sainsbury Centre for Mental Health.

8

Thinking about 'mental health': towards a social model

Peter Beresford

It is time to take stock systematically of the dominant philosophical model underpinning the field of 'mental health'. It is difficult to think of any other area of medicine, let alone thought or practice more broadly, where prevailing understandings have remained so long glued to their nineteenth century origins. Whatever our views about 'mental health' issues, or our personal, professional or organisational position, policy, practice and thinking are all at a time of significant change. This gives added force to the view that the philosophical base of 'mental health' needs to be reviewed. The increasing association of mental health service users with 'dangerousness' and the constant coupling of cruel and murderous activities with 'mental illness', as though 'bad' is tantamount to mad, is a defining feature of early twenty-first century discussion. Prevailing political understandings of globalisation and globalised economies, mean that there is a constant pressure against making adequate public investment to ensure support for people who are not seen to pose a public threat. Service users and progressive practitioners both now frequently express concern about the appropriateness and effectiveness of much of the 'mental health or treatment' and provision that is made, with its emphasis on psychotropic medication.

Historically, there have, of course, been challenges to dominant understandings of 'mental health'. The best known and remembered is probably that of

Edited from P. Beresford, *Journal of Mental Health* (2002), vol. 11, no. 6, pp. 581–4.

anti-psychiatry in the 1960s and 1970s. However, it is debatable how great an impact this has actually had on the routine day-to-day experience most people have of mental health services. More recently, from the mid 1980s, the emergence in the UK and internationally, of the mental health service user/survivor movement, may be seen to represent the basis for a more fundamental challenge to dominant psychiatric ideology.

However, we should remember that psychiatric services and the mental health system are still essentially based on the idea of 'mental illness' and of people being 'mentally ill'. While there is now often a preference to underplay this and talk instead about 'mental health', 'mental health issues' and people with 'mental health problems', the underlying idea remains the same. The dominant 'mental illness' concept carries massive political and professional authority. We should not underestimate the power and credibility invested in it at many levels and among many groups. This includes service users – for many, it is the only conceptual framework they have ever known. On the basis of diagnostic categories following from this idea of 'mental illness', people may be locked up, subjected to compulsory (and health damaging) 'treatment' and have their rights restricted. Yet the intellectual and practical shortcomings of the idea and of the typology and therapeutic responses following from it have long been argued and evidenced. 'Mental illness' constitutes a medicalised individualised interpretation of the phenomenon it seeks to explain, describe and deal with. It is based on a deficit model, which presumes the pathology and inadequacy of 'the mentally ill' and which conceptualises their thoughts, emotions, perceptions and behaviours as wrong and defective. It continues to encourage a search for bio-chemical and genetic explanations (so far with little evidence or success) and the increasing medicalisation of many problems, from the problems of childhood to the effects of war.

Mental health service users/survivors and their organisations have many concerns about such an underpinning ideology for 'mental health' services. This is hardly surprising since it is a philosophy which essentially conceives of them as deviant and which sees the origin of the problem as primarily within them. However, these concerns have more often been the subject of private discussion than public statements. The mental health service users/survivors movement has not yet developed its own alternative philosophy. There seems to have been a wariness about doing so. As one founding member of the UK movement once said to me, if we are seen to question the idea of 'mental illness', then that may just be taken as further evidence of our irrationality, leading to us being further discredited and excluded. This highlights a fundamental and unique problem facing mental health's service users as we seek to develop our own discourse. What is called into question about us; the very basis of our collectivity, is the instrument by which we seek to develop our own discourse and critiques – our minds and thoughts.

However, the interest of mental health service users/survivors in exploring different conceptual frameworks and approaches, has become visible through their development of a different language, which replaces the idea of 'mental illness' with terms like 'madness' and 'mental distress', 'hearing voices', 'asylum' and 'eating distress'. These symbolise the search for a different understanding.

Recently, there has been renewed interest in social approaches to 'mental health' from professionals and their organizations. This has been reflected in the discussions and activities of critical psychiatrists and psychologists. It has also been highlighted by the establishment, in 2002, of a new Social Perspectives Network. This has the aim of promoting: 'the value of social models in modern mental health services and to encourage the integration into the new service structures of the twenty-first century' (SPN/TOPSS England, 2002). A discussion paper, prepared for the Network's launch, stressed that the concern was not to 'struggle for domination with the medical model' and highlighted the individual's interaction with their 'social context' (Duggan with others, 2002, p. 7).

These interests reflect broader concerns of traditional approaches to a social model, both within 'mental health' and elsewhere. These highlight social, rather than, or as well as, individual 'factors' to explain what makes people the way they are. But while such approaches place an emphasis on 'nurture' rather than 'nature', they do not necessarily challenge the underpinning conceptual framework involved, in this case one based on the idea of 'mental illness', or the negative values associated with it. Thus dominant ideology and values may continue to be taken as given.

Lately, more public debate about social approaches has also begun to develop among mental health service users. But it has taken a different turn to professionally led discussions. In April 2002, Greater London Action on Disability held a well-attended conference on 'the social model of madness and distress'. This drew on the social model of disability developed by the disabled people's movement as a key starting point for discussion. The social model of disability, however, represents a fundamental departure from traditional social approaches. Traditionally disability has been understood in terms of a medicalised individual model which focuses on the deficits assumed to follow from (perceived) individual impairments. The social model of disability, however, draws a distinction between individual impairment and disability. Disability is understood to mean the social barriers, discrimination and oppression experienced by people with impairments. The social model rejects assumptions that impairment is pathological or 'tragic'. Instead it has highlighted negative social responses to impairment and their disabling effects (Oliver and Barnes, 1998).

Survivor activists are increasingly considering how such a social model might apply to their situation. There is an interest in developing discussion about the social model of disability to see how it might provide a helpful framework and might need to be adapted for a new 'social model of madness and distress'. Certainly the social model of disability has provided a philosophical basis for a transformed approach to disability among disabled people. It has shifted the emphasis from individual 'adjustment' and 'rehabilitation', to challenging discrimination and securing the human and civil rights of disabled people. It has provided the philosophical basis of the independent living movement, which is framed in terms of ensuring disabled people have the personal assistance, support and conditions to live as independently as non-disabled people. This has resulted in major changes, in the UK and internationally, in disability legislation, policy, practice and thinking. This has fundamental implications for 'mental health' policy and mental health service users and workers.

There is much still to be done to work out what a social model of madness and distress might look like and entail. Hopefully professionals pursuing their own discussions of social approaches will also ensure that service users and their organisations have the opportunities, space, credibility and platforms to take forward their own discussions. 'Mental health' policy, provision and practice are now predominantly based on notions of 'cure', 'care' and 'recovery' tied to a medical model. These often fit poorly with the actual wants and circumstances of mental health service users. The social model of disability suggests a different lexicon to mental health service users, based on ideas of support, personal assistance and non-medicalised provision. What implications will this have for services and practice? Will it mean, for example, that instead of conceiving of a mental health service user as someone who has a crisis when their 'illness' becomes acute, that we might be able to think of ensuring they can purchase, with state support, the kind of ongoing help they need (whatever form that might take) which might often avoid such difficulties developing? Would it mean, as one survivor said, funding the purchase of a microwave so that someone can cook for themselves easily rather than seeing treatment or hospitalisation as the route to their normalisation? Would it mean acknowledging that for many survivors moving from 'welfare to work' which the government prioritises (and which many survivors aspire to), is not helpfully understood in terms of 'recovery' and therefore, the removal of support, but of ensuring the maintenance of flexible support as people need it, so that they can stay in employment and not live in fear of the 'benefit trap'?

It is likely that a social model of madness and distress will offer the basis for a fundamentally different approach to mental health policy and practice, just as the social model of disability has done with disability policy and practice. Already some mental health service users are beginning to benefit from provisions following from the latter, to which they are eligible because of their bureaucratic status as 'disabled people'. This includes access to direct payments putting them in charge of the kind of support they want; taking advantage of the safeguards provided by the Disability Discrimination Act 1995 and, of course, eligibility to disability benefits which enhance their quality of life and life choices by lifting them above low income.

The advancement of a social model in 'mental health' offers the prospect of a radical new approach to understanding and support for service users and workers alike. But it is crucial that this is a discussion in which mental health service users have a lead role. This involvement needs to be as broadly based as possible to reflect difference, according to gender, age, sexuality, ethnicity and class, as well as experience of the psychiatric system. Then we have a chance of developing a truly social approach to 'mental health' for the future.

References

Duggan, M. with Cooper, A. and Foster, J. (2002). *Modernising the Social Model in Mental Health: A Discussion Paper*, Leeds, Social Perspectives Network/Training Organisation for Personal Social Services (England) (TOPSS).

Oliver, M. and Barnes, C. (1998). *Disabled People and Social Policy: From Exclusion to Inclusion*. London: Longman.

SPN/TOPSS England, (2002). *New Network to Promote the 'Social Model' of Mental Health*, News Release, 14 February, Social Perspectives Nework/Training Organisation for Personal Social Services (England) (TOPSS).

9

Recovery: the lived experience of rehabilitation

Patricia E. Deegan

It is important to understand that persons with a disability do not 'get rehabilitated' in the sense that cars 'get' tuned up or televisions 'get repaired.' They are not passive recipients of rehabilitation services. Rather, they experience themselves as recovering a new sense of self and of purpose within and beyond the limits of the disability. This distinction between rehabilitation and recovery is important. Rehabilitation refers to the services and technologies that are made available to persons with disabilities so that they might learn to adapt to their world. Recovery refers to the lived or real life experience of persons as they accept and overcome the challenge of the disability. We might say that rehabilitation refers to the 'world pole' and that recovery refers to the 'self pole' of the same phenomenon.

The recovery process is the foundation upon which rehabilitation services build. This is most evidenced in the simple observation that we can make the finest and most advanced rehabilitation services available to the individuals with psychiatric disabilities and still fail to help them. Something more than just 'good services' is needed, for example, the person must get out of bed, shake off the mind-numbing exhaustion of the neuroleptics, get dressed, overcome the fear of the crowded and unfriendly bus to arrive at the program, and face the fear of failure in the rehabilitation program. In essence, they must be active and courageous participants in their own rehabilitation project or that project will fail. It is through the process of recovery that persons with disabilities become active and courageous participants in their own rehabilitation project.

Edited from P. E. Deegan, Chapter 3 in W. Anthony and L. Spandiol (eds) (1994) *Readings in Psychiatric Rehabilitation*, Boston, Center for Psychiatric Rehabilitation, pp. 149–61.

We see then that recovery is an important and fundamental phenomenon upon which rehabilitation efforts depend. It is therefore surprising that very little has been written in our professional and scientific journals regarding it. Perhaps the phenomenon is elusive precisely because it is so fundamental. Perhaps it is because the recovery process cannot be completely described with traditional scientific, psychiatric or psychological language. Although the phenomenon will not fit neatly into natural scientific paradigms, those of us who have had a disability know that recovery is real because we have lived it. At a recent conference that brought together persons with diverse disabilities, I had the pleasure of talking with Brad, a man who has paraplegia. We shared our stories of recovery

The experience of recovery

At a young age we had both experienced a catastrophic shattering of our world, hopes and dreams. Brad had broken his neck and was paralysed and I was diagnosed as being schizophrenic. We recalled the impact of those first days following the onset of our disabilities. He was an athlete and dreamed of becoming a professional in the sports world. I was a high school athlete and had applied to college to become a gym teacher. Just days earlier we knew ourselves as young people with exciting futures, and then everything collapsed around us. As teenagers, we were told that we had an incurable malady and that we would be 'sick' or 'disabled' for the rest of our lives. We were told that if we continued with recommended treatments and therapies, we could learn to 'adjust' and 'cope' from day to day.

Needless to say, we didn't believe our doctors and social workers. In fact, we adamantly denied and raged against these bleak prophesies for our lives. We felt it was all just a mistake, a bad dream, a temporary setback in our lives. We just knew that in a week or two, things would get back to normal again. We felt our teenage world was still there, just waiting for us to return to it. Our denial was an important stage in our recovery. It was a normal reaction to an overwhelming situation. It was our way of surviving those first awful months.

The weeks passed us by but we did not get better. It became harder and harder to believe we would ever be the same again. What initially had seemed like a fleeting bad dream transformed into a deepening nightmare from which we could not awake. We felt like ships floating on a black sea with no course or bearings. We found ourselves drifting further and further away from the young, carefree people we had been. He lay horizontal and in traction while his friends were selected to play ball for prestigious colleges. I stood drugged and stiff in the hallways of a mental hospital while my classmates went off to their first year of college.

We experienced time as a betrayer. Time did not heal us. Our pasts deserted us and we could not return to who we had been. Our futures appeared to us to be barren, lifeless places in which no dream could be planted and grow into a reality. As for the present, it was a numbing succession of meaningless days and nights in a world in which we had no place, no use, and no reason to be. Boredom and wishfulness became our only refuge (Knowles, 1986).

Our denial gave way to despair and anguish. We both gave up. Giving up was a solution for us. It numbed the pain of our despair because we stopped asking 'why and how will I go on?' (Harrison 1984). Giving up meant that for 14 years he sat in the day rooms of institutions gazing at soap operas, watching others live their lives. For months I sat in a chair in my family's living room, smoking cigarettes and waiting until it was 8.00 p.m. so I could go back to bed. At this time even the simplest of tasks were overwhelming. I remember being asked to come into the kitchen to help knead some bread dough. I got up, went into the kitchen, and looked at the dough for what seemed an eternity. Then I walked back to my chair and wept. The task seemed overwhelming to me. Later I learned the reason for this: when one lives without hope, (when one has given up) the willingness to 'do' is paralysed as well.

All of us who have experienced catastrophic illness and disability know this experience of anguish and despair. It is living in darkness without hope, without a past or a future. It is self-pity. It is hatred of everything that is good and life giving. It is rage turned inward. It is a wound with no mouth, a wound that is so deep that no cry can emanate from it. Anguish is a death from which there appears to be no resurrection. It is inertia that paralyses the will to do and to accomplish because there is no hope. It is being truly disabled, not by a disease or injury, but by despair. This part of the recovery process is a dark night in which even God was felt to have abandoned us. For some of us this dark night lasts moments, days, or months. For others it lasts for years. For others, the despair and anguish may never end.

Neither Brad nor I could remember a specific moment when the small and fragile flame of hope and courage illuminated the darkness of our despair. We do remember that even when we had given up, there were those who loved us and did not give up. They did not abandon us. They were powerless to change us and they could not make us better. They could not climb this mountain for us but they were willing to suffer with us. They did not overwhelm us with their optimistic plans for our futures but they remained hopeful despite the odds. Their love for us was like a constant invitation, calling us forth to be something more than all of this self-pity and despair. The miracle was that gradually Brad and I began to hear and respond to this loving invitation.

For 14 years Brad slouched in front of the television in the hell of his own despair and anguish. For months I sat and smoked cigarettes until it was time to collapse back into a drugged and dreamless sleep. But one day, something changed in us. A tiny, fragile spark of hope appeared and promised that there could be something more than all of this darkness. This is the third phase of recovery. This is the mystery. This is the grace. This is the birth of hope called forth by the possibility of being loved. All of the polemic and technology of psychiatry, psychology, social work, and science cannot account for this phenomenon of hope. But those of us who have recovered know that this grace is real. We lived it. It is our shared secret.

It is important to understand that for most of us recovery is not a sudden conversion experience. Hope does not come to us as a sudden bolt of lightning that jolts us into a whole new way of being. Hope is the turning point that must quickly be followed by the willingness to act. Brad and I began in little ways with small triumphs and simple acts of courage. He shaved, he attempted to read a book, and he talked with a counselor; I rode in the car, I shopped on Wednesdays, and I talked to a friend for a few minutes. He applied for benefits, he got a van and learned to drive; I took responsibility for my medications, took a part-time job, and had my own money. He went to college so he could work professionally with other people experiencing disabilities; I went to school to become a psychologist so I could work with people experiencing disabilities. One day at a time, with multiple setbacks, we rebuilt our lives. We rebuilt our lives on the three cornerstones of recovery – hope, willingness, and responsible action. We learned to say: 'I am hopeful;' 'I am willing to try;' and 'I discover that I can do' (Knowles, 1986). This is the process of recovery that is the ground from which springs effective use of rehabilitation services.

Recovery does not refer to an end product or result. It does not mean that Brad and I were 'cured.' In fact, our recovery is marked by an ever-deepening acceptance of our limitations. But now, rather than being an occasion for despair, we find that our personal limitations are the ground from which spring our own unique possibilities. This is the paradox of recovery, i.e. that in accepting what we cannot do or be, we begin to discover who we can be and what we can do.

Recovery does not refer to an absence of pain or struggle. Rather, recovery is marked by the transition from anguish to suffering. In anguish Brad and I lived without hope. We experienced anguish as futile pain, pain that revolved in circles, pain that bore no possibility other than more pain, and pain that lead nowhere. However, when we became hopeful, our anguish was transformed into true suffering. True suffering is marked by an inner peace, i.e. although we still felt great pain, we also experienced a peace in knowing that this pain was leading us forward into a new future. A biologist who has spina bifida captures this spirit of true suffering in recovery when she writes: 'Suffering is peaceful. You know the pain may kill you, but it won't destroy you. In a very risky way, you are safe' (Harrison, 1984).

For many of us who have disabilities, recovery is a process, a way of life, an attitude, and a way of approaching the day's challenges. It is not a perfectly

linear process. At times our course is erratic and we falter, slide back, re-group and start again. Our experience of recovery is similar to that described by the poet Roethke (1948/1975) who himself experienced major mental illness:

Cuttings

... One nub of growth
Nudges a sand-crumb loose,
Pokes through a musty sheath
Its pale tendrilous horn.

Cuttings
(later)

This urge, wrestle, resurrection of dry sticks,
Cut stems struggling to put down feet,
What saint strained so much,
Rose on such lopped limbs to a new life? ... (p. 35)

Recovery is the urge, the wrestle, and the resurrection. Recovery is a matter of rising on lopped limbs to a new life. As professionals we would like nothing more than to somehow manufacture the spirit of recovery and give it to each of our program participants. But this is impossible. We cannot force recovery to happen in our rehabilitation programs. Essential aspects of the recovery process are a matter of grace and, therefore, cannot be willed. However, we can create environments in which the recovery process can be nurtured like a tender and precious seedling. Some of the principles for creating such environments in rehabilitation programs are given below.

Recovery in rehabilitation programs

As we have seen, recovery is not a linear process marked by successive accomplishments. The recovery process is more accurately described as a series of small beginnings and very small steps. To recover, persons with psychiatric disabilities must be willing to try and fail, and try again. Too often rehabilitation programs are structured in such a way as to work against this process of recovery. These programs tend to have rigid guidelines for acceptance. They tend to have linear program designs in which a person must enter at point 'A' and move through a series of consecutive steps to arrive at point 'B'. Failure at any point along the way will require that participants return to entry level.

Rehabilitation programs can be environments that nurture recovery if they are structured to embrace, and indeed expect, the approach/avoid, try/fail dynamic that is the recovery process. The real challenge of rehabilitation programs is to create fail-proof program models. A program is fail-proof when participants are always able to come back, pick up where they left off, and try again. In a fail-proof environment where one is welcomed, valued, and wanted, recovering persons can make the most effective use of rehabilitation services.

A second point regarding the establishment of rehabilitation environments conducive to the recovery process derives from the understanding that each person's journey of recovery is unique. Of course, there are certain fundamental constituents of the process of recovery that are similar in all persons with a disability, for example, the experience of despair and the transition to hope, willingness, and responsible action. However, people with disabilities are, above all, individuals and find their own special formula for what promotes their recovery and what does not. Therefore, it is important to offer persons in recovery a wide variety of rehabilitation program options from which to choose, such as supported work programs, social clubs, transitional employment programs, consumer-run drop-in centers and businesses, workshops, skill training programs, and college support programs.

Consumer-run self-help groups, self-help networks, and advocacy/lobbyist groups can also be important resources for persons in recovery and should be available as options. Of course, these important resources can only be established and maintained by persons recovering from psychiatric disability. Creating these resources, as well as linking with other persons with disabilities and sharing existing resources, is one of the greatest challenges that face those of us who are recovering.

For some people with psychiatric disabilities, especially those who relapse frequently, traditional values of competition, individual achievement, independence, and self-sufficiency are oppressive. Programs that are tacitly built on these values are invitations to failure for many persons in recovery. For these persons, 'independent living' amounts to the loneliness of four walls in the corner of some rooming house. For these persons, 'individual vocational achievement' amounts to failing one vocational program after another until they come to believe they are worthless human beings with nothing to contribute. For these persons, an alternative type of rehabilitation program, and even lifestyle, should be available as an option. Instead of competitive vocational training based on individual achievement, a cooperative work setting stressing group achievement could be established. The value here is cooperation in the achievement of work goals and the sharing of responsibility for work production so that the group or work community can compensate for the individual during periods of relapse. Residential program options should include the possibility for communal living situations such as the L'Arche communities pioneered by Jean Vanier (Dunne, 1986; Vanier, 1979; Vanier and Wolfensberger, 1974). When these types of options are made available and exist alongside rehabilitation programs based on more traditional values, then we can feel confident that we are offering a truly comprehensive network of services from which persons in recovery can choose their own course of rehabilitation.

The third recommendation for creating programs that enhance recovery involves recognition of the gift that people with disabilities have to give to each other. This gift is their hope, strength, and experience as lived in the recovery process. In this sense, persons with disabilities can become role models for one another. During that dark night of anguish and despair when individuals live without hope, the presence of other persons in recovery can challenge that despair through example. It becomes very difficult to continue to convince oneself that there is no hope when one is surrounded by others with disabilities who are making strides in their recovery!

Hope is contagious and that is why it is so important to hire people with disabilities in rehabilitation programs. Because recovery is a phenomenon that is similar for all people with disabilities, it can be very effective to have persons with divergent disabilities act as role models for one another. Additionally, a person need not be 'fully recovered' in order to serve as a role model. Very often a person with a disability who is only a few 'steps' ahead of another person can be more effective than one whose achievements seem overly impressive and distanced.

Finally, and perhaps most fundamentally, staff attitudes are very important in shaping rehabilitation environments. There are a number of common staff attitudes that are particularly unhelpful to persons in recovery. For instance, too often staff attitudes reflect the implicit supposition that there is the 'world of the abnormal' and the 'world of the normal'. The task facing the staff is to somehow get the people in the 'abnormal world' to fit into the 'normal world'. This creates an us/them dichotomy wherein 'they' (persons with disabilities) are expected to do all of the changing and growing. Such an attitude places staff in a very safe position in which they can maintain the illusion that they are not disabled, that they are not wounded in any way, and that they have no need to live the spirit of recovery in their own lives. Indeed, when the us/them attitude prevails, 'staff' and 'clients' are truly worlds apart. Such an environment is oppressive to those individuals with disabilities who are struggling with their own recovery.

Staff members must be helped to recognize the ways in which they, too, are deeply wounded. Perhaps they have experienced anguish in their lives or perhaps they have known personal tragedy or struggle. To embrace and accept our own woundedness and vulnerability is the first step toward understanding the experience of persons with disabilities. In so doing we discover that we share a common humanity with them and that we are not 'worlds apart'.

References

Dunne, J. (1986) 'Sense of community in L'Arche and in the writings of Jean Vanier', *Daybreak Monograph 20*, Richmond Hill, Ontario: Daybreak Publications.

Harrison, V. (1984) 'A biologist's view of pain, suffering and marginal life'. In F. Dougherty (ed.), *The Deprived, the Disabled and the Fullness of Life*, Delaware: Michael Glazier.

Knowles, R. T. (1986) *Human Development and Human Possibility: Erikson in the Light of Heidegger*, Lanham: University Press of America.

Roethke, T. (1948/1975) The lost son and other poems. In *The collected poems of Theodore Roethke*, New York: Anchor Press/Doubleday.

Vanier, J. (1979) *Community and Growth*, Darton, Longman & Todd.

Vanier, J. and Wolfensberger, W. (1974) 'Growing together', *Daybreak Monograph 2*, Richmond Hill, Ontario: Daybreak Publications.

10

Spirituality and mental health

Suman Fernando

The mental health discourse today in Europe and North America usually refers to mental health problems rather than mental illness and symptoms, but yet much of the thinking continues to be strongly influenced by ideas in western psychiatry and western psychology. These ideas are concerned with concepts built up over the years about 'mental' matters: mental illnesses, mental processes, mental therapies and so on. All the so-called information put out by psychiatry and psychology has been, and continues to be, devised within a reductionist framework, supplemented largely by a mechanistic approach of Newtonian physics (rather than modern physics). This means the reducing of complex systems into their parts, assuming that the function of the whole can be understood by analysing the functions of its constituent parts. The spiritual dimension of human beings cannot be accommodated within this approach and so psychiatry and psychology have no place for spirituality.

In their book *Zen Buddhism and Psychoanalysis*, Erich Fromm and colleagues (1960) propose that psychoanalysis emerged as an attempt, in European thinking, to find a solution to 'western man's spiritual crisis' (1960: 80), a crisis attributed by them to Europe's 'abandonment of theistic ideas in the nineteenth century' with 'a big plunge into objectivity' (1960: 79). Cultures in Asia and Africa did not undergo this change, at least not at that time: and, although undoubtedly influenced later by western ideas, appear to have maintained a spiritual dimension to their thinking in many ways until the present. Thus, it can be assumed that non-western ways of thinking accept spirituality

Edited extract from S. Fernando in *Mental Health and Psychiatry: The Struggle against Racism* (2003), Hove, Brunner-Routledge, pp. 115–21.

as central to human experience, different to 'belief' or 'cognition' or even an emotional state.

The term 'spirituality', like the term 'mental health', does not denote a precise concept but is used widely. In exploring spirituality it is important to note that its essence is not necessarily represented in the written or spoken word nor evident in organised religion. In fact perhaps the opposite may be true for organised religion is more about politics and power (than about spirituality) and sometimes tends to distort, negate or even destroy the spirituality of individuals. Yet, it is true to say that wisdom within the great religions, whether oral or written, may guide one to an understanding of spirituality and spirituality may well form the original basis, the 'spiritual basis', of all religious systems and traditions. In the mental health field many people conceptualise the 'spirit' as a concept similar to the 'mind' but yet different. When people talk of being 'spiritual' they generally mean a feeling of connectedness, the personal being connected to others, the 'I and I' principle of the Rastafarians which 'expresses the oneness between two persons' (Cashmore 1979: 135), connectedness to the 'community' (a community spirit) or even wider to the land or environment (an ecological spirit?), the earth and the sky, the cosmos (a unity with 'atman' the Hindu godhead?). Lack of spirituality may be experienced as an impoverishment of the spirit, a sense of emptiness. Prayer and meditation may then be a way of replenishing this lack of spirituality; joint action in a group setting may equally well do the same and various other culturally determined ways may exist.

The first aim of this section is to provide some impressions of the cultural traditions understood as 'spiritual' that have some bearing on thinking about mental health. Ross (1992) writes about indigenous (First Nations) Americans undergoing spiritual observance in preparing to embark on a task such as making a journey or venturing on a hunting expedition. Nobles (1986) believes that the integration of mind, body and spirit is characteristic of the world views derived from African thinking and Richards (1985) makes a case for this spirituality having survived the transatlantic slave trade to continue in an African-American spirituality. Indeed Du Bois (1970) in his classic *The Souls of Black Folk* originally published in 1903, saw 'spiritual striving' as a characteristic of the cultural ideal of black (African) Americans. Ninety years later, bell hooks (1994) writing in *Outlaw Culture*, regrets the 'spiritual loss' of modern African-American communities in the US and advocates the need for political movements that can effectively address the 'needs of the spirit' (1994: 247). It is my experience that a major demand from users of mental health services in the UK is that the disciplines of psychiatry and psychology should incorporate a spiritual dimension. This section may help to clarify what this means and how it may be brought about.

It could be stated that all religious traditions have their roots in a search for the meaning to life; the search to know, to understand, to become insightful and finally to achieve a goal. And basically spirituality means the realisation of the interconnectedness of all beings, of life as a unitary 'thing'. Then, what is seen as the 'spirit world' is part and parcel of the real world and something that is within every human being. It is likely that 'being spiritual' is implied in the process of attaining a state of salvation, nirvana or a similar equivalent ideal state that a religious system may envisage. Religious leaders and religious systems have built superstructures over the years, pointing to somewhat different paths to be followed, the languages used have differed, and their cultural contexts have been different. And of course politics (of organised religion) has distorted and often corrupted the fundamentals of every religion. However, it is possible to extract from these traditions some aspects of spirituality in, as it were, its raw form separated out from the social and political superstructures around it. Of all the great religions, Buddhism is the one that developed fairly precise methods of reaching spiritual insight and liberation from suffering. As it spread from its original source in north India to other parts of southeast Asia, China, Japan and Tibet, Buddhism accumulated varieties of practices and beliefs. However, its basic premise remains a fundamental adherence to liberation with meditation as a primary means of attaining its goals. I present here a picture of how I envisage Buddhist spirituality.

Buddhist spirituality

The term *bhavana*, or 'cultivation', is the closest Sanskrit equivalent to spirituality in Buddhist writings. Meditation is fundamental to Buddhism and generally the means by which spirituality is experienced. *Bhavana* aims at liberating the mind and realising the ultimate truth, nirvana (Yoshinori, 1995). The freedom attained in Buddhist practice is knowledge or reality, or rather it is reality itself, existence freed from illusions and passions that bind us to a world of ignorance and suffering (1995; xiii). The earliest interpretations of the message of Buddhism is described by Pande (1995) as follows:

> Spiritual life consists in the effort to move away from ignorance to wisdom. This effort has two principal dimensions: the cultivation of serenity and the cultivation of insight. Ignorance is the mistaken belief in the selfhood of body and mind which leads to involvement in egoism, passions, actions, and repeated birth and death. (1995: 10)

The wisdom through which nirvana was reached was characterised by no-self (*anatta*), impermanence (*anicca*) and suffering (*dukkha*). The variations of these characterisations, their elaborations and interpretations, resulted in a variety of Buddhist traditions. Therefore, Buddhist spirituality may seem close to what in western psychology would be seen as self-knowledge through meditation but with one important proviso. A fundamental teaching in Buddhism is the lack of a 'self' as something permanent, the 'non-selfhood of body and mind' (1995: 10), and the realisation of 'self' as illusion is an integral part of liberation. The western psychological approach of analysing the self or understanding the self, is like trying to catch up with one's shadow. In contrast to the Buddhist tradition of downplaying the self as impermanent and illusionary, western psychology elevates the self, the ego, to centre stage as something separate from all other aspects of a personal individuality, as autonomous and very important. As a result, psychological therapies, the western equivalent to 'ways of liberation' according to Watts, (1971: 4), emphasise developing and maintaining self-esteem, integrity and ego-boundaries to protect the self, boost the self, etc. Similarly psychiatry (dealing with the 'abnormal') looks for abnormalities of self-categorised as self-depreciation, hopelessness, guilt, etc. (Box 10.1).

Box 10.1   Self/ego in western psychology and psychiatry

Separate
Autonomous
Important

Represented in psychology as
  self-esteem
  integrity
  ego-boundaries

Represented in psychiatry as
  self-depreciation
  hopelessness
  guilt
  disintegration
  passivity feelings
  dependency
  'enmeshed families'

Clearly there is no absolute distinction between eastern and western traditions or religious systems with respect to spirituality.

Communication and interchange between them has not just taken place in recent times nor is it represented by the sort of 'new age' interest in eastern religions: 'Karma Cola' (to go with Coca Cola) as Gita Mehta (1980) puts it. In the introduction to a translation of the *Bhagavad Gita* (Prabhavananda and Isherwood, 1947) the epic conversation between Arjuna and Krishna, which epitomises the Vedanta philosophy that underpins the Hinduism. Aldous Huxley (1947), a western philosopher and scientist, states 'In regard to man's final end, all the higher religions are in complete agreement . . . Contemplation of truth is the end, action the means.' Huxley goes on to suggest that this was a universal orthodoxy until:

> The intervention of the steam engine produced a revolution, not merely in industrial techniques, but also and much more significantly in philosophy. Because machines could be made progressively more and more efficient, western man came to believe that men and societies would automatically register a corresponding moral and spiritual improvement. Attention and allegiance came to be paid, not to Eternity, but to the Utopian future. External circumstances came to be regarded as more important than states of mind about external circumstances, and the end of human life was held to be action, with contemplation, as a means to that end. These false and, historically, aberrant and heretical doctrines are now systematically taught in our schools and repeated, day in and day out, by those anonymous writers of advertising copy who more than any other teachers, provide European and American adults with their current philosophy of life. And so effective have been the propaganda that even professing Christians accept the heresy unquestioningly and are quite unconscious of its complete incompatibility with their own or anybody else's religion. (1947: 11–12)

Huxley does not mention the role of colonialism, and the racism that accompanied it and has continued even after its demise, in driving a wedge between east and west, by suppressing and denigrating eastern thinking and eastern religions and preventing, for example, eastern systems of medicine from developing. What has happened is that traditions identified in the field of mental health as western are now very different to those identified as eastern. On the whole I believe that the latter is more in line with what is generally considered a spiritual approach to life. That is the justification for my approach in this chapter to explore issues of spirituality and mental health by contrasting east and west. Yet this contrast could equally well be designated as between north and south, broad and narrow or holistic and reductionist.

In Table 10.1, I have shown the main overall differences of emphasis between eastern and western thinking. In eastern cultures human life is conceptualised as an indivisible 'whole' that includes not just the western 'mind'

Table 10.1 Ideals of mental health

Eastern	Western
Harmony	Self-sufficiency
Social integration	Personal autonomy
Balanced functioning	Efficiency
Protection and caring	Self-esteem

Table 10.2   **Underlying eastern and western themes**

Eastern	Western
Understanding	Analysing
Knowing	Gathering knowledge
Being	Having

and 'body' as one but also the spiritual dimension of human life, the feeling of oneness with other beings, other things even. The ideal of self-sufficiency and personal autonomy reflects a western emphasis on developing 'individuality', feeling oneself as an individual separate from others. The down side to this is that the more the sense of being an individual is enhanced the greater is the sense of 'the other', promoting the we – they dichotomy. When race is a factor for marking difference, racism is the result. In Table 10.2 I have attempted to clarify the east–west differences of emphasis a little further. Eastern traditions seem to favour knowing and understanding while the western emphasis is on gathering knowledge and analysing. Thus, for example, when some westerners go to India to seek knowledge they sometimes end up gathering bits of knowledge rather than immersing themselves in an understanding. This difference of emphasis has been usefully conceptualised by Erich Fromm (1976) as the difference between 'having' (possessing) and 'being' (experiencing). Some psychotherapists tend to talk about having thoughts or having feelings, instead of thinking and feeling. The approach then is to objectify what is subjective in order to analyse and reduce the thoughts or feelings to their basics. This is the reductionist analytic approach that may be contrasted with the contemplative or meditative approach to understanding, understanding by awareness versus understanding by analysis.

References

Cashmore, E. (1979) *Rastaman: The Rastafarian Movement in England*. London: Allen & Unwin.

Du Bois, W.E.B. (1970) *The Souls of Black Folk*. New York: Washington Square Press (first published by McClurg, Chicago 1903).

Fromm, E. (1976) *To Have or To Be?* London: Johathan Cape.

Fromm, E., Suzuki, D.T. and de Martino, R. (1960) *Zen Buddhism and Psychoanalysis*. London: Allen & Unwin.

hooks, bell (1994) *Outlaw Culture. Resisting Representations*. New York, Routledge.

Huxley, A. (1947) 'Introduction', in S. Prabhavandanda and C. Isherwood (eds and trans) *The Song of God, Bhagavad-Gita*. London: Phoenix House, 5–19.

Mehta, G. (1980) *Karma Cola. The Marketing of the Mystic East*. London: Jonathan Cape.

Nobles, W.W. (1986) 'Ancient Egyptian thought and the development of African (black) psychology', in M. Karenga and J.H. Carruthers (eds) *Kemor and the African World View. Research Rescue and Restoration*. Los Angeles: University of Sankore Press, pp. 100–18.

Pande, G.C. (1995) 'The message of Gotama Buddha and its earliest interpretations', in T. Yoshinori (ed.) *Buddhist Spirituality*. Delhi: Motilal Banarsidass, 3–33.

Prabhavananda, S. and Isherwood, C. (trans.) (1947) *The Song of God, Bhagavad Gita*. London: Phoenix House.

Richards D. (1985) 'The implications of African-American spirituality', in M.K. Asante and K.W. Asante (eds) *African Culture: The Rhythms of Unity*. Westport, CT: Greenwood Press, pp. 207–31.

Ross, R. (1992) *Dancing with a Ghost: Exploring Indian Reality*. Markham, Ontario: Reed Books.

Watts, A.W. (1971) *Psychotherapy East and West*. London: Jonathan Cape (originally published by Pantheon Books, New York, 1961).

Yoshinori, T. (ed.) (1995) 'Introduction', in T. Yoshinori (ed.) *Buddhist Spirituality*. Delhi, Matilal Banarsidass, xiii–xxvi.

11

Big boys don't cry? Mental health and the politics of gender

Philip Thomas

A young man was brought to see his GP by his sister and mother. Two weeks earlier, his wife had left him for another man. He was distraught, beside himself with grief. He still loved her and couldn't understand why this had happened. He was so upset he had had to have time off work. He had been staying with his mother because he could not face going back to an empty house. He was unable to sleep and had lost weight with worry. He kept breaking down in tears, sobbing violently and unpredictably. In the surgery his face was tear-stained. He was barely able to speak for himself, but the doctor gave him time. He listened and let him talk about what he was going through. He arranged to see the man a week later to talk. Talk about anything he wanted to. As he left the surgery, his mother and sister knocked on the doctor's door. They wanted a word. The mother told the doctor that her son needed to pull his socks up. His sister nodded vigorously in agreement. They were both fed up with him moping about the house like a spare part. All he did was wander around aimlessly, crying continuously. He was getting on their nerves. He should go back to work. That was the best thing for him. He'd be better off there. He'd have his mind taken away from his problems. Men should be out at work.

This scene actually took place. The man, his mother and sister really exist. It implies that our collective talk, or discourse, has peculiar ways of straining

Edited from P. Thomas, *Journal of Mental Health* (1996), vol. 5, no. 2, pp. 107–10.

and distorting the way we see the world. Women have been oppressed by men for centuries. Over the last thirty years, feminism has lain open the misuse of male power and all manifestations of the domination and subjugation of women. However, the swing of the pendulum is so great, that, in terms of gender, we now find it impossible to view men as victims themselves. It seems as if the very nature of language itself has changed following the systematic deconstruction of the patriarchal assumptions underlying the use of words such as 'chairman' or 'mankind'. But there is one very important exception to this: the language of the emotions, and the discourses that are structured around it. What are the consequences of this for the mental health of men?

There is evidence that men and women's brains are organised in different ways. Women possess better language skills, and process information sequentially. Men, on the other hand, possess better visuo-spatial skills, and process information through the identification of patterns. The origin of these differences is contentious. Do they arise through the effects of sex hormones on brain maturation in utero, or are they determined by early interactions between mother and infant? If the biology of difference is debatable, its consequences are incontestable. Consider how words carry gender-specific connotations through the use of metaphor. Words that convey masculine properties have phallic associations. Words such as thrusting (ambition), incisive (comments), or penetrating (move), all suggest masculinity. These are active, doing words, adverbs which qualify verbs, which, in turn, are related to action in the physical, external world, the world of work and space. Words that convey feminine properties use quite different metaphors, those of the uterus as a receptacle. Think of expressions such as 'I felt full of emotion', 'I felt like bursting with pride', or 'I felt empty and drained'. These are metaphors of passive containment, of holding, of being. But there is something else about these expressions. These female metaphors convey emotional states, or states relating to our feelings. There is an endless list of metaphors relating feeling states to containment, and thus femininity. This provides us with an important clue. The very words we use to talk about our feelings are dominated by female metaphors.

These language tricks are reflected in popular culture, where portrayals of gender differences in talk about emotion abound. Observe how male and female characters in soap operas such as Coronation Street communicate. Women are depicted in groupings of mutual support, in which they share intimate details of their personal lives. Before she left the Street for financial reasons, Bet Lynch, the barmaid, functioned in a counselling role usually in support of other female characters. She was sensitively attuned to the emotional states of her younger protégés and frequently directed them to disclose their anxieties. In contrast, most of the male characters are emotionally flat and shallow. The stereotype of the emotionally gauche male is not restricted to television. Recently, the press has carried a series of adverts for British Telecom which presented a striking image of a middle-class father and son. The two men were facing away from each other on opposite sides of the page. The implication was of a profound gulf between fathers and sons, with little communication or emotional contact. Men, it seems, find it difficult to face each other and deal with their emotions.

Differences in social roles determined by gender may play a part in the different rates of mental illness in men and women. Cochrane (1983) has pointed out that traditional female roles deem that women are passive and subservient. They tend to be submissive and compliant, given to emotional displays. He suggests that women who accept such roles are less likely to exert control over their lives, and are thus at risk of depression. Women are more likely to discuss emotional problems than men (Horowitz, 1977), and there is evidence that mental health professionals are no different from the general population in accepting such stereotypical gender differences (Broverman et al., 1970). For the individual woman, the outcome of gender and society's response to it (especially male psychiatrists' responses) would appear to bring with it the risk of being labelled as 'depressed'. Johnstone (1989) has taken this analysis even further in a feminist critique of gender and mental health. She points out that a central feature of the traditional woman's role is the emotional care of others. This means that she must defer to others' needs and put herself last. Such roles are not valued by a society where the masculine attributes of resilience, power and achievement in the social world are valued. Consequently, women feel insignificant and unworthy. They feel inadequate. The situation is complicated by the fact that in mental health it is the discipline of psychiatry, with its medical model of diagnosis and treatment, which dominates. According to Johnstone, this is yet another feature of the pre-eminence of male values over female.

This analysis is important for it highlights the important link between social role, gender and self esteem. What are the implications of this for men? A *Panorama* television programme of 16 October 1995 examined the underachievement of young men at school. The programme interviewed a teacher from the North East of England and seven ex-pupils, four male and three female. All seven had shown promise in their early secondary school years, but this had faded in the men as they approached their GCSEs, and they failed badly in their exams. None had progressed to further education. Only one had a job. As they spoke about their lives, they conveyed a sense of purposelessness amounting to nihilism. In contrast, the girls were at university or college. All were doing well. All were ambitious and had a clear view of where they were going. The message is clear. Feminism is succeeding in liberating young working class women from oppressive gender roles. The result is that they are motivated to go on to higher education and take up careers. In the process they are leaving their male peers behind. This new generation of women, with their thrusting ambition and penetrating intellects, revel in the prospect of going out into the world and making a success of life. They regard education as an integral part of this process, so they work harder at school than the men. In addition, they value education in its own right, because their mothers and grandmothers were denied it. Indeed, it was the male hegemony within working class families that denied women education. But what of the young men?

The same class values that denied women access to higher education and careers also dictated that the only source of male self-esteem was to be found in manual work. In the *Panorama* programme, this emerged as a powerful feature of young working class male identity. One of the men indicated that a job only meant anything to him if it involved the use of his hands and body in strenuous physical activity. Traditionally such work was to be found in the construction industry, or heavy industry such as coal, steel and engineering, but our post-industrial society has witnessed the disappearance of such jobs. The greatest contraction in the labour market has been in these areas. The economic and political consequences of Thatcherism have changed the nature of work in a profound manner. The keyboard has replaced the hod. The telephone has replaced the trowel. Linguistic, not physical, prowess is now required for success in the labour market. Should we be surprised, then, that the inarticulate male withdraws and under-achieves at school? What point is there when the world of labour has shifted its axis in such a way that makes it impossible for them to get what they want out of work? The guts have been ripped out of working class male self-esteem.

Changes in the nature of labour, the rise in male unemployment and the under-achievement of young men at school are the most obvious signs of a profound change in the nature of the social experience of men. We should not be surprised that this has implications for their well-being. There is evidence that the unemployment rate is a powerful predictor of hospital admission rates for serious mental illness (Kammerling and O'Connor, 1993). Jones et al. (1991) found a strongly significant association between parasuicide and unemployment. Suicide is more common in men, especially young, working class men. In social class V the highest suicide rates are to be found in the age range 25–44 years. Suicide rate has a significant positive correlation with unemployment; the higher the unemployment level, the higher the suicide rate (Platt and Kreitman, 1984). The next step for the young men interviewed in the *Panorama* programme, young men who are unemployed, miserable, alienated, withdrawn, socially isolated and who have low self esteem, may well be the surgery or the community mental health team. But will it?

Women's health has quite rightly received much attention over the last twenty years, yet in comparison, men's remains a neglected area. There is no national screening service for cancer of the prostate (the second most common cancer in men) as there is for breast cancer in women. In any case, focusing on these aspects of physical health overlooks the need to examine mental health. Men are not allowed to talk about how they feel. It may be acceptable for a woman to admit to feelings of inferiority, but not so for a man. Men are strong. They don't have feelings, let alone the need to talk about them. Even if they wanted to do so, would they be able to? And even if they could form the words, would they be listened to? The majority of mental health professionals, those who do the caring and the listening, are women. Can they shake themselves free of their own stereotypes about maleness? Can we allow men to have feelings about their lives, just as we have been able to allow women to step out of the shadows, and transcend commonly ordained gender roles? We should not be surprised at the rising suicide rates in young men, as long as we expect them to be unable to talk about their feelings. Here lies one of the greatest challenges to those involved in mental health.

References

Broverman, K., Broverman, D., Clarkson, F., Rosenkrantz, P. and Vogel, S. (1970) 'Sex role stereotypes and clinical judgements in mental health', *Journal of Consulting and Clinical Psychology*, 34, pp. 1–7.

Cochrane, R. (1983) *The Social Creation of Mental Illness*, London, Longman.

Horowitz, A. (1977) 'The pathways into psychiatric treatment: some differences between men and women', *Journal of Health and Social Behaviour*, 18, pp. 169–78.

Johnstone, L. (1989) *Users and Abusers of Psychiatry*, London, Routledge.

Jones, S. C., Forster, D. P. and Hassenyeh, F. (1991) 'The role of unemployment in parasuicide', *Psychological Medicine*, 21, pp. 169–76.

Kammerling, R. M. and O'Connor, S. (1993) 'Unemployment as a predictor of psychiatric admission', *British Medical Journal*, 307, pp. 1536–39.

Platt, S. and Kreitman, N. (1984) 'Trends in parasuicide and unemployment among men in Edinburgh', *British Medical Journal*, 289, pp. 1029–32.

12

Madness and misogyny: my mother and myself

Jane M. Ussher

When I was an adolescent my mother was mad. Because it was the 1970s, she was deemed to be afflicted by her 'nerves'. Had it been 100 years ago, she would probably have been called 'hysterical' or 'neurasthenic'. Today, it might be 'post-natal depression'. Her particular madness manifested itself in what was termed depression. Her unhappiness, pain and fear resulted in withdrawal, apathy, tiredness and a sense of worthlessness. Sometimes she cried. Sometimes she was angry. Being a 'good mother', a well-trained woman, as most of us are, she turned her anger in on herself, rather than outwards on her four children, all under twelve years old. She didn't eat a lot. She 'let herself go' by eschewing nice frocks and neatly curled hair. Her outward anger was less evident: no doubt we missed a lot, intent on pretending that everything was normal at home and that we were a happy family. As the unhappiness had no outlet in this world determined to deny women the right to their tears, to their torment, the anger was tightly controlled – stored up until it reached a breaking point, when cracked cups and saucers set aside specifically for this purpose would be taken out into the back yard and flung at the wall. We children loved it. Our mother was really potty. So we laughed, and felt relieved, because the broken cups were easier to deal with than the tears. The careful storing of any dropped and cracked cup for our mother's occasional smashing we could treat as a shared joke, shared secret; some acknowledgement of her frustration and despair, but harmless. Sometimes at night she walked for hours, wearing out her frustration and anger pounding the darkened

Edited extract from J. M. Ussher, *Women's Madness: Misogyny or Mental Illness?* (1991), Hemel Hempstead, Harvester Wheatsheaf, pp. 3–7.

pavements. Her absence from the house was never commented on, even when we feared she would not return.

Looking back now, I see it all as a blatant cry for help. A plea to be noticed, for someone to listen. But we four children, preoccupied with our own games and rivalries, were the only ones who heard. And we didn't really hear at all. We didn't want to.

When my mother tried to kill herself, I was told she was really mad. They put her in the local mental hospital, the one we joked about at school, taunting each other with cries that 'the white van has arrived to take you away.' Suddenly it wasn't very funny any more. They gave her ECT which left her shaking and crying, and gave her a cocktail of drugs so that she forgot everything. She forgot her pain, her misery, her loneliness, the fears which kept her awake at night and which I can even now only imagine. But she forgot everything else. Sometimes she forgot our names, confusing us, calling each name in turn before reaching the right one. So she must have been mad. My father told me she was. Her nerves had given in. She was ill. And it was a secret. We weren't allowed to tell our friends, or our relatives and we didn't talk about it ourselves. I learnt the lesson of the stigma of madness early in life: shame, fear, guilt, perhaps for many people more debilitating than the symptoms called madness. So we feigned normality, and coped.

Nearly twenty years later all this seems a distant memory. My mother weaned herself off her debilitating drug dose and carried on living. She is no longer mad. She is happy, healthy and independent, having escaped from many of the bonds that tied her. But we never talk of this time.

For years I wanted to know: to know what was wrong, what to do, how to help. My inability to cure my mother in her earlier misery, to make her happy again, spurred me to seek solutions in the abstract, contained and academic way.

I studied psychology; this would be where I would find the answers. Nine years of undergraduate study, postgraduate research and clinical psychology training equipped me with the academic armour with which to enter professional debates on the subject. But do I now have the answers? Unfortunately, I do not. My psychology gives me (or is designed to give me) a legitimate voice in the market place of the mad. It equips me with logical, well-researched explanations for madness. It gives me a myriad of labels with which to classify the different manifestations of madness, ranging from depression, anxiety, phobia, schizophrenia, to the more specific 'illnesses' such as post-traumatic stress disorder, premenstrual syndrome or post-natal depression. Symptoms – whether physical or psychological – can be grouped in neat clusters, and seen as different forms of madness, or 'mental illness' as the experts prefer, or *mental health problems* in our New Age of enlightenment. The mad can be scientifically classified – and then, supposedly, cured.

This knowledge gives me power. I can now use my hard-earned skills to treat other women (and men) deemed mad. I can intervene in their pain, as the psychiatrist treating my mad, sad mother did all those years ago. As she is now happy, no longer throwing cups or hating herself, perhaps they were successful. Who knows whether *I* have been with the people I have tried to help? For I still don't know the answer. What I *do* know is that my mother was not mad, and that her anger, pain and despair were not unique to her. I know that women trapped in unhappy marriages, isolated, lonely, with young, demanding children, no money and no friends are often deemed mad. That to be a woman is often to be mad. If we stay inside our prescribed roles and routes as my mother did, or if we speak out, or move outside our designated paths we become mad. My mother may have been mad because she was adhering to the dictates of her feminine role, staying as wife and mother when she desperately wanted to flee. I can be called mad because I reject that same role. I am publicly called 'neurotic' or 'hysterical' by senior men at work if I speak out or criticise. It's a common pattern. Women members of the British Parliament are continuously hectored and pathologised when they speak. Intelligent educated men still use the threat of the label of madness very cleverly, with no shame. It silences many of us. We are all in danger of being positioned as mad. Forming part of what it is to be a woman, it beckons us as a spectre in the shadows.

Madness is no more a simple set of symptoms or problems – an individual difficulty or illness experienced by each 'interesting case' – than any individual woman's history can be seen entirely independently of the history of *all* women. As we cannot hope to understand an individual woman without looking at the meaning of what it is to be 'woman' in a patriarchal society, so we cannot understand the pain and agony which makes up 'madness' without looking at the meaning of this very concept.

Psychology, or any expert profession, any academic discipline, does not have the answer, even if those who have invested years of their lives in learning and training would have it otherwise. I wish psychology *did* have the answer. But it is a utopian dream. Women are not mad merely because of our hormones, our genes, our faulty learning, our cognition or our unconscious desires. Our madness is not an illness; it is disguised as such by the legalistically worded classifications meted out to women. And why is it *women* who are mad? Why is it that it has *always* been women? Is this madness actually the result of misogyny, as many feminists would claim, and are the symptoms not madness at all, but anger or outrage?

Our misogyny causes us to be named as mad. It dismisses witches, wise women, suffragettes and battered women as mad. Labelling us mad silences our voices. We can be ignored. The rantings of a mad woman are irrelevant. Her anger is impotent.

13

Strategies for promoting the mental health of populations

Eero Lahtinen, Natacha Joubert, John Raeburn,
Rachael Jenkins

This chapter looks at the broad issue of conceptualising and planning strategies for mental health promotion. Our intention is to discuss mental health promotion first and foremost as a population-based exercise – that is, we are primarily concerned with aggregations of people rather than individuals, while at the same time not forgetting that these populations are indeed made up of thinking, feeling, intensely individual people in their family and community environments.

Mental health and its promotion

Our view is that mental health relates primarily to emotions, thoughts, relationships, behaviours and spirituality (Lahtinen, 1998); to individuals' capacity to enjoy life and to deal or cope with the challenges they face (Joubert and Raeburn, 1998); and thus to a positive sense of well-being. This includes individual resources such as self-esteem, optimism, a sense of mastery and coherence, the ability to initiate, develop and sustain mutually sustaining relationships and the ability to cope with adversity (Lavikainen et al., 2000). Nevertheless, most often, especially among professionals within formal and influential

Edited from E. Lahtinen et al., Chapter 17 in H. Herrman, S. Saxena and R. Moodie (eds) (2005), *Promoting Mental Health: Concepts, Emerging Evidence, Practice*, World Health Organization, pp. 226–42.

institutions and organisations, mental health is referred to, researched and debated within a pathological context – the language of which is of deficiency, disability and disorders. This is strongly illustrated by the content of numerous professional journals and reports produced worldwide on mental ill-health.

As most mental disorders are considered to be environmentally caused, there is risk that human suffering, a likely reaction in extreme circumstances, is categorised as a mental problem and thus medicalised. When people are facing major stresses caused by unstable family, social, economic and political conditions, when their basic physical and mental needs are threatened, and when they are stigmatised and isolated while facing such situations, the suffering and the distress is tremendous. The reactions that individuals may display when they are distressed or are fighting for their lives are frequently confused with mental disorders. However, a considerable body of longitudinal research shows that when their basic life conditions are restored, when the suffering experienced is recognised and legitimised, and when it is possible to count on family and social support, the capacity to recover – the resiliency – and the capacity to build meaning out of the suffering is astonishing. Furthermore, the vast majority of individuals are able to learn from adversity and to move on with their life in an enhanced way (for example, Cyrulnik, 1999, 2001, 2003; Henderson, Benard and Sharp-Light, 1999; Pransky, 1991, 1998; Werner, 1994; Werner and Smith, 1992). These kinds of human processes are fundamental to a mental health promotion extended beyond a pathologised clinical and short-term frame of reference.

The approach for promoting the mental health of people that is presented in this chapter is first and foremost based on a fundamental faith and trust in people's humanity, a positive view of mental health and on a strong belief in all individuals, including people with mental health problems or disorders. This involves an inner resiliency, a capacity to 'be, belong and become' on everybody's own terms within supportive environments. We believe that any mental health promotion activities should be based on a 'people-centred' approach (Raeburn and Rootman, 1998) that focuses on empowering individuals and communities to take control over their own lives and mental health while showing respect for culture, equity, social justice, interconnections and personal dignity (Joubert and Raeburn, 1998). For instance, human or social enterprises aimed at promoting the mental health of entire populations should be considered a long-term investment by nations or governments. Such investment obviously requires initial financial and other support but would progressively pay itself off through reduced costs in health and social services. As a structural change, such an approach becomes sustainable because of individuals' and communities' direct involvement and participation, and the strength and productivity they get from their own involvement (see Durning, 1989; Lord and Farlow, 1990; Pransky, 1991; WHO, 2002).

Three levels of action

It is probably helpful to consider the population approach to mental health promotion at three broad levels of analysis: macro or societal, meso or community and micro or individual. Each of these has its own set of conceptual and strategic considerations.

First, at the societal level the major preoccupation is with policy. Policy is often seen as a somewhat regulatory matter, but it can also be seen as representing a statement of principles and values by individuals, communities, and societies relating to their own goals and desired courses of action (Jenkins et al., 2002). While much policy tends to be formulated by experts in their offices away from 'real life', communities need the opportunity to deliberate together about mental health and its contribution to their overall health, sense of well-being and quality of life (Joubert, 2001). In short, there is no reason why policy development should not be a participatory and empowering process in its own right and therefore mental health promoting. An example of a step towards such participatory policy development processes has been provided by a few governments that allow a consultative debate on the Internet on policy proposals. Another example involves relevant stakeholders in participatory country situation appraisals prior to policy development (see Jenkins, 2004 at www.mental-neurological-health.net).

Second, at the meso or community level, the desirable situation is that mental health promotion strategies and activities are decided on, developed and applied by people where they live their day-to-day lives. Here, 'community' includes families, schools, workplaces and various community organisations and settings as well as whole geographical localities and neighbourhoods. For example, in the workplace concerns about significant decreases of productivity in the private and public sectors have resulted in studies that have clearly indicated that in order to reduce high levels of stress, burnout and overall absenteeism, employers and employees have to work together to idenitfy, discuss and agree on managerial and individual practices that need to be improved or radically changed (Marmot, 1997; Marmot and Wilkinson 1999). Organisations and industries that have adopted healthy workplace guidelines and programmes focusing on increasing and fostering a sense of control, initiative, participation, appreciation, self-esteem and self-worth, as well as a sense of belonging and support among employees and employers, have experienced major improvements in their human and business conditions (Lowe, 2003a, 2003b, Lowe, Schellenberg and Shannon, 2003). There are also examples of entire communities facing major social problems (for example, high levels of violence, child abuse, delinquency, dropping out, drug trafficking and teenage pregnancy) that have succeeded in transforming what seemed to be intractable living conditions by primarily focusing on people's innate resiliency and capacity for well-being, for wisdom and for common sense instead of trying to change destructive conditions that kept people immersed in their problems (Durning, 1989: Pransky, 1991, 1998).

The third, micro or individual level is the oldest and most traditional sphere of mental health work. Here, mental health promotion strategies define themselves through various activities or practices that aim to promote, build on, increase or foster primarily individuals' strengths, resourcefulness or resiliency. Life skills such as social competence (responsiveness, cultural flexibility, empathy, caring, communication skills and a sense of humour), problem-solving (planning, help-seeking, critical and creative thinking), autonomy (sense of identity, self-efficacy, self-awareness, task mastery and adaptive distancing from negative messages and conditions) and a sense of purpose and belief in a bright future (goal direction, educational aspirations, optimism, faith and spiritual connectedness) are examples of individual mental health dimensions that are being targeted in programmes designed to increase resiliency in young people (Benard, 1991, 1993a, 1993b; Henderson, Benard and Sharp-Light, 1999; Rowling, Martin and Walker, 2002).

Many of the factors and conditions that impact negatively on the health and mental health of individuals, communities and overall populations often result from situations that go far beyond the direct control of individuals. Analysis of the health status of populations and its determinants has revealed how major economic, political and social decisions taken at the macro level by governments (for example, economic restructuring) can impact negatively on people's lives, health, mental health and well-being (Stephens, Dulberg and Joubert, 1999). At the opposite end of the spectrum, when these decisions are taken within a partnership and participatory approach that fully recognises and supports individuals and communities in their capacity for self-determination, they become instrumental in major social changes that are beneficial to the whole population (Maxwell et al., 2003; MacKinnon, 2003, Phillips and Orsini, 2002). Mental health and social policies that espouse an empowering approach allowing for the participation and reinforcement of individuals' and communities' capacities to take control over their destinies would undoubtedly contribute directly to the health and wealth of populations and nations.

With respect to prevention, treatment and recovery/rehabilitation, the major and powerful characteristic of mental health promotion is that it is closer to the 'natural' way people see and want to live their lives. It can be asserted that human beings are much more likely to be open and responsive to approaches that increase their capacity to cope with life on their own terms, than to ones that are prescribed from above and which victimise and reduce them to their deficiencies or disabilities. In short, an approach to mental health is advocated in a mental health promotion context that is not pathologised or medicalised, but positive and likely to resonate with people in terms of its intuitive appeal and respect for them as resourceful human beings. It is also likely to reduce the stigma currently associated with mental illness-dominated approaches to mental health issues. Indeed, the potential for the application of the kinds of mental health promotion principles espoused here – involving strength-building, resilience, empowerment, positivity and community – is increasingly being used in the treatment and recovery sector (Falloon and Fadden, 1993; Hawe et al., 1998; Rowling, Martin and Walker, 2002). The research suggests that such approaches are highly effective (Barry, 2001; Durlak and Wells, 1977; Falloon and Fadden, 1993; Health Promotion Wales, 1996; Hosman and Llopis, 2000; Pransky, 1991; Tilford, Delaney and Vogels, 1997; Vinokur, Price and Schul, 1995). Our view is that the application of positive mental health promotion principles across the whole mental health sector, and as part of the whole operation and thinking of governments with regard to the well-being of their populations, could usher in a new era of enlightened thinking. When a government puts the positive quality of life of their citizens first, then the nation is sure to prosper.

Conclusion

Effective mental health promotion is based on a positive, non-pathologised approach to mental health that focuses on strengths and resilience building. Mental health promotion as a recognised or formal enterprise is still in its infancy. But mental health promotion as represented here is close to the natural way people see and want to live their lives. As such, it goes right to the heart of the most important matters of human existence and, at a population level, could well be a vehicle for empowerment of people around the world, and for indicating to governments that the well-being and quality of life of the populations over which they preside is of pre-eminent importance. Good mental health is the most important thing we have.

References

Barry, M.M. (2001). 'Promoting positive mental health: theoretical frameworks for practice'. *International Journal of Mental Health Promotion*, 3: 25–34.

Benard, B. (1991). *Fostering Resiliency in Kids: Protective Factors in the Family, School, and Community*. Portland OR, Northwest Regional Education Laboratory.

Benard, B. (1993a). 'Fostering resiliency in kids', *Educational Leadership*, 51: 44–8.

Benard, B. (1993b). *Turning the Corner from Risk to Resiliency*. Portland OR, Northwest Regional Education Laboratory.

Cyrulnik, B. (1999). *Un merveilluex malheur*, Paris. Odile Jacob.

Cyrulnik, B. (2000). *Les vilains petits canards*, Paris. Odile Jacob.

Cyrulnik, B. (2003). *Le murmure des fantomes*, Paris. Odile Jacob.

Durlak, J.A. and Wells, A.M. (1977). 'Primary prevention mental health programmes for children and adolescents: a meta-analytic review', *American Journal of Community Psychology*, 25: 115–52.

Durning, A.B. (1989). 'Grass roots are our best hope for global prosperity and ecology', *Utne Reader*, 34: 34–49.

Falloon, I.R.H. and Fadden, G. (1993). *Integrated Mental Health Care: A Comprehensive Community Based Approach*. Cambridge, Cambridge University Press.

Hawe, P. et al. (1998) 'Working invisibly: health workers talk about capacity building in health promotion', *Health Promotion International*, 13: 285–95.

Health Promotion Wales (1996). *Mental Health Promotion: Forty Examples of Effective Intervention*. Health Promotion Wales (Technical Report No. 21).

Henderson, N., Benard, B. and Sharp-Light, N. (1999) *Resiliency in Action, Practical Ideas for Overcoming Risks and Building Strengths in Youth, Families and Communities*. San Diego, CA, Resiliency in Action.

Hosman, C. and Llopis, E.J. (2000). *The Evidence of Health Promotion Effectiveness: Shaping Public Health in a New Europe. Part Two. Evidence Book* (2nd edn) Brussels, International Union for Health Promotion and Education.

Jenkins, R. et al. (2002) *Developing National Mental Health Policy*. Maudsley Monograph No. 43. Hove, Psychology Press.

Joubert, N. (2001). 'Promoting the mental health of the population: promoting individual resilience and social support'. *Mielenterveys – Finland*, 3: 6–10.

Joubert, N. and Raeburn, J. (1998) 'Mental health promotion: people, power and passion'. *International Journal of Mental Health Promotion*, Inaugural Issue: 15–22.

Lahtinen, E. (1998) *Mental Health Promotion on the European Agenda: Themes from Finland*. Helsinki, National Research and Development Centre for Welfare and Health.

Lavikainen, J., Lahtinen, E. and Lehtinen, V. (2000) *Public Health Approach on Mental Health in Europe*. National Research and Development Centre for Welfare and Health (STAKES).

Lord, J. and Farlow, A.M. (1990) 'A study of personal empowerment: implication for health promotion'. *Health Promotion Canada*, 29: 2–8.

Lowe, G.S. (2003a) *Identifying the Building Blocks of a Healthy Health Care Work Environment*. Ottawa, Canadian Policy Research Networks.

Lowe, G.S. (2003b) *Healthy Workplaces and Productivity: A Discussion Paper*. Ottawa, Minister of Public Works and Government Services.

Lowe, G.S., Schellenberg, G. and Shannon, H.S. (2003) 'Correlates of employees' perception of a healthy work environment'. *American Journal of Health Promotion*, 17: 390–9.

MacKinnon, M.P. (2003) *Citizens' Dialogue on Canada's Future: A 21st Century Social Contract*. Ottawa, Canadian Policy Research Networks.

Marmot, M.G. (1997) 'Contribution of job control and other risk factors to social variations in coronary heart disease incidence'. *Lancet*, 350: 235–9.

Marmot, M.G. and Wilkinson, P. (eds) (1999) *Social Determinants of Health*. New York, Oxford University Press.

Maxwell, J. et al. (2003) 'Giving citizens a voice in healthcare policy in Canada'. *British Medical Journal*, 326: 1031–3.

Phillips, S.D. and Orsini, M. (2002). *Mapping The Links: Citizen Involvement in Policy Processes*. Ottawa, Canadian Policy Research Networks.

Pransky, J. (1991) *Prevention: The Critical Need*. Springfield, MO, Burrel Foundation and Paradigm Press.

Pransky, J. (1998) *Modello: A Story of Hope for the Inner City and Beyond*. Cabot, VT, NEHRI Publications.

Raeburn, J. and Rootman, I. (1998) *People-Centred Health Promotion*. Chichester, Wiley.

Rowling, L., Martin, G. and Walker, L. (2002) *Mental Health Promotion and Young People: Concepts and Practice*. Australia, McGraw-Hill.

Stephens, T., Dulberg, C. and Joubert, N. (1999). 'Mental Health of the Canadian Population: a comprehensive analysis'. *Chronic Diseases in Canada*, 20: 118–26.

Stephens, T. and Joubert, N. (2001) 'The economic burden of mental health problems in Canada'. *Chronic Diseases in Canada*, 22: 18–23.

Tilford, S., Delaney, F. and Vogels, M. (1997) *Effectiveness of Mental Health Promotion Intervention: A Review*, London, Health Education Authority.

Vinokur, A.D., Price, R.H. and Schul, Y. (1995)'Impact of the JOBS intervention on unemployed workers varying in risk for depression'. *American Journal of Community Psychology*, 23: 39–74.

Werner, E. (1994) 'Risk, resilience, and recovery: perspectives from the Kauai longitudinal study'. *Development and Psychopathology*, 5: 503–15.

Werner, E. and Smith, R. (1992) *Overcoming the Odds: High Risk Children from Birth to Adulthood*. Ithaca, NY, Cornell University Press.

WHO (2002). *Community Participation in Total Health and Sustainable Development: Approaches and Techniques*. Geneva, World Health Organization.

Part II

Inequality and policy

14

Introduction

Mick McCormick

Mental distress is closely related to social and material deprivation. This would suggest that the policies aimed at promoting mental health should be primarily economic and social rather than medical and curative – that mental health services need to offer people more opportunities to get their lives back and focus less on medication and symptom control. Such policies would aim to improve the conditions of large numbers of people. In fact, there never has been a comprehensive mental health policy in the UK. Instead, there has been a variety of policies for dealing with a minority of individuals who are clearly designated as 'mentally ill'. This part of the book looks at the historical evolution of these mental illness policies, relating them to their social context and effects. Particular attention is paid to their potentially coercive nature.

There would seem to be a growing consensus among policy makers that social inclusion should be a common goal for mental health services and service users (Spandler, 2007). Working towards social inclusion has been a key government goal since 1997 and is seen as of fundamental importance to people with severe mental health problems. One of the main issues in mental health with the pervasive terms 'exclusion' and 'inclusion' is that progress towards a clear understanding of the concepts is hampered by insufficient practical definition – leading to implicit assumptions 'reinforcing particular dominant cultural values and practices' (Spandler, 2007).

Closely related to social inclusion is the concept of 'recovery'. Recovery is about building a meaningful and satisfying life as defined by the persons themselves, whether or not there are ongoing or recurring symptoms and problems, and a move away from a focus on the removal of symptoms as the prime purpose of mental health services. For example, learning to live with voices may be the focus rather than eliminating them. Recovery represents a movement away from pathology, illness and symptoms to health, strengths and wellbeing.

For many people, recovery is about social inclusion and restoring meaningful and satisfactory roles and responsibilities within a community. These roles take place in society and within local communities rather than within segregated services. Interdependence is encouraged as much as independence. The intention is to support the individual to use the same resources as the general population rather than create parallel but segregated resources. Recovery also requires significant changes to traditional power relationships in mental health services.

All of these important themes are explored in the readings forming this part of the book which begins with Roger Gomm's update (Reading 15) on his article in Mental Health Matters (Heller et al., 1996). The results of this reviewed epidemiological survey of diagnosed mental illness remain very much the same. He demonstrates that mental illness continues to have essentially the same relationship with deprivation as that shown by other kinds of illness. The lesson usually drawn from mapping ill-health against social deprivation is that appropriate policies for promoting health are economic and social rather than curative and medical. It is in this sense that much mental health policy has become policy only for dealing with 'mental illness'.

A number of themes introduced by Gomm are picked up and explored in subsequent articles in this part of the book. For example, Gomm's discussion on the quality of social relationships is explored in detail in Martin Webber's reading (25) on social capital and the issue of social exclusion and inclusion are discussed in readings by Julie Repper and Rachel Perkins (Reading 17) and Helen Spandler (Reading 18).

The other readings in this part of the book concern policies which reflect this public policy conceptualisation of 'mental illness' – usually in a narrow sense defined as the problem of curing and controlling distressed individuals, rather than as a matter of providing individuals and communities with resources with which they may be able to lead satisfactory lives.

The nineteenth century was the age of large lunatic asylums, when mental illness and incarceration became equated with each other. This is outlined in Reading 16 by Annie Borthwick and her colleagues who discuss moral treatment used at The Retreat in York in the nineteenth century and argue that many of the main principles of this treatment at The Retreat are still relevant to contemporary mental health practice. In applying the main principles of moral treatment to contemporary mental health, Borthwick et al. place a great deal of emphasis on seven basic principles for moral treatment and one theme which strikes a chord and is echoed in subsequent articles is that of 'inclusion'. Repper and Perkins (Reading 17) explore issues of discrimination in the context of recovery and social inclusion – offering a critique of anti-stigma campaigns and favouring an analysis of discrimination and power within the context of social exclusion and inclusion. Their contention that a focus on stigma leads to a focus on individuals rather than on socially constructed exclusion – limiting the options available to people with mental health problems – chimes with the themes in Webber's reading (25).

While Spandler (Reading 18) acknowledges the helpfulness of the term social exclusion, she explores whether the notion of social inclusion helps or hinders possibilities for wider social change. She offers more of a critique of the notion of social inclusion and considers some of the problems associated with its wide-scale adoption – arguing that assumptions based on the apparently self-evident common sense desirability of social inclusion may lead to individualised practices guided by judgements as to what constitutes a healthy or normal life.

Media coverage of mental health has long been a concern to service users, academics, carers, professionals and policy makers. In Reading 19, Mark Walsh pursues the theme of commonly held views and perceptions as he investigates the way the mass media disseminate images of mental distress. Walsh demonstrates how the media often take a lead in feeding views and stereotypes of mental distress and goes on to suggest that current mental health policy and procedure are driven by both public and political reaction to a handful of high-profile 'mental health cases' which have been misrepresented by the media. This theme is explored in some more detail by Diego De Leo (Reading 20) as he considers anti-suicide strategies and looks at their failure in the light of a call for closer cooperation and a coordinated and 'scientific' approach to the prevention of suicide. De Leo argues that the complex nature of suicide means that an integrated and inclusive approach is necessary rather than one based on simple, linear policy guidance. In calling for an integrated approach, he argues that the factors that lead to and protect people from suicidal behaviour are both diverse and culturally specific while current national responses and strategies may be motivated more by politics than by public health.

Risk and protection are themes explored by Hazel Kemshall (Reading 21) as she considers the impact of risk reduction and risk taking policies which have arisen with a shift to community care and deinstitutionalisation. She argues that – again as a result of media pressure and unchallenged stereotyping – community care has become preoccupied with risk avoidance and risk management, which has resulted in a largely negative view of user risks and an erosion of user rights. Picking up a theme which resonates through this part of the book, Kemshall argues that as a result of risk being rooted at an individual level, structural factors are either ignored or given only limited consideration.

Issues of risk and protection are brought into sharper focus with Mike Flanagan's reading (22) on the challenge of shared care. Like De Leo, Flanagan calls for an integrated approach for service users with dual problems (mental ill health and substance use). Recognition of the extent of coexistence of mental ill health and substance use is recent (Watkins et al., 2001) and this presents many challenges to mental health and substance misuse services – in the past, service users with such a dual diagnosis have been passed between mental health services and specialist drug services. With the rise in the incidence of drug/alcohol use alongside mental health problems there is increasing concern over this approach to service delivery (O'Neill, 2004). Flanagan explores these challenges to mental health and substance misuse services and suggests that while there is a need for inter-agency collaboration, there are associated tensions which need to be addressed and one main way of addressing these is through a programme of reciprocal training. He goes on to suggest that this reciprocal training may achieve little unless there is a simultaneous alteration to the structure of local services and the development of new systems and supports at a local – as well as national – level.

McKenzie argues that psychiatric services ought to consider the various risk factors experienced by different ethnic groups and suggests that:

> The one-size-fits-all concept of psychiatry is still prevalent. It has come under pressure recently as discussion of institutional racism has come to the fore. But many of the resulting suggestions . . . are insufficiently radical or comprehensive to produce significant change. (McKenzie, 2002)

Taking the theme of risk and racism further, Deryck Browne's reading (23) draws attention to the continuing manner in which black communities are given unequal treatment and are over-represented in both mental health and criminal justice systems. Examples of these inequalities are explored and the inability of a plethora of government initiatives to make any positive impact is considered, together with suggestions for new approaches which could address the causes of these inequalities rather than continue to focus on their symptoms.

Government policies direct the responsibility for risk reduction through compulsory treatment to forensic psychiatrists, and the mental health needs of people in prison or transferred from prison to mental health services often fall under the clinical supervision of forensic psychiatrists. The powers of forensic psychiatrists include making judgements about care, treatment, and potential discharge. John Gunn (Reading 24) offers a brief summary of the development and place of forensic psychiatry and then puts this in a contemporary context by pointing up some of the problems forensic psychiatry faces today – problems which resonate elsewhere in this part of the book (media frenzy; a 'failing' community care system; self-harm and suicide; and dual diagnosis) – before going on to consider the successes of forensic psychiatry.

In the last reading in this part of the book, Martin Webber (Reading 25) explores the significance of the notion of social capital to mental health and although he acknowledges that there is a limited amount of research into the links between social capital and mental health, he suggests that the quality and quantity of everyday support to an individual can be of great importance for their mental health. Equally, he suggests that the quality and quantity of everyday support is affected by the nature of their local community. Like all of the contributors, he acknowledges the close links between mental health and inequality (as outlined by Gomm) – and argues for a more inclusive model. Spandler, too, acknowledges the need for, and usefulness of, strategies to reduce exclusion but warns against using inclusion as the only or inevitable response to exclusion.

References

Heller, T., Reynolds, J., Gomm, R., Muston, R. and Pattison, S. (1996) *Mental Health Matters: A Reader*, Basingstoke, Macmillan.

McKenzie, K. (2002) 'A community-embedded psychiatry', *Openmind*, 114, Mar/April, pp. 14–15.

O'Neill, T. (2004) 'Same place, same time', *Mental Health Today*, July/August, pp. 27–9.

Spandler, H. (2007) 'From social exclusion to inclusion? A critique of the inclusion imperative in mental health', *Medical Sociology Online*, vol. 2, issue 2, pp. 3–16.

Watkins, T.R., Lewellen, A. and Barrett, M.C. (2001) *Dual Diagnosis: An Integrated Approach to Treatment*, Thousand Oaks, Sage.

15

Mental health and inequality

Roger Gomm

Introduction

The link between health and material conditions is well-known and well-documented (for convenient summaries see Marmot and Wilkinson, 2000; DH, 2006a and b, or more briefly, DH, 2004a). A very simple statement will serve to summarise all the research findings on this matter: for nearly every kind of illness, disease or disability, 'physical' or 'mental', poorer people are afflicted more than richer people: more often, more seriously and for longer – unless, of course, they die from the condition, which they do at an earlier age.

Not only have links between material inequality and health been persistently obvious for the last 150 years (Farr, 1860), but inequalities in health have widened dramatically during the life-time of the NHS. They are now greater than they were in the 1930s (DH, 2006a).

Since 1997 reducing health inequalities has become a major aspiration of government policy in the UK (DH, 1999). This has led to the closer monitoring of health inequalities. The most up-to-date picture of the relationship between a range of health indicators on the one hand, and deprivation/affluence on the other can be viewed on Public Health Observatory websites.

Dis-ease rather than disease

'Physical' and 'mental' health both show the same kinds of relationship to differences in material condition. Some obvious 'life and death' matters in the mental health field contribute directly to social class differences in life expectancy. Suicide, which is now the second highest cause of death for younger men, shows a very strong relationship with social class and deprivation (Lewis and Sloggett, 1998; ONS 2007, Figure 7). Suicides are also closely linked to alcoholism, which is itself linked to other mental health issues. Alcoholism is more common among the unskilled, the unemployed (Wood et al., 2006) and the roofless (Tims and Balazs, 1997). It is a direct cause of premature deaths and an indirect cause through the undermining of the drinker's health. Similar remarks can be made about heroin and crack cocaine use, which predominate in more deprived neighbourhoods. Although the number of people using drugs is actually higher in more affluent neighbourhoods, more people end up with severe drug problems in the poorer areas (Chivite-Mathews et al., 2005; Eaton et al., 2006). People who are depressed or otherwise mentally distressed show elevated accident proneness without medication, and an even greater proneness to life-threatening accidents when taking anti-depressant medication (Freeman and O'Hanlon, 1995). Depression shows a very strong social class profile (Brown et al., 1994; Fryers et al., 2003, 2005). The poorer you are the more likely you are to be miserable enough to be regarded as clinically depressed. Clinical depression is strongly associated with coronary heart disease (Hippisley-Cox et al., 1998). Seriously self-harming behaviour – at least ten times more common than suicide and often a precursor – also shows the same social class pattern (Gunnell et al., 1995, Hawton and James, 2005).

Some studies have found schizophrenia up to three times more common among those from working class origins than among those from other backgrounds (Barbigian 1985; McLaren and Bain, 1998). Other studies have not found this association (Mulvany et al., 2001). Evidence seems to be accumulating that there is a strong genetic component in schizophrenia (Turner, 1997). This doesn't necessarily mean that there is no causal link between schizophrenia and deprivation. As Weich and Lewis (1998) argue, a link between mental illness and deprivation may lie in deprivation prolonging and increasing the severity of a condition actually caused by something else.

Very important in numerical terms are the dementias of later life. Alzheimer's disease particularly, and to a lesser extent multi-infarct dementia (MID) again show a greater prevalence among lower socio-economic groups. Here however, it is the number of years of education which seem to be associated rather than material conditions as such (Ott et al., 1995), and the link between social class and dementia tends to be obscured since fewer lower-class people survive into their eighties when the risk of dementia increases dramatically.

There are some 'mental illness' conditions which show a reverse pattern: anorexia nervosa, for instance, although a life-threatening condition, seems more common among well-educated, middle-class young women (Goldberg and Goodyer, 2005) and there are some conditions that show no clear social class pattern. Bi-polar affective disorder ('manic-depression') may be more common among those from middle-class backgrounds (Goldberg and Goodyear, 2005). But people who get diagnosed as manic depressives themselves often end up among the poorly paid or unemployed (Giggs and Cooper, 1987). The processes of downward social mobility and residential segregation associated with mental ill health are clearly outlined in Jones and Moon (1987). So, despite some contrary examples, something like the earlier summary will serve: that for nearly every kind of 'mental' illness, disease or diability, and especially those that afflict large numbers of people, poorer people are affected more than richer people, more often, more seriously and for longer. Embroidered on this general pattern of social-class inequalities are inequalities of gender (Graham, 2000; Sacker et al., 2000, Vågerö, 2000) ethnicity (Nazroo, 1997a, 1997b; Karlsen and Nazroo, 2004), and age (Evans et al., 2003).

'Mental' and 'physical' illnesses are frequently found together in the same person (Meltzer et al., 1995; Evans et al., 2003: Chapter 3). Judged by their elevated rates of mortality from causes in addition to suicide, and from morbidity studies, people regarded as 'mentally ill' are often 'physically unwell' (Brugha et al., 1988; Pasquini and Biondi, 2007), while those who are diagnosed as physically unwell or disabled are often distressed mentally (Broome, 1989). In later life the association of depression with physical ailments, loss of continence, mobility and hearing is well known, as is the association between depression, cognitive impairment, or confusion and infection, drug side effects, poorly controlled diabetes and dietary deficiencies (Holland and Rabbitt, 1991). Poorer sections of the elderly population are either more likely to contract the conditions concerned, or less likely to receive adequate treatment for them (Evans et al., 2003).

The links between 'physical' ailments and 'mental' conditions are many and complex. One source of linkage should be obvious from the discussion so far – a triangular relationship between physical illness, psychological stress and social, environmental, economic and political conditions (Figure 15.1).

If you take any social group, or any neighbourhood with a high rate of premature death, coronary heart disease or long-term and limiting illness, gastric

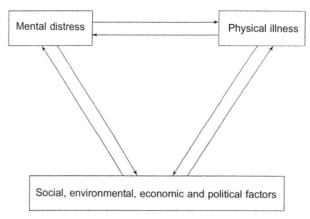

Figure 15.1   The 'illness triangle'

ulcers, childhood accidents, and so on, the chances are that the group or the neighbourhood will be a poor one, and that it will also show a high rate of suicides, depression and anxiety states and schizophrenia. Research on local patterns of health and socio-economic circumstances demonstrates that the census wards that generate most cases for psychiatric admissions, or most cases of suicide, are also those that tend to have the highest death rates (all causes), highest rates of low birth weight babies, and the highest rates of coronary disease (see for instance, Townsend et al., 1985, or Townsend et al., 1988, and the data posted on Public Health Observatory websites).

Material conditions cause ill-health: ill-health causes material conditions

In this unholy triangle causality runs in all directions. Poorer people are more vulnerable to physical illnesses and physical disabilities: being physically ill or disabled is depressing and anxiety provoking. Poorer people are more prone to 'mental illnesses': 'mental illness' lowers immunity (Goodkin and Visser, 1999) and is often associated with health-damaging behaviour such as excessive smoking (Jochelson and Majgoski, 2006) and drinking, drug taking, careless and risky activities, self-neglect, malnutrition and being homeless or without income. Once someone is physically ill, psychological disturbance impedes their recovery. The side effects of psychoactive drugs might be regarded as physical ailments to which people with a diagnosis of mental illness are highly vulnerable (Gabe, 1996). And to complete the triangle, ill health of whatever kind arises not only from social and material deprivation, but sometimes predestines people to unemployment, low incomes and poor housing or no housing at all, all of which make a negative contribution to physical and mental health. Working to the same effect in the reverse direction, it is the parents with the lowest educational qualifications who have the highest risk of having children who suffer from mental disturbances (DH, 2004b: Table 4.6 and Figure 4.10). The children from single parent families are twice as likely to suffer from a mental disorder as the children of a two parent family, those from households where no one is employed are two-and-a-half times more likely, and the children of the poorest 10 per cent of the population are three times more likely to suffer from a mental disorder than those in the richest 10 per cent (Green et al., 2005: Figures 4.1–4.4).

The links between physical ill-health, mental ill-health and material deprivation are not automatic. If they were, Scotland, which has the lowest average incomes and the highest death rates for mainland UK would also have the highest rates of mental illness, which it does not. And Greater London, where incomes are higher and death rates are lower, would not have had a higher rate of mental malaise than did Scotland in the early 1990s (Lewis and Booth, 1992).

Three kinds of factors mediate between material conditions and health (Lynch et al., 2000). One of these is the 'lifestyle' factors so often addressed in health education programmes. Scotland does show higher rates of drinking, smoking and diets predisposing people to coronary disease (Scottish Office, 1992; McLaren, and Bain, 1998). This may explain the co-presence of high death rates and rather lower rates of mental illness than might be predicted from them. Among lifestyle factors are ways of coping with the stresses of life, and these do vary with social class (West, 1995). However, Blaxter (1990) and others have argued that the first step towards adopting a healthier lifestyle is usually an improvement in material conditions.

The second set of factors is constituted by the expectations people have of life and the comparisons they make between themselves and others. It is suggested that while gross material inequalities are important to health, so also are relative inequalities, perceived by people as frustrations of expectations and as indications of their own failure. Wilkinson (1996) is probably the best known exponent of this view.

The third important kind of mediating factor is the quality of social relationships (West, 1995; Evans et al., 2003: Chapter 3) It is interesting in this regard that the mental health of members of minority ethnic groups shows no consistent difference from that of the 'white' population (Nazroo, 1997a), except in the very high rates found among minority ethnic people who live isolated in very small groups among people of other ethnicities (Boydell et al., 2001). The quality of social relationships may be independent of material conditions as in a close, but poor community, but equally, isolation, alienation and fraught relationships may be an associate of poverty as in many inner urban and out-of-town council estates.

Thus while there is no automatic link between material conditions and disease of the physical or mental kinds, poorer people are vulnerable in many ways by comparison with the better off.

Long-term health effects of material deprivation

Research seems to show that there is some very rapid feedback between patterns of inequality and patterns of health. For example, from 1921 to 2001, social class differentials in death rates rose and fell in tune with rising and falling differentials in income (Wilkinson, 1996). Since the war suicide among younger men has shown a close relationship with rates of unemployment (Gunnell et al., 1995; Middleton et al., 2006).

But there is also evidence that past deprivation may show itself many years later in the form of ill health. For example, of men born in Hertfordshire in the 1930s, those who showed a poor weight gain in the first year of life were appreciably more likely to have committed suicide 50 years later (Barker et al., 1995).

Low weight gain is a rough-and-ready indicator of family poverty. By 1983 the mortality pattern for men born in Sweden in 1933 appeared closely related to their experience of earlier adverse life events. Most such life events were of the kinds experienced more by people from manual backgrounds. The greater the number of adverse events, the more likely were the men to be dead before the age of 50 (Rosengren et al., 1993). The various cross-sectional and longitudinal child development studies in Britain show much the same. They chart the effects of low birth weight, early childhood illnesses, family poverty, family disruption, and mentally distressed parents many years later in such multifarious ways as vulnerability to illness in general and to coronary disease, gastric, liver and depressive illnesses in particular, inability to cope with life crises, poor educational achievements, low levels of occupational achievement, alcoholism and difficulties in forming relationships (Wadsworth, 1991). An important sub-group among people disadvantaged as children in these ways are the children of lone parents, and especially the children of teenaged single mothers (Green et al., 2005 Figure 4.1; Nanchahal et al., 2005). Most of these effects seem to be due more or less directly to the material deprivation suffered by such families, insofar as they are much rarer among those who were children of single mothers with more adequate incomes and housing (Spencer, 2005).

Juvenile criminal behaviour is also something which is predictable from the kinds of childhood adversities listed above, and that in turn is associated with elevated levels of mental disorder and elevated mortality before the age of 30: homicides, suicides, accidents, drug overdoses and alcoholic poisoning predominate among the causes of death (Coffey et al., 2003). The inverse relationship between years of education and dementias in later life, mentioned earlier, is another example of the long-term effects of earlier experiences.

As an antidote to this depressing picture it is important to note that adverse circumstances in childhood merely predispose towards adverse outcomes in adulthood. Equally important is what happens to people throughout their lives, and particularly their opportunities for achieving self-esteem and making satisfactory relationships. Although somewhat dated, Rutter (1985) provides a useful summary of 'protective factors' which is still valid today. The implications of long-term studies such as those discussed here is that adversity now breeds adversity later, sometimes much later in advanced old age, but that it is never too late to attempt a remedy. That's the good news. The bad news is that it may be many years before government programmes to reduce health inequalities show any effects.

Increasing inequality in health

In Britain social class differences in life expectancy have widened since the 1930s (DH, 2006a). In 2003 the gap in life expectancy between those of the professional classes and manual workers was two-and-a-half times greater than in 1932. And this is despite the government having made reducing these differences a high priority for the NHS since 1997 (DH, 1999, 2006a and b). The general picture is one where most groups in the population have improved their life expectancy, but richer people have increased theirs much more than poorer people, hence the gap between classes has widened. By 2003 the poor lived 76.2 years on average while the wealthiest lived until 80.3 years old. Up to 2001 there was an increasing health divide between the rich and the poor (Adams et al., 2006) and between the more affluent south of Britain, and northern England and the Celtic fringes (Doran et al., 2004). There have, however, been small, but promising reductions in the gap between classes in deaths from coronary heart disease and cancer (DH, 2006b), and the suicide rate for males has turned down (ONS, 2007).

Widening material inequalities

It is not difficult to chart the growth of material inequality which lies behind increased inequality in health. In Britain, throughout the 1980s and 90s and into the new millennium there was a substantial redistribution of wealth and income in favour of the rich, particularly in the second half of the 1980s. By 2001 the poorest 10 per cent received only two per cent of the nation's total income after taxes and benefits, whereas the richest tenth obtained more than a quarter (Jones, 2007). It appears that the post-tax, post-benefit income gap narrowed a little from 2001 to 2005, but only to the size it was in 1987 (DWP, 2006a). The main factors narrowing the gap are improved benefits for families with children, reducing the number of children in poverty, improved state pensions and lower unemployment (DWP, 2006b).

It has been argued that the same 25 year period has shown the 'feminisation of poverty'. The census of 2001 shows a large rise in the population over 70, which is predominantly female and often poor, and a large rise in female-headed single parent families as compared with 1991. However, in terms of life and death issues the health gap between rich and poor is mainly accounted for by differences between richer and poorer males: female life expectancy has increased much more rapidly than male life expectancy (Sacker et al., 2000), Over the same time span, the changing structure of the labour market has tended to generate jobs for females, albeit not well-paid jobs. While there are still major discrepancies of opportunities in employment between men and women, there have been advances here. At the same time the economy has lost better paid, higher skilled manual jobs once monopolised by males.

A wide range of factors has consolidated socio-economic disadvantage. These include the effects of unemployment and increasing insecurity of employment. Unemployment rates have usually been a good predictor of the mental and physical health of a neighbourhood (Kammerling and O'Conner, 1993; Weich and Lewis, 1998; Mathers and Schofield, 1998). Unemployment is at an historically low level, but it impacts disproportionately on manual workers, on new would-be entrants to the labour market (Lakey, 2000), older workers and ethnic minorities, and has created a new poor of once well-paid, but now unemployed or prematurely retired people (Kapansalo et al., 2005). The collapse of a number of major pension schemes cannot have improved the situation of the latter, and it seems likely that in future a general down-grading of occupational pension benefits will increase the already considerable gap between better-off and poor pensioners.

There is some evidence to suggest that working conditions have been deteriorating as a result of attempts to cut costs and raise productivity, and an increasing proportion of work is provided through small and medium-sized, rather than large employers, and through self-employment. Job insecurity and casualisation have increased markedly. Job insecurity seems to affect physical and mental health adversely (Thomas et al., 2005), more so when there are rumours of redundancy (Ferrie et al., 2001; Vahtera et al., 2004; Weich and Lewis, 1998; Head et al., 2006; Kivimaki et al., 2007). The lower the occupational category the more people are likely to experience physical strain, serious injury and high levels of chemical or noise pollution (Hasan, 1989). Research has consistently shown that those who experience the most workplace stress and illness related to this are low-placed employees with little discretion over the way they work (Rahkonen et al., 2006). The latter has been associated with vulnerability to coronary illness, which in turn is correlated with mental illness conditions (Karasek and Theorell, 1990).

Another increasing inequality derives from the rising prices for public transport and the movement of shopping facilities to out-of-town sites, both of which marginalise those who cannot afford to own cars. Low levels of car ownership correlates closely with many indicators of ill health.

Housing has always been shown to be a crucial determinant of health (Marsh et al., 1999, Shelter, 2000). Since 1980 the main emphasis in housing policy has been to encourage owner occupation and restrict public expenditure. Housing is one of the two major areas of government expenditure that has been reduced in real terms since 1979. (The other area has been defence.) Rising house prices have placed many people in a situation where they cannot afford to buy, and there is a gross shortage of decent and affordable housing to rent. Homelessness in the shape of 'rooflessness' has in fact reduced since 1999 but 'homelessness' in the form of people living in overcrowded or unfit housing may have increased (Communities and Local Government, 2007). Evaluations of urban regeneration programmes suggest that they have done much for the profits of property developers, and not much for the health of the poorer sections of the population (Thomson et al., 2006). The prioritisation of owner occupation and the sale of the municipal housing stock has tended to concentrate the poorest and most vulnerable people in neighbourhoods of intense deprivation with high rates of vandalism, crime, drug use and racial tension. These are precisely the kinds of areas which generate the greatest number of cases for admission to mental hospitals (Goldberg and Thornicroft, 1998).

Conclusion

In much of the literature, and even more so in service planning and delivery, 'physical health' is divided from 'mental health'. Then each category is chopped up finely into discrete diagnoses. This has the effect of teasing out details from the pattern as a whole and viewing them in isolation. Thus studies that investigate only the social correlates of coronary heart disease fail to note the way in which the same circumstances also predict high levels of mental distress. Studies that focus on the epidemiology of mental illness alone may miss the fact that populations vulnerable to 'depression' or 'anxiety states' are also vulnerable to 'physical' diseases and handicaps. The term 'population' is used advisedly here because the distribution of dis-ease is a population phenomenon. It may be that someone is 'mentally ill' without impairment of physical health, but if she or he comes from a vulnerable population, there will probably be a spouse, parent, child or neighbour whose 'physical health' is impaired for the same complex of reasons.

Fragmenting dis-ease into discrete diagnoses is questionable even where treatment is the aim. It colludes with a tendency to treat diseases rather than people and their circumstances. In terms of health promotion or the prevention of illness, it is not just questionable, but downright misleading to think of communities as divided first into individuals who are sick or well and then to think in terms of the division of the sick into those who are mentally and those who are physically sick, and then to sort these each into a diagnostic category. The main effect here is to distract attention away from the social processes that distribute the wherewithal that people need in order to lead healthy lives.

References

Adams, J., Holland, L. and White, M. (2006) 'Changes in socioeconomic inequalities in census measures of health in England and Wales 1991–2001', *Journal of Epidemiology and Community Health*, vol. 60, pp. 218–20.

Barbigian, H. (1985) 'Schizophrenia epidemiology', in Kaplan, H. and Saddock, B. (eds) *Comprehensive Textbook of Psychiatry IV*, Baltimore, Williams & Wilkins.

Barker, J., Osmond, C., Rodin, I., Fall, C. and Winter, P. (1995) 'Low weight gain in infancy and suicide in later life', *British Medical Journal*, vol. 331, pp. 1203–4.

Blaxter, M. (1990) *Health and Lifestyles*, London, Tavistock/Routledge.

Boydell, J., van Os, J., McKenzie, K., Allardyce, A., Goel, R., McCreadie, R. and Murray, R. (2001) 'Incidence of schizophrenia in ethnic minorities in London: Ecological study into interactions with environment', *British Medical Journal*, vol. 323, p. 1336.

Broome, A. (ed) (1989) *Health Psychology: Processes and Applications*, London, Chapman & Hall.

Brown, G., Harris, T., Hepworth, C. and Robinson, R. (1994) 'Clinical and psycho-social origins of chronic depression 2: a patient inquiry', *British Journal of Psychiatry*, vol. 165, pp. 457–65.

Brugha, T., Wing, J. and Smith, B. (1988) 'Physical health of the long term mentally ill in the community', *British Journal of Psychiatry*, vol. 155, pp. 777–81.

Chivite-Mathews, W., Richardson, A., O'Shea, J., Becker, J., Owen, N. and Roo, S. (2005) *Drug Misuse Declared: Findings from the British Crime Survey*, Home Office Statistical Bulletins 04/05, London, Home Office.

Coffey, C., Veit, F., Wolfe, R., Cini, E. and Patton, C. (2003) 'Mortality and young offenders: Retrospective cohort study', *British Medical Journal*, vol. 326, p. 1064.

Communities and Local Government (2007) *Tackling Homelessness*, London, Department of Communities and Local Government. www.communities.gov.uk/index.asp?id=1502899 [accessed 01/03/07].

Department of Health (1999) *Saving Lives: Our Healthier Nation*, London, The Stationery Office.

Department of Health (2004a) *Fact Sheet on Inequality*, www.dh.gov.uk [accessed 02/04/07].

Department of Health (2004b) *Mental Health of Children and Young People in Great Britain*, London, Department of Health.

Department of Health (2006a) *Tackling Health Inequalities: 2003–05 Data Update for the National 2010 PSA Target*, London, Department of Health.

Department of Health (2006b) *Tackling Health Inequalities: Status Report on the Programme for Action*, London, Department of Health.

Department of Work and Pensions (2006a) *Households Below Average Income (HRAI) 1994/95, 2004/05*, London, Department of Work and Pensions.

Department of Work and Pensions (2006b) *New Figures Show Good Progress on Poverty* – Hutton, Press Release 9 March www.dwp.gov.uk/mediacentre/pressreleases2006/mar/cphs 015-090306.asp [accessed 26/05/07].

Doran, T., Drever, G. and Whitehead, M. (2004) 'Is there a north-south divide in social class inequalities in health in Great Britain? Cross sectional study using data from the 2001 census', *British Medical Journal*, vol. 328, pp. 10435.

Doran, T., Drever, G. and Whitehead, M. (2004) 'Is there a north–south divide in social class inequalities in health in Great Britain? Cross sectional study uskng data from the 2001 census', *British Medical Journal*, vol. 328, pp. 1043–5.

Eaton, G., Marleo, M., Lodwick, A., Bollis, M. and McVeigh, J. (2006) *Annual Report to European Monitoring Centre for Drugs and Drug Addiction 2005*, Liverpool, Department of Health/North West Public Health Observatory.

Evans, O., Singleton, N., Meltzer, H., Stewart, R, and Prince, M. (2003) *Mental Health of Older People*, ONS for Department of Health, Scottish Executive and Welsh Assembly Government.

Farr, W. (1860) 'On the construction of life tables: illustrated by a new life table of the healthy districts of England', *Journal of the Institute of Actuaries IX*.

Ferrie, J., Martikainon, P., Shipley, M., Marmot, M., Stansfield, S. and Davey Smith, G. (2001) 'Employment status and health after privatisation in white collar civil servants: A prospective cohort study', *British Medical Journal*, vol. 322, p. 627.

Freeman, H. and O'Hanlon, J. (1995) 'Acute and sub-acute effects of anti-depressants on performance', *Journal of Drug Development and Clinical Practice*, vol. 7, pp. 7–20.

Fryers, T., Jenkins, R. and Meltzer, D. (2003) *Social Inequalities and the Distribution of Common Mental Disorders*, Maudsley, Monographs 44, Hove, Psychology Press/Taylor and Francis.

Fryers, T., Meltzer, D., Jenkins, R. and Brugha, T. (2005) 'The distribution of the common mental disorders', *Clinical Practice and Epidemiology in Mental Health*, vol. 1, p. 14.

Gabe, J. (1996) 'The history of tranquilliser use' in Heller, T., Reynolds, J., Gomm, R., Muston, R. and Pattison, S. (eds) *Mental Health Matters: A Reader*, Basingstoke, Macmillan, pp. 186–95.

Giggs, D. and Cooper, J. (1987) 'Ecological structure and the distribution of schizophrenia and affective psychoses in Nottingham', *British Journal of Psychiatry*, vol. 151, pp. 627–63.

Goldberg, D. and Goodyer, D. (2005) *The Origins and Course of Common Mental Disorders*, London, Taylor and Francis.

Goldberg, D. and Thornicroft, G. (1998) *Mental Health in Our Future Cities*, Maudsley Monographs No 41, Hove, Psychology Press/Taylor and Francis.

Goodkin, K. and Visser, A. (1999) (eds) *Psychoneuroimmunology: Stress, Mental Disorders and Health*, Washington, American Psychiatric Press.

Graham, H. (ed) (2000) *Equal to the Task: Understanding Health Inequalities*, Buckingham, Open University Press.

Green, H., McGinnity, A., Meltzer, H., Ford, T. and Goodman, R. (2005) *Mental Health of Children and Young People in Great Britain* 2004, Basingstoke, Palgrave Macmillan.

Gunnell, D., Peters, T., Kammerling, R. and Brooks, J. (1995) 'The relation between parasuicide, suicide and psychiatric admission and socio-economic deprivation', *British Medical Journal*, vol. 311, pp. 226–30.

Hasan, J. (1989) 'Way-of-life, stress and differences in morbidity between occupational classes', in Fox, J. (ed.) *Health Inequalities in European Countries*, European Science Foundation, Aldershot, Gower, pp. 372–85.

Hawton, K. and James, A. (2005) 'Suicide and deliberate self-harm in young people', *British Medical Journal*, vol. 330, pp. 891–4.

Head, J., Kivimaki, M., Martikainen, P., Vahtera, J., Ferrie, J. and Marmot, M. (2006) 'Influence of change in psychosocial work characteristics on sickness absence: The Whitehall II Study', *Journal of Epidemiology and Community Health*, vol. 60, pp. 55–61.

Hippisley-Cox, J., Fielding, K. and Pringle, M. (1998) 'Depression as a risk factor for ischaemic heart disease in men: population based case-control study', *British Medical Journal*, vol. 316, pp. 1714–9.

Holland, C. and Rabbitt, P. (1991) ' The course and causes of cognitive change with advancing age', *Reviews in Clinical Gerontology*, vol. 1, pp. 79–94.

Jochelson, K. and Majgoski B. (2006) *Clearing the Air: Debating Smoke Free Policies in Psychiatric Units*, London, King's Fund.

Jones, F. (2007) 'The effect of taxes and benefits on household income 2004–05', Office for National Statistics. http://212.58.231.22/articles/economic_trends/ET_May_Francis_Jones.pdf [accessed 18.03.09]

Jones, K. and Moon, G. (1987) *Health, Disease and Society*, London, Routledge & Kegan Paul.

Kammerling, R. and O'Conner, S. (1993) 'Unemployment rates as a predictor of psychiatric admissions', *British Medical Journal*, vol. 307, pp. 1536–9.

Kapansalo, M., Kauhanen, J., Lakka, T., Manninen, P., Kaplan, G. and Holstein, B. (2005) 'Depression and early retirement: Prospective population-based study in middle aged men, *Journal of Epidemiology and Community Health*, vol. 59, pp. 70–4.

Karasek, J. and Theorell, T. (1990) *Healthy Work: Stress, Productivity and the Reconstruction of Working Life*, New York, Basic Books.

Karlsen, S. and Nazroo, J. (2004) 'Fear of racism and health', *Journal of Epidemiology and Community Health*, vol. 58, pp. 1017–8.

Kivimaki, M., Honkonen, T., Wahlbeck, K., Elovainio, M., Pentti, J., Klaukka, T., Virtanene, M. and Vahtera, J. (2007) 'Organisational down-sizing and increased use of psychotropic drugs among employees who remain in employment', *Journal of Epidemiology and Community Health*, vol. 61, pp. 154–8.

Lakey, J. (2000) *Youth Unemployment: Labour Market Programmes and Health: A Review of the Literature*, London, PSI.

Lewis, G. and Booth, M. (1992) 'Regional difference in mental health in Great Britain', *Journal of Epidemiology and Community Health*, vol. 46, pp. 608–11.

Lewis, G. and Sloggett, A. (1998) 'Suicide, deprivation and unemployment: record linkage study', *British Medical Journal*, vol. 317, pp. 1283–86.

Lynch, J., Davey Smith., G, Kaplan, G. and House, J. (2000) 'Income inequality and mortality: importance to health of individual income, psychosocial environment, or material conditions', *British Medical Journal*, vol. 320, pp. 1200–4.

Marmot, M. and Wilkinson, R. (2000) *Sources of Inequality: Social Determinants of Health*, Oxford, Oxford University Press.

Marsh, A., Gordon, D., Pantaziz, C. and Heslop, P. (1999) *Home Sweet Home? The Impact of Poor Housing on Health*, Oxford, Polity Press.

Mathers, C. and Schofield, J. (1998) 'The health consequences of unemployment: The evidence', *Medical Journal of Australia*, vol. 168, pp. 178–82.

McLaren, G. and Bain, M. (1998) *Deprivation and Health in Scotland: Insights from NHS Data*, Edinburgh, ISD Scotland.

Meltzer, H., Gill, B., Petticrew, M. and Hinds, K. (1995a) *The Prevalence of Psychiatric Morbidity among Adults Living in Private Households: OPCS Surveys of Psychiatric Morbidity in Great Britain: Report No. 1*, London, HMSO.

Meltzer, H., Gill, B., Petticrew, M. and Hinds, K. (1995b) *Physical Complaints, Service Use and the Treatment of Adults with Psychiatric Disorders: OPCS Surveys of Psychiatric Morbidity in Great Britain: Report No 2*, London, HMSO.

Middleton, N., Sterne, J. and Gunnell, D. (2006) 'The geography of despair among 1544 year-old men in England and Wales: Putting suicide on the map', *Journal of Epidemiology and Community Health*, vol. 60, pp. 1040–7.

Mulvany, F., O'Callaghan, E., Takei, N. Byrne, M., Fearon, P. and Larkin, C. (2001) 'Effect of social class at birth on risk and presentation of schizophrenia: case-control study', *British Medical Journal*, vol. 323, pp. 1398–401.

Nanchahal, K., Wellings, K., Barrett, G., Copas, A., Mercer, C., Macmanus, S., MacDowall, W., Fenton, K., Ehrnes, B. and Johnson, A. (2005) 'Changes in the circumstances of young mothers in Britain: 1990–2000, *Journal of Epidemiology and Community Health*, vol. 59, pp. 828–33.

Nazroo, J.Y. (1997a) *Ethnicity and Mental Health: Findings from a National Community Survey*, London, Policy Studies Institute.

Nazroo, J.Y. (1997b) *The Health of Britain's Ethnic Minorities: Findings from a National Survey*, London, Policy Studies Institute.

Office for National Statistics (2007) *Corrected Suicide Rates in UK: 1991–2004* www.ons.gov.uk/statbase [accessed 02/04/07].

Ott, A., Breteler, M., van Harskamp, F., Clans, J., van der Cammen, T., Grobbe, D. and Hoffman, A. (1995) 'Prevalence of Alzheimer's Disease and vascular dementia: association with education', *British Medical Journal*, vol. 310, pp. 970–3.

Pasquini, M. and Biondi, M. (2007) 'Depression in cancer patients: a critical review', *Clinical Practice and Epidemiology in Mental Health*, vol. 3, p. 2.

Rahkonen, O., Laaksonen, M., Martikainen, P., Roos, E. and Lahelma, E. (2006) 'Job control, job demands or social class? The impact of working conditions on the relation between social class and health', *Journal of Epidemiology and Community Health*, vol. 60, pp. 50–54.

Rosengren, A., Orth-Gomer, K., Wedel, H. and Wilhelmsen, L. (1993) 'Stressful life events , social support and mortality in men born in 1933', *British Medical Journal*, vol. 307, pp. 1102–5.

Rutter, M. (1985) 'Resilience in the face of adversity: protective factors and resistance to psychiatric disorder', *British Journal of Psychiatry*, vol. 147, pp. 598–611.

Sacker, A., Firth, D., Fitzpatrick, R., Lynch, K. and Bartley, M. (2000) 'Comparing health inequality in men and women: prospective study of mortality 1986–96' *British Medical Journal*, vol. 320, pp. 130–37.

Scottish Office (1992) *Scotland's Health: A Challenge to Us All – A Policy Statement*, Edinburgh, HMSO.

Shelter (2000) *Health and Housing: Homelessness and Bad Housing – Impact on Physical Health*, London, Shelter.

Spencer, N. (2005) 'Does material disadvantage explain the increased risk of adverse health, educational and behavioural outcomes among children of lone parents in Britain? A cross sectional study', *Journal of Epidemiology and Community Health*, vol. 59, pp. 152–7.

Thomas, C., Benzeval, M. and Stansfeld, S. (2005) 'Employment transition and mental health: an analysis from the British household panel survey', *Journal of Epidemiology and Community Health*, vol. 59, pp. 243–9.

Thomson, H., Atkinson, R., Petticrew, M. and Kearns, A. (2006) 'Do urban regeneration programmes improve public health and reduce health inequalities? A sythesis of the evidence from UK policy and practice (1980–2004)', *Journal of Epidemiology and Community Health*, vol. 60, pp. 218–20.

Tims, P. and Balazs, J. (1997) 'Mental illness and homelessness', *British Medical Journal*, vol. 315, pp. 536–9.

Townsend, P., Simpson, P. and Tibbs, N. (1985) 'Inequalities in health in the city of Bristol: A preliminary review of the statistical evidence,' *International Journal of Health Services*, vol. 15, pp. 637–43.

Townsend, P., Phillimore, P. and Beattie, A. (1988) *Health and Deprivation: Inequality and the North'*, Beckenham, Croom-Helm.

Turner, T. (1997) 'ABC of mental illness: schizophrenia', *British Medical Journal*, vol. 315, pp. 108–11.

Vågerö, D. (2000) 'Health inequalities in women and men', *British Medical Journal*, vol. 320, pp. 1286–7.

Vahtera, J., Kivimäki, M., Pentti, J., Linna, A.,Virtanen, M., Virtanen, P. and Ferrie, J. (2004) 'Organisational downsizing, sickness absence, and mortality: 10-town prospective cohort study', *British Medical Journal*, vol. 328, pp. 555–6.

Wadsworth, M. (1991) *The Imprint of Time: Childhood History and Adult Life*, Oxford, Clarendon.

Weich, S. and Lewis, G. (1998) 'Poverty, unemployment and common mental disorders: population based cohort study', *British Medical Journal*, vol. 317, pp. 115–9.

West, R. (1995) 'Psychosocial health' in *Health and Lifestyles Project, A Survey of the UK Population: Part 1*, London, Health Education Authority, pp. 57–86.

Wilkinson, R. (1996) *Unhealthy Societies: The Afflictions of Inequality*, London, Routledge.

Wood, J., Hennell, T., Jones, A., Hooper, J., Tocque, K. and Bellis, M. (2006) *Where Wealth Meets Health: Illustrating Inequality in the North West*, Liverpool, North West Public Health Observatory.

16

The relevance of moral treatment to contemporary mental health care

Annie Borthwick, Chris Holman, David Kennard, Mark McFetridge, Karen Messruther and Jenny Wilkes

Introduction

Moral treatment was the name given by William Tuke to one of the first, and best known, attempts to create a setting specifically to provide a humane, homely environment for people 'afflicted' by the 'loss of reason' (Tuke, 1813). It embodied 'the injunction to treat the mentally ill as though they were mentally well' (Appelbaum and Munich, 1986). This simple yet radical idea developed by Tuke 200 years ago at The Retreat in York became the focus for a revolution in the care of 'insane persons' in the first half of the 19th century, but its success faded as the century progressed. The new asylums that were inspired by its philosophy grew massively in size to become the soulless human warehouses that we now associate with asylum care, and a more biological – and pessimistic – view of psychiatry began to gain acceptance.

During the 20th century interest in providing specially designed social environments to aid recovery from mental disorder has fluctuated. Following World War II some of the large run down mental hospitals were revitalised by the therapeutic community approach which was, as David Clark pointed out, in some degree a revival of the principles of moral treatment (Clark, 1965). However, from the 1970s onwards the emphasis moved increasingly towards care in the community.

Edited from A. Borthwick et al., *Journal of Mental Health* (2001), vol. 10, no. 4, pp. 427–39.

Historical background

The Retreat's founder William Tuke set about establishing an environment where people in mental distress could begin to take responsibility for their own emotions and conduct, in order that they might come into clearer focus with their own personal truth and their responsibility towards others.

The essential elements of this environment were to be comfort, nurture, beauty, purpose, and personal and social responsibility. The Retreat had no new medical theories to propound, it was flying no ideological flags, and it had no self-conscious name for what it was doing. It began as a lay experiment in caring for distressed people, a small 'therapeutic community' based on an extended family model, in which attendants and distressed residents lived, worked and dined together (Porter, 1997).

The term 'moral treatment' to describe this way of working was first adopted by William Tuke's grandson Samuel in his book *Description of The Retreat*, published in 1813, 17 years after its opening.

A number of 20th century commentators such as Scull (1981) have attributed the rise of moral treatment to broader social factors, such as the rise of manufacturing industries, which gave human beings more control over their external circumstances, and led to the belief that self control of internal processes was both possible and desirable. Foucault (1965, 1988) stressed the view that moral treatment was merely an internalised form of repression of deviant individuals, based on a regime that instilled fear and anxiety as its main agents of control. While these views need consideration, it can be argued that neither Foucault nor Scull were familiar with the philosophy and ethics of Quakerism (Stewart, 1992), and that they failed to take into account the fact that Quakers, since their founding, had been outside the mainstream of British society and held neither bourgeois ideals nor the conceptions of madness common during the 17th and 18th centuries. Indeed Quakers had always been characterised by their alienation from the political and social systems in which they lived, and by their recognition of the common humanity of all people regardless of gender, class, status, religion or indeed their mental state.

Identifying the basic principles of moral treatment

In 1996 The Retreat held a conference to mark the bicentenary of its opening on the theme 'Social Values and Mental Health'. The conference, attended by about 100 people including mental health service users, social workers, psychiatrists and academics, posed the question 'Could there be another revolution in mental health care to match the one pioneered by moral treatment?' Out of this consultation exercise emerged a number of core themes or principles. Also drawing on the work of Kathleen Jones (1996) and Mary Glover

(1984), we were able to identify seven basic principles of moral treatment. These are presented in Box 16.1.

Box 16.1   Basic principles of moral treatment

1   *A concern for the human rights of people with severe and disabling mental health problems*
There is a deep seated belief that all men and women are created equal and are equally deserving of care. Each individual is unique and of value. The concern for human rights is closely linked with the ideology of empowerment, closing the social gap between able and disabled people.

2   *Personal respect for people with severe mental health problems*
More than a theoretical recognition of rights, this implies tolerance of odd behaviour, recognition of the need for privacy and dignity, respect for the meaningfulness to the individual of their subjective experiences and respect for individual and cultural differences.

3   *An emphasis on the healing power of everyday relationships*
Kindness, acceptance, encouragement, affection, friendship, the opportunity to give as well as receive and an expectation of responsible behaviour, are all seen as powerful forces in helping an individual to recover his or her mental health. They may be more important in their effects than specific treatment technologies.

4   *The importance of useful occupation*
Useful occupation is seen as important in a number of ways. The structure of the activity can be a calming influence, occupation can be a basis for relating to others and being part of a group, and the sense of achievement and purpose is a source of self-respect.

5   *Emphasis on the social and physical environment*
The Retreat endeavoured to create a family-like living environment as a 'quiet haven in which the shattered bark might find the means of reparation or of safety'. Moral treatment stresses the physical as well as social environment: the setting and the views should be pleasing. Staff are employed for their personal qualities of tolerance, intelligence and integrity. The numbers should be small enough to create a family-like atmosphere, with a culture of solidarity and mutual support built on shared values.

---

6 *A common sense approach rather than reliance on technology or ideology*
There is a mistrust of professions, with their tendency to seek power through claims of specialist knowledge and techniques for eliminating pathology. At the same time a common sense approach can accept the need for supervision to prevent harm or exploitation, recognises that mentally ill people have responsibilities as well as rights, and balances the ideology of empowerment with the recognition that there are limits to the tolerance of antisocial behaviour.

7 *A spiritual perspective*
For Quakers this is expressed in the belief that there is 'that of God' in everyone, an inner light in every individual, however disturbed or withdrawn, which underpins the equality of all human relationship. A spiritual perspective also expresses the sense of there being a deeper or transcendent meaning to our lives that stands outside our everyday concerns.

Applying the principles of moral treatment to contemporary mental health care

If these principles were able to revolutionise the treatment of 200 years ago, to what extent can they still be used as markers of good practice in contemporary mental health care? We have chosen five areas to look at to try to answer this question.

Creation of environments for 'difficult to place' people

Research and anecdotal evidence point to a core group of people with long-term mental illness whose needs are not appropriately provided for in community care settings – the so-called 'difficult to place'. Repper and Perkins (1995) identified these people as 'more likely to be homeless, have a history of contact with forensic services, to manifest a higher level of irresponsible and turbulent behaviours at assessment, to have experienced longer periods of hospitalisation and spent time in a special hospital'.

A concern for human rights. At the launch event of the Health Advisory Service 'Rehab' Good-Practice Network, Perkins (2000) discussed the challenges to rehabilitation services of a 'new generation of people who are seriously socially disabled by their mental health difficulties'. She argued that despite changes in the client group the essential principles still apply: 'helping people disabled by mental health problems to make the most of their lives'.

Personal respect. Shepherd (1995) has described a new kind of institutional solution for difficult to place patients, the 'ward-in-a-house' – small, homely and personal, where 'each resident is regarded as unique and as having unique needs and abilities' and importance is attached to the quality of staff-resident interaction.

The healing power of everyday relationships. In the 'ward-in-a-house' (Shepherd, 1995) responsibility for running the house is shared by the residents and staff. This task-oriented approach 'helps to equalise the relationship between staff and residents and facilitate a sense of working together. It serves to highlight what staff and residents have in common rather than what divides them and in this way helps to reduce staff-patient distance'.

The importance of useful occupation. Durham (1997) in reviewing literature on work-related activity for people with long-term schizophrenia highlights the need for better-developed vocational and social activities.

The social and physical environment. Reflecting on the similarity between the 'ward-in-a-house' and the first institutions for the mentally ill, Shepherd (1995) points to how The Retreat 'prided itself on its small, homely atmosphere and the quality of its accommodation and surroundings'.

A common sense approach. The 'de-emphasis of pathology' in the ward-in-a-house is not blinkered by ideology. Residents are maintained on anti-psychotic medication, and the staff 'don't avoid talking to people about their worries or fears or attempting to treat their symptoms where this is possible' (Shepherd, 1995).

Care in the community

Personal respect, the importance of useful occupation and a common sense approach. The following example illustrates several of the principles of moral treatment in an ordinary community mental health service. A community psychiatric nurse and a psychologist from the same community team facilitated a 20-session closed group for women who had been referred by their General Practitioners for individual therapy following their disclosure of childhood trauma. The group took place on hospital premises on a once weekly basis. Towards the end of the group the suggestion of continuing as a self-support group was raised (by the facilitators), with an offer to assist with choice of venue, reading material and occasional invited attendance to speak on a specific topic.

The healing power of everyday relationships. From within the same service a community psychiatric nurse responsible for the depot clinic (anti-psychotic medication) attempted to organise it so that it also offered some support and social interaction with others. For the majority of those individuals motivated to do so, she would ask that they come to the clinic at the community base, and would spend some time with each individual whilst the others waited together.

The social and physical environment. The importance of the environment for people moving from institutions into the community has been recognised in a major UK study of community care, the TAPS project (Leff, 1997). A member of the TAPS Research Unit writes that 'the gaining of autonomy by mentally ill people within a homely living environment is a value regarded as a cornerstone in the ethos of deinstitutionalism' (Trieman, 1997).

Public attitudes towards mental illness

Since the advent of the community care policy, the promotion of positive attitudes towards mental illness or distress has been a challenge to both service users and providers. Much of the public's understanding comes from the media – television soaps, films, newspapers – and inevitably this does not always carry the messages that those involved with mental health services would wish to portray. Lineham (1996) describes how cases in the media have concentrated on the dangerousness of mental illness and explores how this affects public views on mental illness and special hospitals in particular.

Personal respect. Media representation of mental illness is more often than not negative, focusing on sensational headlines or themes (usually violence) that perpetuate many of the prejudices that are associated with mental health issues. The Brainwaves Media Forum was set up by service users who were concerned about the way in which mental health was dealt with by both mental health organisations and the media. Their aim is to work positively to promote and inform public awareness of mental illness.

The healing power of everyday relationships. Carlile (1996) describes in the *Nursing Times* how his inability to form significant relationships had led to frequent admissions to hospital. His role with a user-involvement project enabled him to develop new relationships, networks and friendships that helped to maintain his mental health. 'It is now 5 years since my last admission, even though I have coped with several crises. Some significant people have supported me and taught me effective ways of responding to difficult situations'.

The importance of useful occupation. Individuals with mental illness appear to have difficulty in accessing and maintaining useful occupation or employment. Welch (2000) has identified individuals with mental health problems as the most socially excluded group in relation to employment. However, recent cases heard through the Disability Discrimination Act 1995 have raised the issues of occupation and employment high onto the agenda of employers.

Training of mental health professionals

A concern for human rights. Alan Leader is one example of a veteran user of mental health services who holds conferences and seminars for professionals in which he promotes the use of user-designed care plans and support networks. His resource pack 'Direct Power' (Leader, 1995) is an example of how simple, everyday language can help people to make decisions and express their wishes and needs when in crisis.

Personal respect. With regard to the training of mental health professionals this means more than just civility or politeness towards people in distress. It means encouraging dialogue with those who may promote different paradigms as a framework for understanding unusual types of human experience. Ron Coleman, a service user and founder member of Hearing Voices Network, has been influential in shaping attitudes to the experience of voice hearing, a phenomenon until recently almost universally regarded as pathological (Coleman and Smith, 1998).

The healing power of everyday relationships. On a smaller scale, and working from The Retreat, Annie and Brian Borthwick use their personal experience of schizophrenia within their family as the basis of their training of nurses, psychotherapists, and others. As with Leader and Coleman, their work challenges accepted professional paradigms and explores the meaning of subjective experience of psychosis.

A spiritual perspective. Brandon (1998) has an interest in non-religious forms of spirituality and believes that true spirituality is expressed in human beings letting go to each other, letting situations be, accepting what is, and letting friendship develop spontaneously. Religious and spiritual beliefs and their influence on mental health are also explored in a summary of user-led research from the Mental Health Foundation (Faulkner, 1997). Faulkner found just over 50 per cent of 400 service users questioned about their coping strategies stated that religious and spiritual beliefs were important to them.

Mental health legislation

Inevitably mental health law is in a tense relationship with the practice of psychiatry, being of a discourse quite alien to the medical, 'scientistic' philosophy which underlies psychiatry. However, we should see it as an ally in the project of establishing a framework within which to sustain the human rights and personal value of people suffering from mental illness.

A concern for human rights. The proposals to amend the Mental Health Act (1983) include the idea that the process of assessment for compulsory detention should specifically focus on assessment of capacity, assessment of risk, assessment of mental disorder and the care and treatment plan. The decision about detention would be made not by the Responsible Medical Officer on the basis of his or her own views about the nature of the mental disorder and the usefulness of treatment, but by an independent Specialist Tribunal. There is no doubt some way to go before the proposals take a final form, but it does seem closer to the principles of moral treatment that such decisions should be taken out of a purely medical frame.

Personal respect. Mental health professionals can readily assume a position of unwarranted authority. To treat people as equal partners in the planning of their treatment, professionals need to be prepared to discuss openly with those who will be affected by their decisions the whole process of their thinking and planning in relation to their care.

A spiritual perspective. Invoking the powers of the Mental Health Act does not appear to offer much opportunity to address the spiritual aspects of a person's needs. It is an experience in which the professional and patient can be most widely and distressingly estranged. The professionals may protect themselves by recourse to omnipotent rationalisation based on the idea that assessment of someone's mental state is an objective process. It is sustaining to the professional and patient alike to recall that we are all part of the same shared process of life, and that the experience of the person who is mentally disturbed speaks to the way we all, individually or as a social collective, live our lives. The respectful and thoughtful use of the powers of the law must reflect this.

Discussion

Moral treatment evolved out of the spiritual values, mutual solidarity and personal experience of Quakers as a pragmatic approach to mental distress which contained or implied a number of principles. Through a consultation exercise with interested professionals and users, including some Quakers, we have identified seven principles.

In attempting to answer the question, 'to what extent can these principles of moral treatment still be used as markers of good practice?' we have looked at five different aspects of contemporary mental health care. What seems to stand out is that the principle of personal respect for people with severe mental health problems — the expectation that service users should have their experiences and views taken seriously — is high on the agenda in all areas.

An emphasis on the healing power of everyday relationships that are mutually respectful, accepting and empowering also appeared to be widely supported as a principle.

Not surprisingly the aspect of mental health care that seems to embody most of the principles of moral treatment is the creation of settings for difficult to place people. As Shepherd (1995) points out these settings can be seen as direct descendants of moral treatment, where useful occupation, a homely environment and the quality of personal relationships play a central role. Another aspect that emerges as strongly influenced by the principles of moral treatment is the training of mental health professionals. This may be the authors' collective rose-tinted spectacles, but it may also be the case that trainers in mental health professions (some at least) are beginning to turn away from the emphasis of the last two decades on techniques of intervention, and are rediscovering, with the added impetus of an increasingly confident and articulate user movement, the importance of the principles we have outlined in this paper.

References

Appelbaum, A.H. and Munich, R.L. (1986) 'Reinventing moral treatment: the effects upon patients and staff members of a program of psychosocial rehabilitation'. *The Psyciatric Hospital*, **17**, 11–19.

Brandon, D. (1998) 'Zen healing'. *Journal of Interprofessional Care*, **12**, 407–10.

Carlile, G. (1996) 'Telling it like it is'. *Nursing Times*, **92**, 50–2.

Clark, D.H. (1965) 'The therapeutic community – concept, practice and future'. *British Journal of Psychiatry*, **111**, 947–54.

Coleman, R. and Smith, M. (1998) *Working with Voices*. Gloucester: Action Consultancy Training.

Durham, T. (1997) 'Work-related activity for people with long-term schizophrenia: A review of the literature'. *British Journal of Occupational Therapy*, **60**, 248–52.

Faulkner, A. (1997) *Knowing our own minds*. London: Mental Health Foundation.

Foucault, M. (1965, 1988) *Madness and Civilization: a History of Insanity in the Age of Reason*, New York: Random House.

Glover, M. (1984) *The Retreat, York. An Early Quaker Experiment in the Treatment of Mental Illness*. York: William Sessions.

Jones, K. (1996) Foreword to *Description of The Retreat* by Tuke, S. (1813) reprinted London: Process Press.

Leader, A. (1995) *Direct Power*. Brighton: Pavilion Books.

Leff, J. (ed.) (1997) *Care in the Community: Illusion or Reality*. Chichester: Wiley.

Lineham, T. (1996) 'Media madness'. *Nursing Times*, **92**, 30–1.

Perkins, R. (2000) 'Challenges Facing Rehabilitation Today'. *Network Newsletter* 1, 3–4 Health Advisory Service Rehab Good-Practice Network.

Porter, R. (1997) *The Greatest Benefit to Mankind*, London: HarperCollins.

Repper, J. and Perkins, R. (1995) 'The deserving and the undeserving: selectivity and progress in a community care service'. *Journal of Mental Health*, **4**, 483–98.

Scull, A. (1981) *Madhouses, Mad-Doctors, Madmen*. Philadelphia: University of Pennsylvania Press.

Shepherd, G. (1995) 'The "Ward-in-a-House": Residential care for the severely disabled'. *Community Mental Health Journal*, **31**, 53–69

Stewart, A.S. (1992) *The York Retreat in the Light of the Quaker Way*. York: Sessions.

Trieman, J. (1997) 'Residential care for the mentally ill in the community'. In: J. Leff (ed.), *Care in the Community: Illusion or Reality*. Chichester: Wiley.

Tuke, S. (1813) *Descriplion of The Retreat, An Institution near York for Insane Persons of the Society of Friends*. Reprinted by Process Press 1996.

Welch, J. (2000) 'Mental block'. *People Management*, 20 January.

17

Challenging discrimination: promoting rights and citizenship

Julie Repper and Rachel Perkins

If mental health services are to assist the recovery of the people who use them, then the way in which these services operate is important. Such services, however, and the people who work in them, cannot be separated from the broader social context in which they exist.

The prejudice and discrimination associated with mental health problems have a profoundly negative impact on people with mental health problems, in both direct and indirect ways. First, the social exclusion which results means that people with mental health problems are denied the rights and opportunities that are available to non-disabled citizens. It is very hard to rebuild your life if, everywhere you turn, you face barriers that make it difficult for you to do the things you want to do. Second, prejudice and discrimination limit the scope for changing mental health services. Mental health workers cannot help but be influenced by the prevailing views of the society in which we live, and the prejudice and discrimination of the electorate heavily influence governmental mental health policy. The *Mental Health National Service Framework* (Department of Health, 1999) and the *NHS Plan* (Department of Health, 2000a) tell us that we must organise services around the needs and wishes of those who use them. At the same time, however, we are required to protect those people whom, it is often assumed, cannot make decisions for themselves, and to protect society from the dangers it is assumed they present (see Perkins, 2001c).

Edited from J. Repper and R. Perkins, *Social Inclusion and Recovery: A Model for Mental Health Practice* (2003), Baillière-Tindall, pp. 183–202.

There is, however, increased recognition, among both people who experience mental health problems and mental health workers, of the need to address the negative stereotypes that underpin discrimination and exclusion. As user/survivor consultant and activist Peter Campbell (2000) wrote:

> The great irony of service user action in the past 15 years is that while the position of service users within services has undoubtedly improved, the position of service users in society has deteriorated. As a result, it is at least arguable that the focus of user involvement needs adjustment.

The nature of stigma

Most definitions of stigma focus on some characteristic of an individual that is devalued. For example, Goffman (1963) defined stigma as 'an attribute that is deeply discrediting' while Cocker et al. (1998) described how 'stigmatised individuals possess, or are believed to possess, some attribute, or characteristic, that conveys a social identity that is devalued in a particular social context'. However, use of the term 'stigma' has attracted much criticism.

Oliver (1990) argued that the concept of stigma focuses attention on the perceptions of the individuals at the expense of an examination of the pervasive and socially constructed exclusion from social and economic life that people experience. As such, stigma is unlikely to be a useful concept on which to base efforts to combat the discrimination and exclusion faced by disabled people, because it is unable to 'throw off the shackles of the individualistic approach to disability with its focus on the discredited and the discreditable' (Oliver, 1990). Sayce (1998, 2000, 2002) and Chamberlin (2001) have extended these arguments more specifically in relation to mental health.

Sayce (1998) argues that the terms we use lead to 'different understandings of where responsibility lies for the "problem" and as a consequence to different prescriptions for action'. Contrasting the concepts of 'stigma' and 'discrimination', she argues that stigma focuses attention on people who are the recipients of rejection and exclusion rather than on those who perpetrate the unjust treatment. This leads to a focus on the impact of stigma on the individual (they are unable to get a job, study, etc.) rather than the mechanisms that result in these disadvantages. She draws parallels with work to combat racism, which has focused on the individual and institutional perpetrators of racism rather than on the individual's experience of the stigma of being black. As Chamberlin (2001) argues, 'the concept of "stigma" is itself stigmatising. It implies that there is something wrong with the person, while "discrimination" puts the onus where it belongs, on groups and individuals that are practising it'.

On the basis of arguments such as these, Sayce (1998) believes that people with mental health problems can learn much from the broader disability movement:

'Stigma' has not provided a rallying point for collective strategies to improve access or challenge prejudice. Instead the disability movement has turned to structural notions of discrimination and oppression . . . the main issue at stake is that we should root thinking and practice in an analysis of unfair treatment.

The aetiology of discrimination

In response to such criticisms of the term stigma, Link and Phelan (2001) undertook a major reconceptualisation of the term. We would agree with those who criticise use of the term 'stigma', and have chosen to use the terms 'prejudice' and 'discrimination'. These focus attention on people and institutions whose behaviour results in exclusion of people with mental health problems from social and economic life. However, following Sayce (2002), we would argue that Link and Phelan's (2001) reconceptualisation of 'stigma' offers a useful analysis of the processes involved in discrimination and exclusion. In their model, Link and Phelan (2001) describe the convergence of a number of interrelated components.

Distinguishing and labelling human differences

This process necessarily begins with the identification of differences between people: intelligence, height, weight, eye colour, mental health status, and so forth. However the labelling of difference alone does not result in exclusion and denial of rights. Some differences lack social salience and are largely ignored (for example, the colour of one's car or the length of one's forearm), many others (such as food preferences or hair colour) are relevant in relatively few situations, but some characteristics are highly salient (for example, sexuality, IQ, skin colour and mental health status).

Stereotyping: linking labelled people to undesirable characteristics

After labelling of the differences comes the linking of negative attributes to these labels. The label 'mental illness' has been associated with a number of undesirable characteristics such as dangerousness, unpredictability and incompetence.

The separating of 'them' from 'us'

Those to whom negatively loaded labels are attached are then separated from the rest of society. They are seen as a distinct class of person. There are 'them' (who have mental health problems) and 'us' (who do not). In the process of separation, the negative attributes ascribed to distinguish 'them' from 'us' are elaborated and extended and 'they' become the thing that they are labelled (Estroff, 1989). Instead of 'people with schizophrenia, anorexia, mental health problems' 'they' become 'schizophrenics', 'anorexics', and 'the mentally ill'. It is noteworthy that this process is far more marked for people with mental health difficulties than for those with other illnesses. 'Mental illness' is not seen as 'an illness like any other'. People have cancer, heart disease or influenza, but they remain one of 'us' who happens to be ill. But people are 'psychotics' or 'manic depressives' and are very definitely different from 'us'. These identities eclipse any other attributes that 'they' have. This 'them' and 'us' divide remains alive and well both within mental health services and beyond.

The importance of power

Most importantly, discrimination and exclusion are dependent on social, economic and political power (Link and Phelan, 2001):

- The power to determine those differences which are salient in a particular culture
- The power to ensure that the culture recognises the differences that have been identified
- The power to separate 'them' from 'us'
- The power to deny 'them' jobs, decent housing, an adequate income, access to education, etc.

The media have the power to promote exclusion, with headlines about 'mad axe murderers' that devalue and demonise people with mental health problems. Employers have the power to exclude people from jobs. People who are not defined as 'mentally ill' have the power to get together and organise 'nimby' campaigns.

People defined as 'mentally ill' have little power to determine the values and practices of the communities in which they live. Organisations for people with mental health problems identify differences between 'service-users/survivors' and 'mental health professionals'. They have linked those labelled as 'mental health professionals' with characteristics they consider undesirable, for example, as agents of social control who deprive people of their liberty and forcibly medicate them with toxic substances. They have separated 'us' (users/survivors) from 'them' (mental health professionals). They have excluded 'them' in so far as they can by rejecting their diagnoses and treatments and campaigning against their right to compulsorily detain and treat 'us'. But people with mental health problems lack social, economic and political power. Therefore such endeavours have had little impact on the prevailing negative stereotypes, nor have they substantially reduced discrimination. Indeed, these very activities have been used as a further rationale for exclusion. The challenge that users/survivors present to accepted psychiatric wisdom is seen as an indication of the 'lack of insight' that accompanies mental health difficulties. Dismissing what people say as a manifestation of their psychopathology is a very powerful way of minimising the impact of any challenge that an oppressed group might make to the way in which its members are defined and treated.

Attempts to decrease discrimination and exclusion cannot avoid issues of power. On the basis of the work of Link and Phelan (2001), and an extensive review of the impact of attempts to reduce discrimination and exclusion, Sayce (2002) argues that initiatives are most likely to succeed if they:

- effectively challenge the power that underpins discrimination

- aim to transform the beliefs of those who have the power to discriminate, and

- work within a comprehensive framework of ongoing anti-discrimination work.

Challenging discrimination

Drawing on the wisdom of ancient Greece, Huxley (2001) described two levels at which social inclusion can be considered: 'demos' and 'ethnos'. At the level of 'demos' social inclusion is concerned with rights and citizenship:

> A nation state can achieve the state of 'Demos' when it is inclusive in its definition and realisation of citizenship and when citizen status leads to equality of social, political and legal rights ... Congruence between Demos and any nation state will be highest where social inclusion and social cohesion are maximised, but obviously not when a large proportion of the people of the country are denied full citizenship. (Huxley 2001)

By contrast, social inclusion at the level of 'ethnos' is concerned not with rights, but with community participation and identification.

'Ethnos' refers to a cultural community rather than a national community ...
[There are] four components that make up an ethnos community: membership,
influence, integration and fulfilment of needs; and a shared emotional connection.
(Huxley 2001)

We would argue that, in helping people to rebuild their lives, mental health
workers need to address social inclusion at the levels of both ethnos and
demos. People need to participate in, and feel part of, the communities in
which they live. They also need the rights that ensure they have access to the
economic, social and cultural opportunities within those communities.
Indeed, we would argue that ethnos and demos are interrelated. People are
more likely to be able to be a part of their communities if they have a right to
those things that are valued in that community (such as decent housing and
jobs). However, they are more likely to enjoy these rights if they are seen as a
part of those communities and can participate in community opportunities
alongside non-disabled citizens.

One of the most direct ways of challenging the separation of 'us' and 'them'
is by achieving direct contact between the two categories, enabling people
with and without mental health problems to come together on equal terms.
One programme within mental health services achieved this via a range of
initiatives designed to increase access to employment within the service for
people with mental health problems. These ensured that 27 per cent of recruits
had personal experience of mental health problems, and people with and without mental health problems worked together on an equal basis (the same positions, terms and conditions and responsibilities; see Perkins 1998; Perkins
et al., 2001b). Attempts have also been made to change attitudes outside the
mental health services by publicising (on national radio, and in a London newspaper, for example Perkins 2001a) this programme's success in enabling
people with mental health problems to work successfully in responsible and
senior positions.

It is important to note that the attitudes of those in positions of power were
critical to the success of this employment programme in lowering the 'them'
and 'us' barriers. Similar programmes that have not enjoyed the active support
of the Chief Executive and Chairman have been notably less successful (Perkins et al., 2000). Such support from those with power may also contribute to
the extension of employment opportunities throughout the National Health
Service via national initiatives encouraging the employment of people with
mental health problems (see Department of Health, 2000a, b, 2001a) and positive ministerial statements:

A key objective of the Government is to enable all disabled people, including those
with mental health problems, to make the most of their abilities at work and in
the wider society and, as the largest public sector employer in the country, the
NHS should also be making a significant contribution to delivering this agenda.

The South West London and St George's Mental Health Trust user employment programme is an excellent example of such initiatives. (Secretary of State for Health in Department of Health 2000c)

However, the impact of such initiatives has been relatively limited. If participating alongside people who do not have mental health problems is to be effective in breaking down the 'them' and 'us' barriers, then it is necessary that people know that those with whom they are working, studying or pursuing social/leisure pursuits have mental health difficulties, and that they allow them to participate on equal terms.

We are not suggesting that legislation alone will reduce discrimination, but we do believe that formal, legal rights at the level of 'demos' are an essential component of promoting inclusion. The challenge to discrimination against women and racial minority groups has occurred at the level of both 'demos' and 'ethnos'. Legislation prohibiting discrimination on the basis of race or gender, and commissions to enforce this legislation (the Equal Opportunities Commission and the Commission for Racial Equality) have gone hand in hand with more educative efforts to change attitudes and behaviour (for example, anti-discrimination campaigns and awareness training).

If we are to assist people to rebuild their lives we must address issues of discrimination and exclusion. In doing this, we have to broaden our vision, looking beyond individual interventions to minimise mental distress and disability. There are many ways in which we can help people to access opportunities on an individual level, but we also have a broader role to play in breaking down the barriers that prohibit such access, for example, by making use of anti-discrimination legislation and endeavouring to change the attitudes of those who have the power to perpetuate exclusion.

References

Campbell, P. (2000) 'The role of users of psychiatric services in service development – influence not power'. *Psychiatric Bulletin*, 25, 87–8.

Chamberlin, J. (2001) 'Equal rights, not public relations. World Psychiatric Association Conference "Together Against Stigma"'. Leipzig, September 2001.

Cocker, J., Major, B., Steele, C. (1998) 'Social stigma', in: Gilbert, D.T. and Fiske, S.T. (eds) *The Handbook of Social Psychology*. Boston: McGraw-Hill.

Cumming, E., Cumming, J. (1957) *Closed Ranks. An Experiment in Mental Health*. Cambridge, MA, Harvard University Press.

Department of Health (1999) *National Service Framework for Mental Health*. London, Department of Health.

Department of Health (2000a) *The NHS National Plan*. London, Department of Health.

Department of Health (2000b) *Looking Beyond Labels. Widening the Employment Opportunities for Disabled People in the New NHS*. London, Department of Health.

Department of Health (2000c) *The Government's Response to the Health Select Committee's Report into Mental Health Services*, October 2000, Cm 4888. London, Department of Health.

Department of Health (2001a) *Making it Happen: A Guide to Mental Health Promotion*. London, Department of Health.

Estroff, S.E. (1989) 'Self, identity, and subjective experiences of schizophrenia: in search of the subject'. *Schizophrenia Bulletin*, 15, 189–96.

Goffman, E. (1963) *Stigma: Notes on the Management of Spoiled Identity*. Harmondsworth, Penguin.

Health Education Authority (1997) *Young People's Resources to Combat Stigma Around Mental Health Issues. Qualitative Research to Evaluate Resource Material*. London, Health Education Authority.

Huxley, P. (2001) Rehabilitation – the social care dimension. In: Proceedings of the 'Reinventing Rehabilitation' Health Advisory Service Rehabilitation Good Practice Network Conference, London. HAS Rehab Good Practice Network Newsletter 5, 2–3.

Jones, L., Cochrane, R. (1981) 'Stereotypes of mental illness: a test of the labelling hypothesis'. *International Journal of Social Psychiatry*, 27, 99–107.

Link, B.G., Phelan, J.C. (2001) 'Conceptualising stigma', *Annual Review of Sociology*, 27, 363–85.

Oliver, M. (1990) *The Politics of Disablement*. Basingstoke, Macmillan.

Perkins, R. (1998) 'An act to follow?' *A Life in the Day*, 2, 15–20.

Perkins, R. (2000) 'I have a vision . . .', *Openmind*, 104, 6.

Perkins, R. (2001a) 'All in a day's work'. In: 'Just the Job' section. *Evening Standard* 8th October, p. 15.

Perkins, R. E. (2001b) 'What constitutes success? The relative priority of service users' and professionals' views of the effectiveness of interventions and services' [editorial]. *British Journal of Psychiatry*, 178, 1–2.

Perkins, R. (2001c) 'Danger and incompetence: mental health and New Labour', *Critical Social Policy*, 21, 536–9.

Perkins, R., Rinaldi, M., Hardisty, J. (2001) *User Employment Programme Progress Report 2001*, South West London and St George's Mental Health NHS Trust, London.

Rogers, A., Pilgrim, D. (1994) 'Service users' views of psychiatric nurses', *British Journal of Nursing*, 3, 16–18.

Sayce, L. (1998) 'Stigma, discrimination and social exclusion: what's in a word?', *Journal of Mental Health*, 7, 331–43.

Sayce, L. (2000) *From Psychiatric Patient to Citizen: Overcoming Discrimination and Social Exclusion*. London, Macmillan.

Sayce, L. (2002) *Beyond Good Intentions: Making Anti-Discrimination Stragegies Work*. London, Disability Rights Commission.

Warner, R. (2000) *The Environment of Schizophrenia: Innovations in Practice, Policy and Communications. London, Routledge.*

18

From social exclusion to inclusion? A critique of the inclusion imperative in mental health

Helen Spandler

Introduction: from exclusion to inclusion?

Over the last few years there has been a significant shift in social policy discourse in the UK from a focus on tackling social 'exclusion' towards one of promoting 'inclusion'. Such a change in focus inevitably has consequences for how we understand, frame and potentially address the ways in which certain individuals and groups are marginalised and excluded. Whilst the concept of social exclusion has attracted much interest and debate (Fairclough, 2000; Humpage, 2006; Levitas, 2004; Burden and Hamm, 2000; Gray, 2000; Lister, 2000), there has been less critical attention paid to social *inclusion* (Ratcliffe, 2000). The notion of social inclusion is difficult to critique because, like other concepts in the Government's 'modernisation' agenda (such as 'choice', 'user involvement' and 'recovery'), it is presented as self evidently desirable and unquestionable. This has resulted in a growing consensus around the need for inclusion which is often framed as a human right or moral imperative. An interrogation of the notion of social inclusion is particularly urgent in the field of

Edited extract from H. Spandler, *Medical Sociology Online* (2007), vol. 2, issue 2, November, pp. 3–15.

mental health because it is being used to reshape services and redesign delivery in ways that could have serious consequences for users of mental health services and the future of mental health provision. Without denying the progressive impetus behind the demand for inclusion, nor the ways the term has been creatively employed by campaigners, service providers and users, this article raises the question of whether it has been too readily embraced as a policy imperative and asks if this has obscured some potential negative consequences.

The notion of inclusion, like 'mental health' itself, is hard to define and has many possible meanings. Whilst 'mental health' is increasingly used as a euphemism for 'mental illness' in service provision, social inclusion and exclusion are increasingly used either interchangeably or, as we shall see, as unproblematic opposites. However, whilst 'mental health' cannot be seen merely as the absence of 'illness', social inclusion cannot be seen as necessarily the absence of exclusion as they have complex interrelated, contested, but independent meanings. Indeed it may be the very flexibility and elasticity of the term 'inclusion' which has allowed it to be used to progress a number of outward looking, non-medicalised and non-stigmatising initiatives inspired by a social model of disability (Bates, 2002). However, notwithstanding its contested meanings, for the purposes of this article I view social inclusion as the policy drive towards 'bringing people with mental illness into mainstream society, enabling access to ordinary opportunities for employment, leisure, family and community life' (Rankin, 2005: 9–10).

Firstly, it is important to acknowledge that many mental health service users do experience profound social exclusion and this often has a number of negative consequences for individuals and communities (Rankin, 2005; Dunn, 1999; Social Exclusion Unit, 2004b). Indeed, one important aspect of the notion of social exclusion was that it drew attention to the many ways that people with mental health difficulties can be excluded, marginalised and discriminated against in a variety of spheres of life (Sayce, 2001; Sayce and Morris, 1999; Social Exclusion Unit, 2004a). However, while exclusion refers to an act with an agent or agents (for example, individuals, groups, institutions or markets) that have the power to exclude (Atkinson, 1998; Kleinman, 1998), inclusion tends to imply a benign effort on behalf of these exclusionary agents to 'include'. The policy shift to 'inclusion' can make invisible the social structures and divisions which generate and sustain exclusion and create an obsession with the choices and responsibilities of the individual rather than the constraining context in which they live.

As this shift occurred, the concepts of social inclusion and exclusion were also increasingly used as if they were polar opposites, as if one was the unproblematic negation of the other (Levitas, 2004). As this logic is followed to its conclusion, the solution to the problem of social exclusion becomes one of promoting a policy direction which stressed the inclusion of individuals. Whilst seemingly 'obvious' and 'logical', the assumptions involved in such conceptual slippage have not been explored or theorised. As a result the two concepts are used unproblematically as diametrically opposed poles within policy making. For example, although the Social Exclusion Unit report on mental health and social exclusion focused on some of the causes of exclusion, its recommendations and subsequent discussions have seamlessly moved towards endorsing inclusion as the way forward without a demonstrated awareness of the complexities of these twin concepts (Social Exclusion Unit, 2004a).

Assumptions of 'inclusion'

While it seems well evidenced that social exclusion has a negative impact on health and well-being, there is an accompanying widespread assumption that 'inclusion' in mainstream social settings is important for mental health and well-being. Thus social inclusion taps into common sense established ideas that 'everyone should be included in the one-nation Britain, that everyone should have a chance to contribute and be involved' (Sayce, 1998: 341). In other words, people with mental health problems should *want* to be involved and take part, as it is undeniably good. However, it is precisely this 'common sense' idea that is problematic. One of the problems with the move to 'promoting inclusion' is that inclusion in practice implicitly assumes that the quality of mainstream society is not only desirable, but unproblematic and legitimate (Levitas, 2004; Fairclough, 2000).

Equally, a fundamental, if implicit, premise of social inclusion is the existence of an 'ideal of common life' (Gray, 2000: 22) which everyone should aspire to. In practice this assumes a general consensus on basic values around involvement in community, work, family and leisure (Burden and Hamm, 2000; Gray, 2000). To be included is to participate in this ideal, and to do so is both 'healthy' and desirable. Despite this shared and 'common sense' belief, the link between inclusion in mainstream social settings and increased mental well-being has not been clearly established (Angus, 2002). Research has also questioned the assumption that inclusion is necessarily lacking or desirable for everyone with mental health difficulties (Seeker et al., 2007).

In addition, social inclusion discourse implies that society is comprised of a comfortable and satisfied 'included majority' and a dissatisfied 'excluded minority'. This focuses attention on the excluded minority and fails to take seriously the difficulties, conflicts and inequalities apparent in the wider society which actually generate and sustain exclusion and mental health problems (Kleinman, 1998; Levitas, 2004; Fairclough, 2000; Burden and Hamm, 2000). Indeed, it is often the pressures and expectations underpinning this ideal of common social life which contribute to mental health difficulties in the first place (Cornett, 2007). This is evident in recent research in the UK which highlights the increasing levels of mental health problems within mainstream society (James, 1997; Layard, 2005a; 2005b; Bird, 1999). Indeed it is not only people with diagnosed 'severe and enduring' mental health difficulties who do not necessarily 'feel at home in mainstream society' (Bates and Davis, 2004: 199).

Consequences of 'inclusion'

The ways in which the socially excluded are constructed within policy and practice discourse can result in a number of potential consequences. In particular, it can lead to a focus on changing the individual's choices and aspirations, rather than the social context which constrains their choices. In assuming that the 'mainstream' is ideal and desirable, it is possible that discourses around mental health are increasingly constructed within a deficit model, which constructs the socially excluded as lacking in the skills and dispositions required for paid work and other mainstream activities. In this way, the problem which needs to be addressed is not social inequality, oppression or discrimination, but cultures of low aspiration and fatalism (Fairclough, 2000). The moral imperative for service users to engage in a way which is defined as appropriate by government, policy makers and services can lead to those who do not co-operate being viewed as dysfunctional.

This is apparent with modern policy concerns about the issue of 'dependency'. Increasingly, service users are constructed as being 'dependent' on welfare services if they use services in particular ways. The notion of dependency is almost invariably constructed in negative terms and is opposed to the ideal of 'independence' (usually through employment). In this way, service users' reliance on benefit payments, services and/or other people with mental health difficulties becomes a 'moral hazard' (Levitas, 2004: 4) which encourages dependency, rather than a social good which prevents destitution or provides support, solidarity and care (Burden and Hamm, 2000). It is interesting to note that some elements of the service user/survivor movement also place a lot of emphasis on independence from services as part of their aspiration for greater autonomy and may view 'getting back to work' (for example) as a particular individual mark of achievement.

If the socially excluded (or service users) are constructed as 'lacking' or 'dependent', the problem then becomes how to 'help, cajole or coerce' those perceived as outsiders back into mainstream society (Levitas, 2004: 7). Social inclusion strategies often target groups and individuals whose behaviour or choices are seen as problematic (single parents, teenage mothers and members of the 'underclass') and try to encourage or impose more appropriate or acceptable modes of behaviour, choices or lifestyles (Kleinman, 1998; Levitas, 2004). Although the mantra of 'individual choice' and 'person centredness' often accompanies social inclusion initiatives, in effect the inclusion imperative inadvertently imposes certain choices as more desirable than others. In other words some choices are privileged and encouraged while others are problematised or pathologised.

Moreover, social inclusion has a *conditional* element in which coercion can be used to ensure compliance (Burden and Hamm, 2000; Humpage, 2006). Thus, alongside seemingly progressive modernisation strategies which promote greater choice, control and independence for welfare service users, we are also witnessing a growth in the social control of people with mental health difficulties. Recent moves towards compulsory treatment in the community, supervision orders and assertive outreach services have often been viewed as mental health 'anti social behaviour orders' (ASBOs) which function to exclude certain undesirable people (and their behaviour) from the rest of society. Such treatment of the issue bears similarity to the way in which the tenants of social housing are compelled to behave 'properly' or have their tenancies revoked (Young et al., 2004). Mental health service users are being urged to exercise greater choice and control, but only if they make the 'right' decisions.

References

Angus, J. (2002) *A Review of Evaluation in Community-Based Art for Health Activity in the UK.* London, Health Development Agency.

Atkinson, A.B. (1998) Social Exclusion, Poverty and Unemployment. In A.B. Atkinson and J. Hills (eds) *Exclusion, Employment and Opportunity.* CASE paper no. 4. London: Centre for Analysis of Social Exclusion, London School of Economics.

Bates, P. (ed.) (2002) *Working for Inclusion: Making Social Inclusion a Reality for People with Severe Mental Health Problems.* London, Sainsbury Centre for Mental Health.

Bates, P. and Davis, F.A. (2004) 'Social capital, social inclusion and services for people with learning disabilities'. *Disability and Society*, 19(3): 195–207.

Bird, L. (1999) *The Fundamental Facts: All the Latest Facts and Figures on Mental Illness.* London, Mental Health Foundation.

Burden, T. and Hamm, T. (2000) 'Responding to socially included groups', in J.H. Perry-Smith (ed.), *Policy Responses to Social Inclusion*, Buckingham: Open University Press.

Cornett, J.A. (2007) 'Becoming-paranoid: displacements of 'paranoia' in circulations of counter-knowledges'. *Journal of Critical Psychology, Counselling and Psychotherapy* 7(1): 4–8.

Cox, T., Leka, S., Ivanov, I. and Kortum, E. (2004) 'Work, employment and mental health in Europe'. *Work and Stress*, 18(2): 179–85.

Dewson, S., Eccles, J., Tackey, N.D. and Jackson, A. (2000) *A Guide to Measuring Soft Outcomes and Distance Travelled.* London: Institute for Employment Studies for the DfEE.

Dunn, S. (1999) *Creating Accepting Communities – Report of the Mind Inquiry into Social Exclusion and Mental Health Problems*. London, Mind.

Fairclough, N. (2000) *New Labour, New Language?* London: Routledge.

Furedi, F. (2003) 'Making people feel good about themselves', Inaugural Lecture: British social policy and the construction of the problem of self-esteem, University of Kent, 24 January 2003.

Gabriel, P. and Liimatainen, M. R. (2000) *Mental Health in the Workplace*. Geneva: International Labour Office.

Gray, J. (2000) 'Inclusion: A Radical Critique'. In P. Askonas and A. Stewart (eds) (2000) *Social Inclusion: Possibilities and Tensions*. Basingstoke: Macmillan.

Humpage, L. (2006) 'An inclusive society: a "leap forward" for Maori in New Zealand?' *Critical Social Policy*, 26(1): 220–42.

James, O. (1997) *Britain on the Couch*. London: Century/Random House.

Kent, P. (2002) *Quality of Life as Distance Travelled: Final Report* prepared for Fairbridge and the Foyer Foundation December 2002.

Kleinman, M. (1998) *Include Me Out? The New Politics of Place and Poverty*. CASE paper No. 11 London: Centre for Analysis of Social Exclusion, London School of Economics, *http://sticerd.lse.ac.uk/dps/case/cp/paper11.pdf*.

Layard, R. (2005a) *Happiness: Lessons from a New Science*. London: Penguin Books.

Layard, R. (2005b) 'Mental health: Britain's biggest social problem?' Paper presented at the No. 10 Strategy Unit Seminar on Mental Health, LSE, 20 January 2005.

Layard, R., Clark, D., Knapp, M. and Mayraz, G. (2006) *Implementing the NICE Guidelines for Depression and Anxiety: A Cost–Benefit Analysis*. Mental Health Policy Group, LSE, May 2006.

Levitas, R. (2004) 'Let's hear it for Humpty: social exclusion, the third way and cultural capital'. *Cultural Trends*, 13(2): 41–56.

Lister, R. (2000) 'Strategies for social inclusion: promoting social cohesion or social justice'. In P. Askonas and A. Stewart (eds), *Social Inclusion: Possibilities and Tensions*. Basingstoke: Macmillan.

NIMHE/CSIP (2006) *From Segregation to Inclusion: Commissioning Guidance on Day Services for People with Mental Health Problems*, National Inclusion Programme National Institute for Mental Health in England (NIMHE), Care Services Improvement Partnership (CSIP), London, Feb 2006.

Rankin, J. (2005) *Mental Health in the Mainstream: Mental Health and Social Inclusion*. London: Institute for Public Policy Research.

Ratcliffe, P. (2000) 'Is the assertion of minority identity compatible with the idea of a socially inclusive society?', In P. Askonas and A. Stewart (eds), *Social Inclusion: Possibilities and Tensions*. Basingstoke: Macmillan.

Repper, J. and Perkins, R. (2003) *Social Inclusion and Recovery: A Model for Mental Health Practice*. London: Baillière-Tindall.

Sayce, L. (1998) 'Stigma, discrimination and social exclusion: what's in a word?' *Journal of Mental Health*, 7(4): 331–43.

Sayce, L. (2001) 'Editorial: social inclusion and mental health'. *Psychiatric Bulletin*, 25: 121–3.

Sayce, L. and Morris, D. (1999) *Outsiders Coming In? Achieving Social Inclusion for People with Mental Health Problems*, London: Mind.

Secker, J., Grove, B. and Seebohm, P. (2001) 'Challenging barriers to employment, training and education for mental health service users: the service users' perspective'. *Journal of Mental Health*, 10(4): 395–404.

Secker, J., Hacking, S., Spandler, H., Kent, L. and Shenton, J. (2005) *Mental health, social inclusion and arts: developing the evidence base*, London: National Social Inclusion Programme, Care Services Improvement Partnership.

Secker, J., Hacking, S., Spandler, H., Kent, L. and Shenton, J. (2007) Mental health, social inclusion and arts: developing the evidence base: Final report from Phase 1: The state of the art in England. November 2005.

Siegrist, J. (1996) 'Adverse health effects of high effort – low reward conditions at work'. *Journal of Occupational Health Psychology*, 1(1): 27–43.

Social Exclusion Unit (2004a) *Mental Health and Social Exclusion: Social Exclusion Unit Report*. London: Office of the Deputy Prime Minister.

Social Exclusion Unit (2004b) *Breaking the Cycle*. London: Office of the Deputy Prime Minister.

Sparks, K., Faragher, B. Cooper, C.J. (2001) 'Well-being and occupational health in the 21st Century Workplace'. *Journal of Occupational and Organizational Psychology*, 74: 489–509.

Young, F., Huntington, A., and Foord, M. (2004) 'No room for nuisance'. *Community care*, 22 April 2004: 42–4.

19

(Mis)representing mental distress?

Mark Walsh

The impact that the mass media can have on our beliefs and personal experiences has been the focus of a substantial amount of academic and interest group research throughout the world. As a result there is now a large body of evidence from international sources to support claims that the mass media do have power and influence over many areas of public belief and perception. This issue is of particular concern to people who wish to challenge and change prejudices and damaging stereotypes that exist about mental distress and the people who experience it. But what evidence is there that the mass media do create and perpetuate these negative stereotypes? And why does this matter?

Research carried out into the representation of mental distress suggests the mass media play an active role in the development and dissemination of a range of negative images in both news and entertainment media. Roth Edney (2004) suggests that the role of the mass media can be summarised in the following terms:

1 the mass media are a primary source of public information about mental distress
2 the media promote false and negative images and stereotypes of mental distress
3 there is a connection between negative media portrayals of 'mental illness' and the public's negative attitudes toward people experiencing mental distress
4 negative media portrayals have a direct impact on individuals living with mental illness
5 there is a connection between negative media portrayals of mental illness and government responses to mental health issues.

It is important to note that the mass media tend to accept the concept of 'mental illness' as unproblematic. Consequently 'mental illness' remains largely uncontested as an explanation of mental distress in news and entertainment media portrayals of issues, experiences and events relating to emotional, psychological or behavioural disturbance. As a result many of the research studies in the field also focus on representations of 'mental illness' and 'mentally ill people' in the mass media. Where these studies are being directly referred to, the term 'mental illness' will be used in this discussion. However, where this is not necessary 'mental distress' will be used instead.

If the initial 'hypothesis' outlined by Roth Edney (2004) is correct, the mass media have the power to establish, disseminate and maintain public attitudes and beliefs about mental distress and the people who experience it. So, is there research evidence to support this hypothesis? Considerable research has concluded that the media are the public's most significant source of information about 'mental illness' (Coverdale et al., 2002; Philo et al., 1994). Philo (1997) also found that media representations of 'mental illness' are so powerful that they can even override people's own personal experiences in relation to how they view mental distress. This suggests that the mass media do indeed play a formative and very influential role in communicating ideas about mental distress to the public.

However, being the primary source of public information about mental distress isn't a criticism of the mass media in itself. Even though research has established that the mass media play a critical role in establishing public attitudes and beliefs, isn't it still possible that they may represent and cover the topic of mental distress in a balanced, positive and even educational manner? This is possible, though research studies repeatedly find that the mass media actually promote false, negative images and stereotypes of mental distress and the people who experience it.

Diefenbach (1997) found that the depiction of 'mental illness' in American television programmes was highly correlated with the portrayal of violent crime. The stereotypical linking of 'mental illness' with violence and violent crime was also evident in research carried out by the Glasgow University Media Group (Philo, 1993). This team of media researchers conducted a content analysis of 562 national and local newspaper items published in April 1993 that referred to 'mental health and illness'. Philo et al. (1996) concluded that 66 per cent of these items focused on a 'mentally ill' person being violent toward others while only 18 per cent offered 'sympathetic coverage'. The common focus on 'violence towards others' was also given a high profile, while 'sympathetic coverage was largely confined to back-page material in newspapers and magazines such as problem-pages and health columns' (p. 116).

In a later study, Rose (1998) also found that nearly two-thirds of news stories that reported on people with psychiatric diagnoses could be classified as 'crime news'. This is despite the fact that this type of news story usually makes up only 10 percent of news reporting. As a result when people read or hear about 'mental illness' they often do so in the context of 'crime'. Imprecise reporting can also compound this skewed presentation of mental distress by the mass media. For example, Coverdale et al. (2002) make the point that inaccurate generalisations about 'mentally ill people' occur because the media rarely provide a specific diagnosis when they present a description of a 'mentally ill' person or fictional character. Arguably the lack of clear diagnostic terms and the general use of 'mental illness' as an explanatory label leads readers, listeners or audiences to make generalised assumptions about the behaviour and personal qualities of all people who receive a 'mental illness' label.

Violence and criminality are not the only negative associations made with mental distress by the mass media. Wilson et al. (1999) analysed prime-time television drama programmes and found that 'mentally ill' characters were often portrayed as simple-minded, helpless and unable to control their lives. Wilson et al. (1999) suggest that character constructions like these communicate the message that 'mentally ill' people tend to be 'unproductive failures'. This type of representation is typically supported by a 'mentally ill' character's lack of employment, poor or absent relationships with family and friends and by their homelessness or poor living conditions. Olstead (2002) argues that a consequence of drama stereotypes like these is that 'mental illness' tends to be presented as a character's main personality trait to the extent that it becomes the only way of defining that person and the main point of any story involving them. This kind of one-dimensional depiction is damaging because people experiencing 'mental illness' are then not recognised or responded to as fully human individuals. Instead an individual's ill-defined 'mental illness' becomes an enveloping identity or master status that explains them.

The mass media's failure to recognise and respect the individuality of people experiencing mental distress has also been highlighted in research studies that draw attention to the absence of the voices and views of people who featured in reporting about 'mental illness'. Macmin (2001), for example, carried out a survey of UK national and regional newspapers and found that only 6.5 per cent of articles published over a two-month period contained service users' perspectives. The absence of first-person accounts of mental distress in the mass media may be one reason for the apparently false and stereotypical portrayals that exist and may give the impression that mentally distressed people are incapable of developing opinions and expressing their views. This type of omission also means that the experience of mental distress is rarely explored or explained in public. Rose (1998) argues that when psychosis is portrayed on television, as well as generally in the media, it is presented as an unclassifiable, incomprehensible and unstable experience that poses a threat to others. But why does any of this matter?

A number of research studies have investigated the impact of negative media portrayals of mental distress. In a study conducted for the UK Department of

Health in 1996, Rose (1998) found that representations of 'mental illness' in the news and entertainment media had a negative effect on public perception and also influenced government responses to public concerns. The findings of this study confirmed those of Philo et al. (1994) that the public believed there was a strong link between 'mental illness' and violence. Arguably, the repetition of stereotypes based on the notion that mentally ill people are 'dangerous', 'violent' and 'unpredictable' misrepresents the majority of people experiencing mental distress and makes their lives harder. The direct experience and comments of those being stereotyped and misrepresented would seem to support this.

The UK mental health charity Mind carried out a survey of people who experience mental distress to find out about their feelings regarding media coverage of 'mental illness' (Baker and McPherson, 2000). The aim was to assess whether media coverage of mental health issues over the previous three years had had an impact on the lives of service users/survivors. Of the 574 people who returned questionnaires, almost three-quarters felt that media coverage of mental health issues had been unfair, unbalanced or very negative. Half of the respondents said that this media coverage had had a negative effect on their own mental health and a third said that this had led directly to an increase in their depression and anxiety. A total of 22 per cent of the participants said they felt more withdrawn and isolated as a result of negative media coverage and eight per cent said that such press coverage had made them feel suicidal. Almost 25 per cent of respondents said that they noticed hostile behaviour from their neighbours due to negative newspaper and television reports. A further 11 per cent said they required additional support from mental health services because of negative press coverage and almost 25 per cent of all respondents said that they had changed their minds about applying for jobs or volunteer positions owing to negative media coverage. Comments such as the following illustrated some effects:

> It makes me worry that I might get as bad as some of the people shown on TV. (Female, aged 59 with a diagnosis of schizophrenia)

> A friend of many years, responding to media reports of killings by ex-psychiatric patients, said that psychiatric patients should all be locked up. (Male, aged 40 diagnosed with depression)
>
> (Baker and McPherson, 2000, pp. 7–8)

In addition to the impact on the public and people experiencing mental distress, research studies suggest that the misrepresentation of mental distress affects the thinking and responses of government policy makers too. Rose (1998) concluded in his report that a link does exist between media representations of 'mental illness' and government responses to the extent that:

it [is] not an exaggeration to say that mental health policy is now motivated by the desire to deal with risky individuals and to assuage the public disquiet. (Rose, 1998, p. 225)

Similarly, Cutcliffe and Hannigan (2001) argue that there is an implicit relationship between negative and inaccurate representations of 'mental illness' in the mass media and the development of current mental health policies and law in the UK. They state that

the shift towards a coercive policy has, in part at least, much to do with the Government's attempts to pander to inaccurate public perceptions, reactions, and intolerance. Furthermore ... the public may have been 'whipped up' into this position of intolerance as a result of misleading, inaccurate mass representations of mental illness and mental health issues. (Cutcliffe and Hannigan, 2001, p. 318)

The portrayal of mental distress by the mass media would, according to the research evidence presented, seem to be narrow, generally negative and stereotypical. The voices and experiences of those who actually experience mental distress are rarely given radio or television airtime or space on the pages of newspapers or magazines. The images and accounts of 'mental illness' that are disseminated tend to portray these people as unpredictable, broken and dangerous 'failures', and certainly not as 'people like us'. The consequences of this misrepresentation can be seen in the enduring public insecurities and hostility towards those identified as 'mentally ill', in the damage that this does to some people's life chances and in the increasing concerns of policy-makers to protect 'us' from the 'monsters' that the media suggest may be lurking in our communities.

References

Baker, S. and MacPherson, J. (2000) *Counting the Cost: Mental Health in the Media*, London, Mind.

Coverdale, J., Nairn, R. and Claasen, D. (2002) 'Depictions of mental illness in print media: a prospective national sample', *Australian and New Zealand Journal of Psychiatry*, vol. 36, no. 5, pp. 697–700.

Cutcliffe, J. R. and Hannigan, B. (2001) 'Mass media, "monsters" and mental health clients: the need for increased lobbying', *Journal of Psychiatric and Mental Health Nursing*, vol. 8, no. 4, pp. 315–21.

Diefenbach, D. L. (1997) 'The portrayal of mental illness on prime-time television', *Journal of Community Psychology*, vol. 25, no. 3, pp. 289–302.

Macmin, L. (2001) *Mental Health and the Press*, Mental Health Media www.mhmedia.com/training/report.html [accessed 06/04/07].

Olstead, R. (2002) 'Contesting the text: Canadian media depictions of the conflation of mental illness and criminality', *Sociology of Health and Illness*, vol. 24, no. 5, pp. 621–43.

Philo, G. (1993) *Mass Media Representations of Mental Health: A Study of Media Content*, Glasgow, Glasgow University Media Group.

Philo, G. (1997) 'Changing media representations of mental health', *Psychiatric Bulletin*, vol. 21, pp. 171–2.

Philo, G., Secker, J., Platt, S., Henderson, L., McLaughlin, G. and Burnside, J. (1994) 'The impact of mass media on public images of mental illness: media content and audience belief', *Health Education Journal*, vol. 53, pp. 271–81.

Philo, G., Secker, J., Platt, S., Henderson, L., McLaughlin, G. and Burnside, J. (1996) 'Media images of mental distress' in Heller, T., Reynolds, J., Gomm, R., Muston, R. and Pattison, S. (eds) *Mental Health Matters*, Basingstoke, Macmillan.

Rose, D. (1998) 'Television, madness and community care', *Journal of Community and Applied Social Psychology*, vol. 8, no. 3, pp. 213–28.

Roth Edney, D. (2004) *Mass Media and Mental Illness: A Literature Review*, Canadian Mental Health Association, www.ontario.cmha.ca/docs/about/mass-media.pdf [accessed 06/04/07].

Wilson C., Nairn, R., Coverdale, J. and Panapa, A. (1999) 'Mental illness depictions in prime-time drama: identifying the discursive resources', *Australian and New Zealand Journal of Psychiatry*, vol. 33, no. 2, pp. 232–9.

Why are we not getting any closer to preventing suicide?

Diego De Leo

In humanistic domains such as ethics, philosophy and anthropology the debate on the legitimacy of preventing suicide seems to have proceeded in parallel with the history of human development (Minois, 1999). Even in the medical world, where suicide has been acknowledged as a primary public health problem within the past century, and where the World Health Organization declared the fight against suicide as a priority for the first time in the year 2000, there is disagreement about the effectiveness of preventive efforts (Wilkinson, 1994). There are many reasons for such scepticism, all of them more or less centred on the extreme complexity of the suicide phenomenon and its relative rarity. A recent *World Health Report* (World Health Organization, 2001) calculated the number of recorded suicide deaths to be 815,000 worldwide (0.0135 per cent of the global population), a burden slightly lower than the estimate of 1 million published in an earlier technical report dedicated to suicide (World Health Organization, 1999).

Traditional difficulties

Despite the huge amount of literature and research on the topic, prevention of suicidal behaviours, both fatal and non-fatal, remains an imperfect art based on scant scientific evidence (Hawton et al, 1998). The most commonly cited reasons for this are inadequate sample sizes for randomised, controlled studies (Gunnell and Frankel, 1994), and programmes of insufficient duration (Goldney, 2000). Moreover, there are numerous biases inherent in suicide

Edited extract from D. De Leo, *British Journal of Psychiatry* (2002), vol. 181, pp. 372–4.

research, notably the use of people who have attempted suicide as research participants; such people only minimally overlap suicide completers, and their use implies the hypothesis of a continuum between non-fatal and fatal suicidal behaviour. Other sources of bias are difficulties in creating clusters of participants with similar problems (for example, problems within similar dyadic relationships), the use of retrospective evaluations, the lack or inadequacy of control groups, and the design of psychological investigations performed on proxies of the deceased (psychological autopsies) (Hawton et al., 1998). On the other hand, little is known (because they are poorly investigated) about factors that are likely to protect against suicide, such as coping skills, problem-solving capabilities, social support and connectedness. Indeed, the multi-determined dimension of suicide poses per se enormous difficulties, even at the level of conceptual models of development of the suicidal process. Clearly, it would be much easier to investigate the prevention of a phenomenon provoked by just one or two possible causes.

Less traditional (more neglected) difficulties

Multi-disciplinary approaches to the prevention and investigation of suicide are often flagged up but virtually never practised. Research teams have difficulties in achieving a balanced composition between biologically and psychologically oriented investigators (both equally important in the study of suicide). This is further complicated by the need to evaluate also other important concomitant factors, such as socio-economic, cultural and religious aspects. A classic example of the impact of non-biological or psychological/psychiatric factors on suicide rates is provided by the observation of epidemiological data on a century of suicide mortality in western countries. Socio-economic events (wars, major economic fluctuations) produce tremendous fluctuations in suicide mortality, particularly in men. The intrinsically large-scale nature of those events provoked effects that, if applied deliberately, would be incomparably bigger than any well-targeted anti-suicide initiative (World Health Organization, 1998). Understandably, the controllability of social events remains hypothetical and their relevance to suicide prevention largely speculative. However, the impact of socio-cultural phenomena should be considered when evaluating suicide prevention programmes, although their interference might render interpretation of outcomes virtually impossible. Categorisation and quantitative/qualitative analysis of these contributory characteristics represent a considerable challenge for every researcher, a process that commonly ends by provoking a rather limiting prioritisation of the many variables involved. Apart from the field of competence of researchers, other factors such as personal attitudes and ideologies, means and funding availability play a major part in hindering the development of meaningful research and prevention on suicide.

Lessons can be learned from approaches to the prevention of life-threatening conditions such as ischaemic heart disease. A significant reduction in mortality from ischaemic heart disease has been achieved only by addressing a wide range of factors: knowledge of family predisposition, exercise, dieting, smoking cessation, cholesterol level control, sophisticated diagnostic techniques that allow early intervention, treatment in highly specialised intensive care units, bypass and angioplastic surgery, and personalised rehabilitation programmes have all contributed to substantial improvements in survival rates and mortality reduction. Suicide is a much more complex phenomenon than myocardial infarction, so it seems illogical that strategies to fight suicide have to be simpler or less integrated than the struggle against coronary artery disease.

Trends in suicide rates

Western countries are facing a general decline in suicide rates that seems reasonably unrelated to the existence of any national plan. Reductions in suicide rates have occurred not only in Finland, Sweden, Norway and Denmark (which had or have a structured strategy), but also in nations such as Hungary and The Netherlands which, like most western countries, do not possess a national prevention programme. The presence of a 'cohort effect' (the ensemble of environmental factors that connote a certain generation) and of its relative size has been postulated several times in suicidology (see, for example, Cantor et al., 1999), although a clear description of the relevant environmental factors (or a hierarchy of their importance) has never been provided. In any case, the fundamental influence of cultural differences means that cohort effects are unlikely to be universally applicable. For example, the American example of the generation born after the Second World War (the 'baby boomers', characterised also by increased suicidality) has not proved fully valid in the European context (Bille-Brahe and Andersen, 2001). Moreover, the marked decline of suicide rates in the elderly over the past 30 years recorded in predominantly Anglo-Saxon countries has not been paralleled by a similar trend in Latin nations for the same generations (De Leo, 1999).

After many years of worrying increases in rates of youth suicide in nearly all western countries, a remarkable decline is now occurring. The motives for such trends are puzzling researchers to the point that the International Association for Suicide Prevention has created a task force, headed by David Shaffer in New York and Annette Beautrais in Christchurch, New Zealand, to study the phenomenon from a transcultural perspective. In addition, the World Health Organization headquarters is promoting a new study, the Suicide Prevention–Multisite Intervention Study on Suicide (SUPRE–MISS), with centres on the five continents, which includes a randomised clinical intervention for people attempting suicide, a biological investigation (into DNA and stress-related hormones), and the comparison of a number of socio-cultural indicators (World Health Organization, 2002).

Inside the labyrinth of anti-suicide strategies

The conflict between political convenience and scientific adequacy in suicide prevention is usually resolved in favour of the former. Thus, strategies targeting the general population instead of high-risk groups (psychiatric patients recently discharged from hospital, suicide attempters, etc.) may be chosen not on the basis of rigorous calculations (Lewis et al., 1997) but just because they might affect a much larger number of individuals and institutions, especially if the desired outcomes also include a number of conditions frequently associated with suicidal behaviours (such as poor quality of life, social isolation, unemployment and substance misuse). Indeed, although a reduction in suicide mortality should be the primary outcome of suicide prevention, interventions that target associated conditions appear more rewarding from a political perspective, especially in the light of the limited duration (3–5 years) that normally characterises the funding government. Many governments do not even fix targets in terms of reduced mortality, nor encourage stringent evaluative practices, because when the time comes for evaluation the term of that government is likely to be over.

Thus, for the above-mentioned reasons and many others not commented on but for which review articles are available (for example, Gunnell and Frankel, 1994), suicide prevention remains essentially a land of hopes and promises but not of certainties. This should not induce discouragement, but must be interpreted as a stimulus to do more and do it better, while endeavouring to avoid past mistakes such as the unidimensional interpretation of suicide, the previous abundance of 'epidemiological safari tours' in developing countries – there is a growing awareness of the sterility of many epidemiological investigations (Eagles et al., 2001) – and the use of popular but largely empty slogans such as 'community capacity building', which lack concrete application.

Moreover, countries should not rely on epidemiological surveys and prevention strategies developed elsewhere. Cultural factors have a major role in suicidal behaviour (Vijayakumar and Rajkumar, 1999) and there are huge differences in the dimension and characteristics of this problem around the world. As an example, the average ratios between the lowest and the highest suicide rates internationally are as large as 1:102.4 for men and 1:35.8 for women (Schmidtke *et al.*, 1999). Cross-cultural comparisons, such as the World Health Organization/EURO Multicentre Study of Suicidal Behaviour (Platt et al., 1992) and the more recent SUPRE–MISS, should be encouraged. They may improve our understanding of causative and protective factors, and consequently help to reorient prevention strategies. Detailed discussion of supposed 'best practices' in the prevention of suicide are beyond the scope of this editorial but are offered, for example, by the World Health Organization (1998) and De Leo et al. (2002).

Conclusion

Despite the strong association between mental disorders and *mors voluntaris*, suicidal behaviour attracts little interest among contemporary psychiatrists, as witnessed by the low number of contributions to suicidology journals. As a consequence, little is new in suicide prevention, and the current recommendations and traditional wisdom are hardly supported by an acceptable level of evidence. Greater use of antidepressant drugs to prevent mood disorders, functional neuroimaging, and genetic and psychometric screening for early detection of impulsive behaviour and suicide proneness seem to hold promise for future prevention strategies. A more rigorous use of available knowledge now seems to be a legitimate expectation.

Suicide research requires major investment, using multi-disciplinary teams to set up more integrated approaches for large-scale, long-term and thoroughly evaluated projects. 'Think big' – to paraphrase the World Health Organization's motto with a famous entrepreneurial slogan of the 1980s – really seems to capture today's priority in suicide prevention. If lack of substantial scientific evidence continues to characterise this area, loss of interest and progressive withdrawal of investment are inevitable. Cooperation between scientists, administrators and politicians is needed more than ever, with a higher level of planning and organisation. Only in this way can we come closer to preventing suicide.

References

Bille-Brahe, U. and Andersen, K. (2001) 'Suicide among the Danish elderly', in *Suicide and Euthanasia in Older Adults* (ed. D. De Leo), pp. 47–56, Goettingen, Hogrefe-Huber.

Cantor, C. H., Neulinger, K. and De Leo, D. (1999) 'Australian suicide trends 1964–1997: youth and beyond?' *Medical Journal of Australia*, 171, pp. 137–41.

De Leo, D. (1999) 'Cultural issues in suicide and old age', *Crisis*, 20, pp. 53–5.

De Leo, D., Bertolote, J. M., Lester, D., et al. (2002) 'Self-inflicted violence'. In *World Report on Violence and Health*, ch. 7. Geneva, World Health Organization.

Eagles, J. M., Klein, S., Gray, N. M., et al. (2001) 'Role of psychiatrists in the prediction and prevention of suicide: a perspective from north-east Scotland'. *British Journal of Psychiatry*, 178, pp. 494–6.

Goldney, R. D. (2000) 'Prediction of suicide and attempted suicide'. In *The International Handbook of Suicide and Attempted Suicide* (eds K. Hawton and K. Van Heeringen), pp. 585–95, Chichester: John Wiley & Sons.

Gunnell, D. and Frankel, S. (1994) 'Prevention of suicide: aspiration and evidence'. *BMJ*, 308, 1227–33.

Hawton, K., Arensman, E., Townsend, E., et al. (1998) 'Deliberate self-harm: systematic review of efficacy of psychosocial and pharmacological treatments in preventing repetition'. *BMJ*, 317, 441–7.

Lewis, G., Hawton, K. and Jones, P. (1997) 'Strategies for preventing suicide'. *British Journal of Psychiatry*, 171, 351–4.

Minois, G. (1999) *History of Suicide. Voluntary Death in Western Culture*. Baltimore, MD: Johns Hopkins University Press.

Platt, S., Bille-Brahe, U., Kerkhof, A. J. F. M., et al. (1992) 'Parasuicide in Europe: the WHO/EURO Multicentre Study on Parasuicide: I. Introduction and preliminary analysis for 1989'. *Acta Psychiatrica Scandinavica*, 85, 97–104.

Schmidtke, A., Weinacker, B., Apter, A., et al. (1999) 'Suicide rates in the world: an update'. *Archives of Suicide Research*, **5**, 81–9.

Vijayakumar, L. and Rajkumar, S. (1999) 'Are risk-factors for suicide universal? A case-control study in India'. *Acta Psychiatrica Scandinavica*, 99, 407–11.

Wilkinson, G. (1994) 'Can suicide be prevented?' *BMJ*, 309, 860–1.

World Health Organization (1998) *Primary Prevention of Mental, Neurological, and Psychosocial Disorders: Suicide*, pp. 75–90, Geneva, WHO.

World Health Organization (1999) *Figures and Facts About Suicide*, Technical Report, Geneva, WHO.

World Health Organization (2001) *World Health Report*, Geneva, WHO.

World Health Organization (2002) Multisite Intervention Study on Suicidal Behaviours – SUPRE–MISS Protocol. WHO/MSD/MBD/02.1. Suicide prevention/SUPRE at http://www.who.int/mental_health/media/en/254.pdf [accessed 18.03.09].

21

Mental health, mental disorder, risk and public protection

Hazel Kemshall

Introduction

Mental health provision is one arena in which needs, rights and risks have long competed. In the Middle Ages the mentally ill were risk managed through expulsion or incarceration and exclusion through the 'ship of fools' (Foucault, 1965). The Enlightenment provided an early example of privatized mental health care through profit-oriented 'madhouses'. The Victorian period and the early twentieth century were dominated by the spectre of the asylum and the concept of containment (Foucault, 1965), although the walls between asylum and local communities were often permeable (Bartlett and Wright, 1999) and 'lunatics' could be just as much 'at risk' in the community as in the asylum (Melling, 1999). The deinstitutionalization of the post-Second World War period was based upon a consensus that large institutions were dehumanizing and prone to abusive relationships with patients. The anti-psychiatry movement in particular recast the asylum itself as a place of risk, and most mental health patients were seen as presenting a low or tolerable risk to the community if released. The latter part of the twentieth century saw the development of community care for the mentally ill. Carpenter (2000) has presented this deinstitutionalization as in part a response to the fiscal crisis of post-1945 welfare provision and advances in neo-liberal techniques of social

Extract from H. Kemshall, *Risk, Social Policy and Welfare* (2002), Buckingham, Open University Press, pp. 90–9.

control – in particular, the dispersal of the asylums' power and social control functions to the individual in the community through the 'psy' disciplines of psychiatry and psychology. The state's overt control is displaced to the control of experts and professionals, and the self-regulation of the individual through adaptation to the preset norms of the normalizing disciplines (Rose, 1985; 1986). As Carpenter (2000: 605) expresses it, the widening of social control is achieved through 'a co-optive rather than a repressive process'. Fiscally, community care (or community neglect, as Scull has dubbed it), has become a cheap alternative for the management of 'labour market casualties' in post-Keynesian markets (Scull, 1979; 1993). Pilgrim and Rogers (1999) have identified four key elements in the development of community care provision:

- fiscal crisis in post-1945 welfare provision, resulting in deinstitutionalization;

- the rise and dominance of drug and physical treatments;

- the influence of cost-effective considerations and concerns with evidence-based treatments;

- the rise and influence of user groups and civil liberty considerations in mental health policy and provision.

This has been paralleled by mental health legislation such as the 1983 Mental Health Act, which reduced the medical orientation of mental health services to incorporate increased emphasis upon individual rights, support services and social needs (Fennell, 1999). Ryan (1996) has expressed the history of mental health risk management in six stages, with distinct risk management strategies and sites of management (see Table 21.1).

Table 21.1   The history of risk management

Period	Risk management strategy	Risk management site
Middle Ages	Expulsion	Banishment and ships of fools
Enlightenment	Confinement	Private jails and madhouses
Victorian era	Incarceration	Asylums
Early twentieth century	Treatment	Psychiatric hospitals
Mid-twentieth century	Decarceration	Community
Late twentieth century	Integration	Community

Source: Ryan (1996: 101). Reproduced with the kind permission of Jessica Kingsley Publishers.

The Community Care Act 1990 was followed by a policy emphasis upon partnership and coordination of services epitomized by the 'Care Programme Approach' (CPA: Department of Health, 1990a), and practice guidance for care management (Department of Health, 1991). Care management and its predecessor, case management, were seen as essential techniques for adequately meeting client need and coordinating disparate resources into 'care packages' (Ryan et al., 1999). Case management was short-lived and focused upon the assessment and delivery of care in the community by health care professionals within a needs-led model (Onyett, 1992). Care management, with its emphasis upon developing and managing care packages, superseded the needs-led approach with service-led control of provision under the umbrella of the CPA. The 1990s saw the tensions between risks, needs and rights in mental health provision sharpen. Risk became central to decisions made by approved social workers to detain mentally ill persons compulsorily under the Mental Health Act 1983. Risk reduction also became central to assessment and provision under the CPA (Davis, 1996). However, as Davis (1996: 109–10) puts it,

Risk is ... emerging as a key but contested concern in the mental health field. It is being discussed in a climate in which political, professional, organisational and service users' interests and territories are being actively re-negotiated. It is thus important in considering risk work to take continuous account of the political, professional and resource interests that are influencing its development and direction.

Davis identifies two such developments: risk reduction and risk taking.

Risk reduction

The risk reduction approach has been fuelled by a series of high-profile mental health enquiries, such as Georgina Robinson (Blom-Cooper et al., 1995) and Christopher Clunis (Ritchie et al., 1994), which exposed flaws in the community care system to meet the care needs of the individuals concerned and to protect the public from risk. The CPA was introduced in 1991 to coordinate both assessment and interventions across a wide range of agencies and professionals, and risk, to both self and others, is seen as integral (Department of Health, 1994a). This was supported by the Blom-Cooper inquiry, which stressed the 'ongoing assessment of risk and risk-management, assuming that risk will change over time and can be managed effectively' (Blom-Cooper et al., 1995: 176). CPA also used risk to prioritize cases, using a tiered approach, comprising 'minimal', 'low support needs which are likely to remain stable' and 'complex' assessments for those whose needs are 'less likely to remain stable' (Davis, 1996). Resource-intensive multidisciplinary assessments are reserved for those individuals 'suffering from severe social dysfunction, whose needs are likely to be highly volatile, or who represent a significant risk' (Department of Health, 1994b). This has focused attention (and services) upon a small residential group of 'high-risk' individuals who are deemed to present a danger to the public. Provision has been skewed towards the identification, assessment, registration and surveillance of this group, and as 'a consequence it fails to engage adequately with the issues of risk as they affect the majority of service users' (Davis 1996: 113).

Risk taking

Risk taking has its roots in user empowerment, service user involvement and anti-oppressive mental health practice, and is seen as a necessary part of life and a right of mental health users (Braye and Preston-Shoot, 1995). Normalization rather than risk reduction is a key feature of this approach, and risk is seen as integral to autonomy, quality of life and citizenship (Ramon, 1991; Brown and Smith, 1992). This approach is underpinned by radical values of empowerment and structural change:

> On the one hand are values located in a long tradition of social care. These urge practitioners to 'treat people better' in the context of allotted roles and place in the social structure. On the other hand are values calling for radical change to, and renegotiation of, existing roles and social structures, to create a fairer society. Thus the traditional agenda is to bring about the adjustment of service users to existing conditions in society, a focus on personal problems. The radical agenda emphasises the structural context in which problems are produced and reproduced. (Braye and Preston-Shoot, 1995: 35–6)

Risk taking is often advocated by user groups, and is used to challenge the oppressive or restraining practices of professionals. It can thereby form an important limit to risk reduction as the bases of decisions to limit rights or choices have to be explicit and competing risks and rights have to be balanced (MIND, 1986; Carson, 1988; 1990; 1994; 1996). It has also been seen as essential to the reduction of stigma, dependency and over-protectiveness, a common feature in the lives of the mentally ill (Barham and Hayward, 1991). However, while community care and risk taking have emphasized client needs and rights, in reality mental health risks have been increasingly negatively defined and community care has become focused on how to increase compliance with community treatments and surveillance (Ryan, 1996). Mental health is now dominated by concerns with low-frequency/high-impact risks of homicide and suicide, with the high-frequency/low-impact risks faced by users in their daily lives largely neglected (Ryan, 2000).

Summary

Deinstitutionalization and the shift to community care have sharpened attention to risk, particularly in assessment and resource provision. However, risk is a 'contested' area in which risk reduction and risk taking can be at odds, and the user's right to take risks is dominated by professional views of risk reduction. Community care has become occupied with risk avoidance and risk management, resulting in a largely negative view of user risks and a deprioritizing of user rights.

Mental health risks in the risk society

Frank Furedi (1997: 4) has argued that the 'evaluation of everything from the perspective of safety is a defining characteristic of contemporary society'. This 'worship of safety' is a key characteristic of life in the risk society, focusing attention on 'hazards' and 'threat' and prudent responses to them. As Furedi (1997: 4–5) puts it, 'By turning risk into an autonomous, omnipresent force in this way, we transform every human experience into a safety situation.' Human activity is characterized by risk aversion, and risk regulation is characterized by the 'precautionary principle'. Paradoxically this can lead us to over-perceive risks and to be fearful even in conditions of comparative safety. Media inflation of risks (Kitzinger, 1999) and a lack of 'lay' trust in expert systems to regulate risks have exacerbated this. Mental health risks are no exception. The Mental Health Advisory Committee to the National Association for the Care and Resettlement of Offenders (NACRO) noted that while community care had 'placed the public at a slightly greater risk' this was not because the risks presented by mentally ill people were unacceptably high, but was due to failures in the system and the resource-led rather than needs-led nature of provision (NACRO, 1998: 48). Mental health risk management failures have also heightened public and policy-makers' views that professional work with this group requires increased regulation and accountability (Sheppard, 1996). Professional decision-making also takes place in a climate of blame, and exhortations to 'defensible decisions' abound (Carson, 1996). Blame serves to strengthen accountability, but also subtly to control information flow and usage, and to reinforce loyalty and solidarity with particular viewpoints on risk: 'News that is going to be accepted as true information has to be wearing a badge of loyalty to the particular political regime which the person supports; the rest is suspect, deliberately censored or unconsciously ignored' (Douglas, 1992: 19). In mental health practice this can result in the legitimization of professional views on risk at the expense of user or carer views. Competing views of risk result, not least between 'lay' public and experts. The subjectivity of risk assessment is now largely accepted (Royal Society Study Group, 1992), but the responsibility of professionals to make the 'right decision' is emphasized by the power of hindsight bias. While the position on practitioner liability is less clear in the UK, cases such as *W* v. *Edgell* (1990) have clearly indicated that professionals should err on the side of public protection (Prins, 1999). Professionals are also charged with deciding acceptable risk, a difficult task in an era of competing perspectives and values on risk.

Mental health has also long been a site of contested concepts, diagnoses, taxonomies and interventions, as evidenced by contemporary histories of insanity and psychiatry (Shorter, 1997; Melling and Forsythe, 1999) and historical sociological analyses of madness and its management (Scull, 1979). As Table 21.1 indicates, definitions of, and responses to, mental disorder are also products of their time. Based upon detailed historical research, Scull has argued that the development of the Victorian asylum owes much to the weakening of community ties and traditional management techniques of mental disorder by the modernization of economic life and labour relations. The 'social casualties' of the emerging modern market environment were dealt with through institutionalization, and the purpose of such asylums was to

model social behaviour around the norms of rational bourgeois expectations. Damaged human capital was repaired and worthless labour was warehoused in the corridors and buildings which quickly became museums filled with lifeless artefacts of humanity. (Melling, 1999: 3)

The 'history of madness' has been characterized as a complex interaction between labour regulation, penal regulation and the development of medical practices to discipline the population (Foucault, 1965), key intersections in the modernization process (Melling, 1999). (It is beyond the scope of this chapter to present a full overview of the 'history of madness'. For further information, and at times competing views, see Foucault, 1965; Scull, 1979; and Melling and Forsythe, 1999.) While such historical constructions are themselves often contested, what is clear is that mental health has long association with the process of modernization and the problem of order. As Harris (1990: 10) puts it, 'Looking at how we comprehend the seemingly irrational few tells us how we comprehend, without even thinking about them, the taken-for-granted seemingly rational many.' Mental disorder is therefore always defined with reference to an often unspoken and implicit norm. Defining mental health, especially as 'risky', is also central to the identification and solidarity of the included, as well as the exclusion of the 'other' (Douglas, 1992). While the asylums have closed, the mentally ill are still with us and have become a site of control and public protection (Bartlett, 1997).

Mental health and social order

Bartlett has argued that the legacy of the asylum runs deep, and is still the defining metaphor of mental health care today.

As Porter (1987: 35) has expressed it, we have a 'deep disposition to see madness as essentially Other'. This is not merely a matter of management or the administration of key services, it defines 'the terms on which people with mental illness are to be accepted in social life' (Bartlett, 1997: xiii). The role of mental health provision and its attendant discipline psychiatry in defining the excluded and alienated other against a rational norm has been well argued:

> Society has progressively defined itself as rational and normal, and by doing so has sanctioned the stigmatizing and exclusion of 'outsiders' and 'aliens'. And the particular device for the walled and locked asylum – which after all ended up housing far larger populations than did prisons – backed by the medical speciality of institutional psychiatry ... underscored the differentness, the uniqueness, of those thus 'alienated' and 'excluded'. (Porter, 1987: 25)

Thus processes of deinstitutionalization can themselves stigmatize and dehumanize, and mentally ill persons in the community can find themselves both alienated and socially isolated.

From mental patient to mental health care

The deinstitutionalization movement gathered pace by the 1960s, and institutional psychiatry was increasingly replaced by the notion of the 'therapeutic community', in which hospitals would provide brief respite and short-term treatment before reintegrating the patient into the community. Significantly, this reintegration was not based upon any acceptance of difference or counteraction of exclusion, but was aimed at abolishing difference through treatments that would normalize (Bartlett, 1997). Patients would accommodate to their environments through the use of drug treatment and medication. For Bartlett, this rendered the community or environment a neutral venue, not a site of dispute, conflict, risk or threat to patients, merely a place to which they could be returned. Social sites would not require management, but individual patients would, and drug regimes, particularly administered through outpatients clinics, fitted the bill. While psychiatry managed to throw off its institutional custodial function, this function was subtly relocated to the community. The long-term and often immutable label 'mental patient' was replaced with the more provisional label 'mentally ill person' (Bartlett,

1997), and in the case management language of the Community Care Programme the person became a 'mental health case'.

Community care provision for the mentally ill has been subject to the same limits of resource constraint and selectivism as other areas of the personal social services. Paradoxically, this has resulted in the invisibility of the majority of mentally ill persons and increased attention to the identification and regulation of a few high-risk cases. This trend is compounded by the tiered priorities for intervention and provision under the CPA, in which instability, significant risk and severe social dysfunction are essential criteria for intensive services. The Mental Health Foundation, in a report on community care provision for severe mental illness, has estimated that there are some 300,000 people with severe mental illness in England and Wales, but the report acknowledges that defining the term 'severe mental illness' is problematic, and conditions change (Mental Health Foundation, 1994). This difficulty is exacerbated by mental health legislation that has traditionally defined mental illness and provided various taxonomies of illness to assist with compulsory admissions and detentions. Such legal definitions of mental illness have a limited role in classifying mental illness when its management is displaced to the community.

The invisibility of mentally ill persons not only prevents appropriate access to services, it also compounds their vulnerability. The vulnerabilities and risks of the asylum are merely displaced to the community, with ex-patients suffering abuse, poverty and social isolation (Bartlett, 1997). The inadequacy of community care services to respond to this group was highlighted in various reports, with the National Schizophrenia Fellowship (1989) using the metaphor of 'Slipping through the net' to describe the problem. Such 'nets of care' come under scrutiny when they are deemed to have failed, and the invisibility of the majority is brought into sharp contrast with the minority who become the subject of inquiries. While the 1975 White Paper *Better Services for the Mentally Ill* (DHSS, 1975) had accepted that the majority of mentally ill people were not especially dangerous and could therefore be appropriately managed in the community, the inquiries of the 1990s in particular focused attention on the few for whom, with hindsight, community care was deemed inappropriate. The Butler Committee in 1975 had attempted to define and introduce a two-tier system of mental health care, with the high-risk minority being selected out for secure hospital accommodation (Home Office and DHSS, 1975). This, and the Glancy report (DHSS, 1974), established the system of special hospitals and regional secure units for the 'dangerously' mentally ill. However, as the more recent Nacro review makes clear, the underlying assumption that it would be possible to identify and separate high- from low-risk patients was misplaced, and reliable risk assessment tools have been illusive (Nacro, 1998; Prins, 1999).

Mental health inquiries and the failure of community care

A major impetus in the move to community care was to ensure greater and more relevant provision for the mentally ill from health and social services, epitomized by the document *Better Services for the Mentally Ill*. Central to government policy on mental health was the introduction of the CPA in 1990 (Department of Health, 1990a; b). The CPA emphasized assessment, a care plan, an allocated key worker for each case and regular review of progress. The CPA represented an acknowledgement that the principles of community care following hospital closures required tighter structures and systems for their delivery. However, resources remained a key issue in the adequate delivery of the CPA (Davis, 1996; Ryan, 1996). Disquiet about the adequate management of mentally ill persons in the community was fuelled by what Grounds (1996) refers to as a new generation of inquiry reports from the late 1980s onwards, in which the focus of attention was homicides perpetrated by mentally ill persons. These reports attracted greater media attention and public disquiet than their predecessors, which had focused on the abuse of patients in psychiatric institutions. The most notable of these were Christopher Clunis (Ritchie et al., 1994), Andrew Robinson (Blom-Cooper, 1996) and the two overviews of inquiries prepared by Sheppard (1997; 1998). The inquiries highlighted specific procedural and systems failures in the care of dangerous and violent mentally ill persons in the community.

The reports highlighted the following:

- inadequate coordination and poor communication between professionals and agencies;
- lack of appropriate resources, including secure beds as well as community provision;
- the need for special supervision arrangements;
- inadequate information sharing and recording;
- inadequate and unreliable assessment of risk and violent behaviour;
- lack of cooperation between agencies;
- patients' rights required greater attention, in particular the right to have their needs met, and to express their needs, wishes and choices;
- legislation required attention, in particular for supervision on discharge from hospital and for compulsory treatment and supervision in the community

(adapted from Nacro, 1998: 24; Sheppard 1997; 1998)

The cumulative impact of the inquiry recommendations and their attendant publicity subtly moved the mental health agenda from care to management, and from treatment and rehabilitation to control and surveillance. Risk and protection began to dominate the mental health policy agenda (Grounds, 1996).

This is evidenced by:

- specific policy development and practice guidance on mental health management of high-risk cases in the community and the development of compulsory community care;

- the increased attention to mentally disordered offenders;

- the development of preventative detention for high-risk cases.

Summary

Risk avoidance and the 'worship of safety' are key features of mental health policy. The 'history of madness' has been characterized as a history of social regulation and normalization of the 'other', in which segregation, surveillance and control of the mentally ill are central. The metaphoric segregation of the asylum is still pervasive in the constitution of community care, with social control functions transferred from asylum to community. Deinstitutionalization is not characterized by reintegration, but by the invisibility of 'low-risk cases' on the one hand and extensive management of more risky individuals on the other, resulting in a two-tier system of mental health provision. Individualization through individual targeting shifts attention from structural issues and social site management to regulating the behaviours of individuals and compensating for any lack of prudentialism or risk management. Responsibility for risk is firmly individual, either of the worker or patient-worker for failing to manage it effectively, or of patients for failing to comply with risk management strategies. The failure of such strategies inevitably attracts public and media attention, and community care has been subject to regular and notorious public inquiries on its shortcomings.

References

Barham, P. and Hayward, R. (1991) *From Mental Patient to Person*. London: Routledge.

Bartlett, P. (1997) *Closing the Asylum: The Mental Patient in Modern Society*, 2nd edn. Harmondsworth: Penguin.

Bartlett, P. and Wright, D. (1999) *Outside the Walls of the Asylum: The History of Care in the Community 1730–2000*. London: Athlone.

Blom-Cooper, L. (1996) *The Case of Jason Mitchell: Report of the Independent Panel of Inquiry*. London: Duckworth.

Blom-Cooper, L., Hally, H. and Murphy, E. (1995) *The Falling Shadow: One Patient's Mental Health Care 1978–1993*. London: Gerald Duckworth & Co.

Braye, S. and Preston-Shoot, M. (1995) *Empowering Practice in Social Care*. Buckingham: Open University Press.

Brown, H. and Smith, H. (1992) *Normalisation: A Reader for the Nineties*. London: Routledge.

Carpenter, M. (2000) ' "It's a small world": mental health policy under welfare capitalism since 1945', *Sociology of Health and Illness*, 22(5), 602–20.

Carson, D. (1988) 'Taking risks with your patients – your assessment strategy', *Professional Nurse*, 3(7), 247–50.

Carson, D. (1990) 'Risk-taking in mental disorder', in D. Carson (ed.) *Risk-taking in Mental Disorder: Analyses, Policies and Practical Strategies*. Chichester: SLE Publications.

Carson, D. (1994) 'Presenting risk options', *Inside Psychology*, 1(1), 3–7.

Carson, D. (1996) 'Risking legal repercussions', in H. Kemshall and J. Pritchard (eds) *Good Practice in Risk Assessment and Risk Management, Volume 1*. London: Jessica Kingsley Publishers.

Davis, A. (1996) 'Risk work and mental health', in H. Kemshall and J. Pritchard (eds) *Good Practice in Risk Assessment and Risk Management, Volume 1*. London: Jessica Kingsley Publishers.

Department of Health (1990a) *Community Care in the Next Decade and Beyond*. London: HMSO.

Department of Health (1990b) *The Care Programme Approach for People with a Severe Mental Illness Referred to the Specialist Psychiatric Services*. London: Department of Health.

Department of Health (1991) *Care Management and Assessment: Practitioners' Guide*. London: HMSO.

Department of Health (1994a) *Guidance on the Discharge of Mentally Disordered People and Their Continuing Care in the Community. Health Service Guidelines*. Local Authority Social Services Letter LASSL (94)4. London: Department of Health.

Department of Health (1994b) *Draft Guide to Arrangements for Inter-agency Working for Care and Protection of Severely Mentally Ill People*. London: Department of Health.

Department of Health and Social Security (1974) *Revised Report of the Working Party on Security in NHS Psychiatric Hospitals*. London: DHSS.

Department of Health and Social Security (1975) *Better Services for the Mentally Ill*. London: HMSO.

Douglas, M. (1992) *Risk and Blame: Essays in Cultural Theory*. London: Routledge.

Fennell, P. (1999) 'The third way in mental health policy: negative rights, positive rights, and the convention', *Journal of Law and Society*, 26(1), 103–27.

Foucault, M. (1965) *Madness and Civilization: The History of Insanity in the Age of Reason*. New York: Pantheon.

Furedi, F. (1997) *Culture of Fear: Risk-taking and the Morality of Low Expectation.* London: Cassell.

Grounds, A. (1996) *Psychiatry and Public Protection.* Public lecture, annual meeting, Mental Health Commission for Northern Ireland.

Harris, R. (1999) 'Mental disorder and social order: underlying themes in crime management', in D. Webb and R. Harris (eds) *Mentally Disordered Offenders: Managing People who Nobody Knows.* London: Routledge.

Home Office and Department of Health and Social Security (1975) *Committee on Mentally Abnormal Offenders (Butler Committee).* Home Office and Department of Health, Cmnd 6244. London: HMSO.

Kitzinger, J. (1999) 'Researching risk and the media', *Health Risk and Society*, 1(1), 55–70.

Melling, J. (1999) 'Accommodating madness: new research in the social history of insanity and institutions', in J. Melling and B. Forsythe (eds) *Insanity, Institutions and Society 1800–1914.* London: Routledge.

Melling, J. and Forsythe, B. (eds) (1999) *Insanity, Institutions and Society 1800–1914.* London: Routledge.

Mental Health Foundation (1994) *Creating Community Care: Report of the Mental Health Foundation Inquiry into Community Care for People with Severe Mental Illness.* London: Mental Health Foundation.

Mind (1986) *Finding Our Own Solutions.* London: Mind.

National Association for the Care and Resettlement of Offenders (Nacro) (1998) *Risk and Rights: Mentally Disturbed Offenders and Public Protection.* A report by Nacro's Mental Health Advisory Committee. London: Nacro.

National Schizophrenia Fellowship (1989) *Slipping Through the Net.* Kingston-upon-Thames: National Schizophrenia Fellowship.

Onyett, S. (1992) *Case Management in Mental Health.* London: Chapman Hall.

Pilgrim, D. and Rogers, A. (1999) 'Mental health policy and the politics of mental health: a three tier analytical framework', *Policy and Politics*, 27(1), 13–24.

Porter, R. (1987) *A Social History of Madness.* London: Weidenfeld & Nicolson.

Prins, H. (1999) *Will They Do It Again? Risk Assessment and Management in Criminal Justice and Psychiatry.* London: Routledge.

Ramon, S. (ed.) (1991) *Beyond Community Care: Normalisation and Integration Work.* London: Macmillan.

Ritchie, J., Dick, D. and Lingham, R. (1994) *Report of the Committee of Inquiry into the Care of Christopher Clunis.* London: Mind/COHSE.

Rose, N. (1985) *The Psychological Complex: Politics and Society in England 1869–1939.* London: Routledge & Kegan Paul.

Rose, N. (1986) 'Psychiatry: the discipline of mental health', in P. Miller and N. Rose (eds) *The Power of Psychiatry.* Cambridge: Polity Press.

Royal Society Study Group (1992) *Risk: Analysis, Perception and Management. Report of a Royal Society Study Group.* London: Royal Society.

Ryan, P., Ford, R., Beadsmore, A. and Muijen, M. (1999) 'The enduring relevance of case management'', *British Journal of Social Work*, 29, 97–125.

Ryan, T. (1996) 'Risk management and people with mental health problems', in H. Kemshall and J. Pritchard (eds) *Good Practice in Risk Assessment and Risk Management, Volume 1.* London: Jessica Kingsley Publishers.

Ryan, T. (2000) 'Exploring the risk management strategies of mental health service users', *Health, Risk and Society*, 2(3), 267–82.

Scull, A. (1979) *Museums of Madness.* London: Allen Lane.

Scull, A. (1993) 'Museums of madness revisited', *Social History of Madness*, 6(2), 3–23.

Sheppard, D. (1996) *Learning the Lessons: Mental Health Inquiry Reports Published in England and Wales between 1969 and 1994 and Their Recommendations for Improving Practice*, 2nd edn. London: Zito Trust.

Sheppard, D. (1997) *Mental Health Inquiries Published During 1997.* Institute of Mental Health Law, Internet publication.

Sheppard, D. (1998) *Mental Health Inquiries Published During 1998.* Institute of Mental Health Law, Internet publication.

Shorter, E. (1997) *A History of Psychiatry: From the Era of the Asylum to the Age of Prozac.* Chichester: John Wiley & Sons.

22

The challenge of shared care

Mike Flanagan

A survey of comorbid substance misuse among people with psychotic illness in a British suburban setting reported a prevalence of 33 per cent (Wright et al., 2000). These figures suggest that community mental health teams (CMHTs) have an important role to play in the holistic care of their client group. Appropriate interventions include harm reduction, early and brief interventions and systematic treatment for those with substance dependence and mental health problems (Pols et al., 1996). Unfortunately though, in many cases, there is reluctance on the part of CMHTs to become involved in the management of substance misuse by their patients. Unnithan et al. (1994) identified three areas of concern among general psychiatrists leading to a reluctance to address substance misuse in their patients:

1 *Role adequacy*: having the necessary information and skills in order to screen and provide appropriate treatment.
2 *Role legitimacy*: whether the management of substance misuse falls within their area of responsibility.
3 *Role support*: the confidence that there is adequate advice and back-up of specialist services.

The issue of dual diagnosis is very serious and causes profound problems for individuals, families and communities. It is now well understood that the misuse of drugs and/or alcohol by severely mentally ill people results in a poorer prognosis and may significantly increase the risk they pose to themselves or others. In this context, *Building Bridges: a guide to arrangements for inter-agency working for the care and protection of severely mentally ill*

Edited from M. Flanagan, Chapter 7 in G.H. Rassool (ed.) (2002), *Dual Diagnosis*, Oxford, Blackwell, pp. 97–107.

people (Department of Health, 1996) was published. This document makes explicit the need for close links between CMHTs and CDATs to be maintained at provider level to ensure that care is properly coordinated.

Utilising such an approach makes clear the individual professional's responsibilities in the overall care plan. Multidisciplinary and multi-agency communication through participation at care planning and review meetings and circulation of the CPA documentation ensures coordination of care. While these arrangements can enhance shared care in theory, in practice philosophical differences and conflict between clinicians and teams will undermine them. The nature of these problems and strategies to assist in overcoming them will be set out. In the case of patients with severe mental illness, the key worker will normally be from the CMHT. The nature and timing of input from the CDAT can be discussed and agreed within the care planning meeting. Such an approach needs to be designed in a flexible, patient centred rather than programme centred way. The interventions need to be tailored to the individual patient's needs. Drake et al. (1993) described nine principles in the treatment of drug misuse in the severely mentally ill. They are:

1 Assertive outreach
2 Close monitoring
3 Integration (or collaborative shared care)
4 Comprehensiveness
5 Stable living situation
6 Flexibility
7 Stage-wise treatment
8 Longitudinal perspective
9 Optimism.

These principles are sensitive to the fact that the severely mentally ill do not identify substance misuse problems and seek help in the way expected of others. They do not respond well to traditional addictions services which put the emphasis on motivation to engage and remain in treatment. While Drake and colleagues developed these ideas as the principles that underpin integrated treatment teams, they are equally applicable as principles to guide practice delivered through simultaneous, coordinated delivery of interventions by more than one team. All of the principles are within the scope of combined efforts but the key to success lies in effective joint working, communication and a shared vision.

Problems with inter-agency collaboration

There are many reasons why historically CMHTs and CDATs have not formed effective partnerships. Wallen and Weiner (1989) identified a number of impediments to a collaborative approach by CMHTs. These include the premature diagnosis of a psychiatric disorder based on the behavioural symptoms of substance misuse, ignorance, fear and a lack of knowledge of chemical dependency and simplistic approaches (for example, 'just say no'). However, Gafoor and Rassool (1998) point out that mental health nurses do possess the core therapeutic skills to work with substance misusers. But they may be reluctant to intervene due to low confidence in their ability to facilitate change in their client's substance use or they may hold negative views towards the outcome of their interventions.

Further reasons why closer cooperation between mental health and substance misuse teams is difficult are because they are often functionally, administratively and geographically separated (Kavanagh et al., 2000). The two systems operate with different treatment philosophies. Though many professionals within the substance misuse treatment setting have a background in psychiatry, their professional lives often diverge from their counterparts in adult general psychiatry (Allen and Gerace, 1996). The emotive response to substance misuse occasionally encountered by some in adult psychiatry becomes a further impediment. Despite both disorders being viewed as aetiologically multifactorial, it is rare for a person with a mental health problem to be viewed as having 'brought it on themself', but this has been the response to inaction on the part of clinicians when substance misuse is encountered.

Even in cases where both teams become concurrently involved in the care of an individual patient, each clinician's treatment outcome expectation can be a barrier to effective treatment. Abstinence may be perceived as the only desirable outcome by the CMHT, and the CDAT may take the view they can only intervene if the psychiatric symptomatology is absent. Clearly, for concurrent treatment to take place there needs to be dialogue and agreement that a reduction/change in use of substances is the appropriate way forward, and abstinence, however, desirable, may not be realistic. A reduction in the use of substances may improve psychiatric symptomatology directly or increase treatment compliance. Even so, psychosocial interventions for patients in the precontemplative phase of the cycle of change, including cognitive therapy (such as motivational interviewing) can be incorporated into the treatment of patients suffering from psychotic illness and substance misuse (Swanson et al., 1999). In this way, a more realistic appraisal of treatment outcome expectation can enable a symbiotic approach from each service.

Overcoming the barriers

Those working in the field will probably be only too familiar with the tendency to lack of cooperation and partnership working between substance misuse services and mental health teams. There is a pressing need for a greater recognition of psychiatric problems and comorbidity by all professionals, both specialist and generic (Gilvary, 1998).

In the long term, to undermine this polarised response to issues of comorbidity, the whole issue of the misuse of substances needs to be integrated far more extensively into the undergraduate and postgraduate training programmes of mental health professionals (Crome, 1999; Royal College of Psychiatrists, 2000). There also needs to be a concerted research programme to determine the most effective model of service delivery before considerable investment is made in a model driven by expediency rather than by an evidence base (Weaver et al., 1999). In the short and medium term, due to the problems described, existing services must be enabled to meet the demands and find ways to work together. Ideally, mental health teams would manage the misuse of substances by their patients and substance misuse teams would address the mental health problems manifested by their patients. However in the real world, the dynamic nature of these inter-related problems, on a continuum of severity, means that at times, a particularly specialist collaborative response is called for.

Much has been written about ineffective collaborative interventions for dual diagnosis. Rodgers (1994) states, 'to pursue and achieve interprofessional collaboration, professionals need to value their sense of worth and relinquish defensiveness'. In order to realise this statement, CMHT staff and CDAT staff need first to be clear about their role and second to be clear about the role of others.

Local strategies to develop new systems

Organising existing service structures to respond to the needs of those with comorbid problems in a timely manner can be achieved in several ways. First there can be an encouragement of arrangements for members of both the substances misuse team and mental health team to develop a particular interest in the issue of comorbidity and act as a liaison between teams. The training of these individuals can be focused in such a way so they become a source of information and supervision for their colleagues. Furthermore they can link with their counterpart in the opposite team and collaborate when people with comorbid problems are referred to their teams. In this way, professionals can work beyond agency boundaries and form 'logical teams' defined by the professionals and workers on the patient's care plan or CPA documentation and not solely by the agency structure. The adoption of more flexible, whole systems ways of working, operating across organisational boundaries, is alien to traditional bureaucratic practice endemic in so many statutory services. Problems often occur in the context of a history of conflict, and a culture of silence or antagonism can result. The response to this situation may be from a managerial or 'shop floor' level but the latter may be more effective. A will to alter the situation at some level is the only prerequisite for change. This may have to come from a managerial or senior level within one of the disciplines. Strategies to address such difficulties have been described in texts on working with diversity within whole systems approaches (Pratt et al., 1999). The driver for change needs to come from the manipulation of key individuals within the whole system (for example, the NHS Trust). Barriers to collaboration are as much about an organisational as practitioner culture (Trevillion, 1995). Change results from supporting new connections between people to challenge and influence a maladaptive situation through the development of a counterculture. The mix of people within such a group should include carefully identified change agents (Pratt et al., 1999):

- different levels of clinicians from both teams and from within the organisation
- people who know how 'to connect' and are interested in doing things differently (some of whom may be 'troublesome')
- the sort of people whose support makes it likely that others will follow.

Bringing together groups of such people within an organisation, with the aim of analysing the problems with interteam collaboration and exploring how shared care for dual diagnosis can be approached is the first step in the management of change.

Conclusion

The issue of dual diagnosis is one of the most pressing issues presently facing the fields of substance misuse and mental health. It is being poorly addressed in most localities, and there are examples of reluctance on the part of some clinicians to become more involved. The challenge is therefore how to enable existing services to address dual diagnosis more effectively through a sharing of knowledge, skills and patient care. Training is central to the long-term strategy to overcome the problems in service delivery for this group. Curriculum planners need to incorporate content on dual diagnosis into undergraduate and postgraduate training programmes in the caring professions. At a local level there need to be programmes of reciprocal training between teams coordinated by clinicians with an interest and training in the issue of dual diagnosis. Where there is resistance to collaboration between teams, organisations have a responsibility to address this comprehensively. Team resistance needs to be addressed through change management strategies, identifying the change agents and altering the mix of individuals within teams. However, the organisational culture may be at the root of the problem. Resistance by individuals needs to be addressed through training and clinical supervision. The development of informal link/liaison roles between CMHTs and CDATs can assist in enabling interteam communication by providing a point of contact for clinicians from each team. These individuals can act as a source of information and supervision for colleagues, ensuring they are not seen as the 'dual diagnosis worker' for the team.

References

Allen, K.M. and Gerace, L.M. (1996) 'Psychiatric nursing', in K.M. Allen (ed.) *Nursing Care of the Addicted Client*. Philadelphia: Lippincott-Raven.

Crome, I.B. (1999) 'The trouble with training: substance misuse training in British medical schools revisited. What are the issues?' *Drugs: Education, Prevention and Policy*, 6, 111–23.

Department of Health (1996) *Building Bridges: a guide to arrangements for interagency working for the care and protection of severely mentally ill people*. Wetherby: Department of Health.

Department of Health (1999) *Safer Services: National Confidential Inquiry into Suicide and Homicide by People with Mental Illness*. London: Department of Health.

Drake, R.E., Bartels, S.J., Teagues, G.B., Noordsy, D.L. and Clark, R.E. (1993) 'Treatment of substance abuse in severely mentally ill patients'. *Journal of Nervous and Mental Disease*, 181, 606–11.

Gafoor, M. and Rassool, G. Hussein (1998) 'The co-existence of psychiatric disorders and substance misuse: working with dual diagnosis patients'. *Journal of Advanced Nursing*, 27, 497–502.

Gilvary, E. (1998) 'Psychiatric perspective: relationships between psychiatric and psychological disorders and symptomatology', in: R. Robertson (ed.) *Management of Drug Users in the Community*. London: Arnold.

Kavanagh, D.J., Greenaway, L., Jenner, L., Saunders, J.B., White, A., Sorban, J. and Hamilton, G. (2000) 'Contrasting views and experiences of health professionals on the management of comorbid substance misuse and mental disorders'. *Australian and New Zealand Journal of Psychiatry*, 34, 279–89.

Pols, R.G., Sellman, D., Jurd, S. Baigent, M., Waddy, N., Sacks, T., Tucker, P., Fowler, J. and White, A. (1996) 'What is the psychiatrist's role in drugs and alcohol?' *Australian and New Zealand Journal of Psychiatry*, 30 (4), 540–8.

Pratt, J., Gordon, P. and Plamping, D. (1999) *Working Whole Systems. Putting Theory into Practice in Organisations*. London: King's Fund.

Rodgers, J. (1994) 'Collaboration among health professionals'. *Nursing Standard*, 9 (6), 25–6.

Royal College of Psychiatrists (2000) *Drugs: Dilemmas and Choices*. Gaskell, London.

Swanson, A.J., Pantalon, M.V. and Cohen, K.R. (1999) 'Motivational interviewing and treatment adherence among psychiatric and dually diagnosed patients'. *Journal of Nervous and Mental Disease*, 87 (10) 630–5.

Trevillion, S. (1995) 'Competence to collaborate'. *CAIPE Bulletin*, 10, 6.

Unnithan, S., Ritson, B. and Strang, J. (1994) 'Organising treatment services for drug and alcohol misusers', in: J. Chick and R. Cantwell (eds) *Seminars in Alcohol and Drug Misusers*. pp. 223–38. London: Gaskell.

Wallen, M. and Weiner, H. (1989) 'The dually diagnosed patient in an in patient chemical dependency treatment program'. *Alcoholism Treatment Quarterly*, 5 (1/2), 197–218.

Weaver, T., Renton, A., Stimson, G. and Tyrer, P. (1999) 'Severe mental illness and substance misuse'. *British Medical Journal*, 318, 137–8.

Wright, S., Gournay, K., Glomey, E. and Thornicroft, G. (2000) 'Dual diagnosis in the suburbs: prevalence, need and in-patient service use'. *Social Psychiatry and Psychiatric Epidemiology*, 35 (7), 297–304.

23

Black communities, mental health and the criminal justice system

Deryck Browne

Introduction

Despite various policy initiatives in recent years, little progress has been made in tackling this important subject. Home Office statistics have consistently borne out the discrimination experienced by black people who come into contact with criminal justice agencies and the Department of Health has admitted that there is an undue emphasis on coercive models of treatment for black mental health patients, with organisational requirements often taking precedence over their individual needs (DH, 2003a). Figures show that black people are increasingly over-represented at each heightened level of security in the psychiatric process from informal to civil detention, and then in detention on forensic sections within the courts and criminal justice system (Cope, 1989). Moreover, the fact that there are such high numbers of black people coming into criminal justice settings, coupled with the discrimination they experience once there, result in the criminal justice system often acting as a gateway to the mental health system for many black offenders. Indeed recent figures show that black communities are over 40 per cent more likely than average to be referred to mental health services through the criminal justice system (Healthcare Commission, 2007).

Edited extract from *Nacro Mental Health and Crime Briefing* (2007).

The criminal justice system

Discrimination from criminal justice agencies

Home Office statistics produced annually under section 95 of the Criminal Justice Act 1991 reveal the extent of the disproportionate involvement of black people with criminal justice agencies as suspects, defendants and prisoners. To fully appreciate the implications of the following figures, it should be remembered that of the population in England and Wales, just 1.1 per cent are Black Caribbean, 0.9 per cent are Black African and 0.2 per cent are from other black groups (Office for National Statistics, 2003).

In addition, higher proportions of black people (particularly young people) were likely to be stopped by police, arrested and once arrested, less likely to be cautioned. Similarly, black people were more likely to be remanded in custody, more likely to plead not guilty and where found guilty they were also more likely to receive longer custodial sentences than their white contemporaries (Fitzgerald, 1993). Even before coming to trial, an analysis of 13,000 case files carried out by the Crown Prosecution Service found that there were more likely to be objections to bail for black males than for white males (John, 2003). Figures such as this reveal that black communities are over-represented at each stage of the criminal justice process from initial contact right through to sentencing.

Gender

Given that there are higher rates of black women in prisons than men, and that there is a higher incidence of black women within psychiatric care than white women, it is concerning that examination of the needs of black female mentally disordered offenders is so conspicuously absent from research literature and policy initiatives. In June 2004, the percentage of foreign national women in prison made up 25 per cent of the female prison population. Notably, over 50 per cent of female foreign national prisoners were from Jamaica with over 90 per cent of these receiving custodial sentences for drug importation (HM Inspectorate of Prisons, 2005). Usually minor players in considerably larger operations, these women undergo the trauma of separation from family, children and their homeland for what are often very lengthy periods, which is bound to have a debilitating effect on their mental health.

Immigration and asylum

Indeed foreign nationals make up one third of all prisoners who are either black or minority ethnic (Reza and Magill, 2006). The proportion of foreign nationals amongst the number of black mentally disordered offenders is likely to increase further in future, given the introduction of the Asylum and immigration Act 2004 which has, for the first time, made it a criminal offence for someone to enter the UK who does not have a passport or who has destroyed travel documents or who, once within the UK, refuses to co-operate with arrangements for their removal. Those claiming asylum or refugee status are likely to have undergone considerable mental stress and trauma and, if this is not effectively addressed, the trauma of the asylum experience could potentially bring to the surface any latent distress they may have experienced previously (Baluchi, 1999).

Resettlement

Discrimination experienced within the criminal justice system is compounded for many black people by difficulties they encounter following release. A 2005 study by Nacro found that black prisoners are less likely than their white counterparts to seek out resettlement services based within prisons (Nacro, 2005). Where black prisoners experience problems shared by the general prison population such as drug or alcohol dependency, family breakdown or poverty, their impact is further compounded by racism in its various forms which will intensify the difficulties they face in being resettled upon release (Nacro, 2005). For example, while homelessness is a problem for many groups, a disproportionate number of black households figure in the homelessness registers of local authorities and historically discrimination against black people has played a part in the allocation of housing stock (Housing Corporation, 1998). The result is that black offenders can end up being excluded and marginalised from mainstream society at a vulnerable time in their lives, which is likely to aggravate any mental health problems present or even lead to their onset.

The mental health system

Routes of referral

It has been found that black people are more likely than white people to experience 'an aversive pathway into mental health services' by means of higher compulsory admission rates to hospital, greater involvement in legal and forensic settings, and higher rates of transfer to medium and high security facilities (DH, 2003b). Research into decision-making in the criminal justice system has shown that professionals often more readily associate black defendants with a sense of danger. One study on black people and the courts, during which a series of interviews was conducted with criminal justice officials including magistrates and probation officers, found that they are 'more likely to err on the side of caution with black mentally vulnerable defendants and to be affected by a heightened perception of dangerousness' (Nacro, 1990). Another study into the operation of the civil sections of the Mental Health Act 1983 (MHA) found too that police officers are prone to associating black people with risk factors (Browne, 1997), with the result that black people are more likely to be detained by police under Section 136 of the MHA and taken to a 'place of safety' within the meaning of the Act – often a psychiatric hospital – thereby opening that channel into the psychiatric services. In 2008 the Independent Police Complaints Commission carried out research which for the first time examined national data on the use of section 136 by all 43 police forces in England and Wales. This showed that the rate of detention for black people, when compared to the general population, was almost twice as high as that for white people (Docking et al., 2008).

The Healthcare Commission census of the same year which looked at 34,000 mental health patients found that black people are in fact 44 per cent more likely to be detained under the MHA than average (Healthcare Commission, 2005). This is largely due to higher than average detention rates under section 37/41 of the MHA, where a person is sent to hospital for treatment via the courts under a restriction order by the Home Office (Healthcare Commission, 2007). Indeed black patients have been found to be almost twice as likely to be referred for treatment via the courts (Healthcare Commission, 2005). Similarly, a study by Nacro established that black people appearing before magistrates were more likely to be remanded in custody for psychiatric assessments and for longer than their white contemporaries, with black defendants also more likely than white defendants to be made subject to hospital orders and psychiatric probation orders. The study concluded that the criminal justice system is one of the key pathways via which black as well as minority ethnic groups enter the psychiatric system, particularly younger black men (Nacro, 1990).

Prison in particular acts as a common point of referral to mental health services for black people, with black prisoners more likely than white counterparts to be referred from prison establishments to psychiatric units (Prins et al., 1993). Cope and Ndegwa (1990) found too in a comparison of white and black patients admitted to a regional secure unit, that black people were significantly more likely to be referred from the prison system while on remand, whereas white patients were more likely to be admitted from the NHS or special hospitals.

Treatment and care

Once within the mental health system, the overwhelming evidence is that black patients' experiences are more negative than those of white patients. Racism, cultural ignorance and stereotypical views can often combine with the stigma and anxiety associated with mental illness to undermine the ways in which mental health services respond to black communities, affecting decisions about treatment, medication and restriction. NIMHE has noted the disproportionately high rate of schizophrenia diagnosed among black mental health patients and the fact that black patients generally remain in hospital on a section for longer than their white contemporaries (DH, 2003a).

The fact that there are disproportionate numbers of black people coming into the mental health services from a criminal justice context means that this group of mentally disordered offenders is often viewed by staff as presenting an increased security risk compared to that posed by other groups. A study into decision-making in the mental health sectioning process showed professionals made a strong link between black patients and a notion of heightened risk (Browne, 1997), with the result that additional safety precautions were frequently seen as necessary. For example approved social workers (who play a key role in the civil sectioning process) are more likely to request a police presence when taking a black patient to hospital. Prins et al. (1993) whose inquiry examined the treatment of black mentally disordered offenders found they are also more likely to be detained in the locked wards of psychiatric hospitals and more likely to be transferred to higher security facilities (and for longer) than white patients.

NIMHE has also found there is a greater likelihood of the use of coercive treatments for black patients than white (DH, 2003a). Figures for 2005 show that black patients are more likely to experience physical seclusion and restraint than other groups (Healthcare Commission, 2005), with the most recent figures for 2006 revealing a particularly high rate of hands-on restraint for this group (Healthcare Commission, 2007). Set against this backdrop, it is perhaps unsurprising that black patients are also less likely to receive benign forms of psychotherapeutic treatment such as psychotherapy and counselling than their white counterparts and more likely to receive higher doses of medication, being 'often subjected to heavy doses of drug cocktails which has led to deaths in HM prisons and special hospitals' (Prins et al., 1993).

Following the publication of the report into the death of David Bennett (Norfolk, Suffolk and Cambridgeshire Health Authority, 2003), there has been increasing debate about separate services for ethnic minorities in general psychiatry and in some parts of the USA, separate in-patient services have been developed (Bhui and Sashidharan, 2003). It has been argued that separate services might better serve black, as well as other minority ethnic, patients and there might perhaps be increased emphasis on communicating (between patient and practitioner) in a culturally informed way (Lyall, 2005). The counter-argument is that the creation of separate services risks the development of a division between those professionals who 'know' how to treat and care for patients from minority groups, and those who 'do not know'. The creation of separate services would appear to be an admission of failure, not only of the current system's ability to provide adequate support and training within existing psychiatric services, but also of its ability to address the fundamental question of why black patients, and especially black mentally disordered offenders, are treated differently to white people in psychiatry.

Conclusion

There is clearly a continued need for government departments and criminal justice and mental health agencies to tackle the many difficult issues that persist in the relationship between black communities, criminal justice and psychiatry. The key strategy documents of recent years have added little of substance to the material produced in the last two decades and many have avoided the focus of black mentally disordered offenders altogether. There is also a need for a concerted and inclusive strategy towards black and minority ethnic mentally disordered offenders which cohesively tackles the particular problems they experience in areas such as immigration, asylum and resettlement. Given that the criminal justice system can act as a gateway to the mental health system, the need for comprehensive action that reforms both systems is all the more pressing, The danger, if this does not happen, is that policymakers in this field will find themselves perpetually addressing the symptoms rather than the causes of these inequalities.

References

Baluchi, B. (1999) *Beyond Urgent: Towards a Strategy for Refugee Health.* London: Kimia Institute.

Bhui, K. and Sashidharan, S.P. (2003) 'Should there be separate psychiatric services for ethnic minority groups?' *British Journal of Psychiatry*, 182, pp. 10–12.

Browne, D. (1997) *Black People and Sectioning: The Black Experience of Detention Under the Civil Sections of the Mental Health Act.* London: Little Rock Publishing.

Cope, R. (1989) 'The compulsory detention of Afro-Caribbeans under the Mental Health Act'. *New Community*, 15 (3), pp. 343–56.

Cope, R. and Ndegwa, D. (1990) 'Ethnic differences in admissions to a regional secure unit'. *Journal of Forensic Psychiatry*, 1 (3), pp. 365–78.

Department of Health (2003a). *Inside Outside: Improving Mental Health Services for Black and Minority Ethnic Communities in England.* London: Department of Health.

Department of Health (2003b) *Delivering Race Equality – A Framework for Action: Mental Health Services Consultation Document.* London: Department of Health.

Docking, M., Grace, K. and Buckle, T. (2008) *Police Custody as a 'Place of Safety': A National Study Examining the Use of Section 136 of the Mental Health Act*, London, IPCC.

Fitzgerald, M. (1993) 'Ethnic Minorities and the Criminal Justice System', *Royal Commission on Criminal Justice Research Study* 20. London: HMSO.

Healthcare Commission (2005) *Count Me In: Results of a National Census of Inpatients in Mental Health Hospitals and Facilities in England and Wales*. London: Commission for Healthcare, Audit and Inspection.

Healthcare Commission (2007) *Results of the 2006 National Census of Inpatients In Mental Health and Learning Disability Services in England and Wales*. London: Commission for Healthcare, Audit and Inspection.

HM Inspectorate of Prisons (2005) *Women in Prison*. London: Home Office.

Housing Corporation (1998) *Black and Minority Ethnic Housing Policy*. London: the Housing Corporation.

John, G. (2003) *Race for Justice: A Review of CPS Decision Making for Possible Racial Bias at each Stage of the Prosecution Process*. London: Crown Prosecution Service.

Lyall, M. (2005) 'Should there be separate forensic psychiatry services for ethnic minority patients?' *Journal of Forensic Psychiatry and Psychology*, 16 (2), pp. 370–9.

Nacro (1990) *Black People, Mental Health and the Courts: An Exploratory Study into the Psychiatric Remand Process as it Affects Black Defendants at Magistrates' Courts*. London: Nacro.

Nacro (2005) *Integrated Resettlement: Putting the pieces together*. London: Nacro.

Norfolk, Suffolk and Cambridgeshire Health Authority (2003) *Independent Inquiry into the Death of David Bennett*. Cambridge: Cambridgeshire Health Authority.

Office for National Statistics (2003) *Census 2001: Ethnicity and religion in England and Wales*. London: Office for National Statistics.

Prins, H., Blacker-Holst, T., Francis, E. and Keitch, I. (1993) *Report of the Committee of Inquiry into the Death in Broadmoor, Hospital of Orville Blackwood and a Review of the Deaths of Two Other Afro-Caribbean Patients. Big, Black and Dangerous*. London: Special Hospitals Service Authority.

Reza, B. and Magill, C. (2006) *Race and the Criminal Justice System: An Overview to the Complete Statistics 2004–2005*. London: Criminal Justice System (Race Unit).

24

Reflections on British forensic psychiatry

John Gunn

History and development

At its simplest, forensic psychiatry can be defined as that part of psychiatry which deals with patients and problems at the interface of the legal and psychiatric systems. The qualified forensic psychiatrist in Britain is expected to treat mentally disordered offenders wherever they are found – in prisons, hospitals and the community. Forensic psychiatrists also give advice to other psychiatrists, to primary care doctors, to lawyers, to the police service, to social workers, and to probation officers; they provide medical evidence and formal reports in legal settings. Forensic psychiatry has a clinical interface with virtually every other psychiatric discipline. It is a subject that uses both long-term care and security, in the broadest sense, as core skills.

Britain and America lead the world development of forensic psychiatry, which is also beginning to develop in other affluent countries. Unusually Britain provides the major role as American forensic psychiatry is heavily focused on legal issues and is much less concerned with therapeutics.

The roots of forensic psychiatry in Britain go back to the beginning of the 19th century when, in 1800, James Hadfield, a war veteran, took a pistol shot at the king. He missed and was arrested. At his trial he was found to be suffering from a serious head injury in a wound sustained fighting for the king in the wars against France. Hadfield was found not guilty by reason of insanity and would therefore have been free to leave the court had not parliament

Edited from J. Gunn, 'Reflections on British forensic psychiatry in 2003', *Mental Health Review* (2003), vol. 8, no. 3, pp. 35–8.

rushed through our first piece of forensic psychiatry legislation in 1800. This required people found not guilty by reason of insanity to be locked up in a mental hospital.

After the Second World War the mental health acts of 1959 (England and Wales) and 1960 (Scotland) introduced informality as the basis of mental health care. The Percy Royal Commission of 1957 stated that 'as far as possible the mentally disordered should be treated using the same informal relationships as occur in every other branch of medicine'. This radical idea dominated mental health care in Britain for the remainder of the 20th century. The Royal Commission also recommended that courts should no longer have anything to do with civil detention other than in appeal tribunals. This brief period of liberal care is about to come to an end.

The 1959 act was superseded by the Mental Health Act 1983, the current legislation in England and Wales, which in turn is about to be replaced by a new mental health act which will return the lawyer to centre stage in mental health legislation and which will put 'public protection' before patient autonomy – a matter of great protest for the Royal College of Psychiatrists; a setback for patients.

Modern forensic psychiatry in Britain developed from recommendations of the Butler report of 1975 that every health region in England and Wales develop its own medium-secure unit and that forensic psychiatry should be established as a distinct sub-branch of psychiatry with its own academic base (Home Office and Department of Health and Social Security, 1975). At that time there was increasing parliamentary concern about the large numbers of patients kept in high security in the special hospitals of Broadmoor, Rampton and Moss Side, and there had been talk of developing regional units for offender patients. The regional secure unit proposal was accepted by the government with the consequence that there is now a secure service within reach of most people's homes which is the focus for the specialised treatment of offenders with mental disorder. Originally such secure units were to take a mixture of diagnostic problems but, as a result of the pressure created by the reduction in beds in other parts of the system, regional secure units have until now largely focused on patients with schizophrenia. One of the changes the government hopes to introduce alongside its new mental health act is the development of specialised services for patients with personality disorder.

The problems of the special hospitals continued until the establishment of the Special Hospital Service Authority (SHSA) in 1990. Sadly this only lasted until 1995 but during that short period the new authority managed to bring the hospitals into line with up-to-date NHS standards, removed many anti-therapeutic and prison-like practices (such as secluding all patients at night) and rekindled a research programme. More recently much of this work has been undone by the government's preoccupation with 'law and order'. The vehicle for this damage has been the Tilt report (Department of Health,

2000), written by an ex-director of the Prison Service with no experience of psychiatric hospitals, which was implemented without consultation. Measures included the building of completely unnecessary extra steel fences and a diversion of staff from nursing duties to so-called security duties. Far from enhancing security and public safety these steps may have increased risks as therapeutic gains have diminished and petty frustrations increased (Exworthy and Gunn, 2003).

In spite of the emphasis of forensic psychiatry on secure services there has been much effort to provide community forensic psychiatry services as well. Following the publication of the Butler Report, there has been a continuous debate about the pattern of service to be provided by forensic psychiatry. Sometimes known as the parallel v. integrated dichotomy (see Gunn, 1978), the issue is whether forensic psychiatry should focus on a defined group of patients and run completely separate services or whether forensic psychiatry should be an adjustment to general psychiatry with flexible boundaries; most forensic psychiatrists are now happier with the integrated model.

Offenders create victims and victims have needs which are frequently neglected but which are an important element in the successful rehabilitation of an offender. Just as importantly most offenders are themselves victims, having had abusive or neglected childhoods. The effective treatment of such offenders may include psychotherapy to help with the healing of those past traumata. Trauma in adult life can lead to both mental disorder and offending, and in severe cases may induce a profound personality change with sufferers becoming aggressive, asocial or even antisocial and coming into conflict with society. Such people need both medico-legal assistance and specialist therapeutic services. The Maudsley Hospital was one of the few places to integrate forensic psychiatry and trauma services and I hope it will become much more commonplace and lead to aetiological research programmes looking at the relationships between trauma in both childhood and in adult life and antisocial outcomes.

Contemporary problems

One of the difficulties faced by psychiatrists in the United Kingdom is the public outrage that occurs whenever a known patient commits a serious offence, particularly homicide. This immediately gives rise to 'mad axe-man' fantasies and the tabloid press implies that there are large numbers of dangerous, unsupervised, mentally ill people wandering the streets about to attack unsuspecting citizens.

Reality is different. Each year in the United Kingdom there are roughly 3,500 to 4,000 people killed on the roads, some 300 of those are thought to be non-accidental (that is, caused by dangerous driving). In addition there are

600 or 700 other homicides and the courts determine that some 80 of those are by mentally disordered people. The total number of homicides has been rising in recent years but the number of homicides caused by the mentally disordered stays constant, so the proportion of cases of homicide committed by the mentally disordered has actually fallen (Taylor and Gunn, 1999). Not a matter for public panic.

The tabloids would also have us believe that there is a national paedophile epidemic and that child killings are on the increase. In fact, approximately five paedophile killings occur each year and this pattern has remained the same for some time. Sex offender registers have been established to enable the police to monitor people with convictions for sex offences once they are back in the community. Most recently, multi-agency public protection panels (MAPPPs) have been set up, usually under the chairmanship of the probation or the police service, to try and monitor all people in a community who are identified as potentially dangerous. At the moment these panels tend to focus mostly on sex offenders but in time they will also look at violent people. There are already calls to get them to monitor violent husbands. As MAPPPs concentrate on those who have a history of mental disorder, they expect hospitals and psychiatrists to work with them in their surveillance work. This can create great difficulties at times because of the differing objectives and levels of confidentiality in the police, probation and mental health services and will be an area of considerable tension for the forensic psychiatrist in the future.

Conclusion

Forensic psychiatry is a fundamental discipline. It is needed by society, but society is ambivalent about it. It deals with 'nasty people' and 'evil monsters' and is probably more stigmatised than any other branch of medicine. Yet in spite of that it has developed a considerable momentum and continues to grow. The profession is now just about large enough to form the critical mass necessary to preserve training and standards and to conduct research. Fortunately the Royal College of Psychiatrists is at present supportive of such developments. The challenge is for another university to take up the crusade where the Institute of Psychiatry left off.

References

Department of Health (2000) *Report of the Review of Security at the High Security Hospital (Tilt Report)*. London: Department of Health.

Exworthy, T. and Gunn, J. (2003) 'Taking another tilt at high secure hospitals'. *British Journal of Psychiatry*, 182, 469–71.

Gunn, J. (1978) 'Management of the mentally abnormal offender: integrated or parallel'. *Journal of Royal Society of Medicine*, 70, 877–80.

Home Office and Department of Health and Social Security (1975) *Report of the Committee on Mentally Abnormal Offenders (Butler Report)*. Cmnd 6244, London: HMSO.

Royal Commission on the Law Relating to Mental Illness and Mental Deficiency (1957) (Percy Commission) Cmnd 169. London: HMSO.

Taylor, P.J. and Gunn, J. (1999) 'Homicides by people with mental illness; myth and reality'. *British Journal of Psychiatry*, 174, 9–14.

25

Social capital and mental health

Martin Webber

Little is known about the association between social capital and the onset of, and recovery from, mental health problems. In fact, it has been noted that the embeddedness of individual social ties within the broader social structure as a function of obtaining access to material goods, resources and services has not yet been researched within mental health services (Lynch, 2000; Berkman and Glass, 2000). However, this appear to be a promising field of enquiry.

Strong ties, or close relationships to friends or family members, can be of great importance to people suffering from mental health problems. If these ties are instrumental in providing support, they can protect people's mental health (Brown et al., 1986; Cassel, 1974). It is also known that positive social support has been found to precede recovery from depression (Brown, Adler and Bifulco, 1988; Leenstra, Ormel and Giel, 1995). However, strong ties may also inhibit free choice (Cattell, 2001; Cooper et al., 1999). This may lead to stress or high expressed emotion within families, known triggers for depression (Cohen and Wills, 1985) or relapse in schizophrenia (Leff and Vaughn, 1981), for example.

It is important to note here the distinctions between social capital, social support and social networks. Social capital represents the resources of other people within an individual's social network. These may be accessed to meet a number of goals such as finding a job, obtaining help with DIY or finding new accommodation, for example. Social support is best perceived from the perspective of the person receiving it and can include both emotional and prac-

Editorial extract from M. Webber, Chapter 5 in G. Tew (ed.), *Social Perspectives on Mental Health*, London, Jessica Kingsley.

tical support. In short, an individual can gain social support from the supply of social capital they hold within their social network.

Implications for mental health services

Emerging evidence about the role of social capital in the mental health of individuals raises a number of questions for mental health services. For example, do people with more social capital recover more quickly from mental health problems? Are they less likely to access support or treatment from mental health services as they have more resources at their disposal within their social network? Do long periods of hospitalisation diminish the value of an individual's social capital that may be important in their long-term recovery? More work needs to be conducted with mental health service users to investigate these and other questions in this emerging research programme.

It is possible that mental health problems, or the interventions of mental health services, can damage reciprocal relationships that are crucial to the transmission of resources or the paying back of social debts. It follows that interventions focusing on strengthening relationships and networks containing useful resources can be beneficial to people with mental health problems. This could possibly explain why supported employment is more effective than pre-vocational training in helping people with severe mental health problems to obtain competitive employment (Crowther et al., 2001), for example. People placed in competitive jobs with support from 'job coaches' or employment specialists are more likely to be exposed to more diverse social networks than those who receive pre-vocational training in sheltered workshops or on training courses. It is possible that resourses embedded within these networks are important to help people to sustain or find new employment.

If there is an association between social capital and recovery from mental health problems, either with or without the assistance of mental health services, it could result in a paradigm shift from a focus on individual pathology to supporting the development of resourceful networks and strengthening interactions with them. This could highlight an important role for social networks beyond the traditional boundaries of the mental health resource centre or psychiatric ward.

Social capital and social inclusion

People with mental health problems face oppression on the street, at work and even at home, perhaps more than any group in society. This results in social exclusion, of which unemployment is perhaps its most visible element (Warr, 1987). For example, the employment rate of people receiving treatment and support from the mental health services rarely reaches more than 10 per cent and, when working, they work fewer hours and earn only two thirds of the national average hourly rate (Meltzer et al., 1995; Office for National Statistics, 2002).

Tackling social exclusion has underpinned much of the 'Third Way' policy agenda of the UK government (Giddens, 1998). Reducing exclusion from social capital has been one of the aims of this policy thrust. This approach has been criticised as downplaying the material roots of inequality (Muntaner, Lynch and Davey Smith, 2000). However, there is evidence that access to social capital may vary according to a range of characteristics including socio-economic status (Ziersch, 2002), ethnicity (Boisjoly, Duncan and Hofferth, 1995) and gender (Campbell et al., 1999). This may be relevant in terms of the way that differential access to social capital may link to the broader processes of social exclusion. For example, poorer people often have less access to resourceful people than wealthier people (Lin, 2000). This difference in access to social capital may reinforce existing mental health inequalities.

Sayce (2001) challenges psychiatrists to embrace social inclusion as a treatment goal in line with Standard One of the National Service Framework (Department of Health, 1999). In support of this objective, Huxley and Thornicroft (2003) argue that mental health professionals are able to exert influence on 'ethnos' sources of social exclusion. 'Ethnos' refers to the shared values, identification and sense of cohesion that are engendered by membership of social groups and communities (Berman and Phillips, 2000). Fostering the growth of social relationships and resourceful networks within the community or, in other words, building the infrastructure for social capital, is a key component of this.

In practice, this requires mental health services to be outward-looking and use resources within the local community rather than provide them internally (Leff, 1996). For example, people referred to community mental health teams need to be encouraged to attend social, leisure and educational activities provided by local services rather than specific mental health day services. This is not to denigrate the latter, which do some valuable work and are valued by their users (for example, Catty and Burns, 2001). Instead, engaging with community resources will provide opportunities for people to develop social networks that may provide potentially important resources for recovery from mental health problems.

References

Berkman, L. F. and Glass, T. (2000) 'Social intgegration, social networks, social support, and health', in L. F. Berkman and I. Kawachi (eds) *Social Epidemiology*. Oxford University Press.

Berman, Y. and Phillips, D. (2000) 'Indicators of social quality and social exclusion at national and community level'. *Social Indicators Research 50*, 3, pp. 329–50.

Boisjoly, J., Duncan, G. J. and Hofferth, S. (1995) 'Access to social capital'. *Journal of Family Issues 16*, 5, pp. 609–31.

Brown G., Adler, Z. and Bifulco, A. (1988) 'Life events, difficulties and recovery from chronic depression'. *British Journal of Psychiatry 152*, 4, pp. 487–98.

Brown, G. W., Andrews, B. A., Harris, T. O., Adler, Z. and Bridge, L. (1986) 'Social support, self-esteem and depression'. *Psychological Medicine 16*, 4, pp. 813–31.

Campbell, C., Wood, R. and Kelly, M. (1999) *Social Capital and Health*, London: Health Education Authority.

Cassel, J. (1974) 'Psychosocial processes and "stress": theoretical formulations'. *International Journal of Health Services 4*, pp. 471–82.

Cattell, V. (2001) 'Poor people, poor places, and poor health: the mediating role of social networks and social capital'. *Social Science and Medicine 52*, 10, pp. 1501–16.

Catty, J. and Burns, T. (2001) 'Mental health day centres: their clients and role'. *Psychiatric Bulletin 25*, 2, pp. 61–6.

Cohen, S. and Wills, T. A. (1985) 'Stress, social support, and the buffering hypothesis'. *Psychological Bulletin 98*, 2, pp. 310–57.

Cooper, H., Arber, S., Fee, L. and Ginn, J. (1999) *The Influence of Social Support and Social Capital on Health*, London: Health Education Authority.

Crowther, R. E., Marshall, M., Bond, G. R. and Huxley, P. (2001) 'Helping people with severe mental illness to obtain work: systematic review'. *British Medical Journal 322*, 7280, pp. 204–8.

Department of Health (1999) *National Service Framework for Mental Health. Modern Standards and Service Models*. London: Department of Health.

Giddens, A. (1998) *The Third Way. The Renewal of Social Democracy*, Cambridge: Polity Press.

Huxley, P. and Thornicroft, G. (2003) 'Social inclusion, social quality and mental illness'. *British Journal of Psychiatry 182*, 4, pp. 289–90.

Leenstra, A., Ormel, J. and Giel, R. (1995) 'Positive life change and recovery from depression and anxiety. A three-stage longitudinal study of primary care attenders'. *British Jounal of Psychiatry 166*, 3, pp. 133–43.

Leff, J. (1996) 'Beyond the asylum', in T. Heller, J. Reynolds, R. Gomm, R. Muston and S. Pattison (eds) *Mental Health Matters. A Reader*. Basingstoke: Macmillan.

Leff, J. and Vaughn, C. (1981) 'The role of maintenance therapy and relatives' expressed emotion in relapse of schizophrenia: a two-year follow-up'. *British Journal of Psychiatry 139*, pp. 102–4.

Lin, N. (2000) 'Inequality in social capital'. *Contemporary Sociology 29*, pp. 785–95.

Lynch, J. (2000) 'Income inequality and health: expanding the debate'. *Social Science and Medicine 51*, 7, 1001–5.

Meltzer, H., Gill, B., Petticrew, M. and Hinds, K. (1995) *OPCS Surveys of Psychiatric Morbidity in Great Britain: Report 2 – Economic Activity and Social Functioning of Adults with Psychiatric Disorders*. London: HMSO.

Muntaner, C., Lynch, J. and Davey Smith, G. (2000) 'Social capital and the third way in public health'. *Critical Public Health 10*, 2, 107–24.

Office for National Statistics (2002) *Labour Force Survey 2002*. London: Stationery Office.

Sayce, L. (2001) 'Social inclusion and mental health'. *Psyhchiatric Bulletin 25*, 4, pp. 121–3.

Warr, P. (1987) *Work, Unemployment and Mental Health*. Oxford: Oxford University Press.

Ziersch, A. M. (2002) *Access to Social Capital. The Implications for Health*. PhD thesis, Flinders University of South Australia.

Part III

Service users' experiences and perspectives

26

Introduction

Jan Wallcraft

Now that service user involvement in health and social care services has been established as government policy, we decided to devote the third part of this edition to the ways in which the literature on personal experience of mental distress and mental health services is having an effect on ways of working. Not all the readings here are by service users and survivors, but all have something to say about service users' lives, their journeys through experiences of breakdown, distress, treatment and recovery, and their views of the mental health system.

The readings are chosen to illustrate how service users and their families are moving from passive recipients, or victims, of an all-powerful mental health system to active involvement in knowledge creation. Thus, we start with reflections on how people have experienced medical responses to their distress, and finish with the role service users are now taking in mental health research, as partners or collaborators and as knowledge creators in their own right.

There is a long way to go still. My aim, stated on behalf of service users in *Healing Minds* (Wallcraft, 1998), is that no therapy or treatment for mental health problems should be considered to be safe or effective if service users and their organisations have not been involved in the design of the outcome measures used. Service users have been the instigators of the new focus on 'recovery' which is now a touchstone for mental health service improvement work. In these readings, the many complex meanings of that often misused term are revealed. Recovery, if it is self-identified, and if the journey towards it is based on people's own choices, strengths, hopes, dreams and life-goals, is the only proper aim of mental health services. With the knowledge about how people recover which is emerging from life-stories, collected narratives and narrative research, it is clear that psychiatric treatments that do not help people to recover or which prevent them from undertaking their own life-journey toward healing (see Barham's story of William, below), can no longer be justified.

In Reading 27, Jeanette Henderson tackles a rarely discussed issue, the shadow that can fall over relationships when one person in a couple is 'sectioned' (a term commonly used for compulsory admission to hospital against the individual's will). Both parties can be left feeling hurt in different ways. The carer may be distressed about the behaviour of their partner which led to the sectioning, or about their own role in it, while the person sectioned may wonder if their partner wanted them out of the way. Henderson points out that neither legislation nor professional practice appear to take account of the impact of the process of admission on couple relationships.

Mary O'Hagan's piece (Reading 28) juxtaposes her own diary notes, during an intense experience of breakdown, with psychiatric and nursing notes on her, which she later obtained. This is a classic account of the clinical gaze seeing only the surface behaviour according to medical and nursing knowledge, and failing to connect with the patient's inner world. While Mary searches for meaning and light in her inner blackness, the doctor regards her with supercilious detachment, noting 'inappropriate laughter' a 'need for control', 'over dramatisation' and seeking to remedy her 'gross psychological turmoil' with Chlorpromazine.

The readings from Peter Barham (Reading 29) and Jeremy Laurance (Reading 30) provide different kinds of narrative, in attempting to recount life journeys of patients and service users. Barham pieces together from medical reports and personal letters, the story of William, an ex-serviceman who had fought in China, and an early example of a 'mad activist' in Barham's terminology. William's health broke down after he was wounded in the Dardanelles at the start of the First World War. Consigned to a long-stay Ministry of Pensions hospital, diagnosed with dementia praecox at the age of only 26, he was kept from his family for 16 years, labelled 'Automaton, incapable of independent life'.

However, his notes also show that he was unhappy with his loss of freedom and worried about what was to become of him. Finally, with the support of his wife, William begged for his release, fearing he would end in an insane asylum. Against all medical advice, he left the hospital with his wife. The power of medical diagnosis was such that the Ministry threatened to reduce his pension for refusing treatment. William and his wife fought for their choice, and were eventually successful, with William declaring he was 'happier at home'.

Jeremy Laurance (Reading 30) interviewed Ron Coleman, a well-known survivor activist, trainer and businessman. He observed Ron give a talk on his own experience of hearing voices, aiming to break his audience's assumption that this is a sign of illness, and noting that Gandhi and Christ heard voices. Ron challenges the conventional wisdom that voice hearers should be discouraged from engaging with their voices in case this makes them worse, arguing instead that common sense alone should tell us that these situations must be worked through, not medicated away.

This theme of hearing voices is taken up in three short pieces placed together in Reading 31. The first of these describes the medical mainstream view, which rules out any dealings with the content of voices, while the next contributions provide a counterpoint from the perspective of two voice-hearers who received conventional treatment but eventually learned to manage their voices themselves. Ivan Leudar and Phil Thomas explain (from a critical perspective) how hearing voices has traditionally led to a diagnosis of schizophrenia, based on Schneider's (1957) classification of first-rank symptoms, and show how once a diagnosis is made, talking to patients about their experiences is seen as pointless. J.Thomas in 'Time-sharing' offers a stark contradiction to the medical view. He learned to deal with his voices by 'time-sharing': allowing the voices to take over for a short time each day has enabled him to get on with his life without medication. Jan Holloway, in 'Learning from voices', describes her journey through several suicide attempts and hospitalisations because of the constant persecution of critical voices which destroyed her self-esteem. She eventually learned to live with them and says that being able to talk about the voices has lessened their power over her.

The commitment of a mental health worker and the impact this had on one woman's recovery is the theme of Reading 32. Alex Williams looks back on her pathway through extreme distress and self-harm. She describes her gradual recovery of hope, despite set-backs, and the importance of attitudes to self-harm and the language used by mental health workers. She makes a plea for mental health workers to maintain connection, optimism and consistency even in the most difficult circumstances.

The reading from Veronica Dewan (33) is the first of three pieces by black women, in which they draw attention to the diversity of meanings encompassed in black people's experiences of distress and treatment. The main common argument is a strong warning about making assumptions about black experience, and a plea for genuine, respectful listening and learning from individuals.

Veronica recounts a number of small but significant acts of kindness and respect she encountered, adding up to two hours fifty-five minutes, during her six year journey through the mental health system. A child of Indian and Irish parentage, Veronica was adopted, and her mental health crises followed difficult life events as a young adult. She points out how vital it is for people entering the mental health system in a fragile state to be respected and heard. This was rare in Veronica's experience as 'so many terrible things happen when we are in hospital ... it takes years to recover from the effects of being personally and collectively ignored', but the kindness of the few helped her to survive and to retain her belief in the goodness of humanity.

Premila Trivedi (Reading 34) is concerned with language and how it is used as part of power-relationships to define and control. She lists the various words used to describe her: 'non-white', 'Asian', 'Indian', 'Gujerati', 'Hindu' and 'woman of colour'. Each of these terms can be used in ways which deny her life experience. She argues that black women must be allowed to define themselves, and have their own terminology accepted. Patricia Chambers (Reading 35) tries to answer the question of what black women want from mental health services. Her main argument is for positive stories and images about, for instance, single mothers managing to bring up their children, women who go back to employment, learn a new skill or return to education. She points out that these are newsworthy stories as well as the other sort. More positive images, along with better support services, would make it easier for people to seek help before their lives went too badly wrong, and would help to prevent the stigma that keeps women with mental health problems unemployed.

Self-management is the theme of the next two readings. In Reading 36, Louise Pembroke talks about how she began self-harming as a teenager when she developed a rare eye condition that threatened her dance career. After negative responses from Accident and Emergency doctors, she was unwilling to go for help, although she was not able to stop self-harming. A sympathetic ophthalmic nurse taught her basic first aid and explained how to minimise the damage of cutting, which gave her more control and allowed her to choose to do it more safely. She compares this with IV drug users learning to use clean needles, rather than being told they have to simply stop taking the drugs.

Amanda Wells (37) accepts her diagnosis of schizoaffective disorder and describes her history of treatment with a wide range of antidepressants and antipsychotics. She has had bad experiences of some drugs, particularly Haloperidol, and drugs that have helped for a while often become less effective for her. However, she finds the newer drugs are improving and she considers it is part of her self-management to continue to take drugs that help her. She does not see why people should tell her she ought to stop taking medicines which prevent her distress, just as other drugs she takes prevent her asthma attacks.

In the next reading (38), Rufus May talks about his life journey from schizophrenic to clinical psychologist. In the process he has learned how to deal with his own voice-hearing and now helps others to manage their problems through self-help and complementary approaches. May describes the problems which led to his seeking spiritual sources of guidance, and eventually believing he was a spy for the secret service. Hospital was a different world, where 'queues for the medication trolley punctuated the boredom and general sense of hopelessness'. May wanted to change the system, and set out to heal himself through work, dance and drama, then he 'acted' sane as he went through psychology training. He argues that many people can live with their own and others' unusual beliefs, and psychologists should help them with this.

Service users in the next reading (39) talk about difficulties they experienced in getting back to work. One anonymous author, well qualified, was appointed to a social worker post. However, the starting date was delayed for months because of the HR department's concerns about the candidate still using mental health services and being on medication. Once the person started in post, their work was over-scrutinised, with any differences of opinion being put down to the medication, with the result that this person left after 10 months. Kalisha Parton refers to a 'service trap' – in other words, service users that do manage to work despite mental health problems find it difficult to access mental health services which are rarely available out of office hours, though when starting a job a person may need support all the more. Also service users who work are often unable to take part in service user involvement events, which also happen during working hours. For employment rates of service users to increase, the writer argues that these problems should be tackled.

In addition to the direct impact of service users taking more control over their lives and learning to manage their own problems or work more often in partnership with professionals, mental health research is in recent years being expected to take account of service users' views. The last three readings (40, 41 and 42) are about the impact of service users' experiences and perspectives on mental health research.

In Reading 40, Jan Wallcraft addresses the problems of researching complementary and alternative therapies which have claims of mental health benefits. Despite evidence of strong demand from service users for access to complementary therapies and dissatisfaction with the limitations and problems often associated with orthodox medicine, there are still problems in creating a level playing field for different types of research to be accepted. Complementary therapies are usually based on a holistic model of mental health. Many want to see mental health move away from the Descartes mind/body split, towards holism, but the government policy of evidence-based medicine is still weighted in favour of randomised-controlled trials. A House of Lords committee on complementary medicines in 2000 recognised they should be seen as differing from conventional medicine in their underlying paradigms. The reading argues that new measures of cost effectiveness, new trial methodology and outcome measures needed to reflect service users' priorities and to evaluate holistic therapies in holistic terms.

Premila Trivedi and Til Wykes (Reading 41) discuss the policy demands from the Department of Health and UK funding bodies for clinical academics to work closely with mental health service users in research projects. Although there are helpful guidelines on the issues that have to be dealt with, there have been few examples of how this partnership research might be undertaken. Trivedi and Wykes researched the process of user involvement in the development of a joint research project. Patients had asked for more information about medication. The clinical research team wanted to investigate the effects of medication education on patient knowledge, insight and compliance. They found that the involvement of a user-researcher changed the focus of the study and its design and content. The experience clarified the contribution that users can make, for example by raising new research questions, by ensuring interventions are kept 'user friendly', and the selection of outcome measures.

Alison Faulkner and Phil Thomas take on user-led research and evidence-based medicine (EBM) in this part's last reading (42). While people want clinical decisions to be based on the best evidence, there is another agenda of engaging patients as partners in health research, which is aimed at making the medical profession more accountable. They examine the value of user-led research in improving the concept of 'evidence'. They find that there is political resistance to seeing psychiatric patients as experts and involving them as full partners in research. Service user-led research has emerged, they argue, in response to this. Despite user-led research looking at issues and outcomes that are relevant and meaningful to service users, it is not featured in psychiatric journals. They question the gold standard of the randomised controlled trial, as people are complex subjects and quantitative studies may produce findings less relevant in the real world than those of qualitative research. A marriage of two types of expertise is the essential ingredient of the best mental health care: expertise by experience and expertise by profession. They argue that psychiatrists should work with service users to find ways of integrating user-led research with EBM, and the Department of Health should value 'partnership' research as much as other research, as 'to do otherwise is to discriminate against psychiatric patients'.

References

Schneider, K. (1957) 'Pimäre and Sekundäre symptomen bei schizophrenia' [Primary and secondary symptoms in schizophrenia], *Feitschritta der Nomrologie Psychiatre*, no. 25.

Wallcraft, J. (1998) *Healing Minds*, London, Mental Health Foundation.

27

Experiences of 'care' in mental health

Jeanette Henderson

Experiences of being 'sectioned'

Formal admission to hospital under a section of the Mental Health Act (often known as 'being sectioned' or 'sectioning') may be a harrowing and emotional experience for both partners.

Some carers were relieved that their partners had been admitted to hospital, in the hope that any treatment prescribed would help the situation. Others expected their partner to have less freedom and to be monitored more closely while in hospital. Some were so exhausted by the time admission took place they felt an overwhelming sense of relief, although this was often accompanied by a sense of grief and bereavement. However, this woman begins with an example of how the experience felt like physical violence, like

> being clouted with something. It's quite unreal. You don't always know at the hospital that this is going to happen. I've had times when yes, they're talking about sectioning and then the next thing I know I get a letter in the post saying it's happened. They've decided after I've gone home . . . you just sit there holding this bit of paper. (Val, carer)

Statistical data gathered on the use of the Mental Health Act in England and Wales gives some indication of the scale of compulsion in admissions to psychiatric hospitals. There were 26,000 formal admissions to hospital in 1999/2000. However, there were a further 20,826 formal detentions after a voluntary admission to hospital (Department of Health, 2000). As Elaine comments:

Edited from J. Henderson, *Journal of Adult Protection* (2002), vol. 4, no. 3, pp. 34–45.

Elaine: It always felt terrible. But each time was different in that there were different circumstances. But I hate it, you know, really hate it.

Jeanette: And since then have you been sectioned?

Elaine: Yes, I've been sectioned, but I can't remember how many times. I think maybe two or three. I'm not sure. Because what's happened is that several times I've been more or less told I've been unofficially sectioned. You're told to go in or be sectioned so what's the choice?

And Teresa:

At the end of the three days I was given the option of I could either stay voluntarily or if I decided not to stay voluntarily then they might section me again, so I said okay, I'll stay voluntarily.

The line between informal admission and 'de facto' detention is a fine one. Elaine and Teresa both experienced threats in their 'voluntary' detentions. None of the 'informal admissions' these women spoke about would be included in statistical data on use of mental health legislation. Were they being assessed for formal admission or detention in hospital, professionals would have a duty to consult Elaine's and Teresa's nearest relatives. It was not possible to establish whether their partners had been consulted about these 'informal' admissions.

At the time of assessment both users and carers seem powerless in the face of professional intervention:

That's when I became very high. I threatened to murder him and I phoned the police and said if you don't get straight round I'm going to murder my husband. They came round and the CPN came round and they sectioned me and put me in hospital. I didn't really know what was going on at all. They kept trying to give me medication but I didn't really know what they were trying to do. I can always remember in the end they rugby-tackled me to the floor and injected me with something and took me off to bed.

Later, Janice continued:

I remember the rugby tackle and I remember thinking surely if they'd have said to me about it I would have taken this injection. I was walking from one room to another because I think I used to pace quite a bit, and it just seemed as if the nurses literally came out of nowhere and rugby-tackled me, pulled down my trousers and injected me with some sort of drug. Then one of them tried to get me to go upstairs to bed and at first I wouldn't go and then I started to become more malleable. And as I started to go upstairs my legs were starting to go. But even as they were putting me into bed I kept saying to them something about 'the light being the only way out' and as I lay there I just kept saying it and saying it and saying it, as if I was trying to keep myself awake.

Such lack of power – the removal of physical and emotional agency from another person – can be nothing other than abusive. Janice was physically abused – in the name of treatment – and, along with the physical abuse of the rugby tackle, came abuse in the way she had her clothes removed. Trousers were pulled down, and then Janice was dragged upstairs. The vulnerable position she found herself in provides some graphic examples of a combination of individual, institutional and system abuse (Penhale, 1999).

When formal admission does take place a partner may have a central role. For example, admission under Section 3 of the Mental Health Act cannot usually take place if the nearest relative objects to the admission. This gives the partner – if they are identified as nearest relative – a great deal of power to put forward their own view (albeit not always easy to exercise when confronted with several professionals):

> I found myself even at odds with the doctors over this recently, which I didn't think would ever happen to me ages ago. They seemed to need my word, I can never remember the exact details, but they seemed to need a yes from me before they could go ahead. The last time it was actually me who refused to give it and made a determined effort to keep Elaine at home. Which did pay off because within a week or so she was really much better again so that was okay. But at other times, all the other times, I suppose I have given my okay. (Richard, carer)

The central role often ascribed to a partner may continue after admission and subsequent discharge from hospital.

The aftermath

Once a period of admission is over the relationship needs to be renegotiated and the partners have to find a way through their experiences. This is a difficult process. Neither legislation nor professional practice appears to consider the impact of the process of admission on the relationship. Both partners must deal with the aftermath:

> For us, during the period I was either high or low, there wasn't really an opportunity to put things behind us. It was a different relationship, and at no time was it our normal relationship until I actually became well at the end of the period. Then once I became well after a time we could actually start to put to bed some of the nasty things we said to each other or did to each other. The bits that destroyed parts of our relationship and we could start to build them back up again. I think if you're either manic or depressed there's no opportunity then to really get the relationship back together again. All you're doing is breaking it down all the time. (Teresa)

Experiences may contribute to feelings of despair and uncertainty about the relationship, and may be attributed to a person – to their personality, or to 'the illness'. The latter is more problematic where the carer or user does not accept mental illness in the first place. Both attributions, however, have subsequent impacts on relationships. Where there is uncertainty, doubts may cause difficulties in accepting events, as Ross, a carer, explains:

> There's the aspect of the cruelty and some of the violence. After the upset you start to deal with it, that person may have forgotten. They would say 'oh, I didn't mean it'. But then for the person who was there it's like, 'well, how do I deal with that?' Because they say they didn't mean it – so where did it come from? There's that shadow

The hurt felt by Val, also a carer, was linked to verbal abuse, when she felt blame and guilt as a result of Peter's admission:

> You feel very hurt really because a lot of the time when Peter was admitted he used to try and put a guilt trip on me. When he felt slightly better it was 'well, I'm only here because you wanted me to be here. It's you who wanted me out of the way, that's why I'm here'.

Elaine felt that power and control were central issues in her relationship with Richard:

> Elaine: I'm not quite sure exactly how [being sectioned] has impacted. It has been important, and it has been in our relationship. In practice since I've been with Richard, he's had a major say in when he thinks that I've got out of control or the situation's unbearable and he thinks that I ought to be in hospital. We haven't always agreed. So that, I think, has had a negative effect on our relationship at times and has been a difficult one to come to terms with.
>
> Jeanette: How do you think you have come to terms with it?
>
> Elaine: Well, I think that on the whole I'm pretty sure that he is reasonable and is acting in both our best interests . . . I have to hold on to that if I'm tempted to feel a bit resentful at times, if he's wittering about whether I'm going over the top, as I might see it. I've realised how important his role was and how it could seem at times as if 'you know' if . . . if I was feeling paranoid I could put the construction on it, well, if he's fed up with me he can throw me into hospital. That was a very, very nasty thought and I have to make sure that I'm not paranoid because I know that isn't really how it has worked.

That 'shadow' Ross mentioned above is cast over both partners. It does not discriminate between service user or 'carer'. In some relationships partners have developed means of dealing with it together. They are open about the impact of their experiences of the period of mental distress on them as individuals, as well as their relationship. In other relationships this process is much less straightforward.

References

Department of Health (2000) *Statistical Bulletin 2000/19: In-patients formally detained in hospitals under the Mental Health Act 1983 and other legislation, England 1989–1990 to 1999–2000*. London: DH.

Penhale, B. (1999) 'Introduction', in N. Stanley, J. Manthorpe and B. Penhale (eds) *Institutional Abuse: Perspectives Across the Life Course*. London: Routledge.

28

Two accounts of mental distress

Mary O'Hagan

This paper is a 'cut and paste' of excerpts from my journal and hospital file written during one of my episodes of mental distress.

I wrote most of the journal entries during my last stay in hospital while I crouched in the safety of a locked toilet. With enormous effort I created coherent sequences of words out of the chaos inside me and recorded them in tiny faint handwriting. This was one of the most intense and profound experiences of my life but down the other end of the long polished corridor, others recorded their own version of my distress in the course of a very ordinary day's work.

Several years later I read what they had written about me and I couldn't believe that my journal and their notes referred to the same person and events. The incongruity between these two accounts of my mental distress is disturbing and I believe exposes the fundamental reason why mental health services so often fail to help people.

My journal entries are in italics. The psychiatrist's and nursing notes are in plain text.

The accounts

Today I went to see a psychiatrist. He is a little man with a beard and glasses and he wrote his notes in small, tidy handwriting. He stared right through me.

Edited in a reading in J. Read and J. Reynolds (eds) (1996), *Speaking Our Minds: An Anthology of Personal Experiences of Mental Distress and its Consequences*, Basingstoke, Macmillan/Palgrave, pp. 44–50.

I kept thinking he could see into every corner of my mind. Every time I moved – the way I sat, where I put my hands – I thought would be used as evidence of my badly diseased mind. I was afraid he had the power to trick me into letting out my biggest secrets. I was too terrified to talk to him.

Mary is a 25 year old Caucasian university student who has a history of Manic Depressive Psychosis. Now appears to be entering a depressive phase. Withdrawn and quiet. Dresses unconventionally. Not an easy patient to relate to. She plays her cards very close to her chest.

I stand alone, unable to move inside a dark bubble. I have no face or hands or feet. My veins are broken and my blood has nowhere to travel. Outside the bubble it is day. A rainbow appears but I cannot see it. I remain in the bubble, broken and hidden from the life around me.

Mary has an inadequate and confused sense of identity. She also has a long-standing picture of being an isolate; tending to live in her own world and always finding it difficult to fit in. In this way she presents a schizoid personality picture.

Today I saw the psychiatrist again. I wanted to cry out and collapse against the wall to show him the pain I am in but I couldn't. I wanted him to show from the core of his being that he understood my pain but he didn't. Instead we had a rational discussion. I asked him:

What do you think is a well functioning human being?

Why do you ask that question? I think you're worried that I will judge you.

Yes, I am worried about that. I want to know if your ideas on human beings are compatible enough with mine for us to be able to talk about me. How do you ensure that your values don't impose on mine?

Let me assure you, it's not my job to judge you. I'm here to help you know yourself better.

But what if you judged me without knowing it?

That was below the belt. You need a high degree of control in your relationships don't you?

Then, somehow we got onto sex. The whole time he just kept gazing into me. I felt terribly uncomfortable and was trying desperately to hide it. The sex talk stripped me right back to the raw. Now all I want to do is shrink back into myself. He had all the power.

Requesting my views on life, sex, religion etc.

1   Why she needs to know my views? Feeling of powerlessness that she knows little about me and my beliefs. Theme of control in relationships and how vulnerable she feels when she cannot label people.
2   Problems with sex relationships – feels loss of control.
3   For further discussion – importance of her control issues.
4   Blood levels satisfactory.

Today I wanted to die. Everything was hurting. My body was screaming. I saw the doctor. I said nothing. Now I feel terrible. Nothing seems good and nothing good seems possible.

I am stuck in this twilight mood
where I go down
like the setting sun
into a lonely black hole
where there is room for only one.

Flat, lacking motivation, sleep and appetite good. Discussed aetiology. Cont. LiCarb. 250 mg qid. Levels next time.

I am lying face down behind a chair in the waiting room of the hospital.

I am a long piercing scream
All screaming on the inside of me
and out of the pores of my skin.
My screaming and myself are one.
This is pure pain.

The doctor comes along and snaps at me to get up. He tells a nurse to put me to bed. I have never ever been in so much shame.

Guilt swoops down on me
and pecks my sense of being good to bits
as I lie here snared between my sheets
like a whimpering animal.

I am full of red hot blame at myself for everything
I cannot bear being so thoroughly bad.

I am carrying hell around inside of me.

On arriving on the ward – spent the entire day curled up on the waiting room floor behind a chair. Could not talk. Impression of over dramatisation but with underlying gross psychological turmoil. She is difficult to engage and to that effect I have admitted her for a period of two weeks in order to consolidate her working relationship with us.

I am locked in here
alone in this black box.
I used to hide its blackness
with colourful decorations.
On its walls I painted windows
with pleasing views on them.

Now I have been stripped right back
to the bare boards of my mind.

My world has been emptied out,
as if burglars broke into my mind
and stole all my power.

On their way out
they pulled down my blinds.

Now, I cannot see the world
and the world cannot see me.

Poor eye contact, slow speech and movements. Stated her head felt empty and fuzzy; vision disordered, things appearing very ugly. Mentioned need to find meaning in her depression – not just a wasteful experience.

A nurse came to me and said 'Go to supper'. I said 'No'. She growled at me for not making an effort, but all my effort is going into making these thoughts and writing them down. The nurse punished me, saying, 'Well, I'm not bringing you any supper, you know.'

Sitting in ladies' lounge with her head in her hands. Very difficult to involve in conversation. Not responding to activity around her.

Is attending the dining room with firm encouragement and eating small meals. Remains very withdrawn but occasionally gives vent to an incongruous sustained laugh – although says she isn't happy. Rx Chlorpromazine BD & Nocte as appears to be preoccupied with thoughts – hopefully medication will break the chain.

Last night they came to me
with Chlorpromazine.
I refused it.
I am afraid medication will dull my mind
and the meanings in there will escape forever.

Refusing medication. States she hasn't been taking it because it doesn't do her any good. Not persuaded by explanations or reassurance.

During the night
between sleeps
I felt bad.
I was on the rack.

Every thought
set off a shrieking alarm in my head.
My body would jerk and go rigid
As if electric shocks went through me
every few seconds.

I nearly didn't make it through the night.
I nearly asked for Chlorpromazine.

Awake at frequent intervals during the night. Found whimpering and thrashing around on her bed at 2.15 a.m. saying 'No, leave me alone.' Said she was frightened. Kept holding and massaging her head.

Every morning the night nurses
pull off my blankets.
They are rough.
I can't fight back.
Even their softest touches bruise me.

A nurse said to me
'Face the world.'
But I am facing the pain inside me.
I cannot face both ways at once.

Mary is not to hide away in her bed. She is to be encouraged to get up for breakfast and engage in ward activities.

My back is hard like a shell.
My front is soft like jelly.

I hate to stand
because I cannot shield my front
from the jabbering gaze of the world.

I must lie
curled up or front down.

Lying in bed under blanket. Face covered by hands. Wouldn't leave bed to talk – 'not safe'. Brief whispered conversation from under her hands. Sleeps worse than usual – can't eat – too frightened – body aching all over.

Everything hurts.
I am burning.

All the life in me
blazing out from the core of me
is getting stuck.
I can feel it
trying to burn through my skin.

I am almost on fire.

Experiencing frightening hallucinations, burning sensations, also brightly coloured shapes when eyes shut. Request Sunnyside notes of EEG. Repeat EEG to exclude Temporal Lobe Epilepsy.

I have lost my self
What is my name?
I have no name.
All I am
is shape and weight
rapid shallow breathing
and a black space inside my head.

Misinterpreting at times. Obsessed with the feeling of not wanting to be in her body – wanted to be a speck of dust. Also concerned as to her purpose of being alive. Describing feelings of 'emptiness'. Sleep poor, appetite poor.

My mind is a pile
of broken up smudgy thoughts.

I am searching for one
that is clear enough to have meaning.

But as soon as I find a thought
it gets sucked into the blackness.

Before, my thoughts were sliding off into nonsense. This terrified me so I tried
to make some sense of things by taking bits out of nonsense and putting them
into a story.

An old woman and her grand-daughter lived by a great ocean. Every day the
old woman went fishing. She yelled in awe to the ocean 'Let me take the life
out of you with my net.' She always returned with fish and cooked them for
herself and her grand-daughter. One day she gave some of the fish to her
grand-daughter and said 'Cook these for yourself.' The girl wailed 'I can't.'
The old woman replied 'You must find your own power.' But the girl didn't
understand and went to bed hungry. That night the girl woke from her
dreams to a booming voice from the sky: 'You have the power of the old
woman and the great ocean flowing into the core of you. Now, take meaning
from the rawness of life and cook it for yourself without fear.'

Remains psychotically depressed. Reported hearing voices but no other
bizarre symptoms noted. Thoughts still coming in 'fragments'. Unable to complete them. Still spending most of time on bed. On 150 mg Doxepin nocte.

Sometimes a speck of light gets into my black hole. The speck is a thought that
has come back into focus.

I am coming up a bit but I feel all weak and wobbly from being on my bed for
days. Before I looked up. This took courage. It was like coming out of a cocoon;
the light was strong; it was strange. The next thing I did was walk around and
say hello to people. It feels good to be halfway back and looking up.

Is beginning to interact. Says she is feeling much better. Asked permission to
[go] out which was refused. Accepted this well. Enjoyed a game of Scrabble,
giggling at times but this was mostly appropriate e.g. at mildly humorous
antics of other patients.

Mary is to be discharged. The family have intimated that they would be glad if I
continued to manage Mary. I will be ready to step in if she has any further psychotic breaks and needs the control of this ward.

29

Wresting his own future

Peter Barham

In the 1920s and 1930s the Ministry of Pensionspromoted institutional treatment as the preferred form of intervention, admitting mentally disabled pensioners to Ministry hospitals for 'hardening' or socialisation into work roles, largely because they had more control over ex-servicemen under these conditions. Separation from families was integral to these regimes because domestic life and influences were perceived as being soft, and subversive of the discipline that such regimes were intended to inculcate. This was 'social reconstruction' at work – a form of *community* care that endeavoured to retain the pensioner as an efficient economic unit as an alternative to banishing him to an asylum. The disclosure that he had all along been a beneficiary of community care would have come as a surprise to William P, since he had been languishing 16 long years in Ministry institutions, mostly on the other side of the country from his home and family, and had quite missed out on seeing his daughters grow up.

Born in 1892, William P had served in China with the South Wales Borderers and been in the fighting at Tientsin. Just two months after returning to England he had been sent to the Dardanelles in time for the landing, where he was wounded and contracted dysentery, his health breaking down generally. At the end of 1915 he was admitted to Maghull where he lay motionless all day, melancholic and lethargic, making no reply to questions, complaining of sounds in his ears like the buzzing of bees, though the authorities managed to elicit from him that in Egypt he had gone with women a good deal, and sometimes been insubordinate. Though he had emerged from his stupor, and returned home to his wife and family in a valley town in South Wales, he seems to have lacked confidence, not least because the economic conditions

Edited extract from P. Barham, Chapter 17, in *Forgotten Lunatics of the Great War* (2007), Yale University Press, pp. 316–20.

did not favour him. From about 1918 onwards he had been a permanent inmate of Ministry of Pensions hospitals, latterly at Orpington in Essex, and was now considered to be suffering from dementia praecox, a 'DP' in the medical shorthand.

The medical reports from the 1920s and early 1930s were consistently bleak: 'No complaints, always "alright". Disinterested. Bored at being asked how he is, fidgety and wants to leave the room. Never volunteers a remark, always distant and inaccessible' (21 February 1927); 'Very fidgety and ill at ease on interview. Never volunteers a remark. No friends. Very inaccessible. Subdued. Merely picking up paper now. Deteriorating slowly' (1 August 1928); 'Man appears resigned to the idea of remaining in hospital. It is extremely unlikely that his present state could have been maintained outside – freedom from all care and worry, regular routine of occupation, good food, occasional interviews have kept him in a stationary state' (15 April 1933). William, however, was rather less inclined to give praise for his institutional good fortune, or to feel himself relieved of care, experiencing certain constraints on his freedom, together with a load of worry about what was going to become of him. Understandably, his family in Wales had also started to voice their concerns, and enlisted the support of their MP. Now put on the defensive, the Ministry medical staff became increasingly rebarbative. 'Pensioner agitating for discharge, cannot say why, no outlook, no plans whatsoever', the doctor curtly commented. 'This man is considered to be a DP, stationary while in hospital. Automaton, incapable of independent life. It is thought that maintenance of his present relatively satisfactory mental state is dependent on retention in hospital and that discharge would be highly experimental' (15 September 1933).

Then, suddenly, 16 months later, there is a divergent appraisal: 'This man has woken up to an extraordinary extent of late, to the surprise of the staff who have known him over a number of years. He has become talkative and the general appearance of DP has, at least temporarily, vanished. His two daughters are waitresses in the Conservative Club, St James Street, and the man now asks for his discharge to keep his wife company. I have known him for ten years and for his present state there has been no counterpart'. William may indeed have woken up, though perhaps he had never been quite as stupefied as the doctor supposed, more likely depressed and befuddled by his circumstances. Unfortunately, however, it is not possible to identify an analogous awakening in the doctor, who continued to ruminate on his deficiencies, and William must have found himself increasingly trapped, not only in an institutional hole, but in a malign administrative and medical mentality with not even a peephole of hope, into which he could only sink deeper.

Learning that it was intended shortly to transfer him to another Ministry hospital, the present one being due for closure, he believed (probably quite correctly) that his fortunes were likely to deteriorate still further, and that in an important respect his life – in the sense of a person having any kind of life to look forward to – was now on the line. 'Entered consulting room and went on his knees in a praying attitude, saying he did not wish to go to Cosham and desired to go home. He has sufficient insight to know that he is not right mentally and he believes that this transfer to Cosham will mean a stepping stone to asylum. His negativism in this respect has reached a climax and there is no dissuading him' (11 May 1935). There *was* no dissuading him either, for the next day, assisted by his wife, he broke with this disciplinary regime and left for home, no mean achievement in the teeth of official threats, the doctor issuing denunciations even as he was walking through the gates: 'discharged against medical advice, his action is part of his negativism and he is not mentally responsible'.

With their 'negativistic' bile, the Pensions medical authorities lacked the insight to see that William was treading the path of hope, for the following month they were still pressing him to return to his station as an in-patient. But William was holding fast, and buoyed-up by his rediscovery of the domestic hearth, he wrote a moving reply, wholly devoid of rancour, that nicely turns the hospital's phraseology on its head and makes William his own occupational therapist:

> The thoughts of further inpatient treatment is an horror to me... I've decided in my best interest that home treatment will benefit me greatly. I feel much happier and more contented here. My Wife is a real Pall to me. She love to have me home and the feelings of being home to me is undescribable after sixteen years of inpatient treatment ... I thank the Medical Advisers and Hospital Staff for there kindness on my behalf. At present, I'm doing occupational treatment in the garden and Wood Work. My Wife fully keep me occupied. Hours pass like minutes.

There were similar protestations of conjugal bliss from Mrs P herself ('after 6 years in hospital I just love to have him home and sir I do all in my power to make him happy') but understandably she was initially also rather ambivalent about the homecoming, more especially in a period when apprehensions gathered like storm clouds about someone who was not strictly 'normal'. Still there are no signs that either of them seriously wavered over the course on which they had now embarked. Over the next three months they would have needed every ounce of their resolve, for the Ministry did everything in its power to undermine their position, proposing at one stage to penalise William for his peremptory refusal of treatment by cutting his pension in half, and sending an inquiry officer, a kind of sleuth in the Ministry's employ, to spy on them in their home town and dig up some incriminating evidence:

> The enquiries were carried out without reference to the pensioner and his wife, although I managed to observe both of them from a shop opposite their house.

Mrs P came to the door and looked up and down the street several times as if she were expecting someone. I noticed she was nicely dressed and had no hat on. She appeared to be rather young, very clean and I assume she had finished her housework for the day. I also observed the pensioner moving about in the front bedroom upstairs and, as far as I could see, he was either painting or doing some form of decoration. Of course, I could not see him clearly. The bed clothes were folded neatly on a chair in the window of the room.

And who could the fresh and bonnetless Mrs P have been waiting for in the street? For her lover, of course, as the malicious Mrs Evans who ran the grocery shop over the way (no doubt the very vantage point from which the Pensions sleuth was observing the suspects) was eager to insinuate. Though she had heard that Mr P was 'mental', she had not observed anything out of the ordinary herself but: 'She told me that, if the man was mental, she would not be surprised, as it would be due to his wife. She said that during the time he was in hospital his wife carried on with several men. . . She said the woman is "fly" . . . Mrs E is about 60 years of age and in my opinion is not a woman who would make random statements'.

Still, the inquiry officer was bound to reveal that his efforts to encourage the townspeople to make out that William was 'mental' had been in vain, for when he called on someone who had known William even before the war, 'this person told me she was surprised he was mental in any way as when she knew him he had always appeared quite normal with the exception of being a little irritable at times. She attributed this entirely to the effects of the war and told me that his people were quite normal and that in her opinion perhaps the man was run down'. Moreover, William's social circumstances were far from propitious, as the officer's report laid bare: 'Even if the man wanted work, he would find great difficulty in obtaining same locally as nearly all the men are unemployed or working 2 days a week only.

Even so, there were officials at the Ministry who did not find this assessment as compelling as it might appear, or saw in it only what they wanted to see, for though the doctor at the Pensions hospital had considered William not to be mentally responsible, it was now proposed (on the logic that if he was not a lunatic in a madhouse then he was very likely a skiver) that 'there is a definite deliberative element in this man's mental condition and that the symptoms are to some extent within his control'. In the event, gently prodded along by the intervention of the local MP, a superior form of medical wisdom did prevail. Summoned to appear before another medical board, William, 'a tall muscular man, apparently well cared for' became 'timid and frightened', with his oft-repeated 'I'm happier at home' exhibiting his fear of being sent back to hospital. Concluding that there was, perhaps, after all some merit in helping him to lead his own independent life, the authorities awarded him a 100 per cent war disability pension for dementia praecox.

30

Life stories – Ron Coleman

Jeremy Laurance

Big Ron stands, feet apart, arms swinging in unison either side of his ample belly, grey shirt open at the collar, frowning at his audience. Hearing voices is normal, he insists. Nothing wrong with it. Some of the greatest figures in history had their private lines of communication.

'If it's good enough for Gandhi and good enough for Christ, why isn't it good enough for us? Why should we always see it as something negative?'

Ron Coleman is enjoying this. His aim in running this workshop is to change people's view of one of the key symptoms of schizophrenia, auditory illusions. Instead of regarding the voices as a delusion, to be dismissed and drowned out with heavy doses of antipsychotic drugs, he argues they should be acknowledged and explored so that the voice hearer can come to own the experience. Ownership is key to recovery, he says.

As a 'recovered' schizophrenic – he carried the diagnosis for ten years from his early twenties and was hospitalised for six years – he is one of the best known ex-users of the mental health system. Now in his early forties, this former Scottish rugby player with blonde highlights and Diesel sandals makes his living teaching others about the shortcomings of the psychiatric system, with its reductionist diagnoses, its refusal to acknowledge the reality of the mental patient's experience and its denial of recovery as the goal of psychiatry.

'I hear seven voices,' he says. 'That doesn't change. What changes is how I relate to those voices. I find when you ask people what their voices say it does make sense. It is essential to contextualise them.'

Conventional psychiatric wisdom has it that voice hearers should not be encouraged to engage with their voices because it makes them worse.

Edited and adapted from J. Laurance, *Pure Madness: How Fear Drives the Mental Health System* (2003), Routledge, pp. 134–8.

Kindly indifference is the accepted strategy, or what Ron calls 'radical non-intervention'. 'It's crap,' he adds.

Instead, voice hearers must be helped to accept their experience and take responsibility for their actions. 'People make choices – to listen, to obey, or not. One of the first things I say [to voice hearers] is that they are responsible for what happens. I will not take responsibility for their actions.'

At this point he pulls two people out of the audience – a man and a woman, strangers to one another – stands them facing each other and then orders the man to hit the woman. The man refuses. Ron repeats the order several times but the man continues to refuse. Triumphantly, he sends them back to their seats. 'You see,' he says, 'you don't have to do what the voices tell you to do.'

It is a powerful piece of theatre and he is an effective speaker – funny, moving, charismatic. He works without notes and has a gift for comic timing which wins over his audience of fifty social workers, nurses and a scattering of mental health service users throughout a day in which he is the only attraction. He intersperses homilies about the treatment of mentally ill people with accounts of his own grim experience: 'When I went into hospital it was always on a section. You must be mad to go voluntarily.'

He traces his own mental problems to the abuse he suffered as a boy at the hands of a Catholic priest in the 1970s: 'You can't fight and you can't run because you are being abused by an adult so what you do is run to a different place – called dissociation. You create a different reality.'

At the same time he took up rugby – and found consolation in the licensed violence: 'I played in the scrum and I would see the priest's face in my opposite number's face and batter it.'

He suffered a second major blow with the sudden death of an early girlfriend and his first true love. He left Scotland at the age of 17 and joined the army. He got a degree in accountancy but had few friends. He was a loner. Then he broke his back playing rugby and was told he would never play again. Six weeks after he came out of hospital he heard his first voice. He was working for a firm of accountants in London in the days when computers were steam-powered: 'A voice behind me said "You've got it wrong". I looked round and there was no one there. I finished up as quick as I could, went to the pub and got bladdered.'

One of the first voices was that of his dead girlfriend urging him to come and join her – a suicide voice. But later many others joined them. Now he has reduced the cacophony to a manageable half dozen – and they no longer have power over him: 'I contend these voices were not created by my biology but by my experience. Guilt was the key factor. When I dealt with the guilt the voices became less powerful. It took me a long time to realise the priest who had abused me was the guilty one [and not me] but when I did I telephoned him and told him he had three days to turn himself in before I went to the police. He went to a life monastery – a closed institution – to contemplate the nature of sin.'

During his decade as a psychiatric patient – in and out of hospital and taking a cocktail of five drugs, some to control the psychosis and some to deal with the side effects of the other drugs – he was always discouraged from engaging with his voices. 'Let's play Scrabble' was the usual reply from the nurses when a patient on the psychiatric ward said their voices were bothering them. This, Ron believes, is profoundly wrong. 'Common sense alone should tell us that these situations must be worked through he said.

In his contribution to *This is Madness: A Critical Look at Psychiatry and Mental Health Services* (Coleman, 1999) he wrote:

> In the early 1980s I was diagnosed as schizophrenic. By 1990 that was changed to chronic schizophrenic and in 1993 I gave up being a schizophrenic and decided to be Ron Coleman. Giving up being a schizophrenic is not an easy thing to do, for it means taking back responsibility for yourself, it means you can no longer blame your illness for your actions. It means that there is no disease to hide behind, no more running back to hospital every time things get a bit rough, but more important than any of these things it means that you stop being a victim of your experience and start being the owner of your experience.

The picture he presents of the mental health system is overwhelmingly negative – although he denies he is anti-psychiatry. He says international studies show recovery rates from schizophrenia are better in Uttar Pradesh, in India, despite its grinding poverty, than in the UK. And what is the reason? Hope, he says: 'They expect people to get better. Here we expect people to remain ill.'

For practical advice on how to help voice hearers he suggests fake mobile phones can be useful for those who wish to answer back to their voices. A person walking down the street gabbling to him or herself risks being carted off to the nearest padded cell, he says, but one muttering into a mobile would not attract a backward glance. 'For 20 pence you can give someone their life back. It's practical and it normalises the experience,' he says.

He tells a joke about a voice hearer who was using his mobile on a train, engaged in animated conversation with one of his voices. The train entered a tunnel and all the other mobile users in the carriage closed their instruments down as they lost reception – except for him.

As he gabbled on he attracted some looks – not of fear but of wonder. After the train emerged from the tunnel, a man approached him. 'I couldn't help noticing,' he began, 'how you maintained reception in that tunnel. Would you mind telling me what network you are on?'

He also hands out a workbook, *Victim to Victor*, which includes a series of exercises to help voice hearers work through their voices, understanding them, organising them and finally accepting them.

Whatever the criticisms of his analysis – flawed and simplistic though it is – the most striking feature of the day is the enthusiasm of his audience. They like what he says, the way he says it and they like him. One senior psychiatric nurse from Birmingham, who has brought six of his staff to the workshop, said: 'Psychiatry is stuck. This is the only new thing happening.'

That captures the essence of the discontent. Here are committed staff, eager to help the thousands of distressed people in need of psychiatric treatment and support, yet all they have at their disposal are drugs which do little more than mask the symptoms and carry a heavy burden of side effects. They are, in the view of many, little better than chemical coshes.

Many of the staff here feel there must he a better and a more humane way – one which makes sense of the mental patient's experience and thereby eases the suffering. But that requires a change in the culture of care.

Reference

Coleman, R. (1999) 'Hearing voices and the politics of oppression', in Newnes, C., Holmes, G. and Dunn, C. (eds), *This is Madness: a Critical Look at Psychiatry and the Future of Mental Health Services*, PCCS Books, Ross-on-Wye, pp. 149–64.

31

Hearing voices

A psychiatric explanation

Ivan Leudar and Phil Thomas

The majority of people who hear voices nowadays are under psychiatric care and on neuroleptic medication. Their experiences have been interpreted within a medical framework which regards voices as a symptom of serious mental illness. This framework precludes any exploration of the content of voices, other than that which the psychiatrist considers necessary to establish those features which she regards as important in establishing a diagnosis. Psychiatrists are only interested in the small number of limited features of voices necessary to make a diagnosis. Some types of voices form part of the group of first-rank symptoms (FRS) described by Schneider (1957). Schneider thought that the presence of one or more of these symptoms, in the absence of organic brain disease, indicated a diagnosis of schizophrenia. FRS include three types of auditory hallucinations: hearing voices speaking your thoughts out loud; hearing two or more voices arguing or having a discussion about you in the third person; hearing one or more voice carrying on a running commentary about your thoughts or actions. These experiences play a prominent role in most modern diagnostic systems, such as ICD-10, which relies heavily on the presence of FRS to establish the diagnosis of schizophrenia. Table 31.1 is an extract from section 17 of ICD-10, the standard system of classification used in the UK.

In practice, most psychiatrists would not refer to a list of symptoms but would rely on a series of questions which they ask patients, first to probe for the presence of VH, second to elicit the nature of these experiences. If the content of the voices indicates that they are of the first-rank symptom type, then

Edited from I. Leudar and P. Thomas (2000) *Voices of Reason, Voices of Insanity*, London, Routledge, pp. 112–14.

Table 31.1   Description of verbal hallucinations from SCAN 10

Information on eleven aspects of hallucinations

17.1	probe for hallucinations	Yes/No
17.3	non-verbal hallucinations	Yes/No
17.4	frequency of verbal auditory hallucinations	Yes/No
17.5	length of utterances	–
17.6	quality of VH	–
17.7	internal hallucinations (inner voices)	Yes/No
17.8	voices commenting on thoughts or actions	Yes/No
17.9	second- and third-person auditory hallucinations	Yes/No
17.12	special features of auditory hallucinations	Yes/No
17.13	insight into auditory hallucinations	Yes/No
17.14	prominence of auditory hallucinations	–

the diagnosis will almost certainly be schizophrenia. There are two exceptions to this. Schneider pointed out that the presence of FRS indicated schizophrenia only in the absence of organic brain disease, so it is important to ensure that there is no evidence of clouding of consciousness, confusion or other clinical features that would suggest that the subject is organically ill. In addition, the psychiatrist will want to establish whether the subject's voices are understandable in terms of a mood change. Voices can occur in severe depression and hypomania, but under these circumstances it is argued that the content of hallucinatory voices is understandable in terms of the mood change, which is then regarded as the primary problem. For example, a profoundly depressed subject may hear voices saying that she is wicked or evil. A hypomanic subject may hear a voice telling her that she is the new Madonna, and that the songs she has written will top the charts. In each case the psychiatrist would argue that the content of these voices is consistent with an underlying mood change, and that this is the primary problem, not schizophrenia.

This is usually as far as the experience will be explored. Once these features have been elicited, then no further explication of voices is considered valuable. In psychiatry voices have little or no meaning. They are, like mind itself, an epiphenomenon secondary to what are regarded as more important biological processes. The pharmacological management of schizophrenia then becomes the priority, and the subject's preoccupation with and self-reports of voices becomes little more than an index of the extent to which the underlying illness is controlled by medication.

This model regards any attempt to get the subject to talk about her experiences as meaningless.

Reference

Schneider, K. (1957) 'Primäre and Sekundäre symptomen bei schizophrenie' [Primary and secondary symptoms in schizophrenia], *Fortschritte der Neurologie Psychiatrie*, no. 25, p. 487.

Time-sharing

J. Thomas

I was 21 and had been at university for a year. I was back home for the summer holiday when my first breakdown hit me. I was labelled with schizophrenia. I blamed the voices for my plight, voices discussing me and, worse, voices commanding me to do idiot things.

To secure my release from the terrible locked hospital ward that held me for so many months, I had to move from blaming voices to accepting them, and then from acceptance to concealment.

Then, as far as the outside world was concerned, I was able to deny and hide these symptoms. I was able to return to university, complete my degree, and hold down a job. Or rather a succession of jobs – for, in my case, 'accepting voices' was by no means foolproof. I kept slipping up, and often these failures would lead to further detentions in hospital. Detentions became more frequent, and for a while the outlook was dismal.

Then, during my last hospital stay, I met another patient called Fred. Fred told me about time-sharing. He claimed it was 'the only well-known, tried and tested way of getting shot of schizophrenia without the drugs'.

I was sceptical: 'If it's that well known, why don't I know about it?' I asked.

But Fred kept on: 'Time-sharing simply means letting in the other side of your brain, the side that is bugging you. It's bugging you because you never let it in to share power – to share control of your own, and of course its own, body'.

'What do you mean by letting it in?' I asked.

'I mean you invite the other side of your own brain to take control of your body for a short time each day. All you have to do is to relax and allow it to take over. It's a sort of self-hypnotism. In return you make your other brain side promise to stop spooking you.'

Eventually I did try time-sharing. I told my carer about what Fred had said, she thought about it for a long time and then said that it could well be true. She told me to tell my other half that I was prepared to time-share with it, that I would let it in and give it control.

Previously published in *Openmind* (2000), 103, May/June, p. 17.

It wasn't easy but gradually it began to work. I used to hate getting up. Now I leave it to my other half I only need take over when I have to meet someone. I now have a working relationship with my other half. It no longer sends me voices or bugs me in any way. Since I do not have to fight to prevent my other half taking control, I have much more energy left to live my own life. I have now been completely well and without need of medication for over thirty years.

Learning from voices

Jan Holloway with Elaine Craig

At first, the voice was barely audible. But as time passed the whisper became louder. I was 33 years old and had never before experienced the plaguing presence of disembodied speech circling around me. Initially, I couldn't hear what the faint, intermittent voice was saying – yet soon it became harsher in timbre and increasingly menacing in content. I did not speak to anyone about it – not even my partner of fifteen years – although I felt a pervasive sense of alienation and confusion.

I became tormented by its continuous criticism, and, in a bid to silence the voice forever, I attempted to kill myself by taking a cocktail of prescribed drugs and alcohol. When this failed, I voluntarily admitted myself to hospital, but remained mute about my voice, ashamed of its presence. On my return to work, the voice began to taunt me again, this time commenting that I was no good at my job and wasn't fit to be a manager. It also told me I ought to drown myself. With my self-esteem eroded by perpetual criticism, I tried to take my own life for the second time.

Again the attempt failed and I was admitted to hospital. Treatment with medication and therapy helped, and the voice was silenced – but only temporarily. As the stress in my life mushroomed – due to family and work pressures – the voice fought its way back into my head. And this time it was not alone; the original voice was joined by a second, and I became a reluctant eavesdropper to their many conversations. Their dialogue concentrated on my laziness, selfishness and worthlessness; and I was, of course, privy to all these debates – but always spoken about as if I was an absent third party.

In the face of such persecution, I became paranoid. On the brink of suicide I admitted myself to hospital and, again, improved a little. Talking about the voices with others who had similar experiences helped – and the medication I was prescribed gave me a palpable sense of distance from my voices. Their presence, however, was still audible.

Previously published as J. Holloway (with E. Craig) in *Openmind* (2000), 103, May/June, p. 16.

Yet tentatively and reluctantly I have learnt to live with them. At times, it is difficult. When at work, I have to remember not to respond to the voices with any sign of recognition. During times of stress, they become louder and more insistent. I have to learn to remain true to myself – the more I compromise for others the more troublesome the voices become. And now that I have found I can indeed function despite their presence, sometimes the voices can be helpful and even bring insight.

In fact, the more I talk about them, the less caught up I become in their opinions about me. The more I use my experience to help others, the more empowered I become. Perhaps paradoxically, it is in listening to the cries of our psychosis that we can begin to find a pathway through the convoluted maze of our own particular distress.

32

The recovery of hope

Alex Williams

The first time I heard the words 'recovery model' was six years ago. It was the first meeting with my community psychiatric nurse. I felt misunderstood. I thought she couldn't have read my file when she said she would work with me to this model. Writing this now I hope to give an insight into what recovery means to me, the pace of change and the joint commitments involved.

I will return to that first appointment and my circumstances then. My CPN had 'inherited' me from psychiatric services I'd been under since I was 17, six years previously. I had been treated for severe anorexia in local and out-of-area Eating Disorder services. A two-year placement I had just left introduced me to and normalised a severe level of self-harm. The move here and difficulties in my first-ever job caused me to start cutting again. Apparently supportive employers then terminated my contract. I lived in a homeless hostel but could make no friends there. After a paracetemol overdose I was admitted the first of many times to the mental health ward. I was broken, defensive, terrified and hopeless. The words 'borderline personality disorder' were added to my records.

My social worker at that time put forward residential care as the only option. The hostel manager had been concerned about accepting me from the start. I was cutting several times a day in a room that smelt of blood. Though I lived only five minutes walk from Accident and Emergency, I nearly didn't reach it one time late at night and had to lie on the benches on the way. But my CPN made a strong case to both the housing department and her colleagues for me to live independently. This would be the first time for me, at the age of 24.

The move, while risky, was to be a major turning point. I decorated this new place of my own. A support worker helped me with practical issues like moving and buying all I needed on a tight budget.

Previously published in *Kent Journal of Mental Health* (2007) issue 2, pp. 16–17.

While a productive 18 months followed, I hadn't gained the personal aware-ness and social skills I needed. I self-disclosed everything to people I'd only just met. I got involved with many activities to impress others, without addres-sing my inner pain and history.

On one long Sunday afternoon alone, I decided to make just one cut again. This led to relentless self-harm. Every day I would blood-let into a bucket, I'd have frequent blood transfusions, after which I'd cut again and return for the same treatment days later. I removed skin and had assessments for grafts. I again took overdoses despite finding them traumatic. Sections of the Mental Health Act were used for short periods of up to a few weeks. This was mainly to give my body a break from my attack on it.

Despite all of these events my CPN never gave up in her faith in my abilities to change my life. She saw that I was a fighter. But she challenged my actions, giving honest information about the consequences including the high chance of death. She also saw how severe anaemia worsened my existing depression. She didn't make me stop cutting and said she couldn't until I found a replace-ment for it. But when it spiralled out of all control she decided to give me the choice of taking time out from seeing her, getting it out of my system, then returning when prepared to work hard on myself.

I slowly started to shift and open my heart to change. I could see services wouldn't be withdrawn as a result. I started to talk about my feelings, my life and fears. My CPN listened, and had the skills to work with me psychodynami-cally. This went further back and deeper than outward signs of distress. It has been very challenging work and to firm boundaries. I wasn't allowed to blame 'illness' for my feelings, but was expected to look at what was going on. I objected to the term 'learnt behaviour' but over time could see how I'd laid down ways of coping in my formative years.

That brings us back to recovery and what it means. It is long-term and not a smooth road. Setbacks shouldn't be taken as 'she's ill again, has there been self-harm?' They are yet another challenge. The intensity of an episode two months ago made me feel scared, confused and vulnerable. But I tried to work through it with my CPN using tools she has given me. Extra support worker time and crisis medication were elements of a package I was able to negotiate around.

I have a respect for my CPN that is a mutual one. She has worked in an evidence-based way, using different approaches including a reflective diary I write every day. Both of the consultant psychiatrists I have been under have also listened and valued my experience. My first consultant took positive risks responding to requests for full psychiatric assessments from medical consul-tant colleagues concerned by the number of unit of blood I used. My GP also did a lot of work often beyond surgery opening hours so I would get the medical treatment I needed.

I write my own care plan, then discuss all changes with my CPN. I have made joint decisions about reducing medication. But I do see a need to use it where sleep deprivation compromises my ability to cope and be safe.

The language mental health workers use is important. I overheard the word 'chronic' self harmer used about me more than once. One psychiatric nurse said to a colleague, in front of me, that 'they've tried everything but nothing has worked with her.' She named different services, including a self harm unit, that had apparently treated me but I hadn't even been referred to. I don't think I was confident enough to say this.

Recovery doesn't mean problem solved or cure. With aspects of my distress it is about living with them. This has been true of my eating disorder. Despite remaining outside of EDUs since I moved here, food is still a difficult issue for me. My anxiety, response to stress and mood are areas of ongoing work. As I see it, recovery goes beyond use of resources past or present. It's about quality of life and how the individual sees and experiences this.

Involvement with community life is flagged up as a contributing factor to recovery. This has always been encouraged and my care plans have included adult education classes, complementary therapies, voluntary work, supported computer training, church and social groups.

I am now able to like and try to be kinder to myself. I wish I had a personal record of the last six years. I destroyed letters and all my diaries to protect those I thought would find them after a death that felt inevitable. I grieve for lost years but wouldn't want them back or to reexamine every event. I try to see the positives like my resilience and my hope one day to give back by helping others.

In writing this, I also wanted to show that change and development can occur in the most difficult circumstances. If you can't see or believe in individual potential what message does that give to the person without hope or any sense of connection? It is always difficult to see someone hurting badly physically and emotionally. But the only response is to continue to take the individual seriously, listen, be truthful and consistent. If the view 'nothing helps' had been taken over my treatment then I probably wouldn't be here now. Instead, I received support to enable me to find my own solutions and take control of my life. I know I am fortunate in this and to be alive to write it.

33

Two hours fifty five minutes

Veronica Dewan

When we are fragile we enter the psychiatric system, when we most need to be treated with compassion, when we need hope and strength to pull us out of despair, why is it so hard for us to remember any acts of kindness?

Between 1991 and 1996 I had several admissions to a psychiatric ward, my crisis followed from competing my first year at university as a mature student, working at nights while doing a full time degree, meeting my birth parents, ending a long relationship with a manipulative male lover and beginning to recognise how much damage had been caused by my adoption. As a woman of Indian and Irish heritage, I had been born and brought up in rural England by white parents.

It has been a tough lesson, learning that care means little more than containment, that treatment means heavy medication. Yet I have worked hard to remember the times I was shown respect, the ways in which my dignity was upheld, to recall who would listen, who would validate my insights. The institution of psychiatry is made up of people; there are people who have helped me and I need to remember them; I still believe in the goodness of humanity.

I remember the Mauritian nursing assistant who shared her home cooked curry with me when I was admitted to the ward after midnight. Whenever I returned to that ward she treated me with kindness. And there was the Polish charge nurse who took me to the playing field beside the hospital and encouraged me to scream. She said she wanted to help me release my anger after hearing me speak about the childhood abuse. The Bajan nursing assistant who

Previously published in *Asylum* (2004), vol. 14, no. 4, p. 8.

held my hand while I cried and shook after I was sexually assaulted by another patient, would often take me for gentle walks around the hospital. And an Irish charge nurse, she was the one who once reached me when I was in the deepest despair, by hugging me.

I have to remember these people because so many terrible things happen when we are in hospital and it takes years to recover from the effects of being personally and collectively ignored, humiliated, misunderstood and misdiagnosed by representatives of the institution of psychiatry. There was the French psychiatrist who disagreed with my English consultant that the only treatment appropriate to me would be medication for life. She was the fourth psychiatrist I had seen in two weeks. She told me she had witnessed how badly her 'mixed race' sons were treated in this country, their father was Indian, and she was insistent that I needed talking treatment. It was the final day of her six-month contract at that hospital and she immediately persuaded the consultant to refer me to psychotherapy. I realise now how lucky I was to meet her in time otherwise I may not have survived.

It was the anniversary of my Indian biological father's death. If I wasn't in hospital I would have visited a chapel that was one of the last places I saw him alive. It had been a difficult relationship, when I was born he denied paternity and as a result I was adopted. As an adult I searched for and found him, even worked for him. He had a serious problem with alcohol and he died six years after we met. I took responsibility to tell the nursing staff that this anniversary would be a difficult day for me, I gave them notice of this several days in advance and each day leading up to the anniversary. When I knocked at the door of the nurses' station that day and asked to be taken to the chapel I was ignored. My Irish primary nurse kept her back to me as she wrote at her desk, her colleagues chatting between themselves and not acknowledging me. My primary nurse spoke without turning around, 'Why are you so demanding? Can't you see we're short staffed? Go back to your room.' I felt humiliation and hurt swelling up inside, and I turned and headed for the door. I was after all an informal patient and had the right to leave at any time. As I reached the stairs four nurses pounced on me, tufts of my hair were pulled out and my arm was bruised and twisted. I was held under Section while the English duty psychiatrist came. When she heard what had happened she took me immediately to the chapel, she was clearly angry at the unnecessary use of force. When I was ready to return to the ward, she said 'Take as long as you need.' Back on the ward a Nigerian nurse who was repeatedly racially abused by patients asked me to try to understand how difficult it was for the staff to meet my demands.

The nurse who hugged me took ten minutes of her time. The nurse who encouraged me to scream spent one hour taking me to the field and back, the nursing assistant who shared her food took an hour to heat it, eat it and have a conversation with me, the psychiatrist who understood the experience of 'mixed race' people took fifteen minutes to assess me, the psychiatrist who took me to the chapel took half an hour. Having spent about eight months in total over a period of six years on the psychiatric ward of a general hospital, it would need several hundred pages to record the neglect and mistreatment I received and witnessed.

34

Are we who we say we are – or who you think we are?

Premila Trivedi

The words we use to describe ourselves are not simple static descriptors of our physical being, but say much about the values and beliefs we hold, our view of own selves and how we see ourselves in relation to others and, perhaps most importantly, how we would like to be perceived. Words are therefore a brilliant way of clarifying who we are. So why do so many people manage to avoid the words I choose to describe myself and instead assign words to me according to how they see me and, from that viewpoint, make conclusions about whom I am? For example:

- The academic researcher who refers to me as non-white, immediately conveying that he recognises white as the norm and sees me outside that 'normality'.

- The consultant psychiatrist who insists I am not black because I am not of African origin, completely ignoring my own (political) interpretation of black and why that term is so important for me.

- The mental health service manager who sees me only as Asian and, in service planning meetings, disregards anything I have to say about issues other than 'Asian issues' and the fact that I may have valid views on those issues too.

- The CPN [community psychiatric nurse} who sees me as Indian and does her liberal best to educate herself about the lives of Indian women but never actually spends much time listening to me, who I say I am and my life experiences.

Previously published in *Asylum* (2004), vol. 14, no. 4, pp. 4–5.

- The OT [occupational therapist] who identifies with me as Gujerati and uses (what she sees as) our similarity to hide our differences and therefore never identifies my needs.

- The hospital Chaplain who sees me as Hindu and tries to interpret everything in my life in terms of my Hinduism, compounding my confusion about my religious faith.

- The feminist psychologist who describes me as a woman of colour in order to place me in her political framework, never questioning whether and how I see myself fitting (or not fitting) into her structures.

- The MH [mental health] survivor who insists he sees me as a person and not a skin colour, thereby discounting a large part of me which has repeatedly aroused negative responses from others and in many ways shaped the course of my life.

So by listening to the words other people use about us, it is fairly easy to identify their attitudes and views on how they see me and my differences. In choosing to use their own words, they dismiss the way I choose to describe myself and (reminiscent of slavery?) assign me an identity that works better for them and does not disturb their sense of self. Thus are power relations structured.

Dalal (2002) has elaborated on this with particular regard to the words black and white. He states that within the English language the clear associations between white and positivity and black and negativity have developed within the context of power relations and are not natural in any sense:

> emotions that are disapproved of start becoming coloured black at about the same time that the European imperialist adventure is taking place . . . and white and black have been honed into powerful devices . . . which are used to lever things into territories of good and bad. (Dalal, 2002)

Thus language has thus become colour-coded and reflects power relations. For some who recognize this and find it uncomfortable, there may be a tendency to avoid the word black and instead use words like 'coloured'. Alternatively, people may re-label the word black in a positive way, for example, by linking it with words conveying strength and purpose (such as Black Power). However, this may cause anxiety and fear and there may be attempts to dismiss such links, as Sivanandum (1990) describes:

> The liberal . . . points out that Black Power itself is an offensive sympathy-losing phrase . . . [because] the connotations of Black created by the white man himself are so frightening, so evil, so primordial that to associate with it power as well is to invoke the nightmare world of divine retribution, of Judgement day.

Thus the words people choose not to use also convey power relations and maybe explains why, even in this day and age, many people do not feel comfortable with the word black when applied to people and try to counter it.

So where does that leave us as black women? As passive, mute victims constantly being defined and boxed up by others or (as in this issue) strong and determined women who are using their personal and creative powers to firmly state who they are, how they wish to be perceived and a challenging of power relations. Unfortunately, in the context of mental health services, that very strength, determination and commitment can get us labelled as challenging, psychotic, schizophrenic and/or personality disordered. But rather than pathologising us, the services should be seeing black women's endurance, resilience, strength and belief in themselves in the positive light it demands, and enable us to define ourselves in our own words without putting their words on us.

I'm not sure the day will come in my lifetime when this will happen, but for now I just ask that we as black women are listened to and our terminology for ourselves accepted. Importantly, such terminology may vary depending on the context, so we may use different terms at different times. But this is an additional means of clarification, not an attempt to confuse or to be difficult. Thus every black woman has the right to define themselves exactly as they want. For me, I am

- Black when I am mindful of my experiences of discrimination and oppression on the basis of my skin colour and am in solidarity with others who have shared similar, better or worse experiences

- Asian as a kind of short hand to acknowledge my difference from African Caribbean women

- Indian when I want to identify the roots and heritage that run deep within me even though I have only ever visited India once

- Gujerati when I want to stress the cultural background against which I have been raised, but which I do not necessarily maintain or ascribe to

- Hindu when I need to show how spirituality has shaped my thinking and being but also caused me confusion which I want recognised.

Non-white, coloured and colour-blind words I never use, and even woman of colour does not feel quite right for me.

So what am I trying to say? Simply that we black women are not a homogeneous bunch. We are shaped by our 'race', culture and ethnicity certainly but also by other factors in our life such as class, gender, sexuality, education, disability and faith. And that complex diversity is the very thing that should make us (as a group) so powerful and strong. How we choose to describe ourselves as individuals at any moment in time (in terms of our race, culture, gender, class, etc.) is critically important and has usually evolved from much personal heart-searching as well as intellectual thought. So please don't dismiss the words and terms we use when we talk to you, and accept we may use different terms at different times. If you curb your enthusiasm to put your perception on us and instead listen carefully to us, you'll find out so much more about us and you may even start to see us more as strong and courageous and less as scary and challenging.

References

Dalal, F. (2002). *Race: Colour and the Process of Racialization: New Perspectives from Group Analysis, Psychoanalysis as Sociology*, London, Routledge.

Sivanandum, A. (1990). 'All that melts into air is solid: the hokum of New Times', *Race and Class*, vol. 31, no. 3, p. 23.

What black women want from the mental health services

Patricia Chambers

I happen to be a black woman who lives under the label of being mentally ill and when I was asked to write this piece I thought to myself it's going to be very short. What can the services give me? They can't give me a good brother to keep me company, share my life and be a companion, it can't give me children, it can't give me a job, it can't rid the Motherland of AIDS. I was in intense thought for weeks. Then the thought came to me, I thought I know what I'd like the mental health services to do for me; I'd like them to seriously tackle stigma in mental health. The dis-respect that I and others (male and female) get when we're brave enough to publicy declare or reveal that we suffer from mental distress and are debatably labelled mentally ill. It wasn't something that I planned for myself or included in my itinerary for my journey through life so should I be ashamed of something that I had NO control over and that ANYONE can have and that they say 'you wouldn't wish on your worst enemy.' Something that has banished me to life-long poverty and broken dreams. It usually happens when you're young and just starting out in life, around your mid-twenties even early thirties is still an age where affliction causes great devastation.

The powers that be need to tell it like it is for people with mental health problems, stories of courage and strength and determination not just letting the image of violence and murder dominate the minds of the general public. I'm not saying that it doesn't happen but that all you hear about in the

Previously published in *Asylum* (2004), vol. 14, no. 4, pp. 14–15.

Harm-minimisation: limiting the damage of self-injury

Louise Roxanne Pembroke

My own experience of realising the concept

As a teenager I knew nothing about first-aid, anatomy, physiology and wound care, I never studied science at 'O' or 'A' level. At 17, I attempted to kill myself and took a Paracetomol overdose believing I would fall unconscious and quietly die in my sleep escaping the intolerable pain of living. Within months of my unsuccessful attempt I was injuring myself, initially superficial scratches, then the cuts became deeper.

Psychiatric hospitalisation only compounded my need to harm myself and the response from staff was frequently angry and hostile. Back at home as my distress and isolation deepened I would go to my local GP surgery with wounds but was frequently referred to Accident and Emergency. There, I learnt what good and bad care meant. One doctor would stitch wounds to the bone of my arm with just a skin suture, not bothering to repair the underlying layers. As the verbal humiliation and hostility increased with each visit to A&E I became increasingly reluctant to attend for fear of the response I would get.

At this point in my life I was struggling with reduced eyesight due to a rare eye condition, was too depressed to continue with a college course I had

Edited from H. Spandler and S. Warner (eds) (2007), *Beyond Fear and Control*, PCCS Books, pp. 163–72.

worked hard to get into, and had very little in my life after psychiatric admissions. Friends were scared of the loony girl who was rumoured to be carving herself up. In short, I lost hope, and didn't think that anyone else believed in me either. Loss of hope jettisoned my need to self-injure and as I became more depressed by the responses to my self-harm this turned into what Gethin Morgan (1979, 1992) refers to as 'malignant alienation'. I became increasingly alienated and withdrawn from everything to the point that I felt death was preferable to the responses to my self-injuring, so I attempted to die again.

Not only did I not know how to look after myself, I didn't care to. My general state of health deteriorated, the ophthalmologist could see this in my eyes and I stopped going to A&E, but my inability to look after myself resulted in septicaemia. The social service run day centre wouldn't accept me on grounds that I was too much of a danger to myself and my GP told me that I risked losing the use of my arm. He might as well have said that my head would drop off because I didn't understand *how* I could lose the use of a limb.

Ros, was my ophthalmic nurse, she had known me since I was 14 years old and seen this bright outgoing girl turn into a slumped shadow of herself. She also grasped just how traumatised I was with the deterioration in my eyesight and the ongoing difficulties and how this must have impacted on someone who was in full-time dance training which requires good sight. Ros knew I was harming myself and during one appointment she asked "What's wrong, are you hurt?", I said I was but that I couldn't face the humiliation of Accident and Emergency so she calmly asked to see the wound. I was adamant there was no way I was going to A&E even if I did get septicaemia again, so she offered to help me look after it so that didn't happen.

It was a bad wound, down to the bone again which I didn't realise because I expected a bone to appear bright shiny white, I didn't realise that bone is covered in a yellowish layer of connective tissue called periosteum.

Ros gave me my first lesson in anatomy and physiology when I was 18 years old. She explained what each layer of tissue was called, what it's function was and what could happen to it if damaged. I learnt that the yellow globular stuff was *fat*, the purplish-brownish bit underneath that which looked like meat at the supermarket was *muscle*. That the white cords which join the muscle to the bone were *tendons* and they were really something I didn't want to damage because *that's* what could have resulted in loss of mobility (now the GP's warnings made sense).

I learnt the difference between veins and arteries and that it was easy to not see a nerve before cutting it. At least most of my serious injuries were *longitudinal*, that afforded me slightly more safety, but that had been luck not judgement on my part.

Ros taught me how to recognise the symptoms of infection and how to minimise the risk of it occurring such as by using clean blades, washing my hands, pulling the wound together with *steristrips* or tape and dressing it with appropriate dressings. Although wounds to the bone really should be repaired properly with each layer of tissue sewn together, she understood that at that point I couldn't face going to A&E and that it was more important to give me the necessary basic knowledge so that I didn't put my life or limb at risk.

This non-judgemental and practical approach was imparted without any lecturing or catastrophising and had a profound impact on me. Ros was the first person who didn't recoil in disgust or be angry, negative or distressed about my need to self-injure. She understood that was where I was at in my life and she *accepted* me whether I harmed or didn't harm. I didn't have to hide it, justify it, or make bargains or promises I couldn't keep, it was such a relief, and, I could ask her for straightforward advice about any aspect of first aid and wound care.

For the first time I had some *control* over my circumstances. I had *choices*, I could *choose* to stop cutting at a certain point, I could *choose* to position the blade the other side of the vein to avoid a major bleed, I could *choose* to make it cleaner and safer. It might not seem like much of a choice but it is when you are striving to stay out of the psychiatric system, cope with extreme experiences and failing eyesight, it's a big deal. Having some physical control over my self-injury was my first step towards engaging more actively with the need to injure and negotiating with that need. Just as IV drug users having access to clean needles is life saving (not that I am in anyway suggesting that self-injury is an addiction, I don't subscribe to that idea).

Likewise good sexual health services would not dictate abstinence to people having multiple sexual partners but promote safer sex by the use of condoms to prevent the contraction of HIV. Some Alcohol Dependency services also address limiting the damage that heavy alcohol consumption can result in.

These services have debated and practised the concept of *harm-minimisation*.

References

Morgan, H. G. (1979) *Death Wishes: The Understanding and Management of Deliberate Self-Harm*, Chichester, John Wiley.

Morgan, H. G. (1992) 'Suicide prevention: Hazards on the fast road to community care, *British Journal of Psychiatry*, vol. 160, pp. 149–53.

37

My right to choose

Amanda Wells

I have been on psychiatric medication for over 12 years now. I cannot say it has always been a happy experience. However, during those times when I have been without medication, I felt so awful that even if taking the tablets was not the most enjoyable thing, I have gone back on them – even begged my GP for them – in preference to going without. At the moment, I am very satisfied with my drug regime: the medication is helping me to be well and I would not dream of stopping it.

My diagnosis is schizoaffective disorder, depressive type, so the appropriate medication is antidepressants and antipsychotics. Currently, I take Effexor and Solian, both at moderate doses so I am more-or-less untroubled by side-effects.

Over the years, I have had just about every drug in the book. Some have been good, some indifferent and some a downright nightmare. It has been a process of trial and error. The worst drug I have ever been on is Depixol depots. These not only gave me side effects that included massive weight-gain and unwanted movements, but also actually made my symptoms worse. I asked to stop Depixol and try something else instead, but I was threatened with being sectioned if I refused the injections. For four years I was coerced into taking Depixol, which was a horrible situation to be in as I knew it was making me more ill.

I finally managed to convince the doctors that the drug was doing me no good at all, and at last they listened to my pleas to try something else. I had been through most of the old antipsychotics by then, but luckily the atypicals had come out so I began working my way through them. Solian is the third one I have tried, and I seem to have struck gold with it. Similarly with the antidepressants; I have been on Effexor since my previous medication seemed to

Previously published in *Openmind* (2003), vol. 123, October, p. 13.

be no longer effective. I do build up a tolerance to certain drugs after a while, which is a problem as then either the dosage or the drug needs to be changed. I get very disappointed when a drug that has been doing well seems to stop working, as I have to begin the process of trial and error all over again. This is a very worrying time as I fear going into major relapse.

I appreciate that some people have terrible problems with certain medications, and that it often proves very difficult to get the powers-that-be to recognise adverse side-effects. I have been on Seroxat a number of times. It did help me a bit, with the only side-effect being a feeling of vertigo and that lightening was running through my head – which I called 'brain cracks'. In the light of current controversy, it seems quite possible that Seroxat can have far more dangerous side-effects. I think that when this is the case, drug manufacturers and doctors would be far better to take such reports seriously and investigate them, as denying the situation only causes people to lose faith.

I have to say that the newer drugs, both antidepressants and antipsychotics, seem to be getting better all the time. I am grateful for the effort and money that goes into developing new medications. Many survivors these days are choosing not to take medication and to find alternative strategies for coping with their distress. It is every individual's right to make that choice for themselves. But for me, now I am on an effective and acceptable regime, I would not want to risk coming off it. I believe it would be odd to choose to be less well than I could be. I also have asthma, for example, but no one suggests I stop taking Becotide or makes me feel inadequate for taking it. Similarly, I don't see why anyone should suggest I stop psychiatric medication.

For myself, I don't see the sense of going through any more distress than I absolutely have to. I would do just about anything if it offered me a chance to feel well – as, luckily, I do now on medication as part of a management programme that also includes seeing a psychologist and a social worker.

To me, medication and self-management need not be mutually exclusive. I would not like to go back to being coerced into medication, as I was with Depixol, and quite understand people's objections to this. But if something is beneficial, isn't it better to include it in any self-management regime?

38

Reclaiming mad experience

Rufus May

Introduction

When I was 18 I witnessed first hand how society's approach to mental health wasn't working. I had been admitted to Hackney hospital, a psychiatric hospital in London, and was told I could not leave. Feeling lost after my girlfriend had left me and on the verge of adulthood, I had invested in a spiritual search for guidance. The messages I picked up from the Bible convinced me I had a mission. Seeking to discover what my mission was, I slowly deduced that I was quite possibly an apprentice spy for the British Secret Service. I was eventually admitted to hospital when I became convinced that I had a gadget in my chest that was being used to control my actions.

The psychiatric hospital was like another world entirely. Queues for the medication trolley punctuated the boredom and general sense of hopelessness. Any resistance to the regime was quashed by forcible restraints and powerful injections. Many friends felt too scared to visit me. That experience, coupled with being given a diagnosis of schizophrenia, made me feel like a social outcast. When my parents were told it was probably genetically inherited, the die seemed irrevocably cast. Ward rounds felt like elaborate religious rituals conducted by the consultant psychiatrist, with an audience of medical students and student nurses observing, while my insanity was confirmed and long term drug treatment prophesied.

I found the medication made me feel empty and soulless, I could not think past considering my basic needs. The psychiatric drugs made me physically weaker and affected my hormones so I became during this time impotent. I was concerned about this. However, to the outside world because of the

Edited extract from a chapter in P. Stastny and P. Lehmann (eds) (2007) *Alternatives Beyond Psychiatry*, Peter Lehmann Publishing, pp. 117–27.

mind-numbing effects of the drugs I was less focused on my spy and spiritual beliefs. The doctors pronounced that I was responding well to the medication. I was determined to stop taking the tablets and injections as soon as I could find other ways of staying calm and centred.

When a friend and fellow patient, Celine, took her own life after being heavily medicated it became a turning point in my life. It was a Caribbean funeral and hundreds of people turned up for it. For me, it contrasted strongly with the absence of support she had had when she had been alive and hearing abusive voices from her past. I realised then that I had found a cause that I could invest my energy into. We, as a society, were making people madder and maybe I could do something about changing that. What if I could make a different kind of come-back to the psychiatric ward as a mental health professional? Then perhaps in Trojan horse style, I could help dismantle the myths of the psychiatric hierarchy. When a junior psychologist informally questioned my diagnosis of schizophrenia, suggesting a temporary psychotic episode instead, it made me think maybe psychology was a way of doing things differently. So my mission was becoming clearer: I would train as a psychologist. I knew I needed to sort myself out to some extent before endeavouring this journey.

My first job straight out of psychiatric hospital was working as a night security guard in Highgate Cemetery in London. I now think that patrolling the heavily wooded grounds in the dark was a deeply therapeutic activity. With no time to daydream, I had to stay aware and face my fears of the dark and the unknown. I also think just walking in close proximity to nature was a very healing process. It was during this time that I successfully came off my psychiatric drugs against doctors' advice.

I then spent several years doing a range of jobs and learning creative ways to express myself using dance and drama. I shifted my focus from thinking about myself to trying to help others while making sure I looked after my mind and body. I used the outdoor gym on Parliament Hill for sports, and breathing exercises as natural ways to manage my moods. 1 was careful to avoid unreliable or abusive friends and stick with people who had stuck by me. Studying sociology helped me understand the wider structures of society, demystifying such things as the class system and power relations between men and women.

For the last 10 years, I have been working as a psychologist with people who have a broad range of mental health problems (see May, 2004). I know that to really help someone who is deeply suffering or confused we need to be very creative and offer a wide range of resources. Over the last eight years, I have shifted my focus from therapy to self-help. This is because self-help networks appear to offer a genuinely more respectful and empowering environment for people to get on with their lives. 1 have also found holistic therapies and approaches to wellbeing very useful both for myself and others, including mindfulness and bodywork (for example, Yoga and Tai Chi).

Unusual beliefs movements

In England, we have taken the principles of the Hearing Voices movement into other areas of mental health. There has now been established a Beyond Belief Network that looks at supporting people with unusual beliefs. The Beyond Belief approach is rooted in the work of Tamasin Knight, a researcher and a mental health human rights campaigner, who has researched how people cope with unusual beliefs that may be termed delusions by mental health professionals (Knight, 2006). She found many people are able to live with unusual beliefs and get on with their lives. Examples of unusual beliefs that psychiatry might describe as 'delusions' are beliefs about spiritual possession, alien abduction, telepathy, and global conspiracy.

Knight highlights the fact that when people are treated by psychiatry they are generally only given treatments that aim to subdue their beliefs or persuade them they are not correct. However, Knight asks if the differences (between people with unusual beliefs who do and don't receive mental health services) are in coping, not in the 'irrationality' of the belief; is it not more ethical to be targeting the *coping* rather than the actual beliefs themselves? Knight suggests that techniques that reduce fear and increase one's sense of control, using problem solving strategies and increasing one's repertoire of coping strategies are all helpful approaches to living with unusual beliefs.

This way of thinking about unusual beliefs follows from the ideas of the Hearing Voices movement that each person should be able to choose how best to understand their reality and that acceptance is an important stage in taking back power to manage one's experiences. It also fits with a social constructionist view that there is no one best way to view reality.

In a multicultural world, it follows that we should not be seeking to promote one allegedly superior (or insightful) world view but helping people live comfortably alongside each other's different understandings and perceptions. My experience in helping people who are thought to have psychotic belief systems over the last ten years suggests that accepting that people have a right to have unusual beliefs is an important approach to take. Traditional mental health services see this attitude as colluding with delusions and making them more real for the person. However, I have found that respecting that people's view of reality is of value and meaningful is often a useful way of joining with someone to look at how they see the world and what might be the best way forward for them. Sometimes I will challenge people's versions of reality but my aim is not to help them see the world more rationally, my aim is to help people get on with their lives and better negotiate their versions of reality with those around them.

Giving people choice about how to approach a distressing belief is important. For example if Jonathan thinks his neighbours are spying on him he can choose whether to investigate the evidence for this, or he can accept his belief as possibly accurate, and choose to focus on building his sense of self value and purpose (that is, not let the 'spies' get to him). This means that if Jonathan's neighbours are spying on him it won't affect him because his mind is focused on more meaningful activities and relationships. Most mental health professionals are not trained to give people this choice. In the United Kingdom, many therapists trained in cognitive behavioural therapy, use guided discovery techniques to subtly guide people to shifting their beliefs without being open about this process or giving them a choice about how best to cope with their beliefs. I have found if people have had their beliefs for a number of years they may be quite attached to them, so ways that work respectful of their beliefs are likely to be much more helpful and less alienating than traditional psychiatric and psychological approaches.

In Exeter, there has been a self-help group called You Better Believe It! that has been going for three years. In Bradford, we have established a similar group called Believe It or Not! Our launch meeting was attended by 60 people and included presentations by Tamasin Knight and an African Shaman called Odi Oquosa. Odi talked about his own experience of using spirituality to overcome trauma and spiritual attack and the power of artistic expression and nature in the healing process. For Odi, madness is an initiation of a healing process; an awakening of the unconscious mind. For this healing to be enabled it is important not to suppress these experiences as western psychiatry has tended to do, rather we need to create artistic spaces where this unconscious state can be expressed symbolically, understood and lessons learned from it by the surrounding community.

The Believe It or Not! group has supported someone who believed they were possessed in seeking spiritual advice and guidance. Another group member who understands his intense experiences of powerful energy as Kundalini has been supported to access a Kundalini yoga class and related self-help literature. Joe was a group member who felt shy and wanted to improve his social confidence and relation-building skills. One meeting Joe presented this poem he had written about an experience he had that was very powerful for him:

As I was walking late one night
Out of the blue there came a light
And the light said relax and don't take flight.
Then all of a sudden, I didn't exist as one.
I was the birds, I was the bees,
I was the whistle in the breeze.
I was the stars, I was the sky,
I was the clouds floating by.
I was the rivers I was the sea,
I was the grass, I was the trees.
And I existed as everything but not as me.
But then I felt that this couldn't last

And there I was stood back on the path.
If that's enlightenment, without any shadow of a doubt
Please light shine on me whenever I am out.

There is a danger that traditional psychiatric services might dismiss this experience as a psychotic symptom. However at the Believe It or Not! group we felt there might be more meaningful interpretations of the experience. As a consequence of Joe's poem and interests we invited a Buddhist guest speaker to the self-help group to tell us about Buddhism. When Joe described his experience the Buddhist told Joe he had a special gift. Joe began attending Buddhist meditation classes taking up regular meditation practice. He also got involved in some voluntary work decorating the Buddhist's monastery. At the same time Joe kept up going to a Christian church and started going out more to Karaoke bars and night-clubs. With his increased powers of relaxation Joe became more socially confident and out-going. He then joined an on-line dating agency. This is an example of how the Believe It or Not! group has been helpful in developing someone's confidence and participation in different communities in Bradford. Within the Believe It or Not! group members tend to hold very different views about the world but develop tolerance and acceptance of other's views. This is a very useful skill to have in the current climate we live in where different ideologies compete for supremacy; a more peaceful world will be one that accepts and values different versions of reality.

References

Downs, J. (2000). *How to Set Up and Support Hearing Voices Groups*. Manchester Hearing Voices Network.

Knight, T. (2006) *Beyond Belief: Alternative Ways of Working with Delusions, Obsessions and Unusual Experiences*. Lancaster.

May, R. (2004). Making sense of psychotic experiences and working towards recovery, in J. Gleeson and P. McGorry (eds), *Psychological Interventions in Early Psychosis*. New York: John Wiley, pp. 245–6.

39

Service users' accounts of finding work

Case study 1

Anon

A social services department in England embarked on a big recruitment campaign in order to fill a number of social work vacancies. Hitherto the department had always been short of social workers. To be appointed to one of the posts all the applicants would have had to pass four stringent stages, namely: (1) the application form itself; (2) a psychometric and IQ test; (3) a preliminary interview; (4) a final interview.

I did quite well in that I came top overall. A number of area teams enquired whether I could come and work with them. Apart from doing well during the various stages of the selection process, they were also impressed by my experience and qualifications. I opted for the team that was nearest to my home.

I got the letter saying that I had been successful and telling me the particular team I would be working for. This was in April. The HR department became concerned when they found out that I had been a user of mental health services and that I was on medication. My doctor had written a letter saying that I was fit for work and that the only time I had taken time off work in the preceding 12 month period was due to a broken jaw (I had been racially attacked in a city centre). I still had to have a meeting with the authority's occupational health team. I had to see the occupational therapist and the doctor twice and wait for the outcome. I received a letter two months later saying that they would like me to see the consultant psychiatrist before starting, which I did. His diagnosis was that I was fit to start work, but I did not receive my letter and contract until September, when six months had passed.

On my first day at work the manager called me into her office and said that she was aware of my medical record but that she would try and be as supportive as she could. I responded by saying that I had been able to do stressful jobs without much difficulty and thanked her for her concern. I soon realised that everything I did or wrote was heavily scrutinised. If I made a decision that she did not agree with she would ask me whether it was the medication that I was taking that was 'affecting my judgement'. Suffice to say, because of the undue strain and stress I was put under I left after 10 months: I couldn't stand being in a 'goldfish bowl'.

Case study 2

Kalisha Parton

While considerable attention has been paid to the perils of the 'benefits trap', there is less acknowledgement of the 'service trap' for mental health service users who are trying to hold down jobs or gain employment.

Why a service trap? Well, if as a mental health service user you work and try to use services simultaneously life becomes difficult. At the point when you may need support most, access to services becomes much harder.

Not only are services inflexible and geared mainly to office hours, but if you have therapy sessions, psychiatrist appointments and care programme approach meetings, it can be difficult to return to the workplace. Also, there is little opportunity to take part in user-involvement initiatives. The only chance to participate is through the management committee of a user-controlled organisation – but that will have a different role and emphasis. It is as though someone who works is not entitled to have an input into service development initiatives other than through surveys.

Part-time work may seem the obvious answer but, apart from the financial implications, even the most supportive flexible employers need to know when you are likely to be in and establish some pattern of working hours during the week. For me, mental health services tend to be on different days of the week and it is difficult to obtain a schedule of appointments a long time in advance.

Direct payments can provide part of the solution but they take organisation, time and energy. They are not a replacement for contact with the professionals. The service trap needs to be tackled urgently if employment rates are to increase. Some of the things that would help include scheduling appointments and user involvement initiatives well in advance; having mental health teams work one day a fortnight till early evening at GP practices if necessary; having

Previously published in *Community Care* (2003), February, p. 23.

a telephone number or e-mail address where users can leave messages; and out-of-hours services that are not focused on crisis management.

Employment is often wrongly seen as a cure. As long as someone is going to work all must be well. For many of us, the end of the working day is when your demons catch up with you. The fact that places of work are just a more valued form of day centre is not widely acknowledged. Perhaps if more professionals had direct experience of juggling with mental health services, employment support and the service trap may change.

40

Holistic approaches in mental health

Jan Wallcraft

Introduction

The 'Healing Minds' report (Wallcraft, 1998) considered a range of complementary therapies and alternative forms of medicine (CAM) able to demonstrate evidence of mental health benefits. These included Ayurveda, traditional Chinese medicine, homeopathy, western herbal medicine and nutritional medicine. The report examined policy and underlying issues relating to holistic medicine in mental health, as well as summarising the evidence base. The report addresses the types of evidence that might be appropriate in holistic mental health research and political blocks that may make it hard to create a level playing field for different types of research to be accepted. This article reconsiders the arguments from the 'Healing Minds' report in the light of more recent developments.

What is holism in mental health?

The term holism was coined by the naturalist Jan Smuts (1927) who defined it as 'the tendency in nature to form wholes that are greater than the sum of the parts through creative evolution'. A more philosophic or spiritual understanding of holism is that mind, body and spirit should be seen as part of an indivisible whole.

Edited and adapted from Chapter 29 in T. Stickley and T. Basset (eds) *Learning about Mental Health Practice* (2008), John Wiley, pp. 555–70.

According to Pert (1998) the origins of the dualistic approach to health, splitting the realms of the psyche (mind or soul) from the somatic (physical body) resulted from a pragmatic deal that Descartes the philosopher who is often considered to be the founder of modern medicine, made with the Pope in the 17th century in order to allow him to experiment on human bodies. This pact

> set the tone and direction for Western science over the next two centuries, dividing human experience into two distinct and separate spheres that could never overlap, creating the unbalanced situation that is mainstream science as we know it today. (Pert, 1998, p. 18)

People increasingly argue that holism in mental health should abandon the Descartes inspired mind-body division. McClanahan et al. (2006) argue that the historic Cartesian mind-body dualism, and the resulting conceptual separation of mind and body, keeps mental health care too separate and stigmatised for holistic thinking.

A House of Lords committee (2000) reporting on CAM recognised a spectrum between reductionism and holism, and said CAM should be seen as differing from conventional medicine in their underlying paradigms:

> The way that many CAM disciplines define health, illness and the healing process can depart significantly from the beliefs that underlie the practice of conventional medicine. It is essential to consider the different paradigms from which conventional medicine and CAM approach health care as these have implications for research and integration.

The Prince's Foundation for Integrated Health argue that 'someone suffering mental distress is not a "patient" to be "treated", but a whole person to be supported in the complex and individual journey of their life' (Prince's Foundation, 2006). The Foundation's strategy is to help transform the 'National Illness Service' into a genuine National Health Service through an integrated service in which orthodox and CAM approaches work together.

Holism in mental health, therefore, can be seen as referring to approaches treating the person as a whole, in the context of their wider environment, concerned with prevention, not just cure, enabling healing and recovery, and using a partnership approach supporting people's natural healing processes.

Service user perspectives

The research that was undertaken in order to produce the 'Healing Minds' report (Wallcraft, 1998), found high demand from service users for access to complementary therapies and dissatisfaction with the limitations and problems often associated with orthodox medicine. However, change is slow. A survey on patient choice in primary care (Mind, 2002) found that people were rarely offered alternatives to medication for mental health problems, and if they did access alternatives they often had to take the initiative, and pay for treatment. The Mind report recommends that complementary therapies should be available as effective treatments for mental health problems and to help reduce negative side effects of medication.

A national consultation carried out by the Prince's Foundation (2006) on integrated mental health care found that people see the biggest barriers to holistic care as lack of funding, the resistance of orthodox practitioners, education and evidence. Many wanted complementary approaches taught in orthodox health training, and called for establishment of an evidence base and appropriate evaluation and outcome measures, including greater attention to patient choice, positive mental health and the recovery approach.

Professional attitudes to CAM

The Healing Minds report (Wallcraft, 1998) demonstrated a shift in the attitudes of the British Medical Association between 1986 and 1993, with a more co-operative attitude emerging from GPs, and gradual acceptance that many patients are seeking non-conventional treatments. Thomas et al. (2001) found that GP fund-holding provided a mechanism to provide CAM; the demise of fund-holding was likely to reduce this access unless Primary Care Trusts (PCTs) are prepared to support patient choice. A leaflet for GPs on Complementary Medicine (DH, 2000) states that 58 per cent of PCTs provide some access to CAM, including acupuncture, aromatherapy, homeopathy and hypnotherapy.

A survey by *Which?* (Porritt, 2003) found that 80 per cent of people with mental health problems are treated entirely by their GP, and most receive medication. Alternatives to drug treatment were often unavailable on the NHS. Porritt argued that alternative therapies with sufficient evidence of benefit should be available free.

It is clear that issues about the benefits and cost-effectiveness of complementary therapies are contested. Canter et al. (2005) reviewed a small group of cost effectiveness studies of complementary therapies, stating that in most of these studies complementary therapies represent additional healthcare costs. They base this finding on their view that the benefits achieved by these therapies have little clinical relevance, i.e. they do not have a sufficiently direct or speedy effect on psychiatric symptoms. However, the orthodox approach to cost-effectiveness is based on value judgements with which service users might disagree.

However, Smallwood (2005) suggests complementary therapies may meet 'effectiveness gaps'; that is, the therapies may address health problems which orthodox medicine does not handle well. They cite mental health as one example. They argue that the use of these therapies to address effectiveness gaps could reduce NHS financial and time pressures.

Meenan (2001) argues for more sensitive measures of the benefits of CAM, suggesting that the process of health care, as well as its outcome, can contribute to its value and benefit to patients, and that this applies particularly to CAM. Therefore, accurate assessment of the health process as well as its clinical outcomes should be included in cost effectiveness analyses.

Government policy and its impact on holistic approaches

Government policy can play a major role in levelling the playing field in which holistic mental health treatments become available to service users. Relevant aspects of policy are: evidence-based medicine, outcomes measurement in mental health, and the recovery approach.

Evidence-based medicine

Evidence-based medicine (EBM) 'is the conscientious, explicit, and judicious use of current best evidence in making decisions about the care of individual patients' (Sackett et al., 1996). Practice based on EBM, is usually considered to integrate individual clinical expertise with the best available external clinical evidence from systematic research.

However, the evidence considered acceptable within EBM is usually weighted towards randomised controlled trials (RCTs) which are considered to be the strongest form of evidence. It is rare that service users have any significant influence on RCTs, and the accepted evidence base is therefore skewed towards research funded by the pharmaceutical industry or agencies representing orthodox medicine, rather than voluntary sector surveys of service users' views and experiences, or studies done by holistic practitioners.

Outcomes measurement and the recovery approach in mental health

Outcome measurement has been described as a 'revolution in healthcare' (Relman, 1988). The Department of Health seeks to bring in routine outcome monitoring of mental health services. At the same time, 'recovery' has been adopted as one of the key concepts in mental health (CSIP/RCP/SCIE, 2007). The recovery movement, originating from the work of service users (Turner-Crowson and Wallcraft, 2002), has argued consistently for outcome measures to reflect recovery goals. Since service users value the benefits of holistic treatment, recovery-focused outcome measures may possibly increase incentives for commissioners and practitioners to move in this direction.

Innovative projects

There are examples of innovative projects that are able to introduce service users to CAM. A voluntary sector project, based in Taunton and West Somerset, called the Service Users Complementary Holistic Project (SUCH), provides holistic treatments to those going through periods of mental distress. SUCH was invited to offer treatment to hospital in-patients, and this work was evaluated. Evaluation work by Collings (2007) found significant improvements in people's wellbeing. People with significant mental distress in their lives valued the direct effects of treatment (relaxing, stress reducing and calming), and the experience of being cared-for, touched and listened to on a one to one basis. Staff at the in-patient unit appreciated the calming effects of treatment on their patients and wanted the project to continue and to expand. A cost-benefit analysis suggested that SUCH's treatments reduced demands on services. Collings argues 'investment in CAM could be viewed as a preventative tool for community mental health teams to contribute to a reduction in admissions'.

Evidence base for complementary and alternative therapies in mental health

The 'Healing Minds' report (Wallcraft, 1998) called for more co-operation between practitioners of CAM and researchers to strengthen the evidence base of the treatments, their cost-effectiveness, and how well they can be integrated with orthodox treatments. It also reviewed some of the paradigm issues resulting from using western scientific methods (which are not holistic in their philosophy) to study holistic therapies, including traditional Indian and Chinese systems of medicine.

A recent Cochrane review of acupuncture for depression (Smith and Hay, 2004) discussed the difficulty of transposing a treatment derived from a traditional Chinese medicine (TCM) into a western medical context. Acupuncture, they explain, is based on the Chinese philosophy of Yin and Yang and the

Five Elements. Westernised medical acupuncture may exclude TCM principles and philosophy. They also note that different styles of acupuncture may have different results. They argue that while stronger RCT based methods are needed for future trials, there is also a need to learn more about the practitioners and their training, their rationale for using acupuncture in depression and the style of acupuncture used.

Similar issues were raised in a further study of acupuncture for people with depression (MacPherson et al., 2004). The authors invited focus groups of service users to discuss their experiences of depression, and to comment on plans for the research study. The focus groups revealed diversity in how people experience depression, leading the authors to question whether it makes sense to see it as one distinct condition.

An observational study was carried out of the acupuncture treatment of ten people with depression. These people were under the care of their GPs and were treated by professional acupuncturists in private practice. The research criteria were: (1) that the research is scientifically rigorous; (2) that it is respectful of the integrity of acupuncture as a system of medicine, and (3) that it takes into account the things that people experience and may value about acupuncture.

The acupuncturists worked within a TCM framework, and practised as they would normally do, using additional treatments such as acupressure, massage, and relaxation as they considered necessary. Standard depression rating scales were used. The people were given diagnoses from within the TCM diagnostic system.

People who had been treated described benefits beyond symptom control, such as having learned more about combating their depression, migraines stopping, feeling less fearful and more motivated. The therapeutic relationship was an important factor. The authors argue that this factor could be shown more clearly with in-depth qualitative interviews. The study did not conclusively demonstrate the value of acupuncture in depression but its main purpose was to look at study design issues. The authors suggest a need for outcome measures that address broader effects of treatment than standard depression rating scales, and argue for the development of trial methodology acceptable to acupuncturists and the scientific community which allows scope for practitioners to be flexible in their treatment repertoire in response to the variable conditions of their patients.

Conclusion

There has been progress in professional attitudes to holism in mental health since the Healing Minds report (Wallcraft,1998). Primary care seems the location offering most promise for change to bring people greater choice of treatment and give more attention to prevention and recovery, in which holistic therapies can play a part.

Debate around holistic therapies centres on scientific and philosophical differences between holistic and orthodox science. Government policy on evidence based medicine has intensified debates about the nature of evidence, but there appears to be no major new investment in researching complementary and alternative therapies in mental health, nor much progress developing new research trial methodology more suitable to assess holistic therapies. The value base underlying current cost-effectiveness measures has been questioned, as it leaves out the process of health care and the therapeutic relationship aspects that would form part of a holistic approach. There are arguments for creating service user-led outcome measures which would include recovery values, which might draw more attention to the need for holistic approaches.

References

Canter, P. H., Thompson Coon, J., Ernst, E. (2005) 'Cost effectiveness of complementary treatments in the United Kingdom: systematic review' *British Medical Journal*, vol. 331, pp. 880–1.

Collings J. (2007) *External Evaluation Report on INSUCH project* (unpublished report) Jane Collings, Ellbridge House Broadhempston TQ9 6BZ.

CSIP/RCP/SCIE (2007) *A Common Purpose: Recovery in Future Mental Health Services* Joint Position Paper 08, Leeds/London, Care Services Improvement Partnership, Royal College of Psychiatrists, Social Care Institute for Excellence.

Department of Health (2000) *Complementary Medicine: Information for Primary Care Clinicians*, London, DH.

House of Lords (2000) *Complementary and Alternative Medicine: Science and Technology – Sixth Report*, Session 1999–2000, 1st Nov 2000, online, available at http://www.parliament.the-stationery-office.co.uk/pa/ld199900/ldselect/ldsctech/123/12302.htm [accessed 17/07/2008].

James, A (2002) 'Prescribing choices: Bromley-by-Bow Healthy Living Centre has pioneered holistic health at primary care level', London, *Openmind*, no. 115, p. 19.

MacPherson, H., Thorpe, L., Thomas, K. and Geddes, D. (2004) 'Acupuncture for depression: first steps toward a clinical evaluation', *The Journal of Alternative and Complementary Medicine*, 10, (6), pp. 1083–91.

McClanahan, K.K., Huff, M.B. and Omar, H.A. (2006) 'Holistic health: does it really include mental health?' *The Scientific World Journal, Holistic Health & Medicine* 1, pp. 128–35.

Meenan, R. (2001) 'Developing appropriate measures of the benefits of complementary and alternative medicine', *Journal of Health Services Research & Policy*, vol. 6 (1) pp. 38–43.

Mind (2002) *My Choice*, individual services survey.

Pert, C. (1998) *Molecules of Emotion: Why You Feel the Way You Feel*, London, Simon & Schuster.

Porritt, F. (2003) 'The hidden costs', *Health Which?* June, pp. 10–13.

The Prince's Foundation (2006) *National Guidelines on Complementary Healthcare in Mental Health: Consultation and Scoping Report*, London, The Prince's Foundation for Integrated Health.

Relman, A. S., (1988) 'Assessment and accountability: the third revolution in medical care', *The New England Journal of Medicine*, vol. 319 (18), pp. 1220–2.

Sackett, D. L., Rosenberg, W. M. C., Muir Gray, J. A., Haynes, R. B. and Richardson, W. S. (1996) 'Evidence based medicine: what it is and what it isn't', *British Medical Journal*, 312 (7023), pp. 71–2.

Smallwood C. (2005) *The Role of Complementary and Alternative Medicine in the NHS*, London: FreshMinds.

Smith, C. A. and Hay, P. P. J. (2004) 'Acupuncture for depression', *Cochrane Database of Systematic Reviews* 2004, Issue 3.

Smuts J. (1927) *Holism and Evolution*, London: Macmillan.

Thomas, K. J., Nicholl, J. P. and Fall, M. (2001) 'Access to complementary medicine via general practice', *British Journal of General Practice*, vol. 51 (462) pp. 25–30.

Turner-Crowson J. and Wallcraft, J. (2002) 'The recovery vision for mental health services and research: a British perspective', *Psychiatric Rehabilitation Journal* vol. 25, no. 3.

Wallcraft J. (1998) *Healing Minds*, London: Mental Health Foundation.

41

From passive subjects to equal partners

Premila Trivedi and Til Wykes

In recent years the Department of Health, the National Health Service (NHS) Executive, research charities and funding bodies have emphasised the importance of user involvement in clinical research (Department of Health, 1998, 1999; Consumers in NHS Research, 1999; Hanley, 1999; Hanley et al. 2001; Royle and Oliver, 2001) because users have 'the experience and skills to complement those of current researchers . . . they know what it feels like to undergo treatments and their various side effects . . . they will have a good idea about what research questions should he asked . . . and how questions might be asked differently' (Goodare and Lockward, 1999), and 'if the needs and views of users are reflected in research it is more likely to produce results that can be used to improve clinical practice' (Department of Health, 2000). Many clinical researchers therefore want to involve users in their research but are often unclear exactly how to go about this. Little detailed information is available about how the process works in practice or the philosophical, conceptual and practical challenges that may arise for clinical researchers when they seek to involve users in research, especially in the field of mental health where the massive imbalance of power that exists in service between professionals and users may make working together in research particularly challenging (Beresford and Wallcraft, 1997; Lindow, 2001).

This review describes our experience of working together for the first time with user-researchers on a study investigating the effects of group medication education sessions on in-patients in our local psychiatric intensive care unit (PICU) (Kavanagh et al., 2002). We use this experience to describe each step in the partnership research process and the challenges we faced along the way.

Edited from P. Trivedi and T. Wykes, *British Journal of Psychiatry* (2002), vol. 181, pp. 468–72.

Ten questions to consider when planning joint research

What is the value of user involvement?

The first question to be resolved should be considered well before any contact with users and involves the clinical research team spending time to consider why they want user involvement: is it merely to satisfy the requirements of funding and regulation bodies (Hanley, 1999, 2001), or is it because there is a considered and genuine belief in the value of user involvement (Goodare and Lockward, 1999)? In our case, members of the research team at the Centre for Recovery in Severe Psychosis (CRiSP) were clear that introducing a user perspective could positively influence the content of their research and make it more relevant to clinical practice.

How will users be involved in the research process?

User involvement in research may occur at many different levels (Lindow, 2001). Our clinical research team was philosophically inclined towards partnership involvement but probably did not fully appreciate just how time-consuming and challenging it should be.

What projects might be suitable for user involvement?

There is scope for user involvement in all clinical research, but certain projects may be more attractive than others – in particular those arising in response to users' requests and those that seek to increase user empowerment (Beresford and Wallcraft, 1997; Church, 1997; Faulkner and Layzell, 2000; Faulkner and Nicholls, 2000; Rose, 2001). In our case the medication education project seemed particularly appropriate because it arose directly in response to requests from patients on the PICU at the Maudsley Hospital for more information about medication. This led to a decision to provide group medication education sessions, and the clinical research team saw this as an important opportunity to investigate (in line with previous studies: Brown et al., 1987; Macpherson et al., 1996; Tempier, 1996) the effects on patient knowledge, insight and compliance. Following further discussion the team came to the conclusion that since the study had been initiated by patients, it was important to maintain the patient focus by having active user involvement, and the decision was made to use the project to involve users actively for the first time in the team's research.

What proposal will be prepared for presentation to users?

Once the decision to involve users has been made, a clear outline of the proposed research should be prepared to present to users. It is probably not useful, however, at this stage to set out a precise proposal with little apparent scope for user intervention. The importance of this became clear to us only when the clinical research team presented their research protocol (with the research question, study design and outcome measures already firmly in place) to users, and received a very firm and negative response (see below).

How will the initial approach be made to users?

One of the most productive ways of approaching users is through relationships that have already been established locally (for example, with user groups, user liaison workers or user development workers), but less direct approaches (such as through posters or advertising in magazines, newsletters and papers) may also be useful and might possibly recruit a wider range of users. In our study, the team knew there was an active user group (Communicate) in the local Trust and, following advice from the Trust's user liaison worker, submitted the research proposal in writing for the group's consideration.

How will users' responses be considered?

One of the most challenging aspects of user involvement for clinical researchers may be considering users' responses to their research proposals, especially if the responses are negative, spirited and passionate. Although it may be tempting to dismiss these responses as those of users with a personal agenda or an 'axe to grind', it is important to remember that responses come about largely through their experience of using services and – since it is this very experience that user involvement is trying to harness – their views, values and opinions need to be taken seriously if they are really to influence research. In our case, users responded by saying that they had considered the proposal carefully but were not prepared to be involved in a project that placed such importance on outcome measures of insight and compliance. They explained that although these outcomes might be extremely important for clinicians, they were anathema to many users who perceived them as echoing the paternalistic and disempowering authority of psychiatry, with 'having insight' too often meaning 'agreeing with professionals' and 'being compliant' meaning 'doing what you are told by professionals' (Perkins and Repper, 1999).

While somewhat taken aback by this strong and negative response, the leader of the clinical research team was sufficiently stimulated to ask for further discussion. This resulted in a series of lengthy meetings between the lead researcher and a member of Communicate charged with making the group's position clear. These meetings were often challenging and not always comfortable, but they served an important purpose in allowing a mutually respectful relationship to build up between clinical researcher and user, which eventually enabled them to agree to look again at the project and consider working on it together in partnership research.

Will research partnerships with users be formalised?

Within any clinical research team there is always a tacit and usually overt agreement, on how individual members of the team will work together, how financial overheads will be shared and how research output will be attributed for assessment purposes. This is also important when users become involved with clinical researchers. An explicit agreement about how they will work together is necessary, addressing issues such as when and how users will be involved in the research, payment of users, acknowledgement of users' contributions, and issues of confidentiality.

In addition to formalising the research partnership between the user and the clinical research team at a team and user group level with the research contract, the research partnership was also formalised at an institutional level by including the user (hereafter called the user-researcher) as a member of the clinical research team on the team's application to the institution's research ethics committee.

How will the proposal be jointly assessed?

The best way of evaluating the outline is to subject the proposal to a series of questions (examples given below) and then adjust the protocol, preferably before starting any practical work. In our study not all of these questions were apparent at the start of the project — some only emerged following user observation of how the research intervention (medication education sessions) was being delivered — and the answers to our questions did not come easily.

How did the research come about and does it address users' priorities?
Our study came about directly as a result of patients requesting information about their medication, was obviously relevant to them, and by providing medication education sessions (in spite of some scepticism from ward staff) showed that patients' priorities were being taken seriously.

What is the purpose of the study and does it contribute to user empowerment?
The original purpose in the study was to provide medication education sessions and assess the effects on patient knowledge, insight and compliance. The

user-researcher pointed out that while insight and compliance might be of major importance to clinicians, users would be interested in the effects of medication education on the empowerment of users, which was completely ignored in the original proposal. Empowerment here means imbuing strength, confidence, authority and power.

What outcomes should be assessed, and are they what users consider to be important?

It was agreed that the outcomes of medication education should be viewed more widely than had been initially suggested, with the focus shifted away from insight and compliance towards measures of patient empowerment. However, at the time there was no standard method for assessing these. In writing the paper the emphasis was specifically shifted away from compliance and it is hoped that, in the future, more work with service users will enable us to develop appropriate methods for assessing patient empowerment (for example, Rogers et al., 1997).

In addition to considering the patient outcome of medication education, we were also aware that the medication education sessions might have important effects on ward staff, some of whom expressed the fear that providing medication education would only make their work more difficult. These fears proved unfounded, and in fact ward staff found that, by clarifying information about medication and helping to dismiss myths about prescribing practices, the medication education sessions actually made their communication about medication with patients much easier.

Is the intervention 'user friendly' and is enough importance attached to delivery of the intervention?

From the start the user-researcher (a former teacher) emphasised that the way the medication education intervention was delivered was important. In particular, she was concerned that if the intervention was seen to 'fail', patients would be blamed for not engaging with the sessions, rather than looking at whether the delivery of the sessions was appropriate. Factors that might influence the success or failure of the intervention included the physical environment where sessions were to be delivered, the skill of the researcher/facilitator/empowerer in fulfilling the many different roles he or she would have to play during the sessions, and the ethos and attitudes of clinical staff towards patients who were taking part in the sessions.

Are the methodology and design of the study appropriate?

Although service user-researchers may not be experts in research methodology or design, they may still be able to make useful contributions to these aspects of a research project. For example, in our study the original proposal was to compare individual patients on the PICU with individual patients on an acute ward, controlling for factors such as length of illness. The user-researcher pointed out that since different clinical teams in the hospital were known to have very different attitudes to medication information, this could markedly affect how patients responded to the medication education sessions. This awareness led us to the specific use of the matching procedure used in our study and thus improved the scientific method of the investigation.

How will data be analysed and the results interpreted?
Although the type of data analysis may be fixed, the interpretations of data may vary considerably depending on who is doing the interpreting, since tables of data rarely come with their own prepackaged explanations and no interpretation is value-free. For example, clinical researchers might (to increase the likelihood of publication and future research funds) emphasise a positive, 'half-full' interpretation, while user-researchers might be more willing to stress a less positive, 'half-empty' version.

How will the project be written up?

Where users have been involved in research, they should also be involved in documentation of the project, certainly in checking that papers submitted for publication reflect the users' impact on the study and properly acknowledge their contribution, for example through co-authorship. In our study there was some debate as to whether the user-researcher wished to be a co-author on a paper which, even after her involvement, still had a major focus on insight and compliance (Kavanagh et al., 2002). Eventually it was agreed that since much more had come out of the study than had been originally intended, two papers should be written, one on the actual medication education study, and the current paper on the process of user involvement in that study. Under these circumstances the user-researcher agreed to be a co-author on both papers.

How will dissemination occur?

The dissemination of clinical research findings generally occurs only in peer-reviewed journals and during academic conference presentations. These usually have an impact only on a relatively small number of clinicians who are research-oriented, and the Department of Health and funding bodies have stressed that a much wider dissemination process is necessary. In particular, dissemination to users is essential since, in the new consumer orientation of the UK NHS, it is not only evidence-based, randomised, controlled trials that determine what interventions are introduced into clinical practice, but also consumer demand (Department of Health, 1999). Furthermore, research 'subjects' (whether they be users or staff) are often the last people to know the results of the project in which they have participated, and are frequently left feeling used and unclear about how the research they have participated in will influence clinical practice (Patel, 1999). One option which has been adopted by CRiSP in the South London and Maudsley NHS Trust is to produce a newsletter for research participants informing them of the latest results of its projects. Alternatively, web pages can be produced or talks organised with service user networks and local community groups. The involvement of users in these types of dissemination is essential so that information is presented in an easily accessible and relevant form and any queries are addressed in an appropriate way.

Conclusions

We have set out the process of involving users in clinical research and have illustrated from our own experience how this may be challenging but also profitable, not only for clinical researchers but for the health services in general. The broader perspective introduced into the content of the study by the user has very much shaped our thinking. We have designed other clinical trials to incorporate such measures as a sense of empowerment, self-esteem and alliance with the clinical team as primary outcomes. Clearly, more research on outcome measures that service users value and that have clear psychometric properties is essential to further collaborative efforts.

We would not want clinical researchers to be unaware of the costs as well as the benefits of a collaboration with service user-researchers. If user-researchers are to be closely involved then a time commitment needs to be given to this process in the research proposal and this must be costed into the project's finances. Service users also need to be paid for their time (as clinical academic staff are). Not only do these costs have to be included in the proposal but they are also difficult to implement, as there are limits to the payment of service users who claim benefits. The commitment to collaboration will be demanding of the research team too as its members come to terms with the competing objectives (Oliver, 1992). These increased demands need to be recognised by research funders if collaborations are to be encouraged in the future.

Many mental health users may not wish to be involved in partnership research (Faulkner and Nicholls, 2000), although a recent local conference in south London indicated that service users can set priorities for research and would like more involvement (Thornicroft et al., 2002). However, the main problem that emerged was their lack of confidence in the research process. We have therefore set up a collaborative organisation between service users and academic staff, the Service User Research Enterprise (SURE), with the aim of helping to increase confidence through training programmes involving both service users and clinical researchers, which we hope will begin to break down the barriers on either side. The research community has much to gain from these collaborations and we hope to play some part in fostering them.

Appendix

Text of partnership research contract designed by the Communicate user group to protect users' interests

Partnership research contract between Communicate and _____

Title of research study _____

Principal and other clinical researchers _____

_____

User-researchers_____

As principal clinical researcher on the above research study involving the participation of members of Communicate, I agree that the study will:

1. Demonstrate to Communicate's satisfaction that the research project contributes to user empowerment and equal opportunities.
2. Involve users in the research process from the beginning to the end as equal partners who share in control of and decision-making about the research.
3. Show that confidentiality, ethics and informed consent will be built into the project at the outset, and that access to user participants will be negotiated in appropriate and empowering ways and they will be informed of the results of the study.
4. Include provision for support and supervision of user-researchers throughout the project.
5. Pay user-researchers the going rate for their contribution, and ensure payment is made in ways and time-frame negotiated with the user.
6. Acknowledge the contribution of user-researchers in all documentation and at all presentations, and provide user-researchers with copies of such.
7. Have the approval of Communicate.

As principal investigator I will take responsibility for ensuring that all others involved in this project are aware of the conditions of this contract and adhere to its principles. If at any time it appears that any of the above criteria are not being met, service users will review their position and reserve the right to opt out of the research project. [To be signed by the principal investigator for the clinical research team and countersigned by the service user-researcher for Communicate.]

Note: The contract is essentially between the clinical research team and Communicate so that if problems arise during the partnership research for individuals they have constituencies to go back to for support and guidance.

Section 4 may also include a statement about what will happen if the user becomes (or is perceived as becoming) 'ill' during the research, so for example users will only be referred to their clinical team if that has been previously agreed.

References

Beresford, P. and Wallcraft, J. (1997) 'Psychiatric system survivors and emancipatory research: issues, overlaps and differences'. *Doing Disability Research* (eds C. Barnes and G. Mercer), pp. 67–87. Leeds: Disability Press.

Brown, C. S., Pharm, D.,Wright, R.G., et al. (1987) 'Association between type of medication education and patients' knowledge, side effects and compliance'. *Hospital and Community Psychiatry*, 38, 55–60.

Church, K. (1997) 'Madness in her method: creating a "survivor frame" for mental health research', *Journal of Psychiatric and Mental Health Nursing*, 4, 307–8.

Consumers in NHS Research (1999) *R&D in the NHS: How Can You Make a Difference?* Leeds, NHS Executive.

Department of Health (1998) *Research – What's In It for Consumers? Report of the Standing Advisory Committee on Consumer Involvement in the NHS Research & Development Programme*. London: Department of Health.

Department of Health (1999) *Patient and Public Involvement in the New NHS*. London: Department of Health.

Department of Health (2000) *Working Partnerships: Consumers in Research Third Annual Report*. London: Department of Health.

Faulkner, A. and Layzell, S. (2000) *Strategies for Living: A Report of User-Led Research into People's Strategies for Living with Mental Distress*. London: Mental Health Foundation.

Faulkner, A. and Nicholls, V. (2000) *The DIY Guide to Survivor Research*. London: Mental Health Foundation.

Goodare, H. and Lockward, S. (1999) 'Involving patients in clinical research'. *British Medical Journal*, 319, 724–25.

Hanley, B. (1999) *Involvement Works: Second report of the Standing Advisory Committee on Consumer Involvement in the NHS Research & Development Programme*. London: Department of Health.

Hanley, B., Trusdale, A., King, A., et al. (2001) 'Involving consumers in designing, conducting and interpreting randomized clinical trials'. *British Medical Journal*, 322, 515–22.

Kavanagh, K., Duncan-McDonnell, D., Greenwood, K., et al. (2002) 'Educating inpatients about their medication: is it worth it?' *Journal of Mental Health*.

Lindow, V. (2001) 'Survivor research' in *This is Madness Too* (eds C. Newnes, G. Holmes and C. Dunn), p. 14–25. London: PCCS Books.

Macpherson, R., Jerrom, B. and Hughes, A. (1996) 'A controlled study of education about drug treatment in schizophrenia'. *British Journal of Psychiatry*, 168, 709–17.

Oliver, M. (1992) 'Changing the social relations of research production'. *Disability Handicap and Society*, 7, 83–7.

Patel, N. (1999) *Getting the Evidence – Guidelines for Ethical Mental Health Research*. London: Mind.

Perkins, R.E. and Repper, E.M. (1999) 'Compliance or informed choice'. *Journal of Mental Health*, 8, 117–29.

Rogers, E.S., Chamberlin, J., Ellison, M.L., et al. (1997) 'A consumer constructed scale to measure empowerment among users of mental health services'. *Psychiatric Services*, 48, 1042–7.

Rose, D. (2001) *Users' Voices*. London: Sainsbury Centre for Mental Health.

Royle, J. and Oliver, S. (2001) 'Consumers are helping to prioritise research'. *British Medical Journal*, 253, 48–9.

Tempier, R. (1996) 'Long-term psychiatry patients' knowledge about their medication'. *Psychiatric Services*, 47, 1385–7.

Thornicroft, G., Rose, D. Huxley, P., et al. (2002) 'What are the research priorities of service users'. *Journal of Mental Health*, 11, 1–5.

42

User-led research and evidence-based medicine

Alison Faulkner and Phil Thomas

Evidence-based medicine (EBM) and clinical governance play a central role in raising the quality of medical care. People want clinical decisions to be based on the best evidence and EBM places scientific knowledge in the service of clinical decision-making. Yet a quite different agenda is engaging patients as partners in health research, to make the medical profession more accountable. Here, we examine the epistemological basis of EBM, and the ethical concerns raised by this. In particular, we examine the value of user-led research in psychiatry in improving the concept of 'evidence' in evidence-based psychiatry.

Modernism and EBM

Medicine is now practised in a post-modern context that potentially conflicts with the modernist agenda of EBM. Modernism originated in the European Enlightenment with the quest for a self-evident truth free from doubt. The path to truth and knowledge was to be via science and rationality. Most historical accounts of psychiatry trace its origins back to the Enlightenment (Bracken and Thomas, 2001), with the subsequent sequestration of the insane in the asylums. As a result, madness came to be accounted for by the scientific and

---

Edited and adapted from A. Faulkner and P. Thomas, *British Journal of Psychiatry* (2002), vol. 189, pp. 1–3.

rational narratives of psychiatry, through the medical technologies of diagnosis and treatment.

A rational, scientific approach to therapeutic decision-making lies at the core of EBM. Although EBM may be valuable in discriminating between the claims made by advocates of different treatments, patients are left feeling that their concerns are forgotten and that they are little more than a disease being treated. There are two possible ways forward. The first involves a debate about the values, power and assumptions that underlie psychiatric knowledge – what we have framed, as 'ethics before effectiveness' (Bracken and Thomas, 2000). The second attends to the concerns of service users, through user-led research.

The ethics of EBM

Although there are ethical arguments for EBM, it also raises serious ethical problems. First, it is a form of consequentialism: the proposition that the worth of an action can be assessed by measuring its consequences (Kerridge et al., 1998). Consequentialism may be acceptable if outcomes are easy to define and measure, and if doctor and patient are in agreement about the nature of the problem. But this is rarely so in psychiatry, where the internal experiences inherent in mental health problems, such as voices or delusions, are not amenable to objectification and quantification. Diagnoses themselves are contentious and based solely on personal accounts and observation. Outcomes such as quality of life may defy definition. Evidence-based medicine is ill-suited to resolve the resultant conflict because it is unable to reconcile the values and beliefs of different stakeholders. Second, doctors define distress in terms of psychiatric disorders; they determine research objectives, carry out research, interpret research data and implement research findings. Patients are expected to acquiesce in clinical decisions over which they have little control. Third, EBM may be at odds with common morality, because it assesses interventions in terms only of efficacy. It does not resolve how we should handle research evidence taken from unethical studies or unpublished studies that have no ethical safeguards.

There are also ethical concerns about modernism in psychiatry. Technological accounts of madness and the coercive role of psychiatry raise serious ethical issues for the rights of people whose freedom may be taken away and who may be forced to receive treatments they do not want (Bracken and Thomas, 2001). The potential for coercion renders the failure to engage psychiatric patients in influencing research agendas even more significant, and demonstrates the importance of an ethical stance on EBM in psychiatry. We argue that the best way of achieving this is by involving service users in research.

Why user-led research is important

There is political resistance to seeing psychiatric patients as experts and to their involvement as partners in helping to set research agendas, coupled with a dominance of clinical neuroscience in the psychiatric and allied journals. User-led research has developed out of frustration with this situation. Research undertaken by and with service users examines issues and outcomes that are relevant and meaningful to service users. To our knowledge there have been no papers published in psychiatric journals dealing with user-led research, despite the recent growth of high-quality research in this area. We argue that there are several reasons why this must change.

Research methodology

The gold standard of scientific respectability in health service research – and the standard upon which evidence is evaluated – is the randomised controlled trial. This may be the accepted way of answering the question 'which is the effective treatment for condition X?', but people are complex subjects for investigative methods that befit the natural sciences. This raises questions about the interpretation and meaning of human behaviour, which is essential in understanding why the findings of quantitative studies may be less relevant in the real world. Why, for example, do many people choose not to take a drug whose efficacy may be well-established? Such questions can best be answered by qualitative research, which is ideally suited to the elaboration and description of personal experience and to establishing the meaning behind people's views or actions.

In pragmatic terms, the value of research evidence is only as good as the questions we ask. Are we asking questions relevant to service users – the people for whom the issue is most crucial? If the questions are inappropriate to start with, the results will be misleading. Clinical effectiveness, if restricted to the narrow definition of 'symptom relief', may fail to take into account relevant aspects of people's lives, aspects that may be crucial in determining an individual's decision to continue treatment, remain in contact with services or indeed survive.

User-led research challenges this by asserting that research should be based in the subjective, lived experience of emotional distress. For example, research on drug interventions rarely takes sufficient account of what it is actually like to take the drug. If clinical drug trials paid closer attention to the lived experience of those who take these drugs, we would have a better understanding of issues such as 'non-compliance'.

Presenting alternative explanatory frameworks

The dominant paradigm in psychiatry renders the views of people with mental illness invalid and negates the person as an individual. The medical model leaves little space for the individual's explanation of why he or she experiences emotional distress (Barrett, 1996). User-led research creates a space for users' understandings of their problems, laying the foundations for alternative explanatory frameworks. When we consider how a diagnosis is made (self-reporting, behaviour), then this approach has intrinsic validity. User-led research primarily attends to what people say about their experience and relies on their self-defined frameworks for understanding this experience, not on professional concepts of illness. This approach has major implications for services and treatment.

Access to marginalised groups

Modernist psychiatry regards itself as universal: applicable to all people at all times. Post-modern critiques challenge this view and open up space for the views and beliefs of marginalised and excluded groups. User-led research also endeavours to enable the views of marginalised communities to be heard alongside those of mainstream communities and to be given equal validity.

Power and empowerment

A discussion of user-led research cannot take place without a consideration of the power differentials involved. Although the status of psychiatrists and patients differs vastly, so also does the status of different research methodologies within the research community. Furthermore, conventional academic and health services research provides career opportunities for professional researchers, potentially at the expense of their research subjects. In the meantime, service users and research participants are rarely paid for their 'involvement'.

User-led research, by focusing on the *research process* as much as on the outcomes, aims to enable service users to take part in carrying out research while gaining skills and confidence in the process. It aims to be inclusive and informative, ensuring that research participants are kept fully informed of the results and of any action subsequently taken. This is rarely the case with traditional research.

Examples of user-led research

There are now many excellent examples of high-quality user-led research. We shall briefly consider two. *Strategies for Living* (Faulkner, 2000) was a qualitative study involving interviewing of 71 mental health service users. Designed and executed by service users, the research explored people's strategies for living and coping with mental distress. The predominant theme to emerge concerned the importance of relationships with others, especially family and friends, and people encountered at day centres and self-help groups. Peer support, the support of others in similar circumstances and the value of self-help received warm and grateful praise. The first experience of meeting others with similar problems, in a group or day centre, was often a significant turning point in people's lives, emphasising the value of acceptance and belonging against a background of stigma and discrimination. This suggests that practitioners should pay more attention to the role of self-help and peer support in overcoming stigma and discrimination. Mental health professionals should facilitate self-management, rather than prioritising interventions aimed at symptom eradication.

Rose (2001) has demonstrated the value of user-led research in defining standards of good practice in mental health care. In her study, user satisfaction was positively correlated with the amount of information provided, especially information about side-effects of medication. User satisfaction was negatively correlated with the subjective experience of being overmedicated. The message is clear as far as psychiatric practice is concerned: good practice does not necessarily depend on rocket science. Simple things, such as ensuring access to high-quality information and taking steps to prevent overmedication, are very significant to service users.

Conclusions

No matter how 'scientific' we aspire to be, clinical decisions always will involve value judgements and it is a serious mistake to pretend otherwise. This makes it essential that psychiatrists reflect critically on the values that underlie the advice they offer and the decisions they make, and that they understand how these values relate to those of patients. Placing user-led research on an equal footing with professional research enables professionals to think more carefully about the values behind scientific evidence. A marriage of two types of expertise is the essential ingredient of the best mental health care: expertise by experience and expertise by profession. Psychiatrists must work in alliance with service users to find ways of integrating user-led research with EBM. For this to happen, concepts of clinical governance must change. Psychiatrists should attach as much importance to user-led research in the processes of clinical decision-making as they do to randomised controlled trials. This has implications for continuing professional development and the training of psychiatrists. It is time for greater openness between the profession and service users, in our academic departments, journals and scientific meetings. The Department of Health in setting national research and development policies in mental health must attach as much weight to 'partnership' research as it does to other health areas. To do otherwise is to discriminate against psychiatric patients.

References

Barrett, R. (1996) *The Psychiatric Team and the Social Definition of Schizophrenia.* Cambridge, Cambridge University Press.

Bracken, P. and Thomas, P. (2000) 'Putting ethics before effectiveness'. *Openmind,* 102, 22.

Bracken, P. and Thomas, P. (2001) 'Postpsychiatry: a new direction for mental health'. *British Medical Journal,* 322, 724–7.

Faulkner, A. (2000) *Strategies for Living: A Report of User-Led Research into People's Strategies for Living with Mental Distress.* London: Mental Health Foundation.

Kerridge, I., Lowe, M. and Henry, D. (1998) 'Ethics and evidence-based medicine. *British Medical Journal,* 316, 1151–3.

Rose, D. (2001) *Users' Voices: The Perspective of Mental Health Service Users on Community and Hospital Care.* London: Sainsbury Centre for Mental Health.

Part IV

Challenges for practice

43

Introduction

Tom Heller and Mark Walsh

The final part of this book explores various challenges to mental health practice. It seems as though mental health practice in the UK has been going through seismic changes for several decades in turmoil that surely must mimic and parallel what is going on in the thoughts and feelings of people with mental health issues in their lives. How is it possible to make sense of all the structural changes and reorganisations that 'coal-face' mental health workers have to endure? As soon as various mental health-care related parts of the NHS seem to have settled into a workable way of going about their necessary business, another 'better and more efficient' way of doing things is introduced from above.

Often the driver for changes and 'reforms' is cost containment, but invariably this is dressed up as managerial assertions that an improved service will be delivered. Early interventions, assertive outreach, adherence therapy and a host of allegedly 'evidence-based' initiatives have been introduced over a period when partnership working in all its organisational and user involvement forms has reshaped the landscape of mental health work. And of course the mental health professions themselves that are entrusted to look after people going through periods of mental distress also seem to be the subject of perpetual revolution as some jostle for supremacy in the hierarchy of status and authority within the world of mental health while others struggle for recognition and to have their voices heard.

At the same time the tools that are available for mental health workers are changing, becoming perhaps more powerful and almost certainly introducing the possibility of more dangerous side effects. Briefer but allegedly more 'effective' therapies have emerged and new mind-altering drugs are regularly introduced in a promotional frenzy and with hopes and expectations that are never quite matched in clinical practice. The power of these new types of medication is matched only by the complexity of their side effects. So, we have new 'solutions' for mental distress in every sense of this term but amid all this upheaval in practice has anything really changed significantly?

Large proportions of service users and survivors who have experienced the mental health services as 'consumers' still come away dissatisfied with the way that they have been treated. There are still precious few reports outside the public relations blurbs of corporate organisational literature of people having positive experiences of mental health services. Will those in authority continue to respond to this in a professionally defensive way and use their power to maintain their status? Or can they possibly be persuaded to treat users and survivors as experts in their own right, acknowledging that service users' experiences can be used to improve personal and institutional responses to people undergoing periods of mental distress? In the face of concerted criticisms from both service user groups and rumblings in the ranks of mental health practitioners the taken-for-granted authority and power of the psychiatric system is now being challenged.

The subject of risk is never far from the surface in mental health practice. Attitude to risk defines the style and content of the working practices of individual mental health workers and helps to determine the way that organisations are perceived by their 'clients'. Increasingly practitioners focus on assessing and minimising risk, often at the behest of employers, regulatory bodies and a media-fed, anxious public. But can therapeutic work ever be effective without a degree of risk being taken by practitioners as well as by those people who seek their help? Would the elimination of risk have the effect of eliminating any chance of a positive therapeutic outcome? It is frequently commented that western societies are becoming increasingly 'risk averse' with safety and strict procedural directives attempting to cover all possible adverse effects. In mental health practice this may lead to over-use of statutory powers of detention, the use of increasingly long-term medication and a generally defensive attitude that can be palpably felt by those approaching the services for assistance. Of course contemporary practice must be aware and make assessments of potential risks to the people using the services, to the public at large and to the workers in the service, but an excessively cautious and defensive organisation may well stifle some of the creativity and therapeutic spirit that would be unlocked in a more liberal atmosphere.

Many of the changes to mental health practice that are imposed on statutory mental health organisations are introduced in the name of 'efficiency'. The mantra of 'modernisation' is repeated to reinforce 'efficiency' initiatives. In many cases this has a simple relationship to cost saving where attempts are made for example to replace experienced mental health workers with people at lower grades. The introduction of various 'health care assistant' grades on mental health wards, 'graduate mental health workers' in primary care and new roles like Support, Time and Recovery workers that span traditional disciplinary boundaries has become a trend that may well be unstoppable but may ultimately prove to be very short-sighted. Do these changes add to and extend provision or simply deskill the mental health workforce? In a similar vein new, formulaic tools and shorthand devices have been designed to obviate the need for experienced (expensive) mental health practitioners. The ultimate expression of this would seem to be computer-aided psychotherapy (Marks et al., 2007). It may be that some people get a degree of benefit from using one of the computer-aided cognitive-behaviour therapy programmes by themselves (Kaltenthaler et al., 2006). However attractive this 'solution' to mental health issues must be to managers and commissioners with an imperative to reduce expenditure and balance rapidly declining budgets in the face of ongoing demands, in time it will surely be re-discovered that there really is no substitute for the personal, human attention of an experienced, highly trained and dedicated therapist when helping people with mental health issues.

In the third part of this book the 'user movement' has been explored and discussed. Patrick Bracken and Philip Thomas (Reading 44) discuss the future of psychiatry and the psychiatric profession at least in part as a response to challenges from the user and survivor movement. At a time when many elements within the psychiatric profession seem wedded to reductionist, technological solutions to the problems that people in mental distress pose, Bracken and Thomas argue strongly for a re-definition of the roles and responsibilities of mental health workers. Placing mental health within a social and cultural context, and insisting that an ethical approach replaces technological ways of working, is advocated as a pre-requisite for those wanting to pursue a 'new direction for mental health'. The debate about how theoretical approaches are acted out in practice is the main theme within Reading 45 by Nick Bowles and his colleagues. In this article three different mental health 'experts' give their views on the way that mental health nurses go about their therapeutic tasks, particularly with regards to performing observations on the people under their care. Phil Thomas, a consultant psychiatrist, develops the concepts that underpinned his theoretical writing in Reading 44. He comments on some of the problems that will inevitably occur if nurses on psychiatric wards use rigid or formal observation techniques that by definition distances them from people on the wards who need their help. His practical work has involved a change of focus for these nurses. Observational distance is rejected in favour of an approach that actively engages nurses with the problems that might have led the people in their care to develop various forms of mental distress in the first place. Diane Hackney has been a user of in-patient mental health services and tells her intimate story of humiliation and loss of dignity that she experienced when she was 'incarcerated' or 'imprisoned' under a mental health regime that failed to respect her basic human rights. Cath Sutherland, a mental health nurse, describes a more humane and more effective nursing approach that is receptive to and respectful of the feelings of people who may be going through periods of enormous mental turmoil.

In Reading 46 Tim Freeman and Edward Peck report on a study of the way that partnership working is implemented in practice. Bringing about some of the top-down organisational changes that are intended to improve the way that statutory organisations work together provides a challenge for managers, but also creates uncertainty for workers in the services and ultimately may prove unsettling for users and survivors of the services, and for their carers. This study evaluates some of the outcomes of structural changes in partnership-focused services, and although the reported evaluation appears positive in many ways, the disruptive nature of major change in service provision for all those involved is easy to comprehend.

The use of medication in mental health work is explored in Reading 47 by Joanna Moncrieff. Based on her book *The Myth of the Chemical Cure* (Moncrieff, 2007), the reading challenges the notion of mental distress being caused by 'chemical imbalances' that could or should be 'corrected' by the use of psycho-active medication. Her assertion is that the commonly used psychiatric drugs in themselves create abnormal brain states that may be unpleasant and potentially harmful. In addition the positive effects of medication are often overstated by drug company funded research, while in practice a less positive picture of the effectiveness of psycho-active drugs frequently emerges.

Jeremy Holmes (Reading 48) also takes a critical look at orthodoxies in the form of psychotherapies, focusing in particular on cognitive behaviour therapy (CBT). This widely-promoted type of therapy is examined in a critical way, particularly with regard to how it has come to dominate the way that psychological interventions are practised and assessed.

Shulamit Ramon and her colleagues (Reading 49) consider the emergent concept of 'recovery' that has become an important development in the way that 'mental illness' is conceptualised by health professionals, carers and people with significant mental health challenges in their lives. The superficially simple concept of 'recovery' has the potential to pose a serious challenge to the way that 'mental illness' has been promoted by many orthodox health workers. In the past mental health professionals have used their dominant position to paint a rather hopeless and dependent picture of people who are experiencing mental turmoil. In particular, the person who experiences psychotic symptoms might be characterised as someone who will never get better and who is destined to remain dependent and subservient. By contrast, the concept of 'recovery' offers everyone hope. The article considers the role of the user and survivor movement in challenging the negative and often bleak prognoses that have been associated with 'mental illness' in the past. In their opinion the pessimistic view of mental distress can become a self-fulfilling prophesy. The article describes the converse way that a positive recovery-focused attitude for health workers and service users can act as an important aid to healing.

The term 'person-centred care' crops up as rhetoric in plenty of official documentation. It is easy to say that the care you intend to provide will be 'person-centred', but hard to define and even harder to implement. Dawn Brooker (Reading 50) explores in depth the meaning of person-centred care in people with dementia. Her article discusses the way that the term has been ill-defined and frequently misused. More importantly her work gives pointers to very practical ways that person-centred care can be conceptualised and delivered in practice. This has wider significance than for people with dementia and similar principles are surely important in all care relationships. The ideas from this influential paper that was first published in 2004 have been developed into a book (Brooker, 2007), and the VIPS model outlined in this article has become incorporated into National Institute for Health and Clinical Excellence Guidelines for supporting people with dementia (NICE, 2006).

The article by Marilyn Duker and Roger Slade (Reading 51) has been taken from a very practical guide (Duker and Slade, 2003) that aims to help people understand the journey and mindset that people with anorexia and bulimia bring to any consultation or conversation. Viewed from the outside the thought processes of people with significantly disordered thinking, such as during an eating disorder, can appear entirely incomprehensible. This can be problematic for both professionals and for family carers as they seek to understand the person's thoughts, feelings and behaviours. People who try to help are likely to feel increasingly frustrated when their exhortations to 'rational' courses of action are continually subverted or not acted on. This article attempts to help people understand some of the ways that a person with anorexia may be re-interpreting the words that a helper or carer may use. This challenges a more common orthodox approach to disordered thinking that might attempt to catalogue but never to understand or normalise the abnormal thoughts.

Jane Shackman (Reading 52) explores ways of working with survivors of major incidents. Her article discusses how people may be helped to cope after seemingly overwhelming, tragic and catastrophic events that have threatened to disrupt all elements of their lives. Survivors of major trauma, civil emergencies and acts of terrorism may develop ways of responding to those major events that are superficially similar, but detailed individual work with each person is needed to ensure that they are supported appropriately. Shackman describes some common themes that characterise people who have been involved in major incidents and proposes some practical ways that people might be helped to cope better if such an incident affects their lives.

Tom Heller (Reading 53) completes this part and the book, with a final reminder of some of the human dimensions that are involved in all mental health work. 'Still doing being human' discusses the tangled web of issues that will inevitably occur when one person sets themselves up as a helper, healer or therapist and another comes to ask for assistance. The interchange that is described in the article takes place between a GP and one of the people on his list, but we hope it can be seen as a way of exploring more universal issues of power, vulnerability and the value of therapeutic work. The article is a challenge to those who would try to de-value the human content of mental health work and a reminder that mental health really does still matter.

References

Brooker, D. (2007) *Person-centred Dementia Care: Making Services Better*, London, Jessica Kingsley Publishers.

Duker, M. and Slade, R. (2003) *Anorexia Nervosa and Bulimia: How to Help*, Buckingham, Open University Press.

Kaltenhaler, E., Brazier, J., DeNigis, E., Tumur, I., Ferriter, M., Beverley, C., Parry, G., Rooney, G. and Sutcliffe, P. (2006) 'Computerised cognitive behaviour therapy for depression and anxiety update: a systematic review and economic evaluation.', *Health Technology Assessment*, vol. 10, pp. 1–168.

Marks, I., Cavanagh, K. and Gega, L. (2007) 'Computer-aided psychotherapy: revolution or bubble?' *British Journal of Psychiatry*, vol. 191, pp. 471–3.

Moncrieff, J. (2007) *The Myth of the Chemical Cure: A Critique of Psychiatric Drug Treatment*, London, Palgrave Macmillan.

National Institute for Health and Clinical Excellence (2006) Dementia: supporting people with dementia and their carers in health and social care, London: NICE http://www.nice.org.uk/guidance/index.jsp?action=byId&o=10998 [accessed 10/05/2008].

44

Postpsychiatry: a new direction for mental health

Patrick Bracken and Philip Thomas

Government policies are beginning to change the ethos of mental health care in Britain. The new commitment to tackling the links between poverty, unemployment, and mental illness has led to policies that focus on disadvantage and social exclusion (DH, 1998). These emphasise the importance of contexts, values, and partnerships and are made explicit in the national service framework for mental health (DH, 1999). The service framework raises an agenda that is potentially in conflict with biomedical psychiatry. In a nutshell, this government (and the society it represents) is asking for a very different kind of psychiatry and a new deal between health professionals and service users. These demands, as Muir Gray has recently observed, apply not only to psychiatry but also to medicine as a whole, as society's faith in science and technology, an important feature of the 20th century, has diminished (Muir Gray, 1999).

According to Muir Gray, 'Postmodern health will not only have to retain, and improve, the achievements of the modern era, but also respond to the priorities of postmodern society, namely: concern about values as well as evidence; preoccupation with risk rather than benefits; the rise of the well informed patient' (Muir Gray, 1999). Medicine is being cajoled into accepting this reality, but psychiatry faces the additional problem that its own modernist achievements are themselves contested. Consider this: although patients complain about waiting lists, professional attitudes, and poor communication, few would question the enterprise of medicine itself. By contrast, psychiatry has always been thus challenged. Indeed, the concept of mental illness has been described as a myth (Szasz, 1961). It is hard to imagine the emergence of

Edited from P. Bracken and P. Thomas, *British Medical Journal* (2001), vol. 322, pp. 724–7.

'antipaediatrics' or 'critical anaesthetics' movements, yet antipsychiatry and critical psychiatry are well established and influential (Ingleby, 1980). One of the largest groups of British mental health service users is called Survivors Speak Out.

Psychiatry has reacted defensively to these challenges and throughout the 20th century has asserted its medical identity (Clare, 1976). Although the discipline survived the antipsychiatry movement of the 1960s, fundamental questions about its legitimacy remain (Thomas, 1997). We argue that the well publicised failure of community care and the UK government's response (in the form of the national service framework) make it essential that we re-examine critically psychiatric frameworks. In this article we develop a critique of the modernist agenda in psychiatry and outline the basic tenets of post-psychiatry – a new positive direction for theory and practice in mental health (Bracken and Thomas, 1998).

Roots of modern psychiatry

Both supporters and critics of psychiatry agree that the discipline is a product of the European Enlightenment and that movement's preoccupations with reason and the individual subject. Although a critical, postmodern position does not mean rejecting the Enlightenment project, it demands acknowledgment of its negative as well as its positive aspects. It means questioning simple notions of progress and advancement and being aware that science can silence as well as liberate.

On one level, the Enlightenment's concern with reason and order spawned an era in which society sought to rid itself of 'unreasonable' elements. As Roy Porter wrote:

> the enterprise of the age of reason, gaining authority from the mid-seventeenth century onwards, was to criticise, condemn, and crush whatever its protagonists considered to be foolish or unreasonable . . . And all that was so labelled could be deemed inimical to society or the state – indeed could be regarded as a menace to the proper workings of an orderly, efficient, progressive, rational society. (Porter, 1987)

According to Foucault, the emergence of large institutions in which 'unreasonable' people were housed was not a progressive medical venture but an act of social exclusion. Psychiatry was the direct product of this act (Foucault, 1971). Porter agrees: 'The rise of psychological medicine was more the consequence than the cause of the rise of the insane asylum. Psychiatry could flourish once, but not before large numbers of inmates were crowded into asylums (Porter, 1987).

On another level, the concern with reason also led to a belief that a framework derived from science was the best way to engage with madness. Psychiatrists like Griesinger seized on the early successes of pathology in explaining some forms of psychosis and asserted that this framework could be extended universally (Ellenberger, 1970).

From Descartes onward, the Enlightenment was also concerned with an exploration of the individual subject. Eventually, this gave rise to the disciplines of phenomenology and psychoanalysis. Our thesis is that 20th-century psychiatry was based on an uncritical acceptance of this modernist focus on reason and the individual subject. We can identify three main consequences of this.

Consequences of the modernist focus

Madness is internal

Perhaps the most influential 20th-century psychiatric text was Karl Jaspers's *General Psychopathology* (Jaspers, 1963). Jaspers worked within the framework of phenomenological psychology developed by the philosopher Edmund Husserl, who promoted phenomenology as a 'rigorous science' of human experience. His method involved 'bracketing out' contextual issues and an intense self-examination, with strong echoes of Descartes' *Meditations* (Bracken, 1999). In this theoretical tradition the mind is understood as internal and separate from the world around it. Jaspers also distinguished the form of a mental symptom from its content: 'It is true in describing concrete psychic events we take into account the particular contents of the individual psyche, but from the phenomenological point of view it is only the form that interests us' (Jaspers, 1963).

This view had an extraordinary influence on European psychiatry. According to Beaumont, Aubrey Lewis described *General Psychopathology* as 'one of the most important and influential books there are in psychiatry' (Beaumont, 1992). Psychiatry continues to separate mental phenomena from background contexts. Psychosis and emotional distress are defined in terms of disordered individual experience. Social and cultural factors are, at best, secondary and may or may not be taken into account (Samson, 1995). This is partly because most psychiatric encounters occur in hospitals and clinics, and there is a therapeutic focus on the individual, with drugs or psychotherapy. It is also because biological, behavioural, cognitive, and psychodynamic approaches share a conceptual and therapeutic focus on the individual self. Even social psychiatry has had an epidemiological priority for the identification of disordered individuals in populations (Shepherd, 1983).

Technical explanation for madness

The Enlightenment promised that human suffering would yield to the advance of rationality and science. For its part, psychiatry sought to replace spiritual, moral, political, and folk understandings of madness with the technological framework of psychopathology and neuroscience. This culminated in the recent 'decade of the brain' and the assertion that madness is caused by neurological dysfunction, which can be cured by drugs targeted at specific neuroreceptors. It is now almost heretical to question this paradigm.

The quest to order distress in a technical idiom can also be seen in the *Diagnostic and Statistical Manual of Mental Disorder* (DSM). This defines over 300 mental illnesses, most of which have been 'identified' in the past 20 years. In their account of this project, Kutchins and Kirk remark: 'DSM is a guidebook that tells us how we should think about manifestations of sadness and anxiety, sexual activities, alcohol and substance abuse, and many other behaviours. Consequently the categories created for DSM reorient our thinking about important social matters and affect our social institutions' (Kutchins and Kirk, 1999).

Coercion and psychiatry

The links between social exclusion, incarceration, and psychiatry were forged in the Enlightenment era. In the 20th century, psychiatry's promise to control madness through medical science resonated with the social acceptance of the role of technical expertise. Substantial power was invested in the profession through mental health legislation that granted psychiatrists the right and responsibility to detain patients and to force them to take powerful drugs or undergo electroconvulsive therapy. Psychopathology and psychiatric nosology became the legitimate framework for these interventions. Despite the enormity of this power, the coercive facet of psychiatry was rarely discussed inside the profession until recently. Psychiatrists are generally keen to play down the differences between their work and that of their medical colleagues. This emerges in contemporary writing about both stigma and mental health legislation in which psychiatrists seek to assert the equivalence of psychiatric and medical illness (Zigmond, 1998). Ignoring the fact that psychiatry has a particular coercive dimension will not help the credibility of the discipline or ease the stigma of mental illness. Patients and the public know that a diagnosis of diabetes, unlike one of schizophrenia, cannot result in their being forcibly admitted to hospital.

A new direction for mental health

Muir Gray's challenge to medicine to 'adapt to the "postmodern environment"' (Muir Gray, 1999) applies particularly to psychiatry, and while some question the Foucauldian critique of psychiatry, there is a general acceptance that his rejection of a simple 'progressivist' version of psychiatry's development is justified (Gordon, 1990). Psychiatry can no longer ignore the implications of this analysis. Our critique may be stated as a series of questions:

1   If psychiatry is the product of the institution, should we not question its ability to determine the nature of postinstitutional care?
2   Can we imagine a different relation between medicine and madness – different, that is, from the relation forged in the asylums of a previous age?
3   If psychiatry is the product of a culture preoccupied with rationality and the individual self, what sort of mental health care is appropriate in the postmodern world in which such preoccupations are waning?
4   How appropriate is western psychiatry for cultural groups who value a spiritual ordering of the world and an ethical emphasis on the importance of family and community?
5   How can we uncouple mental health care from the agenda of social exclusion, coercion, and control to which it became bound in the past two centuries?

If we are unable to address these questions, the failures of institutional care will be repeated in the community. For these reasons, postpsychiatry is driven by a set of contrasting goals.

Goals of postpsychiatry

Importance of contexts

Contexts, that is to say social, political, and cultural realities, should be central to our understanding of madness. A context centred approach acknowledges the importance of empirical knowledge in understanding the effects of social factors on individual experience, but it also engages with knowledge from non-Cartesian models of mind, such as those inspired by Wittgenstein and Heidegger (Rorty, 1979). We use the term 'hermeneutic' for such knowledge, because priority is given to meaning and interpretation (Phillips, 1996). Events, reactions, and social networks are not conceptualised as separate items which can be analysed and measured in isolation. They are bound together in a web of meaningful connections which can be explored and illuminated, even though these connections defy simple causal explanation. This approach also resonates with the work of Vygotsky (Vygotsky, 1978).

We have attempted to use this approach in our clinical and theoretical work on trauma and on hearing voices (Bracken et al., 1995; Leudar and Thomas, 2000).

We also believe that in practical, clinical work mental health interventions do not have to be based on an individualistic framework centred on medical diagnosis and treatment. The Hearing Voices Network (Box 44.1) offers a good example of how very different ways of providing support can be developed (Romme and Escher, 1994). This does not negate the importance of a biological perspective, but it refuses to privilege this approach and also views it as being based on a particular set of assumptions that are themselves derived from a particular context.

Box 44.1   Hearing Voices Network

The Hearing Voices Network was started by Marius Romme (psychiatrist) and Sandra Escher (journalist) in Holland. Romme had been struggling to treat a woman whose voices had not responded to neuroleptic drugs. She arrived at her own, non-medical way of understanding the experience and challenged Romme to appear on television to discuss her experiences. After the broadcast, over 500 'voice hearers' phoned in, most of whom had not been in contact with psychiatric services. This led to the formation of Resonance, a self-help group for people who heard voices and who were dissatisfied with medical diagnosis and treatment for the experience (Romme and Escher, 1999). The Hearing Voices Network was established in Britain in 1990 after a visit by Romme and Escher. The network now has over 40 groups across England, Wales, and Scotland and offers voice hearers the opportunity to share their experiences using non-medical frameworks. The groups are open only to voice hearers who share ways of coping with the experience and discuss their explanatory frameworks (which do not necessarily exclude medical ones). The network operates nationally and internationally, in alliance with sympathetic professionals. It validates voice hearers' own accounts of their experiences and makes it possible for these experiences to become meaningful.

Ethical rather than technological orientation

Clinical effectiveness and evidence based practice – the idea that science should guide clinical practice – currently dominate medicine. Psychiatry has embraced this agenda in the quest for solutions to its current difficulties. The problem is that clinical effectiveness plays down the importance of values in research and practice. All medical practice involves some negotiation about assumptions and values. However, because psychiatry is primarily concerned with beliefs, moods, relationships and behaviours, this negotiation actually constitutes the bulk of its clinical endeavours. Recent work by medical anthropologists and by philosophers has pointed to the values and assumptions that underpin psychiatric classification (Gaines, 1992; Fulford, 1994).

This is an issue for all mental health work, but the dangers of ignoring these questions are most apparent in the problematic encounter between psychiatry and non-European populations, both within Europe and elsewhere (Sashidharan and Francis, 1999). In Bradford we work with many immigrant communities. The Bradford Home Treatment Service attempts to keep values to the fore and strives to avoid Eurocentric notions of dysfunction and healing (Bracken and Thomas, 1999). While recognising the pain and suffering involved in madness, the team avoids the assumption that madness is meaningless (see Box 44.2). It has also developed a number of ways in which service users can be involved in shaping the culture and values of the team (Relton, 1999).

Box 44.2   Postpsychiatry and psychopathology

Postpsychiatry opens up the possibility of working with people in ways that render the experiences of psychosis meaningful rather than simply psychopathological. A 53 year old married Sikh woman had had two admissions to hospital in the previous six years with a diagnosis of affective disorder (ICD F31.2). She was referred urgently by her general practitioner in July 1999, and when seen at home she had pressure of speech and labile, irritable mood and was noted to be preoccupied with religion and past events in her life. Her family complained that she was overactive and spending excessive amounts of money. She was referred to Bradford Home Treatment Service where her key nurse, a Punjabi speaker, explored a number of issues with her and her family.

It emerged that the patient felt in conflict with her elderly mother-in-law, with whom the family shared the house. She believed that the elderly lady, who seemed to govern decisions about her grandchildren's forthcoming marriages, was usurping her position in the family. At the same time she had a duty of care to her mother-in-law, who suffered from diabetes and required her daughter-in-law's help to administer insulin. She also had a bond of loyalty towards her mother-in-law which made it difficult for her to acknowledge the conflict, particularly outside the family.

With her nurse's support, the patient was able to produce her own interpretation of her psychotic behaviour:

- *Overactive behaviour and spending excessively*: to reclaim her role as mother and wife, to increase her contribution to family life, empowerment

- *Overtalkative*: seeking and demanding her husband's time when alone, need to discuss and influence family decisions, openly airing grievances

- *Hostile, irritable*: openly critical of family, challenging and retaliating, disagreeing

- *Preoccupation with past*: to contextualise grievances, add weight to her argument, and elicit understanding

- *Religious preoccupation*: to renew her strength, a way of coping with stress, a focus in her life.

Framing her problems in this way rather than in terms of a medical diagnosis allowed a space in which these issues could be explored gently with the patient and her family. Her husband became more accepting of his wife's grievances and her behaviour. She has kept well over the past 12 months, needing no drugs.

Rethinking the politics of coercion

The debate about the new Mental Health Act in Britain offers an opportunity to rethink the relation between medicine and madness. Many service user groups question the medical model and are therefore outraged that this provides the framework for coercive care. This is not to say that society should never remove a person's liberty because of their mental disorder. However, by challenging the notion that psychiatric theory is neutral, objective, and disinterested, postpsychiatry weakens the case for medical control of the process. Perhaps doctors should be able to apply for detention (alongside other individuals and groups), but not make the decision to detain someone. In addition, the principle of reciprocity means that legislation must include safeguards such as advocacy and advance directives (Eastman, 1994).

Conclusion: postpsychiatry and antipsychiatry

Postpsychiatry tries to move beyond the conflict between psychiatry and antipsychiatry. Antipsychiatry argued that psychiatry was repressive and based on a mistaken medical ideology, and its proponents wanted to liberate mental patients from its clutches (Bracken, 1995). In turn, psychiatry condemned its opponents as being driven by ideology. Both groups were united by the assumption that there could be a correct way to understand madness; that the truth could, and should, be spoken about madness and distress. Postpsychiatry frames these issues in a different way. It does not propose new theories about madness, but it opens up spaces in which other perspectives can assume a validity previously denied them. Crucially, it argues that the voices of service users and survivors should now be centre stage.

Postpsychiatry distances itself from the therapeutic implications of antipsychiatry. It does not seek to replace the medical techniques of psychiatry with new therapies or new paths towards 'liberation.' It is not a set of fixed ideas and beliefs, more a set of signposts that can help us move on from where we are now.

Psychiatry, like medicine, will have to adapt to Muir Gray's 'postmodern environment'. Mental health work has never been comfortable with a modernist agenda, and an increasing number of psychiatrists are becoming interested in philosophical and historical aspects of mental health care. Indeed, psychiatry, with its strong tradition of conceptual debate, has an advantage over other medical disciplines when it comes to the postmodern challenge. Postpsychiatry seeks to democratise mental health by linking progressive service development to a debate about contexts, values, and partnerships. We believe that the advent of postmodernity offers an exciting challenge for doctors involved in this area and represents an opportunity to rethink our roles and responsibilities.

References

Beaumont, P.J.V. (1992) 'Phenomenology and the history of psychiatry'. *Aust NZJ Psychiatry*, 26: 532–45.

Bracken, P. (1995) Beyond liberation: Michel Foucault and the notion of a critical psychiatry'. *Philos. Psychiatry Psychol.*, 2: 1–13.

Bracken, P. (1999) 'Phenomenology and psychiatry'. *Curr. Opin. Psychiatry*, 12: 593–6.

Bracken, P. and Thomas, P. (1998) 'A new debate on mental health'. *Openmind*, 89: 17.

Bracken, P. and Thomas, P. (1999) 'Home treatment in Bradford'. *Openmind*, 95: 17.

Bracken, P. Giller, J. and Summerfield, D. (1995) 'Psychological responses to war and atrocity: the limitations of current concepts'. *Soc. Sci. Med.*, 40: 1073–82.

Clare, A. (1976) *Psychiatry in dissent: controversial issues in thought and practice.* London: Tavistock.

Department of Health (1998) *Saving lives: our healthier nation.* London: Stationery Office.

Department of Health (1999) *Modern Standards and Service Models: Mental Health*. London: Stationery Office.

Eastman, N. (1994) 'Mental health law: civil liberties and the principle of reciprocity'. *BMJ*, 308: 43.

Ellenberg, H. (1970) *The Discovery of the Unconscious: the History and Evolution of Dynamic Psychiatry*. London: Fontana.

Foucault, M. (1971) *Madness and Civilization: A History of Insanity in the Age of Reason*. London: Tavistock.

Fulford, K.W.M. (1994) 'Closer logics: hidden conceptual elements in the DSM and ICD classification of mental disorders'. In: Sadler, J.Z., Wiggins, O.P. and Schwartz (eds) *Philosophical Perspectives on Psychiatric Diagnostic Classification*. Baltimore: Johns Hopkins University Press, 211–32.

Gaines, A. (1992) *Ethnopsychiatry: the Cultural Construction of Professional and Folk Psychiatries*. Albany: State University of New York Press.

Gordon, C. (1990) 'Histoire de la folie: an unknown book by Michel Foucault'. *History Hum. Sci.*, 3: 3–26.

Ingleby, D. (1980) *Critical Psychiatry*. New York: Pantheon.

Jaspers, K. (1963) *General Psychopathology*. Manchester: Manchester University Press.

Kutchins, H. and Kirk, S. (1999) *Making us Crazy. DSM: the Psychiatric Bible and the Creation of Mental Disorders*. London: Constable.

Leudar, I. and Thomas, P. (2000) *Voices of Reason, Voices of Insanity*. London: Routledge.

Muir Gray, J.A. (1999) 'Postmodern medicine'. *Lancet*, 354: 1550–3.

Phillips, J. (1996) 'Key concepts: hermeneutics'. *Philosophy, Psychiatry, Psychology*, 13: 61–9.

Porter, R.A. (1987) *A Social History of Madness: Stories of the Insane*. London: Weidenfeld and Nicolson.

Relton, P. (1999) 'Being out in the NHS'. *The Advocate*, May: 22–4.

Romme, M. and Escher, S. (1994) *Accepting Voices*. London: Mind Publications.

Rorty, R. (1979) *Philosophy and the Mirror of Nature*. Princeton: Princeton University Press.

Samson, C. (1995) 'The fracturing of medical dominance in British psychiatry?', *Sociol. Health Illness*, 17: 245–68.

Sashidharan, S.P. and Francis, E. (1999) 'Racism in psychiatry necessitates reappraisal of general procedures and Eurocentric theories'. *BMJ*, 319: 254.

Shepherd, M. (1983) *The Psychological Matrix of Psychiatry: collected papers*. London: Tavistock.

Szasz, T. (1961) *The Myth of Mental Illness*. New York: Harper & Row.

Thomas, P. (1997) *The Dialectics of Schizophrenia*. London: Free Association Books.

Vygotsky, L. (1978) *Mind in Society: the Development of Higher Psychological Processes*. London: Harvard University Press.

Zigmond, A. (1998) 'Medical incapacity act'. *Psychiatr. Bull.*, 22: 657–8.

45

Formal observations and engagement: a discussion paper

Nick Bowles, P. Dodds, Diane Hackney, Cath Sunderland and Phil Thomas

Introduction

In this paper, three contributors share their experiences of observation in a series of personal accounts, almost 'conversations' on their experience. None have 'all the answers', yet the experiences of psychiatry related here are contemporary and likely to be shared with many others. Phil Thomas is a psychiatrist; Diane Hackney is a service user with personal experience of formal observation and a non-executive director of an NHS Trust, one of a handful of non-executive directors with personal experience of mental health services; Cath Sutherland is a mental health nurse who works in a setting in which alternatives to observations are routinely practised.

From the psychiatrist's chair (Dr Phil Thomas)

To practice psychiatry is to tread an uneasy line between care and coercion. Most people who become psychiatrists do so because they want to try to help people in distress. Yet, paradoxically, coercion is a significant part of their work, and over the last 15 years or so it has become even more prominent.

Edited from N. Bowles et al., *Journal of Psychiatric and Mental Health Nursing* (2002), vol. 9(3), pp. 255–60.

This shift is reflected in the nature of inpatient care, especially the importance attached to nursing observations. I first became aware of this about 10 years ago, when the nursing staff started to ask me what level of observations I wanted my patients on. I was puzzled. What were they talking about? Then I realized that they wanted to know how often I wanted them to check the patient. My confusion was complete when I discovered that one ward's 'level one' was another's 'level four'.

All this made me uneasy. The process was becoming an end in itself. Nurses were no longer expected to talk with patients, but to observe them. Now nurses always have observed patients but the introduction of nursing observations signified a cultural change, a shift from a philosophy that valued human contact, to one in which facts and enumeration were of greater importance. A phenomenon that gains pace, as our attraction to tick-box risk assessments testifies.

Perhaps the inaccurate reporting and distorted publicity that followed a small number of high profile tragedies in the early 1990s, the so-called 'failures' of community care, created a hostile environment for mental health professionals, who in turn adopted defensive practices. Inpatient units had to stop patients escaping and harming themselves and others.

If formal observations were introduced for defensive reasons, then in my opinion they also created a voyeuristic mentality, an intrusive, disengaged gaze on human suffering. Something was lost when nursing observations became the norm on inpatient units.

Because some nurses no longer engaged closely with patients they no longer *knew* anything of value about them. For example, they could tell me how often patients talked to themselves but they were no longer able to convey anything of the lived experience of the patient, how they had ended up in hospital and what strengths the patient possessed that would help them recover. In multidisciplinary team (MDT) meetings I no longer had the impression that nursing colleagues knew anything about the real reasons for patients being in hospital.

I also grew concerned about the little nursing time that was left over in which to care for those patients who were not on observations. It seemed to me that their needs were sometimes subordinate to the ritual of observations.

As a consequence, all of us are worse off, patients are to varying degrees unknown to their workers, nurses are often demoralized and only too aware of the constraints on what they might otherwise be doing with patients; for me, well it's difficult to practice with inadequate information and hard to justify admission when care is substandard and subordinate to control. This is bad psychiatry.

My experience in Bradford over the last 2 years has changed that, i.e. since the nurses 'refocused' their efforts. Now when nursing colleagues report on a patient's progress at MDT meetings, they convey a sense of the person behind the patient. They have a clearer grasp of the issues that went wrong outside the hospital, and the circumstances that led to admission. Consequently our helping strategies are more focused on trying to resolve these circumstances; poor housing, stigmatization in a neighbourhood, problems with benefits and so on.

In short, shifting the focus of nursing interventions away from the institutional functions of control to care and concern for the person is clearly better for patients. It has helped me to practise better psychiatry, and to feel more confident that our involvement in people's lives does more good than harm. It is not, perhaps, always so clear. Sometimes coercion is necessary, but never as an alternative to care.

Unheard voices – a service user perspective (Diane Hackney)

They said that if I told the doctor the truth, nothing horrible would happen to me. They lied. I told the doctor the truth and he put me on continuous observations for 7 of the 12 weeks I was in hospital.

Observations, together with copious amounts of medication, was the sum total of my 'therapeutic treatment' during my incarceration. I choose the word incarceration purposefully because that's what it was – imprisonment. I was allowed no privacy, no dignity, and no respect – not at any time, nor in any setting. It was all in my best interests, I was told. It would give me someone to talk to about my problems. It would keep me safe. It would help me get better. In fact, the absolute opposite happened.

There is nothing more degrading than having to go to the toilet in front of a complete stranger. There is nothing more frustrating than trying to have a meal with someone watching you take each mouthful, and there is nothing more childish than having someone look over you while you sleep.

Let's look closer at the reality of being observed, there's nothing more basic than going to the toilet, we'll start there. I never did manage to use the toilet in front of a nurse, even after I had been taught the 'trick' of flushing the loo before making my deposits in a vain attempt to overcome the embarrassment of the noises that accompany such a natural function. It got to the point where I was becoming physically unwell as I tried to limit the number of times I had to go to the loo, keeping everything in until I was absolutely desperate. Eventually I got 'relaxed' toilet observations that meant a nurse stood outside the cubical instead of inside it with me. They could still hear the noises but at least they weren't actually watching me do 'it'.

There was usually just one time each week when I could go to the toilet like a 'normal' person. As a Roman Catholic, I attended Sunday Mass at a local convent. After each Mass, the nuns would invite the psychiatric patients into their house for coffee and biscuits. Not only was it by far the best cup of coffee in the week, it was also the only time my nurse would let me go to the toilet on my own, presumably assuming that I wouldn't hang myself in a convent loo. Best pee of the week too!

During my first few weeks of continuous observations, I had to visit a dental hospital for treatment. Of course, a nurse came with me and I had relatively little problem with that. It was strange sitting in the waiting room listening to people talking about what they were going to cook for dinner and watching young children running around. It all seemed so refreshingly normal. It is no surprise therefore that I felt absolutely horrified when I got up to go to the toilet and my nurse came with me. I couldn't believe what she was doing. We were 'outside' now. Nobody had told me that the rules applied in the real world too. I looked around at all the people in the waiting room, convinced that they now knew that I was a psychiatric patient being accompanied by a nurse. I don't think I ever told the nurses how this made me feel, my experiences and what they saw me doing were two different things.

As the weeks of continuous observations went by I began to seriously challenge the idea that they were providing me with 'therapy' and support. Sure, they were keeping me safe, but that was about it. Most of the staff I got lumbered with did not, would not or could not make even small talk with me, let alone discuss my illness. Shift after shift, nurses came and went, often with no conversation at all taking place. It always amazed me that the least experienced staff seemed to be given the most distressed patients to work with. They appeared to have no training in mental health issues and, worse of all, no respect for the person they were 'guarding'.

There was one time during my numerous admissions when several of us were on continuous observations and there developed what became called 'the donkey system'. When patients woke up in the morning and saw who their guardian was for the shift, the first question asked of each other wasn't 'how's things this morning?' but 'what's your donkey factor today?' There was a score from 1 to 10 with 10 being the 'worst', but many of the staff got 15 or more! The scoring system was at one level humorous, but it was also more seriously based on whether or not you were going to be able to talk about anything meaningful and helpful during that particular shift. The staff used in continuous observations often appeared bored and unmotivated. I often felt guilty about wanting to move from one room to another as this was regularly met by a lot of tutting and heavy sighs from my nurse. It appears that all this activity was all too much for them now that they had just got settled in one spot or were deeply entrenched in a magazine or book.

But what amazed me most of all was that some patients actually wanted to be subject to observations. There was, and still is, a subculture of illness status amongst patients in a ward setting. There is almost a competition as to who is the most unwell. If you are on observations, the inference is that you are very unwell and need constant attention. All a patient has to do is tell their doctor that they feel suicidal and there you go – continuous observations. Everyone moans about it, but it is a tangible measure and a public show of the perceived level of your distress. It is very easy to 'get lost' in a ward of many patients, each one vying for the nurses' attention. Days can go by without any member of staff speaking to a compliant patient and so getting yourself on continuous observations means that you get that basic attention, and this is so sad.

There must surely be a much more effective way of supporting very distressed people in the inpatient setting. A way that is rewarding for both the patient and the staff; a way that reduces the cost of having to buy in staff just to follow patients around all day. There have got to be ways of helping a person feel safe and supported without reducing them to victims of voyeurism and seriously eroding away their basic human rights.

It is not acceptable that psychiatric patients are doomed to remain prisoners in their illnesses, their guards continuously watching over them just to make sure.

Beyond notions of observations versus engagement – on 'containment' (Cath Sunderland, mental health nurse)

People who are suicidal or present a risk to others make health care workers (and their managers) feel they have to 'do' something. Is it possible that observation is sometimes used because there's little else that feels possible to 'do' with patients like this? Something clearly must be done, so is there an alternative to formal observations?

In settings where 'doing obs' is not immediately possible or is contradictory to therapeutic values, workers would have to do something (anything) different, think harder and engage more or better. In my workplace, as we take a psychoanalytic perspective, this is always our approach, the 'bread and butter' of our work.

My colleagues and I do this 'something different', we call it 'containment'. Being 'contained' in this different way is more often than not an important learning process for our patients, albeit often an uncomfortable one; many of them have had years of experience in acute settings where their distress was reacted to, rather than understood. They often seek to have us react in the expected, routine way, to do so means we 'act in' with their sense that only concrete action works, which leaves them stuck in a cycle of action – reaction – action.

So what is 'containment'? It sounds uncomfortably like the incarceration that Diane Hackney describes above. As Diane describes, acute settings place the emphasis on containing patients through physical means. In our practice, containment means the process of containing the patient's feelings. This involves being receptive to what the patient is experiencing, being able to bear and think constructively about these feelings. When we can do this, the next step is to use the understanding we have gained about the nature of the patient's feelings or anxieties and communicate this to the patient. To do this effectively, the nurse needs to work in a setting where this level of involvement is encouraged and possible, and through peer relationships, line and clinical supervision the nurse also needs containing.

In acute settings, patients' anxieties and unbearable feelings are often not contained but are reacted to. This is understandable, given the intensity of these feelings and the negative consequences for nurses if the patient harms themselves or others. Equally, the emotional labour, which nurses face if they allow themselves to get close to the painful emotional experience of patients, is significant.

It is when patients most need another person to get close to their experience that they tend to act or communicate in ways that powerfully affect staff, raising staff anxiety and triggering concrete patient management procedures, which will commonly include formal observations. Whilst observations may connote a physical proximity between nurse and patient, it rarely involves a meaningful interpersonal interaction or emotional closeness. The patient needs, more than just the presence of a nurse physically, to have their feelings 'contained' with the help of another.

It is 'containing' for patients to have the things they experience named and understood. The nurse can do this if she has been able to listen to the patient, her own feelings and those of the other staff in relation to the patient. If a feeling generated in the staff team is one of anger towards the patient or fear that they are likely to self-harm, then it's probable that this is what the patient will experience. When these feelings are expressed, understood and named, but not acted upon, the patient may experience a release from the normal cycle of unbearable feelings and self-destructive action.

I would argue that mostly patients don't have this experience but instead see nurses and other professionals having to act, to 'do' rather than 'contain'. What these reactions communicate to the patient may be something like this: 'my feelings must be unbearable, I want to get rid of what I'm feeling and so do they, I've made the staff anxious and annoyed so they are putting me on obs to stop themselves feeling that'. In this way, what happens is that the patient has it confirmed that what they feel is unbearable, to them and other people.

Diane spoke above about being incarcerated for week after week, a prisoner of her mental illness and a prisoner because of it. To this perspective I would like to add the sense I have that distressed patients enter into a sort of ever repeating groundhog day of distress and ritualized reaction from staff, the time-honoured roles played out time and again. It is within our hands to short circuit this ritual; emotional containment provides an alternative way of 'doing' and 'being' with patients, whilst maintaining their safety.

46

Evaluating partnerships: a case study of integrated specialist mental health services

Tim Freeman and Edward Peck

Introduction

Common across multiple UK social policy arenas, partnership working became a central feature of New Labour's approach to social policy in the UK (Powell and Glendinning, 2002), an umbrella term covering a multitude of arrangements between public, private and voluntary agencies and service users.

The political imperative of partnership working is clear, and there is also evidence to suggest that the National Health Service (NHS) and social services were recognising the interdependent nature of their services before the 1999 Health Act, making efforts to provide 'joined up' care (Wilkin et al., 2000) and providing a receptive context for partnership policy initiatives. Section 31 of the Health Act 1999 introduced three types of flexibilities, relaxing some of the perceived barriers to collaborative working. These comprised: pooled budgets, allowing the commissioning of comprehensive packages of health and social care; delegation of commissioning responsibilities to a single lead agency charged with commissioning services on behalf of all partners;

Edited from T. Freeman and E. Peck, *Health and Social Care in the Community* (2006), vol. 14(5), pp. 408–17.

and integration of services (or transfer of elements of provision between partner agencies) to deliver services from a single organisation. While the *forms* of partnership working are well described, there is perhaps rather less understanding of the requirements necessary for implementing the approach in practice (Clarke and Glendinning, 2002). A national evaluation of implementation of Section 31 flexibilities (Hudson et al., 2002) provided some clues, identifying the importance of local commitment, trust and leadership, and the promotion of holistic professional work practices. The implication is that, while the policy framework supplies the context in which changes may be pursued, their enactment requires fine-grained local relationships and working practices.

Case study context

The Mental Health National Service Framework (Department of Health, 1999) identifies a range of required specialist and generalist community-based mental health services. Crisis assessment and treatment teams (CATTs) offer an alternative to inpatient care for people when they are experiencing acute mental health crisis. Teams deliver home-based multidisciplinary treatment, are available 24-hours a day and are charged with targeting those individuals who would otherwise require an inpatient stay, treating them with the minimum restriction and disruption to their lives. Assertive outreach teams (AOTs) are charged with providing bespoke and proactive care for people with enduring mental health problems in their own homes. They are used to engage service users who have difficulty managing their own daily lives – the aim is not to get them to accept other services so much as enable them to live fulfilled lives. While such specialist teams have been developing since the 1980s in the USA, Australia and increasingly the UK, coverage has been patchy and the structures and models of teams vary significantly.

Subjects and methods

In order to provide a rich overview, data was triangulated from three sources: a series of focus groups with users and carers who had been in direct contact with both the new specialist team(s) and previous generalist provision (November 2004); semistructured interviews with each specialist and generalist team manager concerning the operation of the teams within their locality (October 2004); and quantitative self-completion questionnaires to each member of staff within the teams, in order to assess role clarity and job satisfaction within each of the new specialist teams and more traditional, generalist Community Mental Health Teams (CMHTs) (October 2002 and October 2004).

Results

Semistructured interviews with team managers identified a number of pressures involved in collaborations across integrated service providers of mental health services. The issues reported below are a county-wide aggregation of views from across the five localities.

Pressures for fragmentation and integration

The segmentation of provision into tiers of specialist services incorporating personnel from health and social services resulted in legitimate disagreements between clinical professionals over what to do for the best during an emerging crisis episode, which could result in increased distress for both client and carer. In one example, a client known by CMHT services to be high-risk when ill was assessed and referred to CATT as needing admission – but rejected by CATT, who wanted to work with the client to avoid admission. The carer was concerned, expressing a desire for an inpatient stay and unsure of what CATT would be able to provide. The client's mental health quickly deteriorated, resulting in an inpatient stay following a second CATT assessment hours later. Cases are often complex, requiring difficult decisions by a number of people, and where relationships between multiple teams are strained the potential for negative unintended consequences is increased.

For most localities, there was little sense that the existence of specialist teams had freed CMHT capacity or enabled generalist CMHTs to develop interventions consistent with an emphasis on personal development, as anticipated. Much of the work of AOTs concentrated on clients who used to 'slip through the net' – new work with a previously excluded group, rather than a reallocation of existing work between teams. Similarly, discharge from crisis intervention services back into CMHTs had implications for CMHT capacity because, although crisis interventions are tapered down before discharge, additional CMHT visits may be required during the short-term.

Only one of the five localities (East) experienced the anticipated reduced pressure on CMHTs, attributed to a combination of: accident and emergency department liaison relieving pressure during inpatient stay; primary care counselling services dealing with demand for lower-level counselling interventions; generally good levels of staff recruitment and retention in CMHTs relative to other localities; and a historical acceptance by AOT of some 'time consuming' rather than disengaged CMHT clients.

Benefits and difficulties for staff

Above all, respondents identified that the team approach may be experienced as helpful and supportive. Clients are discussed so that multiple professional perspectives may be explored, providing opportunities for informal learning across professional boundaries. The co-location of teams increases the potential for informal 'water cooler' contact, typically enhancing working relationships, and this contrasts starkly with the feelings of isolation and sole responsibility which are often reported within generalist teams with high caseloads. Additionally, specialist tiers promise the time and space to develop social inclusion work with clients who have previously been difficult to engage, and this may be experienced as professionally satisfying, and staff similarly report the 'short-term', challenging and intensive nature of crisis intervention work as professionally rewarding. This is largely a result of the opportunities provided to work in a therapeutic way rather than simple containment, and although ultimately backed by the sanction of inpatient admission, such working relationships generally foster a negotiating style between staff and patient rather than a simple hierarchy. For generalist workers, the availability of specialist crisis services can take the pressure off and reduce staff worry about the level of support they can offer to clients during crisis.

While generally positive, there were concerns that clients with borderline personality disorders may 'play the system' and make liaison between teams difficult. Additional concerns were expressed that integrated specialist teams could be experienced as unsettling, particularly with regard to the blurring of professional roles as a result of multidisciplinary working practices. The staffing needs associated with 24-hour cover and its associated shift patterns were identified as potential problems.

User and carer perspectives

Four separate focus groups were held with users and carers to explore perceptions of the new teams.

User perspectives
Service-user focus group participants regarded specialist integrated services positively because of: a combination of the perceived sensitivity and trustworthiness of staff; the provision of social care; staff ability to liaise with other services; and staff responsiveness to changes in level of need. These indicate the importance of staff *enactment* of procedures and protocols; it is not the existence of partnership documents that is valued so much as the practical benefits which result from their application. While there was much support for the work of the specialist integrated teams, one participant drew attention to

the importance of the relationship between client and worker, and revealed the range of opinions held by users toward inpatient stays, in which notions of sanctuary and asylum vie with more negative images of lack of privacy and safety. This suggests a range of alternative frames of reference in considering judgements of team effectiveness and the reduction of inpatient stays. Somewhat ironically, the staff rotas required to provide extended crisis cover may risk service continuity as experienced by users, who value crisis intervention by *known* individuals with whom they have had previous contact.

Carer perspectives

Carer focus group members shared many positive aspects of integrated teams with users, including sensitivity, responsiveness and provision of social activities, and the sensitivity and responsiveness of the team to *carer* concerns was also valued (Box 46.1) – again drawing attention to the *enactment* of roles and personal qualities of staff. The potential loss of 'sanctuary' provided by inpatient stay was considered from the perspective of carers – while traumatic, inpatient stays could be experienced by carers as periods of respite, and the burden of providing care during acute episodes, notwithstanding support

---

Box 46.1   Positive aspects of specialist integrated mental health services (carers)

Sensitivity and trustworthiness

'[My son] is able to be truthful with them because they have built up a relationship and he trusts them.'

'Over time they were able to introduce different workers, after gaining his trust, but it was good the way they did this gradually.'

Responsiveness and dignity

'They are able to tap into expertise at very short notice. For example, if [my son] is getting ill, they can assess the situation, and if he does need to see a doctor, the doctor will go to his flat, see him there, change medication or whatever and all within a short space of time – and the nurses will do several sessions and a programme of interventions, not just an assessment but some care as well.'

Social activities

'They will take her shopping or out for a meal, this is very good. They always ask her where she would like to go, and then take her out. This is very good for her – she wasn't always like this, but she trusts them.'

Reassurance and easing of carer burden
'It's nice to know that there is somebody else at the end of the line to take responsibility with you – that is the biggest thing.'

'Before, if [my son] was unwell, I would have to make decisions in a vacuum: do I take him to A&E? The GP? Then I have to get him there. And it's always my decision and responsibility to take the next step, which because he is unwell he doesn't want to take. Now I can let the team know that he seems worse this week, and they can assess and make an informed decision.'

Sensitivity to carers
'They always trust me – it is never treated as unimportant. If I panic, they react appropriately: I am never made to feel that it wasn't necessary.'

from a crisis team, could prove difficult. While some expressed concern over the potential withdrawal of valued specialist interventions, others identified potential tensions between carer and user preferences, and expressed ambivalence over the role of the teams in working with both carer and user. This raises the possibility of different frames of reference between users and carers when considering outcomes or the lived experience of different constituencies of service users/carers.

Staff experience of integrated provision

A pre-post quantitative census design was used to assess differences in role clarity and job satisfaction over time.

Role clarity and job satisfaction scales comprised a number of subscales, each with multiple indicators. Each subscale is scored between 0 and 100, with low scores meaning higher achievement.

Whole-sample inter-year comparisons

Scores for each of the job satisfaction and role clarity subscales are graphically presented in Figure 46.1. Scores typically showed moderate to good levels of achievement, with scores for 2004 generally indicating a slight improvement on those for 2002. The score for perceived team effectiveness fell from 37.7 to 20.1, indicating a considerable improvement in staff perceptions following the adoption of integrated specialist provision.

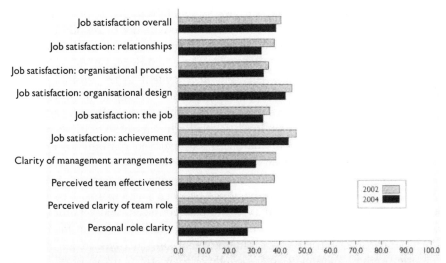

Figure 46.1   Outcome scale scores (mean) for whole sample for 2002 and 2004. Scales are scored between 0 and 100, with a low score meaning a better outcome.

Discussion

The present results identified the difficulties involved in evaluating the impact of complex service interventions on user, carer and staff perceptions of service quality. The authors were able to identify a wide range of concerns held by different stakeholders during an initial diagnostic phase of the evaluation, and were careful to include a range of quantitative and qualitative data in their case study design. However, difficulties were posed by: the complexity of the proposed service interventions themselves; the highly heterogeneous *local* contexts with different histories and experiences of specialist integrated provision; and the dynamic *national* policy context requiring swift implementation of standard models of care.

The present quantitative outcome study (that is, staff perceptions of role clarity and job satisfaction) faced a number of problems. First, there were issues over the appropriate unit of analysis for data collection and reporting. Given the focus on team-based activity and the team-based nature of the intervention, the most appropriate unit of analysis would be the team. It would be inappropriate to use individual-level data to assess change, since this would inflate the (statistical) significance of differences caused by confounding. As well as these technical considerations, there were the practical difficulties posed by significant amounts of staff turnover, recruitment and redeployment, which also effectively ruled out the comparison of tied data from individuals at T1 (2002) and T2 (2004).

Additionally, the present authors' assessment of staff perceptions faced problems of attribution to the intervention. The dynamic policy environment necessitated changes to provision in line with National Service Frameworks simultaneously in all localities, removing the possibility of non-intervention comparison groups. Heterogeneity was also evident in the localities themselves, each with a wide range of prior experience of integrated working with potential to influence the extent to which participants were able to engage with the changes. While some localities had a history of extensive specialist team provision (albeit not compliant with National Service Framework specifications), others had little or no experience and little history of joint working between primary and secondary care, let alone social care agencies, and these differences generated complex dynamics between participants. The present authors' qualitative data from users and carers additionally points to the importance of the *enactment* of interventions by individual team members – the interventions are themselves complex social constructions, reliant on interpretation and interaction between people for their effects to emerge.

References

Clarke, J. and Glendinning, C. (2002) 'Partnership and the remaking of welfare governance', in C. Glendinning, M. Powell and K. Rummery (eds) *Partnerships, New Labour and the Governance of Welfare*, Bristol: The Policy Press, pp. 33–50.

Department of Health (1999) *National Service Framework for Mental Health Services: Modern Standards and Service Models*, London: Her Majesty's Stationery Office.

Hudson, B., Young, R., Hardy, B. and Glendinning, C. (2002) *National Evaluation of Notifications for Use of the Section 31 Partnership Flexibilities of the Health Act 1999*, Manchester: National Primary Care Research and Development Centre,

Powell, M. and Glendinning, C. (2002) 'Introduction', in C. Glendinning, M. Powell and K. Rummery (eds) *Partnerships, New Labour and the Governance of Welfare*, Bristol: The Policy Press, pp. 1–14.

Wilkin, D., Gillam, S. and Leese, B. (2000) *The National Tracker Survey of Primary Care Groups and Trusts: Progress and Challenges 1999/2000*, Manchester: National Primary Care Research and Development Centre.

47

Deconstructing psychiatric drug treatment

Joanna Moncrieff

The use of drugs is the central form of treatment in modern day psychiatry. Most people who are referred to psychiatrists are prescribed one form of drug or another and many psychiatric patients take several drugs simultaneously for years on end. Psychiatric institutions revolve around the rituals of drug administration and devising and supervising drug regimes forms a large part of the work of almost all mental health professionals.

Drugs occupy this pivotal role in mental health care because they are viewed as 'chemical cures' (Moncrieff, 2008). By this I do not mean they are believed to reverse or eliminate psychiatric disorders entirely. They are regarded as cures because they are claimed to work on the underlying biological defect that is thought to give rise to particular psychiatric symptoms. It is the idea that they act in a specific way, on the basis of a disease, that gives modern psychiatric drugs the status of medical treatments. It marks them out from earlier drugs used in psychiatry, which were regarded as forms of chemical restraint. However, contrary to the majority of professional and public opinion, there is no evidence to support this view. We have been sold a myth about the nature of psychiatric drugs, a myth that has blinded us to their real nature. Psychiatric drugs are psycho-active drugs, like alcohol, cannabis and heroin. Their effects on people with mental disorder can easily be explained by the fact that, like other psycho-active drugs, they alter the way the brain functions, the way people think and feel, both while they are being taken and sometimes for ever.

Models of psychiatric drug action

To provide a clear way to think about the nature of psychiatric drugs, I have outlined two alternative ways of understanding how they might affect people.

Table 47.1   Alternative models of drug action

Disease-centred model	Drug-centred model
Drugs help correct an abnormal brain state	Drugs create an abnormal brain state
Therapeutic effects of drugs derive from their effects on an underlying disease process	Therapeutic effects derive from the impact of the drug induced state on behavioural and emotional problems
Paradigm: insulin for diabetes	Paradigm: alcohol for social anxiety

I have called these different 'models' of drug action the disease-centred model and the drug-centred model. Their contrasting features are summarised in Table 47.1.

The disease-centred model is the standard view that psychiatric drugs work by correcting an underlying disease of the brain. According to this model, drug treatment makes your brain more normal by helping to reverse a biological process. The disease-centred model is based on the way most drugs work in physical medicine. Insulin, for example, compensates for the underlying deficiency of insulin in diabetes and anti-asthma drugs help to reverse the lung problems that cause wheezing. Even pain killers, although they do not target the underlying disease, work by acting on the biological pathways that give rise to pain.

Like most medical drugs, psychiatric drugs are named and classified according to the diseases they are thought to reverse or treat. Thus drugs that are thought to help correct the disease process that leads to depression are called 'antidepressants'. Drugs that are thought to rectify the abnormality that gives rise to the symptoms of schizophrenia or psychosis are known as 'antipsychotics' and drugs that are believed to correct an underlying mood control defect are referred to as 'mood stabilisers'.

The alternative way of thinking about psychiatric drugs is what I have called the drug-centred model. According to this view, psychiatric drugs, like all psycho-active drugs, distort the functioning of the nervous system and by doing so they produce altered mental states. Far from correcting an underlying biological abnormality, they create an abnormal state. When we think of recreational drugs we refer to these altered mental states as 'intoxication'. Psychiatric drugs also produce states of intoxication. The features of these states vary according to what sort of drug is taken. Just as the effects of cannabis differ from those of alcohol or heroin, so the effects produced by antipsychotics are different from those produced by benzodiazepines or Prozac, for example. The characteristic features of the intoxicated or drug-induced state depend on the chemical structure and nature of each drug.

The drug-centred model suggests that drugs can sometimes be helpful because the features of the drug-induced state superimpose themselves onto the manifestations of the mental disorder. An example of this is the long-accepted benefits of alcohol in people with social phobia or social anxiety. Alcohol is not thought to be helpful because it corrects a deficiency of alcohol within the brain, nor because it corrects another chemical imbalance. It is thought to help because one of the characteristic features of alcohol intoxication is that it reduces social inhibitions, which may be helpful for someone who finds social situations anxiety-provoking.

However, by stressing that drugs are chemicals that alter the normal functioning of the body and the brain, the drug-centred model highlights the negative effects of drug use. Drug-induced effects do not simply target psychiatric symptoms. They affect all areas of mental and emotional functioning. In addition, since drugs are extraneous chemicals, the body tries to counteract their effects, with both predictable and unpredictable consequences.

Evidence on psychiatric drugs

The idea that psychiatric drugs work in a disease-centred fashion has never been properly evaluated because it is simply assumed to be the case. In fact, since the idea was adopted in the 1960s the psychiatric community have largely forgotten that there is any other way to think about the effects of psychiatric drugs.

Psychiatric drugs, like other medical treatments, are tested to see if they are effective in placebo-controlled randomised trials. In these trials, people are randomly allocated to be given either the real drug, or a dummy pill, called a placebo. The improvement in symptoms in both groups is then measured using various rating scales, consisting of items thought to be relevant to the condition concerned. If the drug is found to be superior to placebo, it is declared to be efficacious. However, these trials assume that drugs act in a disease-centred way, and that any psycho-active effects they have are trivial and do not influence the outcome. But psycho-active effects are bound to impact on psychiatric symptoms. Therefore you can only tell whether a particular drug acts on a disease process if you first rule out the impact of the psycho-active (and physical) effects a drug produces. For example, antidepressants have been shown to be slightly superior to placebo in randomised controlled trials. However, they all produce drug-induced effects that may influence results. Many have sedative effects, for example, which will improve items that relate to poor sleep, anxiety and agitation, which are included in all depression rating scales.

Placebo-controlled trials only establish that a drug is different from a dummy tablet. They do not indicate how or why that is the case. To establish that a drug acts in a disease-centred way, a number of things need to be demonstrated. Preferably, as in many areas of medicine, you would show how a drug interacted with a demonstrable disease process. However, no specific pathology has ever been demonstrated for any psychiatric condition. It has been suggested that schizophrenia and psychosis are caused by an increased amount of a chemical called dopamine in the brain and that depression is caused by a lack of the chemicals serotonin or noradrenalin. However, these are simply theories. The strongest evidence put forward to support them is that drugs such as antidepressants and antipsychotics act in a disease-specific way, but this is just an assumption, as I have already stated. Contrary to popular belief, there is no consistent independent evidence that there are specific abnormalities of dopamine in psychosis or schizophrenia or of serotonin or noradrenalin in depression (Moncrieff, 2008). Indeed, the idea that psychiatric disorders are caused by a chemical imbalance has largely been promoted by drug company literature (Lacasse and Leo, 2005).

In the absence of a demonstrable disease mechanism to justify a disease-centred model, it should at least be possible to show that drugs that are claimed to act in a disease-centred way are superior to other drugs. However, there is little evidence for this either. Drugs that have been shown to be superior to placebo or equivalent to antidepressants in depression trials include benzodiazepines, opiates, many antipsychotics and stimulants (Moncrieff and Cohen, 2006). In addition, antidepressants themselves come from many different chemical classes and can have few pharmacological properties in common. Thus it appears that almost any drug that has noticeable effects has an impact on depression.

Studies that compared antipsychotics with sedative drugs also fail to confirm the superiority of antipsychotics. Although two studies showed that an early antipsychotic was better than barbiturates (Casey et al., 1960a; Casey et al., 1960b), comparisons with benzodiazepines do not find antipsychotics to be superior overall (Wolkowitz and Pickar, 1991). One randomised study from the 1960s, which compared an early antipsychotic to opium found the two drugs were equally good at producing improvement (Abse, Dahlstrom and Tolley, 1960).

Characteristics of some psychiatric drugs

Antipsychotics

Drugs that are now known as 'antipsychotics' were first introduced into psychiatry in the 1950s. To begin with they were viewed as acting in a drug-centred fashion. Pierre Deniker, one of the first psychiatrists to use these drugs, described how they produced a neurological 'disease', which replaced and suppressed the symptoms of schizophrenia (Deniker, 1960). Before they became known as antipsychotics, they were named after the particular effects they induced. Deniker and colleagues named them 'neuroleptics' after their ability to 'seize hold' (*lepsis* in Greek) of the nervous system. In Britain they were referred to as 'major tranquillisers' for many years.

From a drug-centred perspective the old antipsychotics work by inducing a state similar to Parkinson's disease. Parkinson's disease is caused by reduced activity of dopamine, in a part of the brain called the basal ganglia, which controls movement and also influences thought. It consists of a general slowing up of physical and mental activity and an inhibition of motivation and emotional responses. These effects may reduce the impact of psychotic symptoms, but they do not just target symptoms, and their general 'de-activating' effects are often disliked by users (Breggin, 1997).

The new atypical antipsychotics are a mixed bag of drugs. Some appear to act in a similar fashion to the older drugs, and have prominent dopamine-blocking properties. Some of them, like olanzapine and clozapine, appear to act slightly differently. They are less likely to induce Parkinson's symptoms, but they cause a marked increase in appetite and many people who take them gain extraordinary amounts of weight. They also induce a psychological state characterised by mental impairment and emotional indifference. It is usually recommended that people who have psychotic breakdowns should take antipsychotic drugs on a continuing basis in order to prevent a relapse. However, the data supporting this idea are weak because studies involved people who have been on long-term drug treatment prior to the study. The people who were allocated to receive placebo were therefore likely to suffer withdrawal effects and may have even experienced an iatrogenic psychotic episode induced by withdrawal (Moncrieff, 2006). In addition, long-term treatment causes the body to produce more dopamine receptors, which may counteract any beneficial effects and may produce the drug-induced condition known as Tardive Dyskinesia. This consists of abnormal involuntary movements, which can be permanent and are probably associated with general intellectual decline (Waddington et al., 1993).

Antidepressants

Drugs that are now referred to as 'antidepressants' were also first introduced in the 1950s. Initially they were regarded as useful because they were similar to stimulant drugs like amphetamine. Gradually the idea arose that, unlike stimulants, they could work in a specific way to reverse the underlying biological basis of depression and help return someone to normal. The idea that they were drugs with psycho-active effects was forgotten and ignored.

The earliest drugs that came to be called 'antidepressants', drugs classed as monoamine oxidase inhibitors, had similar effects to stimulants. In contrast, the tricyclic antidepressants, such as amitriptyline, are chemically similar to early antipsychotics, and share many of their effects. They are extremely sedating, impair mental functioning and some have been shown to block dopamine in animal studies (Moncrieff, 2008). Selective Serotonin Re-uptake Inhibitors (SSRIs) have only mild psycho-active effects in volunteer studies (Dumont et al., 2005). They make people a bit drowsy, they are unpleasant to take at high doses, and in clinical studies they occasionally make people agitated. There has been heated debate about whether they can induce suicidal behaviour. Several, but not all, large scale analyses suggest SSRIs are associated with increased suicidal thoughts and acts, especially in children (Gunnell, Saperia and Ashby, 2005; Whittington et al., 2004). This may be a result of the unpleasant agitation and activation they can induce (Teicher et al., 1990).

Given this account of the actions of antidepressants, it is difficult to see how they can be useful in people with depression. Indeed, it is difficult to justify the prescription of mind-altering drugs to people with depression, except maybe the careful use of sedatives to improve sleep, or calm agitation or anxiety. Being in a drugged state may effectively distance someone from their current emotions, but it is unlikely to help them recover in the long-term. Indeed, it may act as barrier to dealing with the interpersonal problems that so often contribute to depression.

Stimulants

Stimulant drugs, which include amphetamine and Ritalin, are still referred to by the altered state of artificially enhanced arousal that they produce. They increase heart rate, reduce sleep and at high doses people become more active. However, at lower doses, they produce a state of calmness and heightened and highly focused attention, without increasing activity (Breggin, 2001). They are used for the treatment of children and increasingly also adults who are diagnosed as having hyperactivity or attention deficit disorder. Despite their name they are also regarded as a disease-specific treatment. Psychiatric literature is full of speculations about how they may affect the hypothetical pathology of Attention Deficit Hyperactivity Disorder (ADHD) and little attention is paid to their well-recognised psycho-active effects. Although taking low dose stimulants may enhance attention in the short term, their effects appear to wear off, as with other drugs. The results of a large, long-term trial have not found any benefits of stimulant treatment in children with ADHD compared to other types of non drug based treatment (Jensen et al., 2007). There are also negative consequences of the drug induced state. Animals treated with stimulants become overly focused on trivial, repetitive and meaningless tasks. Likewise, adults and children taking these drugs can develop obsessive-compulsive behaviours, like repeated checking and they also show reduced initiative and can become overly placid, depressed and 'zombie-like' (Breggin, 2001).

Political influences on views of psychiatric drugs

Since there is no evidence to support the idea that any class of psychiatric drug works in a disease-specific way, the question arises as to how this view of drug action became so dominant. The answer may lie in the way it supports the interests of powerful social groups.

The psychiatric profession wants to portray its interventions as specific treatments for specific diseases in order to present itself as a branch of general medicine. This was seen as the key to raising the status, pay and conditions of psychiatrists and their patients. It was also used to counteract competition from other professions involved in managing people defined as having psychiatric disorders, and as a way of rebutting the attacks of the anti-psychiatry movement in the 1960s and 1970s.

The pharmaceutical industry has been an ally in the profession's aim to present its treatments as specific. The disease-centred model presents drug treatment as essentially benign because drugs are claimed to reverse an underlying abnormality, and the alterations they induce are glossed over and relegated to the status of 'side effects'. Therefore the disease-centred view has enabled the industry to massively expand the market for psychiatric drugs. Literature about antidepressants like Prozac, for example, stresses the idea that people with depression have a chemical imbalance that can be rectified by taking the drug. A similar message has been used to market antipsychotic drugs to people diagnosed with schizophrenia and bipolar disorder. Millions of people around the world have been persuaded that their brain chemistry is awry and that they need to take a pill to be normal (Rose, 2004).

However, it is ultimately the support of the state that has allowed the disease-centred view of psychiatric drugs to become dominant. Since the nineteenth century western governments have supported a medical view of madness by sponsoring the psychiatric profession to take main charge of the care of people with mental disorders. The medicalisation of madness and distress enables governments to avoid the difficult political issues that these conditions raise: How does society care for adult dependents, for example, how should it respond to antisocial, disruptive and dangerous behaviour, and why is it that so many people are discontented with their lives and find it difficult to function in modern society?

People have used psycho-active substances to manage mental anguish for a long time. Drugs that suppress mental and emotional activity may be helpful at a time of extreme mental turmoil, but they impact on all areas of mental life and the price is often a heavy one. The portrayal of psychiatric drugs as disease-specific treatments has helped to strengthen the view that mental disorders are simply medical diseases that can be solved with the right technical intervention. But our knowledge about psychiatric drugs does not support this position. Psychiatric problems remain essentially human problems that require a human, not a technical, response.

References

Abse, D.W., Dahlstrom, W. G., and Tolley, A.G. (1960) 'Evaluation of tranquilizing drugs in the management of acute mental disturbance', *American Journal of Psychiatry*, vol. 116, pp. 973–80.

Breggin, P. R. (1997) *Brain Disabling Treatments in Psychiatry: Drugs Electroshock and the Role of the FDA*, New York, Springer Publishing Company.

Breggin, P. R. (2001) *Talking Back to Ritalin: What Doctors aren't Telling you about Stimulants and ADHD.* Cambridge, Massachusetts, Perseus Publishing.

Casey, J.F., Bennett, I.F., Lindley, C.J., Hollister, L.E., Gordon, M.H. and Springer, N.N. (1960a) 'Drug therapy in schizophrenia. A controlled study of the relative effectiveness of chlorpromazine, promazine, phenobarbital, and placebo', *Archives of General Psychiatry*, vol. 2, pp. 210–20.

Casey, J.F., Lasky, J.J., Klett, C.J. and Hollister, L.E. (1960b) 'Treatment of schizophrenic reactions with phenothiazine derivatives. A comparative study of chlorpromazine, triflupromazine, mepazine, prochlorperazine, perphenazine, and phenobarbital', *American Journal of Psychiatry*, vol. 117, pp. 97–105.

Deniker, P. (1960) 'Experimental neurological syndromes and the new drug therapies in psychiatry', *Comprehensive Psychiatry*, vol. 1, pp. 92–102.

Dumont, G.J., de Visser, S.J., Cohen, A. F. and van Gerven, J. J. (2005) 'Biomarkers for the effects of selective serotonin reuptake inhibitors (SSRIs) in healthy subjects', *British Journal of Clinical Pharmacology*, vol. 59, no. 5, pp. 495–510.

Gunnell, D., Saperia, J. and Ashby, D. (2005) 'Selective serotonin reuptake inhibitors (SSRIs) and suicide in adults: meta-analysis of drug company data from placebo controlled, randomised controlled trials submitted to the MHRA's safety review', *British Medical Journal*, vol, 330, no. 7488, p. 385.

Jensen, P.S., Arnold, L.E., Swanson, J.M., Vitiello, B., Abikoff, H.B., Greenhill, L.L., Hechtman, L., Hinshaw, S.P., Pelham, W.E., Wells, K.C., Conners, C.K., Elliott, G.R., Epstein, J.N., Hoza, B., March, J.S., Molina, B.S., Newcorn, J.H., Severe, J.B., Wigal, T., Gibbons, R.D. and Hur, K. (2007) '3-year follow-up of the NIMH MTA study', *Journal of the American Acadamy of Child and Adolescent Psychiatry*, vol. 46, no. 8, pp. 989–1002.

Lacasse, J.R. and Leo, J. (2005) 'Serotonin and depression: a disconnect between the advertisements and the scientific literature', *PLoS Medicine*, vol. 2, no. 12, p. e392.

Moncrieff, J. (2006) 'Does antipsychotic withdrawal provoke psychosis? Review of the literature on rapid onset psychosis (supersensitivity psychosis) and withdrawal-related relapse', *Acta Psychiatra Scandinavica*, vol. 114, no. 1, pp. 3–13.

Moncrieff. J. (2008) *The Myth of the Chemical Cure: A Critique of Psychiatric Drug Treatment*, Basingstoke, Palgrave Macmillan.

Moncrieff, J. and Cohen, D. (2006) 'Do antidepressants cure or create abnormal brain states?', *PLoS Medicine*, vol. 3, no. 7, p. e240.

Rose, N. (2004) 'Becoming neurochemical selves' in Stehr, N. (ed.) *Biotechnology, Commerce and Civil Society*, New Brunswick, New Jersey, Transaction Publishers.

Teicher, M.H., Glod, C. and Cole, J.O. (1990) 'Emergency of intense suicidal preoccupation during fluoxetine treatment', *American Journal of Psychiatry*, vol. 147, no. 2, pp. 207–10.

Waddington, J.L., O'Callaghan, E., Larkin, C. and Kinsella, A. (1993) 'Cognitive dysfunction in schizophrenia: organic vulnerability factor or state marker for tardive dyskinesia?', *Brain Cognition*, vol. 23, no. 1, pp. 56–70.

Whittington, C.J., Kendall, T., Fonagy, P., Cottrell, D., Cotgrove, A.and Boddington, E. (2004) 'Selective serotonin reuptake inhibitors in childhood depression: systematic review of published versus unpublished data', *Lancet*, vol. 363, no. 9418, pp. 1341–5.

Wolkowitz, O.M. and Pickar, D. (1991) 'Benzodiazepines in the treatment of schizophrenia: a review and reappraisal', *American Journal of Psychiatry*, vol. 148, no. 6, pp. 714–26.

48

All you need is cognitive behaviour therapy?

Jeremy Holmes

Introduction

Psychological therapies increasingly form an integral part of government planning for mental health care, and cognitive behaviour therapy tends to be seen as the first line treatment for many psychiatric disorders. Cognitive behaviour therapy is often known as CBT. The therapy attempts to dissect a person's psychological difficulties into their component parts in order to analyse and then deal with them. It may be important for the person to understand the source of their mental distress and differentiate, between an external situation that has become difficult and their own feelings and reactions to that situation. The therapy may be undertaken individually or in groups, or even via self-help books or computer programmes. Because of the short term nature of the therapy and the fact that CBT skills can be rapidly assimilated, the therapy has become popular with managers of the health service and with those looking for speedy resolution of mental health problems. However, the superior showing of cognitive behaviour therapy in trials may be more apparent than real. Psychotherapy is concerned with people in a developmental context and cannot be reduced to the technical elimination of 'disorders'. Psychotherapy research and practice must move beyond 'brand names' of different therapies to an emphasis on common factors, active ingredients, specific skills, and psychotherapy integration.

Edited and adapted from J. Holmes, *British Medical Journal* (2002), vol. 324, pp. 288–90.

Cognitive behaviour therapy as treatment of choice?

In many recent government publications due homage is paid to psychotherapy as a multifaceted, pluralistic enterprise in which a range of therapies is required to meet patients' various needs. Yet, when detailed recommendations are examined there is no doubt that cognitive behaviour therapy is promoted as the therapy of choice. Thus the National Service Framework (Department of Health, 1999) cites cognitive behaviour therapy as the first line treatment for depression, eating disorders, panic disorder, obsessive-compulsive disorder, and deliberate self harm. This follows from the framework's practice of classifying quality of evidence. For most diagnoses, cognitive behaviour therapy tends to get the accolade of 'level 1' evidence – at least one randomised controlled trial and one good systematic review. Other therapies achieve honourable mentions, but usually as also-rans. A similar theme emerges in the Department of Health's guidelines: cognitive behaviour therapy comes first for depressive disorders, panic disorder, agoraphobia, generalised anxiety disorder, post-traumatic stress disorder, bulimia, and chronic fatigue (Department of Health, 2001). It seems that the traditional 'Dodo bird verdict' for psychotherapy research – 'everyone has won, and all must have prizes' (Luborsky et al., 1975) – has finally been superseded.

What are analytic, systemic, eclectic, or pluralistically minded therapists to make of this? Should they abandon hope, and immediately devote their continuing professional development time to retrain in cognitive behaviour therapy? Or, like the late Douglas Adams' Arthur Dent when faced with the imminent destruction of his planet (Adams, 1978), is it still appropriate to say 'Don't panic'?

Cognitive behaviour therapy undoubtedly has much in its favour. It is an attractive, efficient therapy that is relatively easy to learn and deliver and produces good results in many instances. In addition, cognitive behaviour therapy researchers have set standards in detailed descriptions of their methods ('manualisation'), monitoring of adherence, and tailoring treatments to specific disorders that have had a major impact on psychotherapy practice and research generally. Psychoanalytic resistance to quantitative investigation, and consequent marginalisation in an increasingly evidence-based world, has been successfully challenged. Psychoanalytic and systemic therapists now recognise the importance of high quality research, including randomised controlled trials, and many investigations are under way or near completion that would have been unthinkable a decade ago (Fonagy, 1999). Cognitive behaviour therapy provides a benchmark for efficient outcomes, and this has sharpened the minds of psychotherapy researchers worldwide.

Limitations of cognitive behaviour therapy

When it comes to making mental health policy, however, several aspects of cognitive behaviour therapy are open to question. Firstly, the foundations on which it rests are not as secure as some of its proponents would have us believe. The National Institute of Mental Health study of depression, the largest of its kind in the world, is now over three decades old, although its findings are still being digested (Elkin, 1994). In this study, cognitive behaviour therapy fared less well than the two other main treatment arms, interpersonal therapy and clinical management plus antidepressants.

Secondly, there is still much to learn about the impact of different psychotherapies, including cognitive behaviour therapy, on the long term course of psychiatric illnesses. Thus, depression is increasingly seen as a relapsing chronic illness, and without long-term comparative follow up studies it is surely premature to champion any one therapy as the treatment of choice.

Thirdly, there is continuing uncertainty about the effectiveness of different psychotherapies (that is, their clinical relevance) as opposed to their efficacy (ability to produce change under 'laboratory' conditions). Cognitive behaviour therapy works well in university-based clinical trials with subjects recruited from advertisements, but the evidence about how effective it can be in the real world of clinical practice is less secure. In the London depression trial, for example, couple therapy performed better than antidepressants for treating severe depression in patients living with partners, but cognitive behaviour therapy made an unexpectedly poor showing, having been discontinued early in the trial because of poor compliance from a particularly problematic (but clinically typical) group of patients (Leff et al., 2000).

Fourthly, as the Department of Health's guidelines suggest (Department of Health, 2001), absence of evidence is not the same as evidence of absence. Most studies show absolute rather than relative efficacy that is, cognitive behaviour therapy is usually compared with waiting list controls, no therapy at all, or some sort of bland pseudotherapy rather than with another form of psychotherapy. As in drug trials, comparing good treatments with those that may be better is a much greater research challenge than demonstrating that a particular treatment is better than nothing.

Finally, and perhaps most important, leading cognitive behaviour therapists themselves now question aspects of their discipline and recognise some of its limitations. Linehan (1993) argues that standard cognitive behaviour therapy for patients with conditions as complex as borderline personality disorder is unlikely to be effective. Her integrative therapy, dialectical behaviour therapy, combines acceptance and acknowledgement of defences (a psychoanalytic idea laced with Zen Buddhism) with cognitive and behavioural techniques for change. Similarly, Teasdale (2000) questions the 'zap the negative cognitions' approach in major depressive disorder, believing that 'mindfulness techniques' such as meditation are also needed to help patients divorce themselves from their emotional pain. In the treatment of personality disorder Young (1990) argues for a 'schemabased' approach, taking account of transference, which looks increasingly psychoanalytic in flavour (Bateman, 2000). We are entering a 'postcognitive behaviour therapy' world, which goes beyond brand name therapies to considering the active ingredients of therapy, specific competencies and techniques, and the similarities and differences between different approaches at both theoretical and practical levels (Holmes and Bateman, 2002).

In sum, it is hard to escape the suspicion that cognitive behaviour therapy seems so far ahead of the field at least in part because of its research and marketing strategy rather than because it is intrinsically superior to other therapies.

Cognitive behaviour therapy in primary care

If this is so, it puts further pressure on psychoanalytic therapy, counselling, and systemic therapies to prove their worth. More recent studies comparing cognitive behaviour therapy with counselling in primary care showed no significant differences in outcomes (Hemmings, 2000). Such results show the dangers of tying government policies too closely to specific research findings. An earlier review (Freidli and King, 1996) had suggested that counselling was ineffective. That conclusion is now clearly open to question, but health authorities and commissioners or health maintenance organisations react slowly and are unlikely to follow the latest psychotherapy research literature, despite the updating mechanisms built into the national service frameworks. Cognitive behaviour therapy and monetarism could be seen as the medicine needed to sweep aside complacency and old fashioned practice, especially where resources are limited. But there is a danger of imposing cognitive behaviour therapy in general practice just as its therapists in secondary care are moving beyond it.

Beyond psychotherapy brand names

The drug treatment paradigm has enormous power in medicine. Research in psychological therapies, especially cognitive behaviour therapy, has been shaped by the 'drug metaphor' (Shapiro, 1996). This implies specific treatments for specific conditions and that anything that lies outside the paradigm lies beyond the bounds of science. This approach has been beneficial in that it has forced psychotherapists to submit themselves to randomised controlled trials if they are to claim scientific credibility, and means that consumers and practitioners can be secure in the knowledge that their therapies are of proved worth.

However, the drug metaphor has also had a distorting and potentially damaging effect in psychological medicine. Psychotherapy is essentially concerned with people, not conditions or disorders, and its methods arise out of an intimate relationship between two people that cannot easily be reduced to a set of prescribed techniques. One of the most robust findings in psychotherapy research is that a good therapeutic alliance is the best predictor of outcome in psychotherapy (Hovarth and Symonds, 1991) which suggests that specificity needs to be sought at a much deeper level than therapy brand names. Indeed, it may well be that cognitive behaviour therapy with its clear structure, optimistic outlook, and active involvement of the patient is successful precisely because of its power to create a good alliance.

Another negative aspect of the drug metaphor is the neglect of a developmental perspective in psychiatry. Psychiatry is not just about patients' disorders, but people who are on a developmental trajectory. Experience shapes present reactions in ways that cannot be captured simply by the Diagnostic and Statistical Manual notion of co-morbidity between 'Axis 1 disorders' (illnesses like depression) and 'Axis 11 disorders' (personality) (American Psychiatric Association, 1994). For example, there is good evidence that insecure attachment patterns in childhood act as vulnerability factors for adult psychiatric illness and, in particular, that patients with borderline personality disorder are likely to have had disorganised attachment patterns (Holmes, 2001). We need a psychotherapy that is sophisticated enough to take the development of the mind into account and to capture the often unexpected 'emergent meanings' that arise in therapy – the antithesis of the predetermined narrowly technical approach with which cognitive behaviour therapy is sometimes identified.

Even if the drug analogy is to some extent inescapable, there are still grounds for questioning the current undue emphasis on cognitive behaviour therapy. Just as no one antipsychotic or antidepressant drug can cure all ills, so a wide range of psychological therapies are needed if we are to meet the variety of psychiatric illnesses and human developmental experience. The current apparent triumph of cognitive behaviour therapy harks back to the ideological divide between behaviourism and psychoanalysis in the 1920s. Patients in the 21st century deserve therapies that transcend old rivalries and concentrate on effectiveness, common factors, the search for active ingredients that go beyond brand names, and development of the skills needed to deliver them.

References

Adams D. (1978) *Hitchhiker's Guide to the Galaxy*, London, Methuen.

American Psychiatric Association (1994) *Diagnostic and Statistical Manual of Mental Disorders*, 4th edn, Washington, DC, APA.

Bateman, A. (2000) 'Integration in psychotherapy: an evolving reality in personality disorder', *British Journal of Psychotherapy*, vol. 17, pp. 147–56.

Department of Health (1999) *National Service Framework for Mental Health: Modern Standards and Service Models*, London, DH.

Department of Health (2001). *Treatment Choice in Psychological Therapies and Counselling*. London, HMSO.

Elkin, I. (1994) 'The NIMH treatment of depression collaborative research programme; where we began and where are we?' in: Bergin, A. and Garfield, S. (eds) *Handbook of Psychotherapy and Behaviour Change*, Chichester, John Wiley.

Fonagy, P. (ed.) (1999) *An Open Door Review of Outcome Studies in Psychoanalysis*, London, International Psychoanalytic Association.

Freidli, K. and King, M. (1996) 'Counselling in general practice – a review', *Primary Care Psychiatry*, vol. 2, pp. 205–16.

Hemmings, A. (2000) 'Counselling in primary care: a review of the practice evidence', *British Journal of Guidance Counselling*, vol. 28, pp. 233–52.

Holmes, J. (2001) *The Search for the Secure Base: Attachment Theory and Psychotherapy*, London, Routledge.

Holmes, J. and Bateman, A. (eds) (2002) *Integration in Psychotherapy: Models and Methods*, Oxford, Oxford University Press.

Hovarth, A. and Symonds, D. (1991) 'Relationship between working alliance and outcome in psychotherapy: a meta-analysis', *Journal of Counselling Psychology*, vol. 38, pp. 139–49.

Leff, J., Vearnals, S. and Wolff, G. (2000) 'The London depression intervention trial: randomised controlled trial of antidepressants v. couple therapy in the treatment and maintenance of people with depression living with a partner', *British Journal of Psychiatry*, vol. 177, pp. 95–100.

Linehan, M. (1993) *Cognitive-Behavioural Treatment of Borderline Personality Disorder*, New York, Guilford.

Luborsky, L., Singer, B. and Luborsky, B. (1975) 'Comparative studies of psychotherapies: is it true that 'everyone has won and all must have prizes?' *Archives of General Psychiatry*, vol. 32, pp. 995–1008.

Shapiro, D. (1996) 'Finding out about how psychotherapies help people change', *Psychotherapy Research*, vol. 5, pp. 1–21.

Teasdale, J. (2000) 'Prevention of relapse/recurrence in manic depressive psychosis by mindfulnessbased cognitive therapy', *Journal of Counselling and Clinical Psychology*, vol. 68, pp. 615–21.

Young, J. (1990) *Cognitive Behaviour Therapy for Personality Disorders: A Schema Focussed Approach*, Sarasota, FL, Professional Resource Exchange.

49

Recovery from mental illness as an emergent concept and practice in Australia and the UK

Shulamit Ramon, Bill Healy and Noel Renouf

Early explorations of the concept of recovery

During the past two decades the concept of recovery has become a familiar part of the language of mental health policy, services and research literature (Anthony et al., 2003). There seems to be a consensus within the literature that the main impetus for this development came first from the consumer movement, most particularly within the United States during the late 1980s and early 1990s (Roberts and Wolfson, 2004). The professional literature began to incorporate the concept from the early 1990s in the United States followed by New Zealand, and more recently across nearly all countries within the first world, resulting in a move away from the long prevailing view of mental illness as a chronic unremitting disorder to a more optimistic position which incorporates the notion of recovery (Tooth et al., 2003).

The impact of a number of long term outcome studies of people with major mental illnesses is identified as a further factor in the emergence of recovery in professional language across the field (Anthony, 1993). Harding's (Harding

Edited from S. Ramon, B. Healy and N. Renouf, *International Journal of Social Psychiatry* (2007), vol. 53, pp. 215–22.

et al., 1987) US study is the one most often quoted, in which she reports recovery levels as high as two-thirds of the people followed up over more than 30 years. Yet her work is only one example among a number from across most industrialised countries to highlight evidence that, since the 19th century, there have been significant levels of recovery among many populations. Warner (2004) has identified 85 outcome studies of schizophrenia, beginning in 1919 with work by Kraepelin through to 1994, including populations from virtually every continent and the landmark WHO cross-national studies from the 1970s and 1990s (Jablensky et al., 1992). In analysing these studies Warner has utilised two terms, 'complete recovery', meaning 'loss of psychotic symptoms and return to pre-illness level of functioning', and 'social recovery', meaning a regaining of 'economic and residential independence and low social disruption'. His conclusions are that, in almost all of the studies over a period of 75 years, complete recovery occurs in the range of 20–25 per cent and social recovery in the range of 40–45 per cent of the populations studied. The only exception to these findings occurred during the decade of the Great Depression when recovery rates dropped significantly as unemployment rose dramatically.

A more recent follow-up study (Harrison et al., 2001) reported on the International Study of Schizophrenia (ISoS), coordinated by WHO, which drew on respondents from 14 culturally diverse populations. In part this study sought to overcome some of the challenges to the quality of methodologies utilised in many earlier long term follow-up studies. Its conclusions, whilst somewhat less positive than many earlier studies, nonetheless reinforced the notion of optimism about potential for recovery from major mental illness:

> The overarching message of ISoS is that schizophrenia and related psychoses are best seen developmentally as episodic disorders with a rather favourable outcome for a significant proportion of patients . . . the ISoS findings join others in relieving patients, carers and clinicians of the chronicity paradigm which dominated thinking throughout much of the 20th century. (Harrison et al., 2001: 515)

Thus it is puzzling as to how the 'chronicity paradigm' came to have such a dominant place in mental health systems in the first place. One possible explanation for the persistence of this view is provided by Tooth et al., (2003), drawing upon Anthony's 'radical view about chronicity', which asserts that it was seen as essentially being a feature of the disorder whereas it has come to be seen more recently more as a product of the health services and community stigma. Moreover, professional explanations of the meaning and nature of schizophrenia, such as the idea that it is incurable, can all too readily become self-fulfilling prophesies (Allott et al., 2004).

The alternative view has been apparent in a wide variety of ways apart from these long-term follow-up studies since the very beginnings of the modern mental health system. More positive views prevailed over time, as early as the establishment of Tuke's Retreat in York in 1792 (Roberts and Wolfson,

2004), which have been associated with significantly better outcomes than those achieved at other times in contexts of pessimism about prognosis (Jones, 1968; Scull, 1979; Anthony, 1993; Warner, 2004).

Without using the term recovery, the Italian Psychiatric Reform (Ramon, 1989) and Social Role Valorisation (Wolfensberger, 1983; Ramon, 1991), developed in the 1980s, also left behind the cure from symptoms and focused instead on leading a more fulfilling and socially inclusive life, even with the symptoms/disability remaining. So did the focus on users' own strategies of living with voices, developed and nurtured by Romme and Escher from Maastricht in the Netherlands, and transferred into a successful network of local self-help groups in the UK (Romme and Escher, 1993).

The rediscovered concept

Why now?

As already mentioned earlier, recovery rates similar to those reported today have been evidenced since the 19th century, but the concept in its new meaning outlined below emerged in the 1990s and is coming to prominence only now. We think this is to an extent because several factors have come together at this stage, as Table 49.1 highlights.

The new meaning of recovery

The rediscovery of the concept of recovery in mental health is usually dated to the publication of Anthony's 1993 paper in the US in which he defined recovery by stating that

> a person with mental illness can recover even though the illness is not 'cured'. Recovery is a way of living a satisfying, hopeful, and contributing life even with the limitations caused by illness. Recovery involves the development of new meaning and purpose in one's life as one grows beyond the catastrophic effects of mental illness. (Anthony, 1993: 15)

Writing five years earlier, Deegan (1988) suggested that recovery is a process. The focus on the journey there, rather than on reaching its end, is a metaphor, which many users prefer. Liberman and Kopelowitz (2005) point out that recovery is both a process and an outcome. Used in this way, their term recovery marks the separation of controlling symptoms and cure in the usual medical sense from the business of leading a better life, indicating a potentially fundamental shift in psychiatry, while retaining the use of medication as part of the strategies available to service users. Table 49.2 details the central elements of this journey.

Table 49.1   Factors contributing to putting recovery on our cognitive map

Factors	Explanation
Factor 1 Not due to new medication	It is not due to the impact of new medication, as evidenced in the continuous rate of observed positive outcomes since the 1940s. Likewise it is not due to having information of good outcomes based on longitudinal studies, as a number of such studies existed before the 1990s. Could it be that the world of psychiatry ignored all of these studies because they were not coming from the US, unlike Harding's Vermont project (Ciompi, 1980; Huber et al., 1980; Harding et al. 1987).
Factor 2 De-institutionalisation	It has provided an arena in which most people with mental illness do not live in hospital any more, and thus have more opportunities to lead an ordinary life. This led to the development of community-based rehabilitation focused services.
Factor 3 Users' first person/ expert by experience knowledge	It is more valued today than before by some, though not all, service providers (Tooth et al., 1997; Wallcraft, 2005). They have articulated the recovery concept more than other stakeholders (Anthony, 2000: Roberts and Wolfson, 2004).
Factor 4 The social model of disability	Created by physically disabled people. It argues that we all have strengths and weaknesses, which we have learned to live with. If a disabled person cannot lead an ordinary life this is the outcome of social barriers, rather than of an individual's inability. This is by now accepted by most service users in mental health too, as well as by some professionals (Repper and Perkins, 2003; Roberts and Wolfson, 2004; Beresford, 2005).
Factor 5 The acceptance of the strength model	It follows from the social model of disability, as does the acceptance of the need to promote social inclusion to counteract the impact of the stigma which continues to be attached to people experiencing mental illness. The focus on actively fostering social inclusion in mental health also dates from the end of the 20th century (Saleebey, 1992, Rapp, 1998).

Table 49.2   The innovative elements in the new meaning given to recovery

- It is not about going back to a previous pre-illness state
- Instead it is about forging a new way of living controlled by the newly found **self-agency** of users
- Recovery is from the trauma of psychosis, treatment, stigma, lack of skills and opportunities for valued activities (Wallcraft, 2005)
- **Inter-dependency** and self-help are encouraged; other people can be a source of support and confirmation of self-worth
- **Hope** is a core component (Repper and Perkins, 2003)
- Developing one's own coping strategies sits side by side with strategies for **giving** to others
- It requires a **systematic** effort, which entails **risk taking**, as well as risk avoidance
- The right to fail is an integral part of the new meaning (Deegan, 1996)
- Unlike the original meaning of the term recovery, the new meaning is partly created by users and adopted by them, and has transformative implications (Wallcraft, 2005)
- It entails a move from a **deficit** model of living with mental illness to a strengths perspective (Saleebey, 1992; Rapp, 1998) which Davidson (2003) aptly called **living outside** of illness. Whereas the deficit model is based on an assumed overall, often permanent, vulnerability of the person expressed in difficulties to function and symptoms which contribute to malfunctioning, the strengths approach assumes that people with mental illness have abilities and ambitions which motivate them to put these abilities to use

The new meaning attached to recovery entails also a re-look at what psychosis is about. On the basis of interviews with people who had persistent and recurring psychosis, Bock (1999) suggests that 'psychotic experience is a very specific human balancing act of contradiction and social compromise, an ambivalent condition of the simultaneously incompatible, finally an illness which contains the seed of health in it' (Bock, 1999). This view, shared by Topor et al. (1997), is reminiscent of Laing's views (Laing, 1965) labelled as 'anti-psychiatry' and fought against by the psychiatric establishment in Britain since the 1970s. Topor et al. (1997) propose that psychosis can offer a turning point as it comes at the heels of a breakdown in which the person hits bottom, where the catalyst factors form an unexpected change which forces the individual to make a decision. Others, such as Davidson (2003), focused on the threat to the person's core identity within the psychotic experience, consequently focusing on the trauma which this experience entails for the person robbed of any type of certainty (McGorry, 1992).

A number of authors look at the dimensions of and stages in recovery, without proposing that all dimensions and all stages need to happen for recovery to take place (Ralph, 2000; Davidson, 2003; Tooth et al., 2003). Rogers et al., (1997) identified through a 'Making Decisions Empowerment Scale' the relevance of self-efficacy/self-esteem, power/powerlessness, community activism, righteous anger and optimism/control over the future as the key components. Ridgway (2001) compared four early users' recovery narratives, which confirm the importance of most of the dimensions already outlined above, as illustrated in Table 49.3.

Table 49.3   Users' recovery dimensions (Ridgway, 2001)

- Recovery as the reawakening of hope after despair
- Breaking through denial and achieving understanding and acceptance
- Moving from withdrawal to engagement and active participation in life
- Active coping rather than passive adjustment

Critique of the concept

The definitions of recovery encapsulating its new meaning tend to be wide and multifaceted. This is an advantage in terms of allowing for individualised flexibility. However, it is also a disadvantage at the conceptual and implementation levels, as the concept may thus be rendered meaningless. Furthermore, given that psychiatry combines aspects of both care and control and that each radical departure within it relates to this issue too, recovery can be perceived as a new phase in shifting responsibility even more than before to the individual service user, away from society, service systems, structural factors, or government. Scull (1977) has proposed that decarceration (de-institutionalisation) became a socially acceptable option when governments and professionals were sure that those with mental illness could be regulated in the community. In a world preoccupied more and more with risk management and reducing public funding for any type of welfare, the promise of self-regulation would be attractive, even if it competes with the wish of professionals to maintain their overall control as a reflection of monopolised expertise. Users afraid that services will no longer be at their disposal if they do not achieve recovery, as suggested by Roberts and Wolfson (2004), are perhaps not far from the mark in a system which finds it very difficult to provide individualised support within a programme aimed at a hypothetical group of users. The issue of control does not in our view detract from the potential of the concept to bring about much needed fundamental changes in mental health theory and practice. It reminds us, however, of the need to critically analyse the rediscovered concept, clarify and consolidate its meaning and its implications at all relevant levels.

Contemporary research about recovery

Earlier reference was made to the long history of follow-up studies which reveal much better outcomes, more recently defined as degrees of recovery, than was commonly thought to be the case for people diagnosed with some variant of psychotic disorder (Warner, 2004). These findings rely on a particular view of recovery, one which is grounded in outcome measures derived from clinical notions of illness and health. Thus Roberts and Wolfson (2004), citing the most recent International Study of Schizophrenia (Harrison et al., 2001), comment that these studies 'rely heavily on the absence of symptoms, social disabilities and resource utilisation as outcome indicators' (p. 39). As a result, outcomes thus described bear no necessary relationship to the new meaning of recovery and the core ideas identified in consumer literature, like recovering lost potential, or regaining some degree of control, however great or small, over one's personal and social life.

At the same time, arguably one of the great strengths and driving forces of the movement has been its rich and diverse research underpinnings. From the very beginning, personal stories have been and continue to be a powerful developer of and source of validation of key ideas and practices (Deegan, 1988, Deegan, 2003). Much of this literature has both constructed and validated the importance of approaching people as individuals with their own unique journeys within a recovery set of meanings. Whilst personal narratives have been one of the great strengths of the body of evidence, they can sometimes be minimised in importance, even marginalised, within the wider research community where positivistic approaches assume higher status. Nonetheless the cumulative impact of stories specifically about recovery journeys over the past 20 years has had myriad and often major impacts on service users, their families and carers, many professionals and the guiding mental health policies that have emerged in the past few years (Australian Health Ministers, 2003). More conventionally, Mancini et al. (2005) describe an extensive literature, which utilises qualitative methodologies where researchers have gathered, sorted and analysed numbers of stories from individual subjects as part of constructing a theory of recovery. Examples of this form of research range from straightforward use of structured interviews, through more open models of inquiry to collaborative studies with service users and service users themselves as researchers. A key issue here is how service users can continue to maintain a sense of ownership of ideas of recovery whilst at the same time seeking to move policy and practice towards real fidelity with the core principles of recovery as both an outcome and a process.

As a result there is the continuing issue of how can a research tradition drawing much of its strength from qualitative approaches survive and have influence in an era which increasingly appeals to 'evidence-based practice', where evidence means the product of positivistic research, e.g. the so called 'gold standard' of randomised controlled trials. Anthony et al. (2003) attempt to address this issue and conclude that:

> The notion of evidence-based practices and recovery-oriented services can work well together. However, if evidence-based practice research is to inform the development of recovery based services, then the concept of evidence-based practice must he broadened... Recovery-oriented system designers, programme planners and clinicians must be aware that their current efforts remain guided by the best available evidence, while we accumulate the best evidence possible. (p. 112)

Another emergent way of dealing with this issue is to speak more of 'practice-based evidence' (Ferguson, 2003; Merighi et al., 2005) so that the voice of the consumer is privileged and thus given something like equivalent status with the more conventional modes of presenting evidence.

Policies and practice in Australia

Australian policy parameters have been set since 1989 by a series of National Mental Health Plans. The first published document in the National Plan was the 'Rights and Responsibilities of Consumers' (Australian Health Ministers, 1991). Given the date of publication, it is not surprising that this document makes no explicit mention of recovery as either an outcome or a process. The importance of this document rests with it being the first explicit policy statement about service users and their part in service development and provision beyond being passive recipients of professional decisions about treatment. In that sense it is arguable that it is implicitly an acknowledgement of some degree of optimism about outcomes for service users and thus a prefiguring of later recovery-based policy statements.

The first Australian National Mental Health Plan of 1992 (Australian Health Ministers, 1992) is primarily focused on directing a massive restructuring of mental health services away from their historic segregated and isolated position, into mainstream health services. This policy focus was both a product of and an accelerator of hospital closures, and as a result also identified that a new and comprehensive range of services must now integrate provision across hospital and community. Once again there is no explicit reference to recovery although the document assumes improved outcomes.

The Second Plan of 1998 (Australian Health Ministers, 1998), whilst maintaining the commitment to system reform outlined in the first plan, adds a very significant emphasis on early intervention, health promotion and illness prevention. It is in this context that the first explicit references to recovery occur in a national policy document. Nonetheless it makes only a few references to recovery, mostly in the context of statements about either early intervention or rehabilitation, and even there the concept is more implicit than explicit (Rickwood, 2004).

However, the Third National Mental Health Plan of 2003, whilst reaffirming the directions of the first two plans, represents a quantitative and qualitative leap forward in the recognition of the concept of recovery being at the core of service provision. It claims a commitment to recovery is one of the guiding principles of national policy:

> Recovery is both a process and an outcome and is essential for promoting hope, well-being, and a valued sense of self-determination for people with mental illness. A recovery orientation emphasises the development of new meaning and purpose for consumers and the ability to pursue personal goals. Mental health service providers should operate within a framework that supports recovery. (Australian Health Ministers, 2003, p. 5)

The notion of recovery has been evident in the work of Australian service user groups (the preferred Australian language being consumer groups) and organisations such as the Victorian Mental Illness Awareness Council, and the non-governmental (NGO) sector has been promoting and applying the use of recovery in its literature and many programmes' guidelines since the early 1990s (The Mental Health Services Conference of Australia and New Zealand, 1994; VICSERV, 1998). The core business of this sector has been the provision of psychosocial rehabilitation rather than clinical services (McKenzie. 1994). The peak body for the NGO sector in Victoria initially developed a model of psychosocial rehabilitation based on the 15 principles identified by Cnaan et al. (1988). In 1993, at a sector forum:

> It was felt that the two necessary conditions for effective psychosocial rehabilitation were first the generation of hope and second the facilitation of social relationships. It was stressed that these were most effectively achieved in settings consistent with the characteristics of community-managed disability support services quite separate and distinct from any clinical service. (VICSERV, 2005)

This statement entails a discernible and implicit engagement with the idea of recovery in the context of differentiating out from public mental health clinical services. In part this reflects the very different nature of the two sectors in terms of programme purpose, staffing and time. It also reflects what is arguably the base from which a more active role for service users has been built over the intervening years so that now service users have key roles in most NGO organisations from membership of Boards to frontline service delivery and evaluation.

The most notable example of an interest in recovery in the public mental health system has been the work of McGorry beginning with his seminal paper in the Australian context, 'The Concept of Recovery and Secondary

Prevention in Psychotic Disorders' (McGorry, 1992) through the now nearly 20 years of work on early intervention in psychotic disorders (McGorry and Yung, 2003), with its emphasis on the place of optimism, hope and recovery principles in programme design. This work continues to be influential; the recently published national guidelines for the treatment of schizophrenia and related disorders (McGorry, 2005) emphasise not only early and active use of medications but also give equal space to psychosocial interventions and how attention to the individual's social and cultural environment necessarily underpins recovery and the regaining of a better quality of life. The earliest work was conceptualised most particularly in terms of how early intervention, especially with assertive use of medications, could prevent, or at least minimise, the development of secondary morbidities (Anderson, 2001). In that sense such interventions aid recovery from the illness in a way broadly consistent with mainstream medical ideas and practices. Although this model of recovery has broadened out to emphasise a more central role for psychosocial interventions, it nonetheless remains more a set of exemplary practices framed and delivered by professionals, albeit within a high quality and innovative clinical setting, rather than one led by users' definitions of their recovery goals and related journeys.

Whilst the question remains, however, about how wide and how deep this commitment to recovery is evident in the mainstream public mental health services, there are nonetheless many examples of innovative practices that incorporate key ideas espoused in the literature and policy documents. For instance, an issue in 2003 of *Australasian Psychiatry*, a publication of the Royal Australian and New Zealand College of Psychiatry, contained a special section of four papers on service users, services and recovery. One of those papers (Tooth et al., 2003) reports on a qualitative research project designed to gather consumer views on factors important to recovery from schizophrenia. Among the conclusions reported in the paper was the fundamental need to understand the unique individual stories of people in recovery from schizophrenia. Yet they report that a very common experience was that:

> To date, health professionals have not been particularly good at hearing how this illness has impacted on the person's life; nor have they been particularly good at trying to understand what impact the clients had on the course of their illness and then trying to facilitate changes. (Tooth et al., 2003: S76)

There is also anecdotal evidence of varying degrees of uptake of the idea of recovery in practice. For instance, some community mental health services are incorporating the language of recovery in their descriptions of programmes and in some instances in their formal treatment plans. The most inclusive and probably the largest annual conference in the mental health field in Australia, 'The Mental Health Services Conference' (The MHS), defines itself in the following terms:

The MHS provides a forum for: the exchange of ideas; professional development; networking and debate, for mental health professionals, consumers, carers
(families), and managers. The MHS aims to promote positive attitudes about
mental health and mental illness, and to stimulate debate that will challenge
the boundaries of present knowledge and ideas about mental health care. (The
MHS, 2004)

Indeed, their annual conferences typically involve service users in various
paper and workshop presentations, give a central place to recovery issues and
present a number of annual achievement awards including one for the best
national recovery-based programme.

Some recent examples in Australian social work indicate a significant depth
of commitment to recovery and associated ideas. Ryan et al. (2004) have
reported on a series of studies on the idea of expertise in mental health social
work and have identified three core qualities, namely 'belief, optimism and
caring', which are identifiable in the work of their expert practitioners. Gardner et al. (2005) report on their collaborative work with a prominent NGO
mental health agency to develop strength-focused tools 'measuring change for
people using mental health recovery programs'.

Policies and practice in the UK

Recovery appears for the first time in a UK policy document in its new meaning
in 2001 (Department of Health, 2001). The document repeats US principles,
endorses recovery as a good idea, but does not propose a specified way of implementation. A guiding statement on recovery, which includes a document on
emerging best practices, appeared in 2005 (NIMHE, 2005). The document is
based on the work of the Ohio Mental Health Department, amended by British
contributors. This process-focused detailed set of guidelines includes issues
such as the person's status, the clinicians' role and community supporting
role in the contexts of clinical care, peer support and relationships, family support, work/meaningful activity, power and control, stigma, community involvement, access to resources and education at the different phases of recovery.

In 2002 the National Institute for Clinical Excellence, which is responsible
for validation of new health interventions, published a set of guidelines concerning outcomes of recovery from schizophrenia (NICE, 2002). These now act as
the list of criteria for each Mental Health Trust. Roberts and Wolfson (2004,
Box 1) compare the NICE guidelines with the Ohio outcomes measurements
(Ohio Department of Mental Health, 2003), renowned because of their origins
within the users' movement. The British guidelines are clearly written from
the perspective of clinicians and fail to take into account not only issues of self-
definition of what recovery means to individuals, but also key issues such as
hope-inducing interventions and giving users control over their own lives.

Unlike in the US, there has been a considerable emphasis on social inclusion in UK government welfare policies since 1997. A Social Inclusion Unit has existed in the Prime Minister's Office since 1997 when New Labour came to power. New Labour sees itself as the party which fosters social inclusion as a key component in its social policy. The focus on social inclusion within mental health policies begins in 1999, in the National Service Framework (NSF) for Mental Health, which was the first such framework to be published. Social inclusion appears in the NSF in connection with Standard 1, focused on mental health promotion, stating that such promotion cannot take place without tackling social exclusion and discrimination. Again, no guidelines for implementation were included. Presently there is a social inclusion programme within the NIMHE (Morris and Bates, 2003). Its direction complements the new meaning of recovery in enabling users to achieve more and use their potential better, be more in control over their own lives, become more socially competent and less isolated. It shares the strengths approach and the social model of disability without saying so, and attempts to reduce stigma. Repper and Perkins (2003) suggest that social inclusion is an integral part of recovery, as in their view recovery cannot be sustained without it.

Involving users on local and national planning groups (for example, the NSF), a preliminary condition for any user-led policy, has been a UK trend for the last five years. Such involvement is not without its problems in terms of tokenistic participation by users, ensuring pay for participation to people who live on benefits, and the extent to which mental health statutory organisations take account of what users are saying when in conflict with professional perspectives. Relatively little is invested in developing this type of participation, and consequently it is usually the same users who participate on most committees. Only a few instances in which users' views have led to tangible policy changes can be cited. Table 49.4 illustrates these changes.

While a clear policy and implementation process for Britain is not yet there, the necessity of an attitudinal change among UK professionals, if they are to move away from the emphasis on the deficit model and the stigmatising

Table 49.4 NIMHE recovery-related developments

Regional fellows for *experts by experience*, as a means of valuing users' experience and ensuring that it is heard.

Fellows in recovery – the national lead is working in a part-time capacity. He has initiated several training programmes for both users and service providers focused on the US-led WRAP (Wellness Recovery Action Plan) approach to recovery (Copeland, 1997) in a number of regions since 2001.

Several regions have appointed regional recovery fellows, whose role is to stimulate recovery-related activities, including the collation of recovery stories.

emphasis which comes with it, is recognised by a number of writers and activists (for example, Allott, 2004; Allott et al., 2004). A number of UK self-help approaches, such as the one outlined by Coleman and Smith (1999) on overcoming hearing negative voices through using a self-help manual, are mentioned in addition to the focus on WRAP.

Repper and Perkins (2003) propose a model which includes hope-inducing interventions, a much needed focus, but one which has not yet been picked up by UK official publications on recovery. UK mental health policy makers have adopted formally the recovery approach in addition to the related focus on social inclusion. While the latter is now at the beginning of the implementation process, the first is yet to get there, as highlighted in Table 49.5.

Table 49.5   Obstacles to the implementation of the UK recovery policy

1. A service system built on programmes aimed at user populations, rather than at the provision of individualised packages. For example, although it is possible to give users control over buying agreed services and hiring staff, it is proving very difficult to move funding from existing programmes to individualised budgets, even if the service provided by a programme is perceived as not good enough and is under-utilised.
2. All service providers and purchasers would need to change their attitudes and move away from not only the deficit model, but also from the pessimism inherent in the system, as well as be more ready to undertake calculated risks.

Conclusions

Despite widely available evidence of good rates of recovery for people with mental illness, mental health systems are only now starting to emerge from a 'chronicity paradigm'; in both Australia and the United Kingdom the language of recovery is becoming commonplace. The patterns are somewhat different, however. In Australia, service user (consumer) groups have been the main drivers, and it is the non-governmental organisation sector, with its background in psychosocial rehabilitation models, that appears best able to implement recovery models. The use of recovery language in Australian policy and clinical mental health services is not yet generally being translated into radically reformed services. In the UK, the policy change – again drawing on service user perspectives – has perhaps been stronger and clearer, but the task of implementation largely lies ahead.

In any case, what seems critical is that the new meaning of the term recovery should not be lost as it is taken up more widely. Recovery is not about going back to a pre-illness state, and means something very different from the 'old' emphasis on controlling symptoms or cure. Rather, it is a complex and multifaceted concept, both a process and an outcome, the features of which include strength, self-agency and hope, interdependency and giving, and systematic effort, which entails risk-taking. The concept has been rediscovered, and as an emergent concept and practice in the UK and Australia it remains to be seen to what extent policies and practices will follow suit.

References

Allott, P. (2004) 'What is mental health, illness and recovery?' in *Good Practice in Adult Mental Health* (eds T. Ryan and J. Pritchard). London and Philadelphia: Jessica Kingsley, pp. 13–31.

Allott, P., Loganthan, L. and Fulford, K.W.M. (2004) 'Discovering hope for recovery from a British perspective: a review of a selection of recovery literature; implications for practice and systems change'. In *International Innovations in Community Mental Health* (special issue: eds S. Luire, M. McCubbin and B. Dallaire) *Canadian Journal of Community Mental Health*, 21, 13–33.

Anderson, J., Dunbar, L. and McGorry, P.D. (2001) 'Feasibility and effectiveness of early intervention in psychotic disorders: the EPPIC model'. In *Mental Health in Australia: Collaborative Community Practice* (eds G. Meadows and B. Singh). Melbourne: Oxford University Press.

Anthony, W.A. (1993) 'Recovery from mental illness: the guiding vision of the mental health service system in the 1990s'. *Psychosocial Rehabilitation Journal*, 16, 11–23.

Anthony W.A (2000) 'A recovery-oriented service system: setting some system level standards'. *Psychiatric Rehabilitation Journal*, **24**, 159–69.

Anthony, W.A., Rogers, E.S. and Farkas, M. (2003) 'Research on evidence-based practices: future directions in an era of recovery'. *Community Mental Health Journal*, 39, 101–14.

Australian Health Ministers (1991) *Mental Health Statement of Rights and Responsibilities: Report of the Mental Health Consumer Outcomes Task Force*. Canberra: Australian Government Publishing Service.

Australian Health Ministers (1992) *National Mental Health Plan*. Canberra: Australian Government Publishing Service.

Australian Health Ministers (1998) *Second National Mental Health Plan*. Canberra: Mental Health Branch, Commonwealth Department of Health and Family Services.

Australian Health Ministers (2003) *National Mental Health Plan 2003–2008*. Canberra: Australian Government Publishing Service.

Beresford, P. (2005) 'Developing self-defined social approaches to madness'. In *Mental Health at the Crossroads. The Promise of the Psychosocial Approach* (eds S. Ramon and J.E. Williams). Aldershot: Ashgate Publishing.

Bock, T. (1999) *Lichtjahre, Psychosesn ohne Psychiatrie*. Bonn: Psychiatrie-Verlag.

Ciompi, L. (1980) 'Catamnestic long-term study on the course of life and aging of schizophrenics'. *Schizophrenia Bulletin*, 6, 606–18.

Cnaan, R.A., Hlankertz, L., Messinger, K.W. and Gardner, J.R. (1988) 'Psycho-social reliabititation: toward a definition'. *Psychosocial Rehabilitation Journal*, 11, 59–77.

Coleman, R. and Smith, T. (1999) *From Victim to Victor: Working with Voices*. Gloucester: Handsell.

Copeland, M E. (1997) Wellness Recovery Action Plan (WRAP). West Dummerston, VT: Peach Press.

Davidson, L. (2003) *Living Outside Mental Illness: Qualitative Studies of Recovery in Schizophrenia*. New York: New York University Press.

Deegan, G. (2003) 'Discovering recovery'. *Psychiatric Rehabilitation Journal*, 26, 368–76.

Deegan, P.E. (1988) 'Recovery: the lived acceptance of rehabilitation'. *Psychosocial Rehabilitation Journal*, 11, 11–19.

Deegan, P.E. (1996) 'Recovery as a journey of the heart'. *Psychosocial Rehabilitation Journal*, 19, 91–7.

Department of Health (UK) (2001) *The Journey to Recovery: The Government's Vision for Mental Health Care*. London: Department of Health Publications.

Ferguson, H. (2003) 'Outline of a critical best practice perspective on social work and social care'. *British Journal of Social Work*, 33, 1005–24.

Gardner, F., Lehmann, J., Brown, G. and Brooks, M. (2005) 'Noticing change: developing strength-focused tools in a mental health service'. *Australian Social Work*, 58, 1–25.

Harding, C.M., Brooks, G.W., Ashikaga, T., Strauss, T.S. and Breier, A. (1987) 'The Vermont longitudinal study of persons with severe mental illness: II. Long term outcome of subjects who retrospectively met DSM-III criteria for schizophrenia'. *American Journal of Psychiatry*, 144, 727–35.

Harrison, G., Hopper. K., Craig, T., Laska, E., Siegel, J., Wanderling, J., Dube, K.C., Ganev, K., Giel, R., Ander Heiden, W., Holmberg, S.K., Janca, A., Lee, P.W.H., Leon, C.A., Malhotra, S., Marsella, A.J., Nakane. Y., Sartorius, N., Shen, Y., Skoda, C., Thara, R., Tsirkin. S.J., Varma, V.K., Walsh, D.C. and Wiersma, D. (2001) 'Recovery from psychotic illness: a 15- and 25-year international follow-up study'. *British Journal of Psychiatry*, 178, 506–17.

Huber, G.M., Gross, G., Schuttler, R. and Linz, M. (1980) 'Longitudinal studies of schizophrenic patients'. *Schizophrenia Bulletin*, 6, 592–605.

Jablensky, A., Sartorius, N. and Ernberg, G. (1992) 'Schizophrenia: manifestation, incidence and course in different cultures. A World Health Organisation ten-country study'. *Psychological Medicine Monograph*, Supp. 20, 1–97.

Jones, M. (1968) 'Therapeutic community principles within the hospital, and in the outside community.' *Psychotherapy and Psychosomatics*, 16, 84–90.

Laing, R.D. (1965) *The Divided Self*. Harmondsworth: Penguin.

Liberman, D.P. and Kopelowitz, A. (2005) Recovery from schizophrenia: a concept in search of research'. *Psychiatric Services*, 56, 735–42.

McGorry, P.D. (1992) 'The concept of recovery and secondary prevention in psychotic disorders'. *Australian and New Zealand Journal of Psychiatry*, 26, 3–17.

McGorry, P.D. (2005) 'Royal Australian and New Zealand College of Psychiatrists' clinical practice guidelines for the treatment of schizophrenia and related disorders'. *Australian and New Zealand Journal of Psychiatry*, 39, 1–30.

McGorry, P. D. and Yung, A.R. (2003) 'Early intervention in psychosis: an overdue reform'. *Australian and New Zealand Journal of Psychiatry*, 37, 393–8.

McKenzie. L. (1994) 'Psychiatric disability and mental illness – is there a difference?' *New Paradigm*, June, 3–11.

Mancini, M.A., Hardiman, E.R. and Lawson, H.A. (2005) 'Making sense of it all: consumer providers' theories about factors about taking and impeding recovery from psychiatric disabilities'. *Psychiatric Rehabilitation Journal*, 29, 48–55.

Merighi, J., Ryan, M., Renouf, N. and Healy, B. (2005) 'Reassessing a theory of professional expertise: a cross-national investigation of expert mental health social workers. *British Journal of Social Work*, 35, 709–25.

Morris, D. and Bates, P. (2003) *Making Inclusion Work: Social Inclusion Resource Pack on Service Mapping and Outcome Measurement*. Leeds: NIMHE.

National Institute for Clinical Excellence (NICE) (2002) *Schizophrenia: Core Intervention in the Treatment and Management of Schizophrenia in Primary and Secondary Care*. London: NICE.

National Institute for Mental Health in England (NIMHE) (2005) *NIMHE Guiding Statement on Recovery*. London: NIMHE.

Ohio Department of Mental Health (2003) *Ohio Mental Health Recovery and Consumer Outcomes Initiatives*. www.mh.state.oh.us/initiatives/outcomes/outcomes. html.

President's New Freedom Commission on Mental Health (2003) *Achieving the Promise: Transforming Mental Health Care in America*. Final Report. DHSS Pub. No. SM. 03–3832. Rockville, MD: Department of Health and Human Services.

Ralph, R. (2000) *Can We Measure Recovery? A Compendium of Recovery and Recovery-Related Instruments*. Available: http://www.hsri.org.

Ramon, S. (1989) 'The impact of the Italian psychiatric reform on North American and British professionals'. *International Journal of Social Psychiatry*, 35, 120–7.

Ramon, S. (ed.) (1991) *Beyond Community Care: Normalisation and Integration Work*. Basingstoke: Macmillan.

Rapp, C. (1998) *The Strengths Model: Case Management with People Suffering from Severe and Persistent Mental Illnesses*. New York: Oxford University Press.

Repper, J. and Perkins, R. (2003) *Social Inclusion and Recovery. A Model for Mental Health Practice*. Edinburgh: Ballière-Tindall.

Rickwood, D. (2004) 'Recovery in Australia: slowly but surely' (guest editorial). *Australian e-Journal for the Advancement of Mental Health*, 3. www.auseinet.com/journal/vol3issl/rickwoodeditorial.pdf.

Ridgway, M. (2001) 'Re-storying psychiatric disability: learning from first person narrative accounts of recovery'. *Psychiatric Rehabilitation Journal*, 24, 335–43.

Roberts, G. and Wolfson, P. (2004) 'The rediscovery of recovery, open to all'. *Advances in Psychiatric Treatment*, 10, 37–49.

Rogers. E.S., Chamberlin, J., Ellison, M.L. and Crean, T. (1997) 'A consumer constructed scale to measure empowerment among users of mental health services'. *Psychiatric Services*, 48, 1042–7.

Romme, M. and Escher, S. (1993) *Accepting Voices*. London: Mind.

Ryan, M., Merghi, J.R., Healy, B and Renouf, N. (2004) 'Belief, optimism and caring: findings from a cross-national study of expertise in mental health social work'. *Qualitative Social Work*, 3, 411–29.

Saleebey, D. (ed.) (1992) *The Strengths Perspective in Social Work Practice*. New York: Longman.

Scull, A. (1977) *Decarceration: A Radical View*. Englewood Cliffs, NJ: Prentice-Hall.

Scull, A. (1979) *Museums of Madness: The Social Organization of Insanity in 19th Century England*. London: Allen Lane.

The Mental Health Services Conference of Australia and New Zealand (The MHS) (1994) *Surviving Mental Illness: Families, Consumers and the Mental Health System*. Balmain: The Mental Health Services Conference.

The Mental Health Services Conference of Australia and New Zealand (The MHS) (2004) 'Welcome to the MHS', http://www.themhs.org/ (accessed 27 October 2005).

Tooth, B., Kalyanasundaram, V. and Glover, H. (1997) *Recovery from Schizophrenia: A Consumer Perspective*. Brisbane: University of Queensland Centre for Mental Health Nursing Research.

Tooth, B., Kalyanasundaram, V., Glover, H. and Momenzadah, S. (2003) 'Factors consumers identify as important to recovery from schizophrenia. *Australian Psychiatry*, 11, S70–S77.

Topor, A., Svenson, J., Bjerke, C., Borg, M. and Kufas, E. (1997) *Turning Point: On the Road to Recovery from Serious Psychiatric Illness*. Stockholm: FoU-enhetern/psyykiatri, VSSO.

VICSERV (Psychiatric Disability Services of Victoria) (1998) *Reconnections: Strengthening the culture of recovery, VICSERV Conference Papers*. North Fitzroy: VICSERV.

VICSERV (Psychiatric Disability Services of Victoria) (2005) 'What is psychosocial rehabilitation?' http://www.vicserv.org.au/library/papers/whatispsr.htm (updated 6 May 2005).

Wallcraft, J. (2005) 'The place of recovery'. In *Mental Health at the Crossroads: The Promise of the Psychosocial Approach* (eds S. Ramon and J.E. Williams). Aldershot: Ashgate Publishing.

Warner, R. (2004) *Recovery from Schizophrenia: Psychiatry and Political Economy (3rd edn)*. New York: Brunner-Routledge.

Wolfensberger, W. (1983) Social role valorisation: a proposed new term for the principle of normalisation'. *Mental Retardation*, 21, 234–9.

50

What is person-centred care in dementia?

Dawn Brooker

Introduction

The term person-centred care has become all pervasive on the UK dementia care scene. It has been suggested that it has become synonymous with good quality care (Morton, 1999). It seems that any new approach in dementia care has to claim to be pc (person-centred) in order to be P.C. (politically correct). The term is used frequently in the aims and objectives for dementia care services and provision in the UK and the US although what lies behind the rhetoric in terms of practice may be questionable (Packer, 2000a).

Prior to the writing of the late Professor Tom Kitwood, the term 'person centred care' was not used in the dementia care field. The first Kitwood reference (1988) to person-centred approaches was to distinguish them from approaches that emphasised the medical and behavioural management of dementia. Kitwood (1997b) later used the term to bring together ideas and ways of working that emphasised communication and relationships. The term was intended to be a direct reference to Rogerian psychotherapy with its emphasis on authentic contact and communication (Rogers, 1961).

Defining person-centred care

As with many terms that are frequently used, however, there is a tendency for person-centred care to mean different things to different people in different

Edited and adapted from D. Brooker (2007) *Person-Centred Dementia Care: Making Services Better*, Jessica Kingsley.

contexts. In my discussions with practitioners, researchers, people with dementia and their families, it is obvious that the concepts in person-centred care are not easy to understand or articulate in a straightforward manner. To some it means individualised care, to others it is a value base. There are people who see it as a set of techniques to work with people with dementia and to others it is a phenomenological perspective and a means of communication.

Person-centred care as it relates to people with dementia has become a composite term and any definition needs to take this into consideration. The elements of the composite can become so convoluted, however, that the definition loses focus and shape.

Person-centred care encompasses four major elements all of which have been defined as person-centred care in and of themselves by some writers. These elements are

1   Valuing people with dementia and those who care for them. (V)
2   Treating people as individuals. (I)
3   Looking at the world from the perspective of the person with dementia. (P)
4   A positive social environment in which the person living with dementia can experience relative well being. (S)

Continuing the style that Kitwood (1997c) had for representing complex ideas in the form of equations, this is expressed as:

$$\text{PCC (person-centred care)} = V + I + P + S$$

This equation does not suppose a pre-eminence of any element over another, nor are they directional. They are all contributory.

I   Valuing people with dementia and those who care for them (V)

Rogers certainly had a value base of a non-judgemental acceptance of the unique aspects of each individual person. This found its therapeutic expression in unconditional positive regard. An additional complexity for person-centred care within the context of dementia is the definition of the term 'person' (Hughes, 2001). The philosophers Locke and Parfit, whose definition of being a person depends on consciousness of thought and continuity of memory, would mean that an individual with dementia would not be seen as the same person as their dementia progressed, or indeed as a person at all in the most disabling stages of dementia. Using this definition, as dementia destroys the brain it also destroys the person. Hughes (2001) provides an argument for taking a view of the person that is a 'situated-embodied-agent' rather than one that defines a person by consciousness of thought. Defining the concept of person in this way means that we should aspire to treat people with dementia at all stages of their disability, in the way in which all people would wish to be treated. Similarly, Kitwood (1997) described the person with dementia as:

> a person in the fullest sense: he or she is still an agent, one who can make things happen in the world, a sentient, relational and historical being. (Kitwood, 1997a, p. 541)

and

> to be a person is to have a certain status, to be worthy of respect. (Kitwood and Bredin, 1992a, p. 275)

Post (1995) also argues for solidarity among all human beings regardless of their mental capacity. Person-centred care is also about seeing all people as valued. This may be better articulated as a value base that positively discriminates on behalf of all persons who are vulnerable. This has certainly been extended to the staff who work with people with dementia (Kitwood, 1995; Woods, 2001).

On first contact, the moral and ethical basis for person-centred care is rather like 'mom and apple-pie'. How could anyone disagree that treating people as whole human beings is the right and civilised way to respond to people with dementia? However, a cursory look around service provision or a discussion with people with dementia and their families suggests that people with dementia are not valued by society (see for example Ballard et al., 2001; Innes and Surr, 2001; Marshall, 2001; Macdonald and Dening, 2002). Society places a high value on youth and intellectual capacity. Those who are elderly and particularly those with dementia are at risk of prejudice which has been called hyper-cognitivism (Post, 1995). This is a special type of ageism, the victims of whom have cognitive impairment. My personal opinion is that this should be termed 'Dementia-ism' to help clarify who are the main victims. It is related to other powerful prejudices such as sexism, racism, ageism but it also exists independently of all of these. Within services for people who are elderly, those who have dementia often appear to have to suffer a double jeopardy of age and cognitive disability. This discrimination is evident in service provision, resource allocation, research funding, media coverage, policy priorities, professional training and status.

Dementia-ism underpins many of the shortfalls within service provision. Its eradication has to form part of the definition of person-centred care, if people with dementia are to be admitted as full members of the people club. If this part of the definition is not made explicit in value statements, training, staff selection, standards, policies and procedures, national frameworks etc. then services will not maintain a person-centred approach for long.

2   Treating people as individuals (I)

The most concrete implication of person-centred care, that sometimes becomes its whole definition, is about taking an individualised approach to assessing and meeting the unique needs of people with dementia. This element of the definition encompasses all those ways of working that consider men and women with all their individual strength and vulnerabilities, and sees their dementia as part of that picture rather than defining their identity. This approach again has resonance with the work of Carl Rogers for whom each client was a unique and whole person.

Clare at al. (2003) also give emphasis to the whole individual:

> Dementia is more than simply a matter of brain decay. People contribute a unique personality and a set of life experiences, coping resources and social networks. (Clare et al., 2003, p. 251)

Likewise, Stokes (2000) sees the uniqueness of individuals as a major part of his definition of person-centred care. He expands this model in a very practical way to work with people with dementia who are in distress. Archibald (2003) defines person-centred care as:

> People with dementia are individual and, as such, each has a different pathway through the illness and so different care needs. (Archibald, 2003, p. 3)

Marshall (2001) takes a slightly different emphasis:

> [person-centred care] means, in brief, that care is tailored to meet the needs of the individual rather than the group or the needs of the staff. (Marshall, 2001, p. 175)

Still inherent in this view is that the people with dementia are the focus rather than the categories into which professionals and staff might place them.

The National Service Framework (Department of Health, 2001) has chosen this aspect of person-centred care on which to focus. The aim within this standard is about treating people as individuals and providing them with packages of care that meet their individual needs. By inserting a problem focus into the definition, however, in some ways can make it difficult to continue to see the whole person. It then becomes similar to the term 'patient-centred care' or 'resident-focused care' which is also sometimes used interchangeably with person-centred care (Hibbard et al., 2003). Although this is clearly linked to the individualised element of person-centred care, it can be constraining in that the person with dementia can only express those individual needs that are covered by being a patient. There is an element of person-centred care here but the term suggests that the person is defined by their status as patient rather than their individuality. It does, however, signify a desire to focus on the patient (or resident). This is usually done with the intent of protecting the vulnerable from being disempowered by a large bureaucratic organisation and as such would be in accordance with the first element within the definition of person-centred care presented above.

3 Looking at the world from the perspective of the person with dementia (P)

Person-centred care is part of the phenomenological school of psychology. In this, the subjective experience of the individual is seen as reality and hence the starting point in explaining their behaviour and therapeutic approaches to change this. Rogerian person-centred therapeutic approaches would see entering the frame of reference of the individual and understanding the world from their point of view as key to working therapeutically.

Likewise, Feil's Validation Therapy takes entering the subjective world of the person with dementia as its starting point (Feil, 1993). Kitwood (1997a) certainly recognised the centrality of understanding the individual needs of people with dementia to give a focus for interventions. Stokes (2000) also highlights understanding the subjective experience as key to a definition of person-centred care. Clare et al. (2003) define person-centred approaches to dementia care as focusing on 'understanding the experience of dementia in terms of the person's psychological responses and social context, and aim to tailor help and support to match individual needs.' Thus they take the starting point for meeting individual needs as understanding the experience of the person with dementia.

Putting oneself in the shoes of someone with dementia is not an easy or trivial process. Kitwood (1997b) described 'seven access routes' by which dementia care practitioners could deepen their empathy toward people with dementia. Dementia Care Mapping was in part an attempt to help care practitioners put themselves in the place of people with dementia when evaluating the quality of care. Kitwood described DCM as

> a serious attempt to take the standpoint of the person with dementia, using a combination of empathy and observational skill. (Kitwood, 1988, p. 4)

It has only really been in the past ten years or so that researchers have written seriously about the perspective of individuals with dementia (Downs, 1997; Harris, 2002). In dementia research, phenomenological research into the early experience of Alzheimer's disease is now well established (Keady, 1996; Clare, 2002). In quality of life research, self report measures on subjective well-being (Brod et al., 1999) and satisfaction with care (Mozley et al., 1999) have been developed relatively recently. Similarly, in dementia care practice, engaging directly with people with dementia in a therapeutic sense is a relatively new phenomenon (Bender and Cheston, 1997). The work of Killick and Allen (2001) has been extremely influential in the UK in helping practitioners attend to the person with dementia in imaginative, creative and reflective ways. Without these insights that put the person with dementia at the centre of care, how can we define any approach as person-centred?

4   A positive social environment (S)

This part of the definition is about the care that promotes relationships between the people. Rogers (1961) saw relationships as key to therapeutic growth and change. He highlighted the importance of the relationship and therapeutic alliance in person-centred counselling. As verbal abilities are lost, the importance of warm, accepting human contact through non-verbal channels becomes even more important than before. More recent research (Bowers et al., 2001) based on a series of in-depth interviews with people in long-term care found that 16 out of the 26 residents interviewed highlighted relationships, particularly friendships and reciprocity in care givers, as being important.

Kitwood's view of person-centred care for people with dementia was that it took place in the context of relationships – *Person to Person* was the title of Kitwood and Bredin's publication (1992b), which was the first practical book describing the constitution of person-centred care. Personhood is central to Kitwood's writing on person-centred care. He defined it as 'A standing or status that is bestowed on one human being by others in the context of relationship and social being. It implies recognition, respect and trust' (Kitwood, 1997c, p. 8). Bond (2001) also includes the context of relationships within his description of personhood:

> individuals do not function in isolation, they also have relationships with others; all human life is interconnected and interdependent. (Bond, 2001, p. 47)

Again, ensuring that people with dementia have the opportunity for social and loving relationships with those around them seems so obvious that surely we do not need a definition of care to tell us this? However, again, even a cursory examination of care provision shows that this is not the norm. Kitwood's writing on the Malignant Social Psychology and the importance of interpersonal process in dementia clarify why this seems so difficult to achieve in practice (Kitwood, 1990 and 1993).

With the onset of dementia individuals are very vulnerable to their psychological defences being radically attacked and broken down. As the sense of self breaks down, it becomes increasingly important that the sense of self is held within the relationships that the person with dementia experiences.

These relationships cannot be developed through the traditional therapy hour as in person-centred psychotherapy. Rather the development of relationship occurs through the day-to-day interactions. The psychological needs are identified as comfort, attachment, occupation, identity and inclusion (Kitwood, 1997a). Although these needs can be seen as universal, the disabilities associated with dementia, mean that they have to become the main foci of person-centred care in this context if personhood is to be maintained. Kitwood described what a positive social psychology might look like for people with dementia rather than the negative malignant social psychology which prevailed in his earlier writing. He used the term Positive Person Work to describe ten different forms of interaction that would maintain personhood (Kitwood, 1997a, pp. 90–93).

The practice of caring for very vulnerable people with dementia in large groups with low staffing levels, however, can place care workers in an intolerable bind when trying to provide a positive social psychological milieu. How to balance the needs of one individual who requires lots of attention against the needs of the wider group, who may be equally needy but make less show of it, is one that faces dementia care practitioners day in day out. Case studies (Packer, 2000b; Trilsbach, 2002) pay testament to the imaginative and committed work of many care practitioners in this field.

A number of ways of working with people with dementia can be captured under the umbrella term of person-centred care. The British dementia care scene has been described as having gone through a renaissance in the past ten years (Brooker, 2001). Life story work, reminiscence, creativity, play, doll therapy, pet therapy, sensory therapies, psychotherapy have all been written about with people with dementia. Central to these ways of working is the facilitation of social confidence and communication at an emotional level (Woods, 2001).

Rather than seeing people with dementia as the ones having problems and those who are caring having none, Kitwood (1995) suggested that many of the problems experienced in dementia care are interpersonal. They occur in the communication. He suggests we need to view the relationships between 'carers' and 'cared for' as a psychotherapeutic relationship and, in this respect just as in psychotherapeutic work, the helpers need to be aware of their own issues around caring for others.

In person-centred care, the relationships between all people in the care environment should be nurtured.

Conclusions

Fundamental improvements in person-centred care for people living with dementia will not occur until the policy agenda is aligned with the agenda for people with dementia. In clinical gerontology, in the fields of practice and research, we need to be able to articulate what it is we mean by person-centred care if we are to influence that agenda. Person-centred care for people with dementia does not equate with person-centred counselling any more than it equates just to individualised care. It has become a short-hand term for encompassing a whole movement in dementia care which is more far-reaching than either of these things. It is easy to be woolly with such an over-used term. Of course, the acronym VIPS also stands for Very Important Persons which is an easier ways of defining the outcome of person-centred care for people with dementia.

References

Archibald, C. (2003) *People with Dementia in Acute Hospitals, Stirling*, Dementia Services Development Centre.

Ballard, C., Fossey, J., Chithramohan, R., Howard, R., Burns, A., Thompson, P., Tadros, G. and Fairbairn, A. (2001) 'Quality of care in private sector and NHS facilities for people with dementia: cross sectional survey', *British Medical Journal*, vol. 323, pp. 426–7.

Bender, M. and Cheston, R. (1997) 'Inhabitants of a lost kingdom: A model for the subjective experiences of dementia', *Ageing and Society*, vol. 17, pp. 513–32.

Bond, J. (2001) 'Sociological perspectives' in C. Cantley (ed.) *Handbook of Dementia Care*, Buckingham, Open University Press.

Bowers, B. Fibich, B. and Jacobson, N. (2001) 'Care-as-service, care-as-relating, care-as-comfort: understanding nursing home residents' definitions of quality', *The Gerontologist*, vol. 4, pp. 539–45.

Brod, M., Stewart, A., Sands, L. and Walton, P. (1999) 'Conceptualization and measurement of quality of life in dementia', *The Gerontologist*, vol. 38, pp. 25–35.

Brooker, D. (2001) 'Working with people with dementia: therapies and activities' in C. Cantley, (ed.) *A Handbook of Dementia Care*, Buckingham, Open University Press.

Clare, L. (2002) 'We'll fight as long as we can: coping with the onset of Alzheimer's disease', *Aging and Mental Health*, vol. 6, pp. 139–48.

Clare, L., Baddeley, A., Moniz-Cook, E. and Woods, R. (2003) 'A quiet revolution', *The Psychologist*, vol. 16, pp. 250–4.

Department of Health (2001) *National Service Framework for Older People*, London, DH.

Downs, M. (1997) 'The emergence of the person in dementia research', *Ageing and Society*, vol. 17, pp. 597–607.

Feil, N. (1993) *The Validation Breakthrough*, Cleveland, Health Professions Press.

Harris, P. (2002) *The Person with Alzheimer's Disease. Pathways to Understanding the Experience*, Baltimore, Johns Hopkins University Press.

Hibbard, J., Jansen, D. and McFarling, L. (2003) 'Behind the steering wheel', *Journal of Dementia Care*, vol. 11, pp. 12–3.

Hughes, J. (2001) 'Views of the person with dementia', *Journal of Medical Ethics*, vol. 27 pp. 86–91.

Innes, A. and Surr, C. (2001) 'Measuring the well-being of people with dementia living in formal care settings: the use of Dementia Care Mapping', *Aging and Mental Health*, vol. 5, pp. 258–68.

Keady, J. (1996) 'The experience of dementia: a review of the literature and implications for nursing practice', *Journal of Clinical Nursing*, vol. 5, pp. 275–88.

Killick, J. and Allen, K. (2001) *Communication and the Care of People with Dementia*, Buckingham, Open University Press.

Kitwood, T. (1988) 'The technical, the personal, and the framing of dementia', *Social Behaviour*, vol. 3, pp. 161–79.

Kitwood T. (1990) 'The dialectics of dementia: with particular reference to Alzheimer's Disease', *Ageing and Society*, vol. 10, pp. 177–96.

Kitwood T. (1993) 'Towards a theory of dementia care: the interpersonal process', *Ageing and Society*, vol. 13, pp. 51–67.

Kitwood, T. (1995) 'Cultures of care: tradition and change' in T. Kitwood and S. Benson, (eds) *The New Culture of Dementia Care*, London, Hawker Publications.

Kitwood, T. (1997a) 'The uniqueness of persons with dementia' in M. Marshall (ed.) *State of the Art in Dementia Care*, London, Centre for Policy on Ageing.

Kitwood, T. (1997b) 'The experience of dementia', *Aging and Mental Health*, vol. 1, pp. 13–22.

Kitwood, T. (1997c) *Dementia Reconsidered: The Person Comes First (Rethinking Ageing)*, Buckingham, Open University Press.

Kitwood, T. and Bredin, K. (1992a) 'Towards a theory of dementia care: Personhood and wellbeing', *Ageing and Society*, vol. 12, pp. 269–87.

Kitwood, T. and Bredin, K. (1992b) *Person to Person: A Guide to the Care of those with Failing Mental Powers*, Essex, Gale Centre Publications.

Macdonald, A. and Dening, T. (2002) 'Dementia is being avoided in NHS and social care', *British Medical Journal*, vol. 324, p. 548.

Marshall, M. (2001) 'The challenge of looking after people with dementia', *British Medical Journal*, vol. 323, pp. 410–1.

Morton, I. (1999) *Person-centred Approaches to Dementia Care*, Bicester, Winslow Press.

Mozley, C., Huxley, P., Sutcliffe, C., Bagley, H., Burns, A., Challis, D. and Cordingley, L. (1999) ' "Not knowing where I am doesn't mean I don't know what I like": Cognitive impairment and quality of life responses in elderly people', *International Journal of Geriatric Psychiatry*, vol. 14, pp. 776–83.

Packer T. (2000a) 'Does person-centred care exist?' *Journal of Dementia Care*, vol. 8, pp. 19–21.

Packer, T. (2000b) 'Facing up to the bills', *Journal of Dementia Care*, vol. 8, pp. 30–3.

Post, S. (1995) *The Moral Challenge of Alzheimer Disease: Ethical Issues from Diagnosis to Dying*, Baltimore, Johns Hopkins University Press.

Rogers, C. (1961) *On Becoming a Person: A Therapist's View of Psychotherapy*, Boston, Houghton Mifflin.

Stokes, G. (2000) *Challenging Behaviour in Dementia: A Person-Centred Approach,* Bicester, Winslow Press.

Trilsbach J. (2002) 'Mary teaches us that caring is a continual learning process', *Journal of Dementia Care,* vol. 10, pp. 22–6.

Woods, R. (2001) 'Discovering the person with Alzheimer's disease: cognitive, emotional and behavioural aspects', *Aging and Mental Health,* vol. 5 (supplement 1), S7–S16.

51

Getting through: how to help with anorexia nervosa and bulimia

Marilyn Duker and Roger Slade

Whatever a sufferer's weight, food and body control are always central, though at some stages and in some situations this centrality can be quite difficult to detect.

Sufferers whose weight is around their average expected body weight (AEBW) and whose current pattern is stuffing-starving or binge-vomiting will at this stage be totally focused on the problem of how to avoid food and eating, and how to regain the control they lose as, humiliatingly, they cyclically fail to avoid it. Nevertheless they have the capacity to think in complex and varied ways. At low weight, on the other hand, it is the total preoccupation with food and the contraction of intellectual capacity that together create the inability to think about anything else. At this stage, centrality of food control is the consequence of an actual inability to conceptualize much beyond food itself, and a consequence of the black and white, or polarized, thinking that renders this sufferer incapable of grasping the possibility of there being any intermediate positions at all.

Adjusting for the centrality of food control

Irrespective of weight level, the centrality of food/body control is the key to diagnosing anorexic illness, and necessarily so in its underweight stage. It is

Edited and adapted from M. Duker and R. Slade, *Anorexia Nervosa and Bulimia: How to Help* (2003), Buckingham, Open University Press, pp. 166–80.

the presence of this core attitude that will confirm that it is anorexia nervosa the helper is meeting in any particular case.

> I must absolutely plan what I eat, I must know in advance, otherwise I can't organize anything else. Once I've done that I'm all right. Then I know where I am. I don't often eat out, or anything like that. I usually prefer my own company anyway. (At 85 per cent AEBW — i.e. visually not remarkably thin)

With practice helpers and others can quickly learn to tune in to the authentic ring of the anorexic conviction that life is possible only as long as food and body are in control. Statements about food/body regulation will tend to be delivered with a confident assurance. A sufferer can also have a certain social poise that tends to deflect questioning, that turns suspicion aside.

A person's extreme thinness will, of course, make it easier to hear the central importance of food and body control in the things she/he says. But as we have said, sufferers are not always identifiable by their thinness.

Because anorexic commitment to food/body control is in the nature of a lens or prism through which every comment, question, observation, encouragement or suggestion passes, all the 'being' or life statements sufferers make about themselves need to be translated by the helper into food statements, or equally, food-burning statements. At the same time, where the helper uses life statements, he or she must be aware that sufferers will receive and understand these inversely as food statements. Thus when the helper asks how a sufferer is feeling, and the reply is 'I'm feeling fine', the helper must understand that this means 'I'm in control.' In other words, this person has not eaten anything she/he did not mean to eat, has probably eaten less than the amount she/he planned to allow him/herself, and is currently feeling 'good', and 'safe'. The underlying account will run something like: 'I haven't eaten all day, so I can allow myself salad this evening, and a slice of cold chicken (8cm square) and still be in control.' There are probably familiar and reassuring aches felt, because there has been time to run the two miles to the appointment with the helper, instead of taking a bus, and more calories burnt off than would otherwise have been.

Conversely statements such as 'I don't feel very good today', or 'I feel terrible' translate as 'My eating is out of control.' The experience, and underlying account, in this case runs something like:

> It's 12.30 and I've eaten a whole 200 grams of cottage cheese. I only ever eat 100 grams at 12.30. It's made me go completely to pieces. I'm terrified. I might eat and eat and never stop. I hate myself when I can't stick to what I know I ought to.

It must be remembered too that statements about 'feeling terrible' will be made with most urgency and greatest conviction by the hospitalized 28.6 kg

(4st. 7lbs) sufferer – i.e. 59 per cent AEBW (skeletal) who has just gained the first 0.5 kg (barely 1lb) of weight.

Helpers who, by translating thus, can step imaginatively into the anorexic world will more easily understand the situation from its perspective and so genuinely be able to accept the positive statements sufferers make about themselves as being true for them, however unlikely that may seem from the way they currently look! Genuine acceptance, which will be felt by the sufferer, is fundamental in assisting change.

Where no adjustment is made for the anorexic mindset, attempts to reach a sufferer rapidly arrive at their uncomfortable impasse.

Helper: I wonder if there's anything worrying you?
Anorexic: [blandly]: No.
Helper: Nothing at all?
Anorexic: No. Nothing's worrying me. [Translated: I've really got my eating under control, and I'm not worried about anything when I've got that sorted out.]
Helper: You look rather worried.
Anorexic: No, I'm all right. [Translated: The only thing that's worrying me now is you. I'm scared you're going to start pressuring me. I've got it organized and I don't want to be undermined by you or anyone else.]
Helper: But other people are worried about you. Your parents, for instance. That's why you're here.
Anorexic: Yes, I came because I know they're worried, but I don't see there's any need for them to feel like that. I'm OK.
Helper: I'm rather concerned about how thin you are.
Anorexic: But I'm not. I'm fine. There's no need for you to worry about me. You can see I'm all right.

Here the helper thinks: 'But she's skeletal. What does she mean?' and conversation grinds to a halt. A helper on the other hand who continually adjusts for the sufferer's perspective has the possibility of moving into that world and communicating with the sufferer in her or his own terms. This not only avoids an impasse. It demonstrates to the sufferer that the helper understands the position. It is a way of really meeting this person. Thus the above conversation might instead take the following course.

Helper: Is there anything worrying you?
Anorexic: [blandly]; No.
Helper: Nothing at all?
Anorexic: No. Nothing's worrying me. [Translated: I've got my eating in control, and I'm not worried about anything when that's all right]

Helper:	You look a bit worried to me . . . [Deciding to try a 'move' towards her] I imagine the people who think you're thin pressure you a lot to eat more. And I'm wondering whether, right now, you're worried I might start pressuring you like everybody else?
Anorexic:	[appearing startled, and then finding herself agreeing]: They're always trying to make me eat all this food. But I don't want it.
Helper:	[indicating acceptance of her last statement by mirroring her determined tone]: No, you don't want it. But it's probably very hard to make them understand that you feel much better when you don't eat. You can get more done, perhaps?
Anorexic:	[still rather surprised that this therapist appears to understand]: Yes. I do, but they won't believe me.
Helper:	And I guess you do eat something?
Anorexic:	[opening up]: Oh yes, I eat the things I like. [Translated: I like eating a small range of low-calorie foods such as . . .]
Helper:	What kind of things do you like?
Anorexic:	[enthusiastically]: Vegetables. I love vegetables. And cottage cheese. I eat a lot of cottage cheese. [Translated: That is, a small amount which is always exactly the same so I still feel safe.]

In meeting the sufferer by adjusting for this centrality, it becomes possible to help bring the detail of the need for control into the open. This is one essential step towards sufferers eventually allowing themselves to experiment with risking some change.

Adjusting for altered thinking

As starvation progresses sufferers think about a smaller range of things, they think about them in an increasingly polarized way, and everything that is thought about is thought about in food terms. These are the main intellectual changes created where food intake is persistently inadequate for daily requirements.

The changes intensify as weight falls, and become less severe as weight rises. This means that, of the adjustments the helper needs to make, the exact adjustment required for altered thinking will depend utterly on *this* person's weight level on *this* day, and how it has recently altered: whether it has gone up or down, and how fast.

Intellectual change can be masked for a considerable length of time by habitual performance. For instance, while weight drops, sufferers are likely to continue to obtain high marks for academic work at first because they will make up with many hours of dedicated, repetitive learning what they cannot do by abstraction, or by the creative synthesis of new ideas. How well they perform will also depend somewhat on their particular history within the illness, the significant factor usually being the length of time they have been maintaining a low-weight state and at the same time fulfilling day-to-day obligations.

It is pointless for a helper to present low-weight sufferers with the 'grand analysis' in the hope that, by telling them their starvation is progressively impairing their intellectual capacity, they might be encouraged to eat. Attempting to get through by rational argument is as unproductive as attempting to discuss complex issues with a person who is continually under the influence of alcohol. They only have the capacity to respond in the most simple, polarized way, and in any case will not want to believe anything that is out of line with their own rigid views, or contrary to their 'improved' experience of themselves.

It is far more effective a strategy for the helper to make mental adjustments, and so talk about specific deficits that can be judged as most likely to be happening to each sufferer at their particular current weight in the hope that they themselves will be able to recognize that those things the helper is mentioning have begun to occur in their own life.

Helper: You've lost another pound. I know that's not worrying you . . .
Anorexic: No.
Helper: [aware that the girl is now around 72 per cent AEBW]: I'm aware it's easier for you not to eat. Your weight's gone down again. But I wonder . . . Have you noticed yourself changing any other way?
Anorexic: [silent, and looks blank]
Helper: I wonder if you're feeling the cold much more? And taking longer about doing things . . . Because perhaps your concentration might be a bit patchy? Or as though you've got gaps in your memory?
Anorexic: [in a changed tone] Funny you should say that. I don't concentrate as well as I did. It's hard to keep my mind on things. When I'm at work . . . even writing letters, it takes ages.
Helper: You're noticing that yourself.
Anorexic: Yes. I don't remember things. I have to keep asking.
Helper: It wasn't like that a few weeks ago . . .
Anorexic: No.
Helper: So as your weight is going down, you can't work as well as you did.
Anorexic: [grudgingly] Mmm. I suppose so.

Such an intervention can be risky unless the helper is sure she or he has recognized the appropriate stage. Sufferers will be highly offended at the idea that they cannot concentrate if they feel they can. Yet when there is a bland denying of any problem at all, an appropriately judged intervention that homes in on a specific deficit may make its mark.

A helper may find it useful to imagine polarized or altered thinking as a template that is set on every aspect of the person's experience. It is a template that can help make sense of the totally assured, holier-than-thou attitude the sufferer has at one time (that is, when all is organized and feels in control), and the total self-hatred and self-disgust the same sufferer experiences at another time (that is, when control has been lost). There are no intermediate positions. A shift from one extreme to the other can occur as a result of unplanned eating of an amount of food that, to anyone not anorexic in their thinking, will seem insignificant – such as four grapes, or a single bit of a sandwich – or it can occur as a result of not getting to get to the gym *exactly* at 12.45 p.m.

Adjusting for low self-esteem

Anorexic or bulimic sufferers' extremely low self-esteem may not be in the least apparent. Whether they come across as entirely confident and superior or as depressed and self-effacing will always be tied closely to their current sense of being in control of food and weight, or how exercised they feel.

Whether or not their low self-esteem is evident, a helper should allow for its presence, by adjusting for it from the first moments of meeting and actively engaging in ways likely to promote a sense of self-worth. Simple measures such as acknowledging their presence by greeting them by name, giving eye contact in so far as they seem able to cope with this, talking *to* them rather than *about* them, listening to and genuinely acknowledging what they say, and giving them plenty of time to express their position are all helpful in this respect.

A particular adjustment that will need to be made is for the way absence of self-worth colours the way sufferers relate to others, ensuring a pattern of either finding every possible fault with other people, dismissing others as worthless and inferior, or finding every possible fault with themselves and dismissing themselves. Either way, the sufferer is protected from the burden of engaging with anyone, including any helper.

Sufferers who have tried to express their feelings of worthlessness and inadequacy will have been used to having these feelings dismissed. They will be accustomed to others seeing them as highly talented, as confident, poised, well-qualified, as socially advantaged. So they anticipate that this helper too will see them the same way. A helper who does take this view will create an impasse as the sufferer feels obliged to sustain the 'false front'. If on the other hand a helper can gently demonstrate awareness of the mismatch that exists between the way the world sees the anorexic/bulimic and the way sufferers see themselves, this again can provide an awakening, a point of genuine meeting and understanding that might stir the possibility of developing a helping relationship, or assist in keeping a fragile or incipient relationship alive.

Helper:	[at a first meeting with a sufferer who appears resentful, silent and withdrawn] … and your parents seemed proud to tell me you've just got your degree … I guess most people see you as very successful … I suspect that's not quite the way you feel yourself … [Watching the girl's face colour slightly] … even though you got a first.
Sufferer:	[rapidly] I didn't deserve it.
Helper:	You don't believe you deserved it You feel a fraud?
Sufferer:	[quietly] Mmm

Though they will fear being 'so transparent' it can, even so, be a great relief to meet someone who seems to know just how worthless and ineffectual they feel, and how much they loathe themselves, yet who does not blame or chide them for feeling like this; who in fact seems, bewilderingly, to accept them, though they cannot see why.

Like any other human being, an anorexia nervosa/bulimia sufferer is quite normal and ordinary in wanting and needing attention, acknowledgement, respect. Indeed, all of these are essential if a person is to begin to allow the development of a self that does not depend on food/body control. But their feelings of unworthiness prevent sufferers from taking the attention and acknowledgement they need. These are undeserved, in their eyes … The dilemma is that they both want and do not want attention. Where the helper empathizes accurately, and gives appropriate attention and acknowledgement even in recognizing this ambivalence and the tangle of feelings it creates, then communication can become effective.

Adjusting for different physical experiences

The helper will need to be aware of, and adjust for, the many physical sensations familiar to sufferers in their starved state, but outside the experience of the adequately fed person. It is also essential to bear in mind the very distinct contrast there is at low weight between the physical feeling of being empty and the changes to this feeling when even quite small quantities of food are eaten. Large amounts eaten regularly will leave a sufferer feeling 'like one great big digestive tract'.

Failure to appreciate that at low weight the sufferer is speaking from a place that is physiologically different from that of those who are adequately fed has vitiated many medical research projects and investigations, and there is no progress to be made in terms of therapy by making the same mistake. Where the helper allows for different physical sensations, then statements sufferers make about 'feeling disgustingly full', or 'being swollen and bloated', when they have eaten as little as half an orange become quite coherent and intelligible. A helper who understands them as accurate expressions of their physical experiences at low weight is more likely to be able to keep communication open.

Adjusting for different implicit values

The helper's difficulty in communicating with sufferers about the way they experience their bodily states does not arise only because at low weight they are making statements about their physical experiences from a different physiological baseline. Like everyone else anorexia nervosa/bulimia sufferers use their mental faculties to understand and creatively interpret their bodily sensations in terms of their values and their beliefs about themselves. So they interpret all the physical experiences they associate with non-eating and exertion as morally positive, and all those associated with eating or rest as morally negative.

When a self-starver is obviously too thin and still rigidly refusing food, there is the greater temptation for the helper to assume that the sufferer here 'must be able to realize that she cannot go on like this'. It can be useful, as with polarized thinking, for the helper again to imagine a template set on the sufferer's values that completely reverses the ideas of good and bad, safe and unsafe. This helps adjust for the fact that the sufferer is using these ideas in an inverted way.

Nurturing a sense of self

No helper can work with anyone, anorexic/bulimic or otherwise, without their being willing to come to the next appointment. This most minimal cooperation is more likely to be given to the helper who, by making the appropriate adjustments, conveys an accurate and genuine understanding of the way the sufferer feels. There is a balance to be achieved between creating the appropriate safety and engaging a sufferer's curiosity, which may occur initially as a result of the unusual responses received from a helper who is informed, even though such responses also open up risk. Either provides a point from which minimal cooperation can be negotiated, such as coming for a next appointment.

Acknowledging the need for control and thus at first not breaking down the little self-esteem a sufferer has is, in the long term, far more conducive to recovery. *The person who dismisses what the sufferer says is dismissing the person she or he currently is.* Interventions that attack control destroy the only thing the anorexic or bulimic wants, and, in so doing, destroy all that this person is. Such interventions ensure the continuation of hopeless feelings, despair, confusion and failure. They perpetuate the sense of being 'something less than human'.

Whatever their current weight, sufferers need to find out for themselves in quite practical ways how destructive their mindset is. As they discover this, they will need support and practical information about how they might begin to change. Such information will be the most valuable and enduring where it is learnt gradually through their own first-hand experience. Meanwhile the kind of beginning that can be made in setting this process in train will always depend on each sufferer's physical state, current weight and pattern of food/body control, the circumstances in which they are living and the speed at which weight is falling. Given that the natural progression of the illness is for weight to drop, an assessment of the amount of time there is available before it becomes dangerously low is crucial to the helper's decision about what, at any point, should be the immediate focus of help.

52

Responding to people affected by major incidents

Jane Shackman

Major incidents

Most people, wherever they are in the world, are becoming used to hearing about major incidents, even as events are unfolding. It may be a terrorist attack, flooding, a major fire or explosion, a school shooting. It may be a natural disaster or perpetrated by other people.

In a major incident a large number of people will probably be affected and there is likely to be confusion, fear and anxiety. People may be injured or killed, others will be witnesses, bereaved, separated from loved ones or displaced. These events may be seen as a challenge to the mental health of the people involved.

The random nature of a major incident means that it may happen to you, or to your family, friends, colleagues or neighbours. Imagine how you might feel if you were directly affected in some way. What kind of response would you make, both personally and professionally? What might people require from you? Thinking of the issues in advance may help you to feel better prepared if a major incident touches your life or the lives of those around you.

This article draws on my work with Victim Support developing services to victims of terrorist attack, and from supporting people affected by the bombings in London on July 7th 2005 and other major incidents. Evidence shows that early and appropriate assistance after an incident will have positive outcomes for people's mental health. (Ellen and Shackman, 2008).

Features of a major incident

After a major incident many people may be seriously injured or killed. There may be a delay in identifying who has been affected, so people who fear the death of someone close may face a period of agonising uncertainty. Witnesses and survivors are often exposed to disturbing scenes of people in pain or dying. Injuries are often severe, and can result in long-term disabilities, loss of employment or changes in lifestyle.

There is damage at the immediate site of the incident and probably also in the surrounding area and people may be displaced on a short or longer-term basis.

Depending on events, some people will find themselves stranded in places they were simply passing through, on a journey or visit. Family members may be far away and it can take a long time before people are reunited. Other people will travel home after an incident and find that no one in their surroundings knows about what happened, much less understands what they have been through. People can feel very isolated.

If people are caught up in a major incident when they are away from home, they can find themselves without basic essentials. They may be separated from their bags, wallet or phone, unable to call family or friends or pay for anything needed like food, clothing or transport home. Dependency on others to meet these needs may feel difficult for people who have already gone through an experience that was out of their control.

In major incidents, assistance needs to be provided on a large scale usually involving a number of agencies working together. The difficulty in gaining an overview of the situation complicates the process of obtaining and communicating reliable information.

Some families searching for news make attempts to go to the site of the incident, which is almost certainly chaotic as the responders deal with the rescue operation. Many bereaved people also want to visit the site to pay respects and perhaps to see where the person died.

Accountability

Attempting to understand 'what happened' and 'who made the mistakes' is an important part of recovery for survivors and their families, especially if the incident has been deliberately caused by others. After incidents such as the shootings at Virginia Tech which took place in April 2007 in the USA, or a terrorist attack or rail crash, there is likely to be a need to hold others to account, but often this is not possible as those responsible may no longer be alive. After a natural disaster there may also be blame attributed, such as why people and homes were not properly protected in the New Orleans flooding during August 2005.

Investigations into what happened can take many months or even years, and people may not get answers to their questions for a very long time if at all.

Common reactions

People caught up in a major incident have experienced something beyond their control, threatening their safety and their lives. Everyone reacts differently and a range of reactions is normal and to be expected. These reactions may be emotional, physical, social or cognitive; emotional, may include shock, fear, helplessness or feeling overwhelmed; physical, commonly may involve disturbed sleep, headaches, stomach upsets and other physical symptoms; social, could involve withdrawal, irritability or conflict with others; cognitive, may include difficulty in concentrating or decision-making, confusion or distressing thoughts or images.

People may question 'Why me? Why did it happen?' They can become preoccupied with what would have happened if they had done something differently that day and thus avoided being involved in the incident. Some people experience 'survivor guilt', where they question why they survived yet others died or were badly injured (Ellen and Shackman, 2007). Feelings of guilt may prevent some people from accessing assistance because they feel they do not deserve it.

Those affected may become preoccupied with what they did or didn't do to help others. Friends and family members may attempt to prevent the survivor expressing such feelings of guilt and self-blame; however, survivors need a space to express these thoughts and feelings. Many people feel angry, whether general anger that the incident happened, or anger directed at particular individuals or groups seen to be responsible or unhelpful in some way.

People may experience a powerful sense of loss. This could include loss of life, health, occupation or property. Less tangible losses could be loss of security or faith that life has a certain consistency, safety and meaning (Hodgkinson and Stewart, 1998). It is important for those assisting survivors of major incidents to remember that the reactions and symptoms people have are normal reactions to an abnormal experience. Some reactions can feel frightening for people and for those in contact with them, and may lead them to question their mental health.

It is often helpful to reassure people that their reactions are normal and in most cases these symptoms subside over time.

Duty of care in community to respond

Professionals have an important role to play in responding to a major incident, but everyone is a member of the community and has a duty to respond as best they can. Natural disasters or terrorist attacks can bring people together to help and support each other in different ways that do not require specialist knowledge or skills (Gist, 2002). The aim of all support offered should be to build resilience in those affected. Many of those who receive good support and assistance in the early stages after a major incident are able to resume their lives, albeit in an altered way (Yates et al., 1999).

Resilience is the process of adapting to traumatic events. The word 'resilience' comes from the Latin 'salire' (to spring, spring up) and 'resilire' (to spring back). Researchers and clinicians working with survivors (Gist, 2002; Wessely, 2005) have found that resilience is a common response, not extraordinary. Resilience does not mean that people do not experience difficulty or acute distress. In fact, the road to resilience is likely to involve considerable emotional, physical and practical challenges, which may last for many months or years. The ways in which people affected by major incidents are assisted in the early stages will have an impact on building their resilience both in the short and longer-term.

People are best supported by those they know and they naturally call on their social and community structures in times of grief and distress. Professionals can be of most help by supporting these networks (Gist, 2002; Wessely, 2005). The way in which assistance is offered is also important. Four particular aspects of support foster resilience:

Information

Providing accurate information is crucial in enabling people to make decisions and feel more in control. Most people want to be reunited with families or friends as soon as possible. Those directly affected, if not badly injured or hospitalised, often want information about what has happened and how they can travel home.

Families and friends are likely to be searching for those who are missing and hoping for immediate and accurate information about the affected person's whereabouts. The nature of major incidents means that in the immediate aftermath information is difficult to obtain so people may face a long and difficult wait for news. People's ability to absorb and retain information may be reduced in a crisis and they may ask for the same information a number of times. Supporters can help by writing down information for later reference.

Sometimes those affected begin by asking for information, but may really want to talk about what has happened.

Practical assistance

Practical assistance is often greatly needed and appreciated and in the immediate aftermath people are likely to have more practical than emotional support needs. Some people may appreciate help in working out practicalities.

Practical assistance could include contacting family, care of dependent relatives, children or pets, shelter, travel, food, clothing and financial help. Sometimes it can be helpful to prompt people to think what they might need in advance, for example checking whether they still have their house keys.

People are often separated from their personal belongings and can become preoccupied in getting even small things back. This can be seen as an attempt to put their life back together again.

Choice and control

People affected by a sudden and traumatic event often experience a temporary loss of control and this may be the most fundamental form of intangible loss (Mirowsky and Ross, 1989). The more control a person has, and can be given, the better their mental health is likely to be. The ability to make choices and decisions and to problem solve are key features of resilience. Supporters can assist a person to identify his individual choices: what he wishes to do himself and what he wishes to have help with. They can promote choice by providing options where possible, and helping the survivor to decide what he would like to happen, for example with regard to travel or accommodation.

However, not everyone wants help and supporters should be careful not to overwhelm or push a survivor into receiving support as a result of their own need to be of help.

Validation

To validate someone's experience means to make it valid and acknowledged. This helps the survivor frame the event, make sense of their experience, and begin to move past it. When another person validates a survivor, her thoughts, needs and feelings, whatever these might be, she is more likely to feel valued and worthwhile. A survivor who feels validated is free to think more clearly and rationally and can begin to understand herself and make sense of her experience.

Acknowledgement of how a person is feeling and thinking in the immediate aftermath of a major incident can be immensely reassuring. Some people are calm and organised while others are panic-stricken, frightened or distressed. Reassurance that affected individuals' immediate reactions are normal and are likely to abate in time can be very helpful.

In addition to the assistance offered by others, people affected by major incidents find their own ways of building resilience, for example by meeting together in support or self-help groups with others affected by the same incident.

Counselling or formal 'critical incident stress debriefing' sessions are now generally regarded as unhelpful in the early stages and indeed early specialist intervention is contra-indicated by much research (Gist, 2002; Wessely, 2005; Summerfield, 2005). It is common after a traumatic event for people to have intrusive thoughts, flashbacks and dreams about what has happened for a short period of time. This can trouble people but is not a sign of mental ill-health (van der Kolk and McFarlane, 1996). Van der Kolk and McFarlane (1996) advise that this repeated replaying of upsetting memories modifies the emotions associated with the trauma and usually creates a tolerance for the content of the memories.

Such reactions usually diminish over time, but if troubling reactions persist and people report difficulties in social, occupational or other important areas of functioning, this is likely to indicate that more specialised assistance is required.

Researchers and clinicians point out that the majority of people survive terrible events without developing psychiatric disorders such as Post Traumatic Stress Disorder (PTSD). The Traumatic Stress Clinic in London screened people affected by the 7 July 2005 bombings for PTSD and found they were a relatively robust population. The clinic cautioned against suggesting, diagnosing or even thinking of PTSD in the first few weeks saying that support is what people need, not formal mental health services (Ellen and Shackman, 2007).

Personal growth and life changes

As time passes after being affected by a major incident, many people are able to integrate the experience into their lives and see things in a broader perspective. Some see opportunities for self-discovery and change as a result of adversity, including improved relationships, seeing new possibilities and having a greater appreciation for one's life. There may be a greater sense of personal strength or spiritual development.

Many survivors make significant life changes, develop new plans, change jobs or career, or do other things that create meaning and something positive from what happened. As one survivor commented a year after being affected:

> Being able to see this is a really bad thing, but positive things can come out of it. Not letting it completely kind of cripple you ... the hopeful thing for me is that we can learn something from it. That I can now go on and do different things, the possibilities I can see in life now are far more than I could have done a year ago, completely because of what happened. (Ellen and Shackman, 2007, p. 20)

Some people speak of more fully appreciating the precariousness of life, valuing their own and other people's lives more, and being determined to do something that feels more meaningful with their lives. Some people put their energies into campaigning or fundraising, or become active members of self-help groups. Others set up their own charities or work in helping agencies.

What do responders need to know?

Statutory and voluntary agencies should no longer be totally surprised by the scale and impact of major incidents and the general principles of how to respond. Nevertheless, there appears to still be a need for appropriate training and awareness-raising across the statutory and voluntary sectors.

Such sessions could be offered to all those workers who might come into contact with those injured, affected or bereaved by a major incident. This would enable them to be more confident of how to respond, and reassured that a human and supportive response may be all that is needed by many in the immediate aftermath.

Looking after yourself

It is important not to forget the needs of supporters doing this work, as working with and hearing the distressing experiences of survivors, injured and bereaved can have a profound impact (Ellen and Shackman, 2008). In addition, supporters may be directly or indirectly affected by the incident themselves. They may get very involved in the work and continue without a break.

It is vital that workers look after themselves with good self-care practices, which ensure they remain both emotionally and physically nourished during an intense period of work with survivors. They should attempt to protect themselves by maintaining a balance between the work and personal aspects of their lives. It is equally important that they are well supported and supervised by the agencies they work for.

People involved in supporting people affected by major incidents have spoken of the rewarding nature of the work. They often feel that they have done little, but they have done their best in times of great need.

Acknowledgements

Sincere thanks to Paula Ellen who encouraged me to draw on the work that we did and continue to do together, and to Jill Reynolds for her critical reading of this article and helpful comments.

References

Ellen, P. and Shackman, J. (2007) *Building Resilience: Report and Recommendations for Victim Support on Delivering Services to Victims of Terrorist Attack*, London: Victim Support.

Ellen, P. and Shackman, J. (2008) *Incident Care Team Training Handbook for Association of Train Operating Companies*, unpublished training handbook.

Gist, R. (2002) 'What have they done to my song? Social science, social movements and the debriefing debates', *Cognitive and Behavioral Practice*, 9(4) pp. 273–79.

Hodgkinson, P.E. and Stewart, M. (1998) *Coping with Catastrophe: A Handbook of Post-disaster Psychosocial Aftercare*, London, Routledge.

Mirowsky, J. and Ross, C.E. (1989) *Social Causes of Psychological Distress*, Hawthorn, New York, Aldine de Gruyter,

Summerfield, D. (2005) 'Coping with the aftermath of trauma: NICE guidelines on post-traumatic stress disorder have fundamental flaw', *British Medical Journal*, 331, p. 50.

van der Kolk, B.A. and McFarlane, A.C. (1996) 'The black hole of trauma' in B.A. van der Kolk, A.C. McFarlane and L. Weisaeth (eds), *Traumatic Stress: the Effects of Overwhelming Experience on Mind, Body and Society*, New York, Guilford Press.

Wessely, S. (2005) 'Don't panic! Short and long term psychological reactions to the new terrorism: the role of information and the authorities', *Journal of Mental Health*, 14(1) pp. 16.

Yates, S., Axsom, D. and Tiedman, K. (1999) 'The help-seeking process for distress after disasters', in R. Gist and B. Lubin (eds) *Response To Disaster: Psychosocial, Community And Ecological Perspectives*, Philadelphia, Brunner/Mazel.

53

Still doing being human

Tom Heller

Jeff had obviously steeled himself for his visit to the surgery. He sat down with his head already bowed and in a soft, low voice told me how bad he was feeling. I had to lean forward to catch the words. In between sentences, while he was composing what he would say next, his tongue came out from between his lips and then disappeared again. I don't think I said a single word as he told me how he was feeling. The whole process of talking in this way appeared difficult and was almost certainly very unusual for him. He couldn't sleep, he was feeling crap, he didn't feel much like eating and his wife and kids were complaining that he was losing his temper all the time. He looked up tentatively. What was I going to do about it?

Well yes, what am I going to do about it? This is in the middle of the 'drop-in' surgery time and I have already seen plenty of people before Jeff and several more are waiting. What protocol will help me to help him? Who can I shuffle him off to see and save me any further effort? What part of my training can I call up to make our interaction meaningful?

I realised that I hadn't ever seen Jeff as a patient before, although he had brought his kids in from time to time and I remembered him vaguely from those encounters. Otherwise I don't know much about him and the computer has almost no entries under his name except that he seems to have broken various bones over the years. He's 42 years old and for some reason a few years ago he had his cholesterol taken: the reading was 6.7 mmol/l. Big deal! Although some clinicians might think that this is a slightly raised value it really seems to be the least of his problems.

But I recognise that if I just sit still for a while and give him some space and encouragement he'll tell me about his abusive past. And so it comes to pass. He tells me that he was humiliated and abused physically and sexually by his older step brothers from age three to seventeen when he left his family home and joined the Army. He learnt fifteen ways to kill people and no ways to communicate with other human beings. He could sink nine pints a night and dig a trench in the morning. He served in Northern Ireland on just one tour of duty and then left the Army, apparently by mutual agreement. He hadn't been much of a soldier and he was bullied in the barracks by his comrades who became surrogate step brothers. The reason why there isn't much about him on the computer becomes apparent ... he's been in and out of prison rather a lot in the intervening years. In prison he became a regular visitor to the gym and now has the typical shape of a body-builder sadly gone to seed. His belly is big and falling over the top of his jeans. I bet his cholesterol is higher than 6.7 now.

So what interventions could help him feel better? Are there any and how much effort will it take for him and for me? And this knotted situation is obviously not just him, is it? He's sort of re-creating the miserable life that he suffered as a child for his own children in their turn. He doesn't appear to have many resources. He can't read or write well enough to fill in any official forms and to be honest I don't think he has much skill in the way of communicating his 'emotional intelligence' or vocabulary to discuss more than his most superficial feelings. He's not paid his rent for five months and the Council are threatening to evict him. One thing is clear in his mind – it really is my job to help him out and make him feel better. I've probably got some pills that will do just the job.

But how can I help? What is the difference between me as a professional health worker and any other person trying to act in a humane way? What sort of step brother will I prove to be? There's a wide range of choices for each of us at this crucial point in his story.

What are Jeff's expectations of me and the way I will behave? He's definitely taking a risk because he doesn't know me very well. Perhaps I've seemed to be approachable when dealing with his seven year old daughter's tonsillitis, or perhaps he's just desperate and would spill the beans to anyone sitting in my chair. After his most nasty aggressive outburst at home his partner has told him to get himself sorted out or leave home. He's vulnerable and wouldn't have anywhere else to go, he might lose both his home and contact with his children. I think I can actually feel his desperation.

Without getting too pretentious about what is going on between doctors and the people who come to consult with them I sometimes feel that when the door closes and the consultation starts this is 'the still point in the turning world' (Eliot, 1935). In this instant both Jeff and I are the products of our own complex and dynamic psychodynamic pasts. He will never know about my upbringing, how I relate to my own family of birth, my partner or our children. But for sure my upbringing has affected the way that I have turned out, my need to be needed as a doctor and my ability to cope with the stuff of daily life. He will never know what is going on for me more immediately either. Have I had a difficult time recently? Are there problems in my personal or professional life; what mood am I in? So the relationship is already very unequal in terms of status, power, knowledge and capacity. Are we just about to re-enact the child to stepbrother relationship that has caused him so much trouble in the past?

Previously when describing my relationship with people who have become addicted to illicit substances I have wondered if the relationship is all about parenting (Heller, 1993). Am I like their parent trying to provide them with some boundaries and constancy in their lives? Dealing out just the right amount of opiates and forbidding them extra 'sweeties' until the time comes when they are grown up enough to take their own decisions. Holding them in a safe place until such time as they have developed the skills for themselves to face the cruelties of the outside world. But for Jeff it all seems too early to presume any such relationship and he certainly doesn't care about any transactional analysis spin that might be imposed on our brief encounter.

We both have choices at this early stage in the relationship. He will never find out much about me, but it's obviously my job to find out lots and lots of stuff about him. Even with his limited vocabulary, or perhaps because of his apparently limited communication skills, I'll need to be working hard at several different levels. There's the level that can be observed or even captured on video camera. My words and body language are desperately important; he'll run for cover like a frightened fawn if I blunder at this stage. But really I'm like the rapidly paddling duck, trying to keep calm above the surface but with little webbed feet below the surface of the water scrabbling away. What is going on in my mind? I think I can identify at least five different parts of my 'inner consultation' (Neighbour, 1987).

Technical stuff about mental health issues

OK, what part of my professional training can I call upon at this stage? Have all the lectures and research papers that I have been privileged to experience equipped me to be more nuanced and sophisticated and avoid the usual lunge for the prescription pad? Is there any possible outcome other than Prozac? To be honest my reading has perhaps complicated rather than clarified some issues. Is there such a thing as depression? We are all somewhere on a continuum between low and high mood. No wonder Jeff is feeling lousy, he's been stressed to the limit and anyone would be feeling the way he's feeling under such strain. But what makes this an illness? In previous centuries might he have sought help from the church rather than from the NHS for any pickle that he finds himself in? Our little GP surgery is just about the only helping agency left standing in this multiply deprived Council estate. Social workers, community workers and youth workers have all been pulled out of the area long ago. So even if I don't personally think that Jeff's got an illness he certainly seems to have gathered all the symptoms that modern diagnostic manuals (DSM-IV for example) could use to slot him into a diagnosis of depression. Would it help to ask Jeff a set of formal questions to give him a 'depression score' even though the effectiveness of these screening and case-finding instruments has been called into question (Gilbody et al., 2008)? If so, then which score chart should I use? and what help can I get from official guidelines and protocols? Luckily NICE (National Institute for Health and Clinical Excellence) have fairly recently produced and distributed quick reference guidelines for the management of depression (NICE, 2007) but I am not really going to go rooting through a bunch of glossy handouts or even flick onto the internet with Jeff sitting there with an expectant and increasingly desperate look in his eyes. I should be able to deal with this after 39 years of being a doctor.

Pills or no pills?

An attempt to fully answer this question would take up all the words I have been allocated for this article, and possibly the whole book. Over the years of my personal practice I have noted the trajectory of several classes of new antidepressants; introduced with great hope they are promoted as a sure-fire way to help people ... this honeymoon phase is followed both by the realisation that they aren't as effective as hoped for and that side effects prove to be more serious and more intractable than at first suggested. The role of drug companies as the motor for this roller-coaster ride is becoming increasingly apparent. I think that Jeff may benefit from some medication, but I decide that the first consultation is probably too early to make this decision.

Emotional stuff

We have already established that I am allowed to find out about how Jeff is feeling, but that he will never have access to my feelings. But does this make what's going on for me irrelevant? Is it possible for me to treat everyone the same? Would that be good medicine or bad medicine? I have been aware of the local campaign to keep the British National Party (BNP) out of the community where I work. It appears that it's only the depth of deprivation and the lack of organising power on our estate that has so far prevented BNP expansion into our neck of the woods. A candidate attempting to be a local councillor has put his name forward and I had previously noted that Jeff was one of the registered nominators. That's the problem with doctors being involved in the local community. You might get to find out something about your local GP, but she (or he) will know a lot about you as well. I've seen Jeff driving round the estate in his battered white estate car with the red cross of St. George on the bonnet and now he's declared himself to be a supporter of the local BNP candidate. He can't know that I'm the son of Jewish immigrants who were granted asylum in this country only after a period of internment. The emotional stuff has turned political. Can I rise above the emotions that his political or quasi-political activities bring up for me? Is this legitimate 'evidence' that I can use positively to help me understand how he's feeling about his life on a poverty-torn estate. Perhaps even more to the point Jeff doesn't know that his wife, Kim, had been to see me a couple of weeks ago and told her side of the story of their relationship and showed me the bruises. This isn't just time for emotional and political dilemmas, it's all getting into the realms of ethical tangles as well.

The organisational milieu: resources and referrals

The NHS hasn't covered itself in glory recently when it comes to organising local psychiatric services. I promise not to get too nostalgic and go on about a rose-tinted past, but there was a time when our local mental health team were very involved in the work of local primary health care teams. Community Psychiatric Nurses were regular attenders at our clinical case discussion meetings in the practice and the consultant psychiatrist regularly made himself available to us for advice. There seemed to be a steady, mutually-respectful interchange of information and clients. Somehow we have let this deteriorate and there are now seemingly impenetrable gulches between 'us' and 'them'. Referrals to the specialist services take ages before the poor client is even allocated a worker, who then repeats the assessments that we have already made before they may go onto another waiting list, perhaps to see a psychiatrist or psychologist . . . and further assessments. Anyone working in, or relating to, current NHS mental health services will recognise the tortuous (mad?) scenario that I am describing. The poor (usually locum) consultant psychiatrist will only have their prescription pad to turn to. People referred into the service have usually gone through several crises by the time they get to see a psychiatrist and may come away clutching a prescription for mega doses of an anti-depressant that we had been trying to avoid prescribing all those months ago. In any case a referral to the local mental health care team doesn't seem to be sufficient response to the human story that Jeff unfolds before me.

Luckily for Jeff an organisation to help male survivors of sexual abuse has continued to exist in our locality. This excellent but sadly much reduced organisation is run on a shoe-string mainly by volunteers and survivors themselves. The daily drop-in service no longer exists, but there is a phone number to ring to leave a message and they will get back to you if they can. I promise Jeff that I will find the phone number for him . . .

Of course there are other resources that have been established by the local statutory mental health services that might be of help to people who have ongoing challenges to their mental health. Our local mental health managers seem to have invested heavily in self-help booklets for distribution to people who are going through difficult periods in their lives. The big glossy publications with titles such as *An Introduction to Coping with Panic* (Young, 2007) and *An Introduction to Coping with Phobias* (Hogan, 2007) look really good and consciously try to steer a delicate balance between patronising people who are already well read and being off-putting for those with a limited capacity. Other resources are computer-based and people working in primary care settings are encouraged to signpost people towards internet based devices for 'treating emotional problems'. The current favourite seems to be MoodGym (http://moodgym.anu.edu.au) which has been designed to reduce depression symptoms using a form of cognitive behaviour therapy training (Christensen et al., 2004). I do not seem to be alone in questioning how really effective or sustainable computer based CBT programmes are for people with significant mental health issues in their lives (Marks et al., 2007).

In any case Jeff can't read or write well enough to fill in any of the exercises in the self-help booklets and he hasn't ever used a computer for anything other than games. It seems as though he's unlikely to travel to the nearest group session of 'Beating the Blues' that has been arranged by the mental health managers ... so really it us up to the two of us. Two human beings facing each other ...

Jeff looks up again, well what am I going to do?

What will help Jeff and how to communicate it to him?

Jeff and I are mirroring each other's poses. He's hunched forward on the edge of his chair because of the tension he is feeling and I am straining forwards to try to catch his rather mumbled words. It's not easy this consultation, or any consultation if you take them each seriously. But I do have some tricks up my sleeve that I can fall back on. I've been taught a triumvirate of things that really do seem to work for people who may have a label of 'depression' pinned to them.

Firstly they will have to try to sort out some of the things in their lives that need sorting. If there are outstanding housing problems, debt or disputes with the neighbours no other clever interventions or chemical mood altering tablets will make much difference. In recent years this approach has been graced by the title 'Problem-solving therapy', but it's what we have been doing, or should have been doing for years. It seems that this approach has an evidence base and some people find that adding antidepressant medication makes it work even better (Gellis, 2008). So Jeff will have to have some help to sort out some of the sortable-outable things in his life.

Secondly, Jeff can be taught not to think bad things about himself. We can all learn to stop reinforcing negative thoughts and stop in our tracks if we recognise that we are winding ourselves up or down into a worse state than is necessary. Again this simple technique has been developed into an entire industry, now called CBT (cognitive behavioural therapy). But I think that Jeff, even with his limited literacy skills, will be able to grasp this concept and apply it to his own world and thoughts.

Thirdly I discuss the way forward for Jeff. To get to where he wants to get, to climb out of the hole, will not happen all at once. It will be the result of many small steps. We will set ourselves small tasks each time we meet and check out progress at regular intervals. The focus has shifted from questioning what I can do about his situation. Slowly the focus changes to the things he has to do himself in order to function again and be fit enough to tackle some of the real issues that have put him in the position he now finds himself.

I slowly go over the things that I will do before we meet again; I promise to send him the phone number of the survivors of sexual abuse organisation and write a letter of support to the housing department. I ask him to come to see me in an appointment slot next week and report progress. I will be alongside him as he takes his first adult steps out of his difficulties.

Postscript: The title of this essay is adapted from the title of the work by Harvey Sacks 'On doing being ordinary' (1984). In my essay I have made no attempt to follow the work of Sacks or his methods of conversation analysis. However the title of his work has always stuck in my mind when I think about the qualities that doctors should bring to each consultation. Mental health workers need to be ordinary as well as human as we go about the extraordinary tasks involved in our daily work.

References

Christensen, H., Griffiths, K. and Jorm, A. (2004) 'Delivering interventions for depression by using the internet: randomised controlled trial', *British Medical Journal*, vol. 328, pp. 265–70.

Eliot T.S. (1935) *Burnt Norton*, Orlando, Harcourt.

Gellis, Z. (2008) 'Problem-solving therapy for depression in adults: a systematic review', *Research on Social Work Practice*, vol. 18, pp. 117–31.

Gilbody, S., Sheldon, T. and House A. (2008) 'Screening and case-finding instruments for depression: a meta-analysis', *Canadian Medical Association Journal*, vol. 178, pp. 997–1003.

Heller, T. (1993) 'The real person within', *British Medical Journal*, vol. 307, p. 1013.

Hogan, B. (2007) *An Introduction to Coping with Phobias*, London, Robinson.

Marks, I., Cavanagh, K. and Gega, L. (2007) 'Computer-aided psychotherapy: revolution or bubble?', *British Journal of Psychiatry*, vol. 191, pp. 471–3.

Neighbour, R. (1987) *The Inner Consultation: How to Develop an Effective and Intuitive Consulting Style*, Lancaster, Kluwer Academic Publishing.

NICE (2007) 'Depression: Management of Depression in Primary and Secondary Care', London; National Institute for Health and Clinical Excellence http://www.nice.org.uk/nicemedia/pdf/CG23quickrefguideamended.pdf [accessed 7/3/2008].

Sacks, H. (1984) 'On doing "being ordinary" ' in J. Atkinson and J. Heritage (eds) *Structures of Social Action*, New York, Cambridge University Press.

Young, C. (2007) *An Introduction to Coping with Panic*, London, Robinson.

Index

Key: **bold** = extended discussion; b = box; t = table.